Kaizen Desk Reference Standard

The complete guide for applying Kaizen to continuously improve business results

Kaizen Desk Reference Standard

Raphael L. Vitalo, Ph.D., Frank Butz, and Joseph P. Vitalo

Published by:
Lowrey Press, a division of Vital Enterprises
777 Hatchet Mountain Road
Hope, Maine 04847
www.lowreypress.com

To order
Vital Enterprises
777 Hatchet Mountain Road
Hope, Maine 04847
Tel: (207) 763-3758
Fax: (207) 763-3710
Online: www.vitalentusa.com

Technical Editor: Nita Congress
Images Copyright: New Vision Technologies Incorporated

Publisher's Cataloging-in-Publication
(Provided by Quality Books, Inc)

Vitalo, Raphael L.
    Kaizen desk reference standard : the complete guide for applying kaizen to continuously improve business results / Raphael L. Vitalo, Frank Butz, Joseph P. Vitalo. -- 1st ed.
    p. cm.
    Includes index.
    LCCN 2003101105
    ISBN 0-9722810-4-5

    1. Total quality management. 2. Industrial management.
I. Butz, Frank. II. Vitalo, Joseph P. III. Title.

HD62.15.V58 2003   658.4'013
                           QBI03-200147

Printed in the United States of America

Kaizen Desk Reference Standard

Contents

Preface

As Frank Butz passionately reminds us, Kaizen is about people. Yes, its immediate focus is on improving work processes and business results. And yes, its method makes a unique contribution to accomplishing this purpose. But the energy, heart, and lasting benefit of Kaizen are in enabling people to emerge as productive achievers.

There are three steps people must take to emerge as productive achievers. First, they must find the one endeavor in life they are truly passionate about. Second, they must devote themselves fully to realizing the highest level of achievement to which they are capable. Third, they must think about each execution of that endeavor and extract from it learning for further improving their success.

Kaizen enables these activities by providing a framework that supports people's initial success and their continuous learning. The Kaizen process described in the *Kaizen Desk Reference Standard* is a proven producer of value. Built into it are activities that guide learning and enable continuing development as a Kaizen leader. If Kaizen excites you, as we hope it will, it can be the vehicle by which you dedicate yourself to excellence and grow in your power and capability to produce benefit.

Kaizen makes two demands. First, it requires that you commit yourself to bettering others as well as yourself because only then will you effectively engage a team of workers in improving their workplace. And only when you can think beyond yourself will you recognize all the issues that affect the production of successful and lasting improvements. Second, Kaizen demands that you risk failure. Only when you are willing to fail in the pursuit of excellence will you challenge—and work to improve—the status quo.

If you can satisfy these requirements, mastering and applying Kaizen can be your springboard to broader personal success. Once you have taken performance in any domain to its highest level, you can use the learning and proficiencies you develop as a basis for transferring your success to any other arena of human activity.

Introduction

Preview

This section explains the purpose of the *Kaizen Desk Reference Standard*, its organization, and how to use it for support in leading a Kaizen event.

Topics

► Importance of Kaizen

► Why a *Kaizen Desk Reference Standard*?

► Organization of the *Kaizen Desk Reference Standard*

► How to Use the *Kaizen Desk Reference Standard*

   ► Personal Development

   ► Professional Achievement

► Locating Guidance

   ► Print Version

   ► Electronic Version

► Kaizen Tool Kit

► Improving the *Kaizen Desk Reference Standard*

Kaizen (pronounced *ki-zen*) is the Japanese word for continuous improvement. As we use the term, it is a method that strives toward perfection by eliminating waste. It eliminates waste by empowering people with tools and a methodology for uncovering improvement opportunities and making change. Kaizen understands waste to be any activity that is not value-adding from the perspective of the customer. By value-adding, we mean any work done right the first time that materially changes a product or service in ways for which a well-informed and reasonable customer is willing to pay.

Importance of Kaizen

Waste consumes resources—both human and material—pointlessly. People implementing wasteful processes are themselves wasted. They are robbed of the satisfaction of engaging in meaningful tasks that produce outputs customers value. Moreover, they are degraded as humans because engaging in activities that are not meaningful treats their energies and earnest efforts as commodities of little value. When constrained to execute these imperfect processes without the opportunity to make them better, people are denied the exercise of their capacity to learn and improve and thereby grow to the full measure of their capabilities. As for material resources, the financial and material investments in enterprise are prevented from achieving the greatest returns possible.

The application of Kaizen reverses the consequences of waste. Kaizen events have repeatedly demonstrated that the level of value-adding activity in unimproved, labor-intensive work processes is less than 5%—or, put another way, that only 5% of the resources invested in such work processes leverage return to owners, while a full 95% is squandered. Kaizen teaches people to see and eliminate this waste. By empowering people to uncover improvement opportunities and make change, Kaizen respects their humanity and allows them to apply their most valuable qualities toward making the enterprise successful. Kaizen enables people to grow to the full measure of their capabilities, enriching their own personal and professional lives while enhancing the human capital of the business. Through progressive and continuous elimination of waste, Kaizen lets performers continually increase the amount of the material resources that leverage *payback* and not simply *payout*.

Why a *Kaizen Desk Reference Standard*?

To date, the Kaizen process has not been systematized or well documented. Although there are many books on Kaizen, their messages are largely about the philosophy of Kaizen or principles to guide one's thinking either about Kaizen or during the performance of Kaizen. Previous books have not provided a rigorous, streamlined process for executing Kaizen nor the detailed knowledge needed to ensure excellent performance. Ironically, this absence of a systematic and documented process stands in opposition to continuous improvement. Without a defined work process as a standard, there is no reference for learning and no opportunity to enhance performance. In other words, Kaizen, as currently practiced, offers no opportunity to Kaizen itself.

The *Kaizen Desk Reference Standard* redresses this deficiency by providing a step-by-step process with detailed guidance and tailored tools to support the execution of Kaizen. It provides workers the opportunity to study and learn Kaizen on their own and supplies an aid for doing Kaizen. To achieve these ends, the *Kaizen Desk Reference Standard* includes:

- a work process map for executing Kaizen;

- detailed task guidance explaining how to execute each component of the process including milestones, tasks, and steps and the rules to apply in making decisions along the way; and

- tools such as checklists, spreadsheets, forms, announcements, and role descriptions to help in defining the scope of an event, preparing to execute it, conducting the event including documenting what was done and analyzing the results it produced, and following up to ensure that the process improvements make sustained contributions to the business.

Organization of the *Kaizen Desk Reference Standard*

The *Kaizen Desk Reference Standard* is organized into the following units.

- **Introduction** - explains the purpose of the *Kaizen Desk Reference Standard*, its organization, and how to use it for support in leading a Kaizen event.

- **Overview of Kaizen** - presents an overview of the goal of Kaizen and our system for accomplishing this goal.

- **Kaizen in Action** - describes a Kaizen event conducted according to the *Kaizen Desk Reference Standard*.

- **Milestone A. Document a Scope for the Kaizen Event** - guides in gathering information that defines the boundaries of and reasons for performing a Kaizen event.

- **Milestone B. Analyze Whether to Conduct the Kaizen Event** - explains how to evaluate whether holding the Kaizen event is likely to produce the business benefits sought by the people requesting the event.

- **Milestone C. Prepare for the Kaizen Event** - guides in readying the people, setting, and resources needed to conduct the Kaizen event.

- **Milestone D. Perform the Kaizen Event** - tells how to execute the Kaizen event in a manner that energizes people and eliminates waste in the target work process.

- **Milestone E. Institutionalize the Process Improvements** - guides in ensuring that work process or workplace improvements provide ongoing and maximum benefits for the business.

- **Customizing the Kaizen Process** - advises about tailoring the Kaizen process to meet special requirements including accelerating the process, addressing office applications, and planning for multiple Kaizen events within the same business.

- **Ending Note: Of Sanctity and Sacrilege** - provides a cautionary note to those who may desire the monetary gains Kaizen produces but not the added capability and desire of people to participate in conducting the business.

- **Glossary** - defines specialized words used in the *Kaizen Desk Reference Standard*.

- **User Evaluation and Feedback Form** - provides a questionnaire that requests your feedback about the *Kaizen Desk Reference Standard* in our effort to continuously improve its effectiveness.

How to Use the *Kaizen Desk Reference Standard*

You can use the *Kaizen Desk Reference Standard* to support you both personally and professionally. Personally, use it as a learning resource to develop your ability to improve work processes and contribute to a business's success. Professionally, use this book as a real-time resource to guide you in leading Kaizen events and as a baseline for improving the Kaizen process.

Personal Development

To use the *Kaizen Desk Reference Standard* as a learning resource, begin by building a mental image of what Kaizen is and how it is executed. Strengthen this image by reflecting on it and representing it on paper for yourself. Use the *Overview of Kaizen* unit to build your image. Add flesh to your mental image by reading the unit *Kaizen in Action*. Check whether the example of Kaizen it describes matches the image of Kaizen in your mind.

If you prefer building your understanding of a new skill by first seeing it performed, then reverse this process. Read the unit *Kaizen in Action* first and then build your mental image. Use the *Overview of Kaizen* unit to test your image of Kaizen.

In either case, cycle between these two units until you have a sure sense of what Kaizen is about. Use the *Glossary* to explain terms with which you are unfamiliar.

Once you are satisfied with your internal image of Kaizen, create a schedule for study that systematically takes you through this entire book one unit at a time. Proceed through the *Kaizen Desk Reference Standard* in accordance with your schedule. Apply the following method to fill out your mental framework with the detailed knowledge you uncover. This strategy allows you to build your learning incrementally and root it deeply in your mind.

1. Read the guidance provided in the selected *Kaizen Desk Reference Standard* unit. Continue to use the *Glossary* to explain terms with which you are unfamiliar.

2. Try applying the guidance to a work process with which you are highly familiar.

   Tip: As you study, imagine doing the Kaizen process on your chosen work process. For example, when you study *Milestone A. Document a Scope for the Kaizen Event*, first assume the role of the manager of the work process and provide the information needed to produce the scope document. Then assume the role of the Kaizen leader who must apply the *Kaizen Desk Reference Standard* guidance for Milestone A and for each remaining milestone.

3. Write out any questions, issues, or problems you detected and search back in the standard for additional guidance that may help resolve your concerns.

4. Discuss the guidance and unresolved questions or concerns with someone who is qualified in leading a Kaizen event using the *Kaizen Desk Reference Standard.*

   Tip: If you do not have access to a qualified Kaizen leader, consider enrolling in our training program for preparing Kaizen leaders. See details at our website, http://www.vitalentusa.com. Bring your questions and concerns to the training so that we can personalize our instruction to address your particular needs. For help with specific issues, use the Kaizen Forum provided at our website. Post your questions to the forum and benefit from the responses offered by other Kaizen practitioners.

Professional Achievement

Professionally, you will apply Kaizen in two contexts. The first is when you are asked to resolve a deficiency in the operating results of a particular work process (e.g., inadequate throughput, excessive unit cost, untimely delivery of outputs). This type of request is what usually triggers the first use of Kaizen in a work process. The second context is when you will lead return events on the same work process. This recycling of Kaizen to drive continuous improvement is typically supported by managers once they have had an opportunity to see Kaizen in action. It then becomes clear how Kaizen can reveal new opportunities for improvement even when the current operating results seem satisfactory.

The *Kaizen Desk Reference Standard* is a real-time resource to guide you in leading Kaizen events under either of these circumstances. It contains knowledge that will assist you in describing an initial request to remedy problematic operating performance as well as knowledge that enables you to detect opportunities for improvement even when the owners of a work process are satisfied with current performance.

To use the *Kaizen Desk Reference Standard* as a real-time performance aid, consult the book prior to beginning each component of the Kaizen process. Use the review to refresh your understanding of what you need to do and what principles you should keep in mind as you make decisions. Next, consult the book while executing the component on an as-needed basis. The electronic version is especially handy for this purpose, as you can rapidly access guidance using the locator aids embedded in it (see below). Finally, consult the book after you complete each component to verify that you accomplished it correctly. Use the Check Steps section at the end of each milestone, task, and step guidance as a quick way to verify that you performed the component correctly and the Output section to ensure that you generated each required product.

You can also use the *Kaizen Desk Reference Standard* as a baseline solution for executing Kaizen. At the end of each event, make time to reflect on the process and outcomes you produced by applying the knowledge in this baseline process. Extract learning about yourself and the method and develop ways to elevate your execution of Kaizen along with any insights into how to make the Kaizen process better. Please share those ideas with us using the feedback mechanism described below (page 7). Consider using our *Status, Reason, Learning, Direction* (*SRLD*^{SM}) product to support your learning efforts. Information about *SRLD*^{SM} is available at our website. Also consider becoming a member of our website and using our Kaizen Forum to benefit from the ideas and learning of other Kaizen leaders.

Locating Guidance

To use the *Kaizen Desk Reference Standard* for either personal or professional purposes requires that you understand how to navigate it to locate the knowledge you need.

Print Version

The *Kaizen Desk Reference Standard* has several locator aids to assist you in finding specific information. These include:

- a table of contents,
- a preview page marking the beginning of each unit, and
- an index of topics at the end of the book.

Electronic Version

The electronic version of the *Kaizen Desk Reference Standard* includes all the locator features of the print version with some additions. In the electronic version, you can click on "buttons" (see Exhibit 1, next page, for examples) to move to the referenced text. The right side of the table of contents, for example, has each listing set as a button. Similarly, each listing in the index has an associated button so you can quickly jump to the guidance identified. There are buttons located throughout the electronic version of the *Kaizen Desk Reference Standard* to make access to guidance rapid and easy.

In addition, you may find any word or topic in the electronic version of the *Kaizen Desk Reference Standard* by pressing CTRL+F and entering it into the pop-up form that appears. You may search for the exact word you enter or similar words based on the option you select. Adobe Acrobat Reader® will locate the first instance of a match. You may proceed to subsequent instances by pressing CTRL+G.

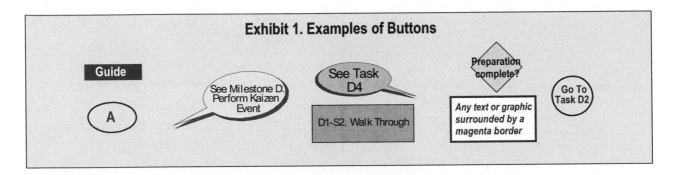

Exhibit 1. Examples of Buttons

Kaizen Tool Kit

The Kaizen Tool Kit brings together, in electronic format, many of the forms and other materials referenced in the *Kaizen Desk Reference Standard.* The Kaizen Tool Kit is on the CD-ROM that accompanies the print edition of the *Kaizen Desk Reference Standard* or on the CD-ROM containing the electronic edition. Insert the CD-ROM into your computer drive, and the Kaizen Tool Kit installation program will open automatically. If it does not, locate the autorun.exe file on the CD, then double click on the file. This action will initiate the installation of the Kaizen Tool Kit. You will need to have Adobe Acrobat Reader® 4.0 or higher installed on your computer. An installation copy of Adobe Acrobat Reader® 5.0 is provided on your CD-ROM[1] and it will be installed for you, if you give permission. You also need Microsoft Word 2000® and Microsoft Excel 2000® to use the items in the Tool Kit. Tool Kit materials are listed in the beginning of each unit of the *Kaizen Desk Reference Standard* in the Materials, Tools, and Other Resources section. Once the installation is completed, a shortcut icon will appear on your desktop. Clicking on this icon will open the Kaizen Tool Kit and provide you access to its contents.

Improving the *Kaizen Desk Reference Standard*

Vital Enterprises is committed to continuously improving the contents and presentation of this *Kaizen Desk Reference Standard*. To this end, we have included a feedback questionnaire at the end of this book; an electronic version of the form is provided in the Kaizen Tool Kit. Please complete the electronic questionnaire and provide your ideas on how this book may be improved to serve you better. Print and mail the questionnaire or fax your feedback to: Raphael L. Vitalo, Ph.D., Vital Enterprises, 777 Hatchet Mountain Road, Hope, Maine 04847 (Fax: 207-763-3710). As an alternative, visit our website and complete the feedback form online. By providing feedback on the *Kaizen Desk Reference Standard* online, you will have the opportunity to become a member of our website and obtain access to our Kaizen Forum and other services dedicated to supporting new learning by users of the *Kaizen Desk Reference Standard*. For more details about these services, see our website.

---

[1]Adobe Acrobat Reader is also available free of charge at http://www.adobe.com.

Overview of Kaizen

Preview

This section presents an overview of the goal of Kaizen and our system for accomplishing it. It identifies the inputs you need to undertake a Kaizen event, the outputs you should generate, and the method by which you transform these inputs into outputs. It also provides an overview of how you evaluate the success of the event and the coordination you must do to ensure success. Finally, it provides a map integrating our understanding of Kaizen.

Topics

► Goal

    ► To, For, and By

    ► So That

    ► Conditions

    ► Standards

► Inputs

► Outputs

► Process

► Feedback

► Coordination

► Timeline

► Image of Kaizen

There is a minimal set of ideas one needs to build an image of any task. These include the goal of the task, the resources needed prior to starting it (inputs), the results the task must produce (outputs), the method by which it transforms inputs into outputs (process), the tests done to ensure successful execution of the task (feedback), and a list of the individuals or groups to communicate with while performing the task (coordination). This section provides you with these essential ideas for our system of Kaizen.

Goal

Each goal we define includes six components: a "to" statement that tells the summary result to be produced, a "for" statement that tells who is to benefit from accomplishing the goal, a "by" statement that names the action to be implemented to produce the result, a "so that" statement that lists the benefits to be produced for each benefiting party, a "conditions" statement that lists the circumstances that must exist prior to undertaking the goal, and a "standards" statement that lists the criteria that define success.

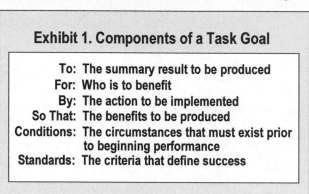

Exhibit 1. Components of a Task Goal

To:	**The summary result to be produced**
For:	**Who is to benefit**
By:	**The action to be implemented**
So That:	**The benefits to be produced**
Conditions:	**The circumstances that must exist prior to beginning performance**
Standards:	**The criteria that define success**

To, For, and By

As we said previously, the summary result Kaizen produces is the elimination of waste in a work process. It achieves this end by empowering people to uncover improvement opportunities and make change through the use of Kaizen. We see the application of Kaizen as focused on benefiting the business and work process on which it is being applied, the customers of the business, and all other stakeholders. These other stakeholders include employees, suppliers, and the community in which the enterprise and its customers operate. The application of Kaizen must provide inclusive benefits to all parties in order to ensure a long-term advantage. Unless all stakeholders prosper, the business will not have the ability to grow, since continuous growth requires ever stronger alliances between a business and its customers, employees, suppliers, and the communities within which it operates. The success of each party in a common activity is the best strengthener of alliances.

So That

What are the benefits that Kaizen produces for its stakeholders? For the *business itself*, Kaizen elevates the yield of its work processes, generating improved top-line (e.g., revenues and profits) or bottomline (e.g., cost reduction) results depending on the precise improvements made. It also elevates employee abilities, providing the company with a greater capability to grow. For *customers*, it provides products and services that better satisfy their values. For *employees*, it provides an opportunity to remove barriers to success and satisfaction and the tools with which to do it. For *suppliers*, it can stimulate new challenges and create new opportunities to learn about and strengthen their relationships with the business sponsoring the Kaizen event. For *communities*, it provides more fulfilled community members and work processes that better address community concerns (e.g., safety).

Conditions

Certain conditions must be satisfied in order to apply Kaizen. These conditions include the following:

- waste exists in the workplace;
- business leadership and membership are aligned with respect to making improvements that will eliminate waste and benefit all stakeholders inclusively; and
- the Kaizen leader possesses the capacity, skills, and proficiency levels needed to interpret and execute the guidance in the *Kaizen Desk Reference Standard*.

If these conditions are not met, the Kaizen process should not be initiated. For example, without the presence of waste, there is no point in applying Kaizen. Without alignment of leadership and membership with respect to making improvements that will eliminate waste, there will be no action to execute the improvements the Kaizen event generates. Also, if the alignment between leaders and members is directed exclusively to their profit and not inclusively to producing benefits for all stakeholders, it will fail to produce a long-term advantage. With respect to the requirements of the Kaizen leader, Kaizen events are typically physically demanding. The Kaizen leader, as well as the team members, works intensively; frequently, the changes made require physical labor (e.g., rearranging the workplace, fabricating new tools). Leading the event also requires a high level of proficiency in communication, problem solving, and decision-making. The Kaizen leader must be able to see, ask, listen to, and understand the people and context in which he or she is applying Kaizen and process this information to make appropriate decisions. The leader must be able to engage, involve, enable, and support team members in the performance of Kaizen. Without these proficiencies, the Kaizen leader will falter in empowering his or her team to conceive, select, and execute actions toward elimination of waste in the target work process.

With respect to satisfying these conditions, our experience has been as follows. First, we have not encountered a work process absent of waste. Second, employees rapidly align to Kaizen because it provides them with an opportunity to make their work more effective and therefore more satisfying. Third, any worker with the desire to achieve and produce benefits for him- or herself and for others can master the Kaizen process. Fourth, the one condition that is most often problematic is leadership's commitment to change. This may seem counterintuitive in that one expects that leadership has the greatest reason to seek business success. Yet, in our experience, leadership is frequently addicted to an "announce and declare" approach to improvement. Leaders announce that an improvement will occur and then declare it achieved. The leadership effort required to bridge the two moments is absent. This effort frequently requires nothing more extraordinary then getting the alignment of the upper and mid-level managers who report to top leadership and establishing cooperation across organizations. While it is possible to produce business benefits at a local level given local management support, the full magnitude of the benefits a Kaizen event can produce requires replicating its improvement ideas across a company—and that requires leadership alignment.

Standards

Every goal we define lists criteria that enable a performer to judge his or her success. For Kaizen, the success criteria include the following elements.

1. **Measurable business and work process benefits accomplished as defined in the mission and goals of the event.** The mission defines the work process improvement that the Kaizen event will make (e.g., reduced unit cost, speedier cycle time, improved safety) and the business result that it will produce. The goals define the types of waste the Kaizen team will remove and the degree of removal the team will achieve.

2. **New or improved work standards developed during the Kaizen event applied to the work process (or submitted for approval).** The new or improved work standards refer to the work process or workplace changes that remove waste defined in the goals and thereby accomplish the mission of the event. Usually, these new work standards are implemented during the event. Sometimes, a business requires the Kaizen team to pilot the new standard during the event and make a formal application for change of the work standard using the results of the pilot after the event is done.

3. **Sustained or improved safety.** Every Kaizen event must make changes that, at a minimum, sustain the current level of safety in the workplace and preferably improve it.

4. **Performers elevated in their business participation, ownership, teamwork, confidence in their ability to make change, and capabilities to achieve success.** The Kaizen event gives the team of performers who participate in it a new understanding of their business and an introductory experience to bettering it. This experience fires their enthusiasm to participate. The process they learn during the event gives them a pathway for making continuing improvements. The tools team members acquire provide them with the means to effect these improvements.

5. **New learning about Kaizen, its application, and the Kaizen leader's capabilities generated.** Each Kaizen event should generate new learning that improves Kaizen and you as a Kaizen leader.

6. **New opportunities for Kaizen events identified.** Every Kaizen event identifies improvement opportunities that the team cannot address in the event. These opportunities become follow-up action items.

7. **Documentation of the event completed.** Every event must be documented so that what was done and what it produced can be shared with people not present at the event. The documentation closes the loop on accountability and provides a learning resource to others.

The *Kaizen Desk Reference Standard* explains in detail each of these expected results and provides guidance to support you in accomplishing each.

Inputs

Before you begin the Kaizen process, you must know the identity of the specific business and target work process you will improve. Companies are frequently made up of multiple businesses, each producing a unique product or service output. Even small companies may offer both a product (e.g., fire suppression systems) and related services (e.g., installation and maintenance). Each of these offerings (system hardware, system installation, and system maintenance) are separate businesses in that each produces a different output and requires different expertise.

You also need a source for information to define the scope of the event, including basic business information, target work process information, and the business's expectations for the Kaizen event. This source must be informed in each of these areas and willing to share that information with you. Finally, you need authorization to proceed from the management of the business hosting the Kaizen event. With these few resources, you can begin the Kaizen process.

Outputs

At the completion of the Kaizen process, you and the Kaizen team should produce the results listed in the standards section of the Kaizen goal.

Process

Our Kaizen process is accomplished through a set of milestones (see Exhibit 2, next page). Three milestones, performed in sequence, guide you in getting ready to do the event. Another milestone performs and completes the event. One last milestone follows up to ensure that the changes made in the event produce continued benefits for the stakeholders.

Exhibit 2. The Kaizen Process	
	Milestone
Getting Ready	Milestone A. Document a Scope for the Kaizen Event Milestone B. Analyze Whether to Conduct the Kaizen Event Milestone C. Prepare for the Kaizen Event
Doing	Milestone D. Perform the Kaizen Event
Following Up	Milestone E. Institutionalize the Process Improvements

Feedback

The *Kaizen Desk Reference Standard* provides guidance to test and verify the achievement of each of the success criteria stated in the standards section of the Kaizen goal. The feedback activities directed to this end include the following elements.

- **Measuring the results produced by the Kaizen event, including both operating and monetary results.** Measuring operating improvements includes detecting changes in the presence of waste and value-added activity in the work process, the cycle time of the work process, employee productivity, resource usage, and throughput. Measuring monetary results includes calculating net savings and gains from the event.

- **Documenting the results produced by the event.** Among other information, the documentation must contain a description of the mission and goals of the event, measurements of the work process both before and after the Kaizen team made changes, the status of operating and monetary improvements, and a list of additional improvement actions that can be pursued following the event.

- **Evaluating achievement of the event's purposes.** Team members test whether the mission and goals of the event have been realized using the measurements developed in the event. The team also uses the results of the event to judge whether safety has been maintained or improved.

- **Evaluating the impact of the event on the team using the Kaizen Participant Feedback Form.** Team members complete an evaluation of their experiences during the event. The Kaizen leader summarizes this feedback, and it is used in verifying that employees benefited from the event and in mining learning from the completed event.

- **Mining learning from the completed event.** The Kaizen leader reflects on the results of the event, concludes whether the event satisfied its success criteria, and explores the reasons for the results it produced. From these ideas, the Kaizen leader develops learning to improve Kaizen and his or her future performance as well as a set of immediate actions to further enhance the event's accomplishments.

Coordination

In performing a Kaizen event, the Kaizen leader and Kaizen team must communicate with all parties that could either affect the success of the event or be affected by its conduct or results. These parties are called stakeholders (Exhibit 3).

Exhibit 3. Stakeholders

■ Sponsor	■ Union
■ Event coordinator	■ Maintenance supervisor
■ Manager of the target work process	■ Safety supervisor
■ Manager of the target work process manager	■ Work standards supervisor
■ Designated representatives of other organizations that must be consulted before modifying the target work process	■ Customer
	■ Suppliers
■ Work process performers	■ Community

Kaizen event stakeholders always include the sponsor of the event (if he or she is not one of the following individuals), the manager of the target work process and that person's manager, the performers of the target work process, and the head or his or her designee of each organization outside the target work process that must be consulted before modifying the target work process. The sponsor is the person who originally requested the event. If the employees are unionized, the union to which they belong is another stakeholder.

Other parties likely to be stakeholders to the Kaizen event include the maintenance supervisor, safety supervisor, and work standards supervisor (i.e., the person responsible for maintaining the formal work instructions employees must follow). Each of these stakeholders is a point of interface and communication for the Kaizen leader and Kaizen team.

The customers of the outputs of the work process are always considered stakeholders in the Kaizen event. Communication with customers, however, is either indirect or direct, depending on the immediacy of the event's impact on them. When there is no foreseeable immediate impact of the event on the customer, communication is indirect: information about key customer values regarding the product or service to which the target work process contributes is gathered from a knowledgeable person within the business. If, on the other hand, the event will have immediate consequences for the customer, direct contact is necessary. For example, if the event will take place at a customer's site, affect the customer's work activities, or change customer product delivery schedules, you must engage the customer directly in the event so that his or her perspective is fully heard. Suppliers are another set of potential stakeholders to an event. Communication with suppliers is essential if the event will potentially affect what they supply or how they supply it. Moreover, customer and supplier representatives should be included on the Kaizen team when there is likely to be an immediate effect on them. Communication with the community is usually indirect. Information about community concerns is reflected in the regulations that govern health, safety, and the environment and is shared by employees who are community members.

Timeline

The timeline for completing a Kaizen event is almost entirely driven by the business for which it is conducted. Exhibit 4 (page 17) depicts the typical timeline for performing a *first* Kaizen event within a target work process. Usually four calendar weeks transpire between the request to perform a Kaizen event and the first day of the event. Of this time period, the Kaizen leader needs only three workdays to complete his or her tasks. The remaining time is to accommodate the availability of people and information and to ensure that all parties are informed about and ready to participate in the event. Subsequent events in the same workplace require less calendar time since people are familiar with Kaizen and energized in supporting it. See *Customizing the Kaizen Process* for ideas about accelerating Kaizen.

Image of Kaizen

We used a system format in representing our mental image of Kaizen. A system is a set of components that together accomplish a goal. Kaizen is a human system, meaning that it is executed by people as opposed to machines. Using his or her expertise, the Kaizen leader applies the components in the following manner. First, the leader verifies that all required inputs are present. Then, the leader executes the process to transform inputs into outputs. As the leader executes the process, he or she communicates with the various stakeholders listed in the coordination component. Along the way and when the process is completed, the leader uses the feedback component as a prompt to gather information and test whether he or she has implemented the system successfully. Exhibit 5 (beginning on page 18) portrays our version of the minimal set of ideas one needs to understand what Kaizen is about and how it accomplishes its purpose. Use it to check your understanding of Kaizen. Then enrich your understanding by reading the *Kaizen in Action* unit.

Exhibit 4. Timeline for Completing a Kaizen Event

Conditions for Event Satisfied		Start Kaizen Process
Milestone A	Document a Scope for the Kaizen Event	■ Kaizen leader creates a folder for the proposed event and acknowledges receipt of the request. ■ Kaizen leader documents a scope for the Kaizen event. **Minimum Time Period:** 1 calendar week
Milestone B	Analyze Whether to Conduct the Kaizen Event	■ Kaizen leader analyzes whether the event is appropriate to hold. ■ Kaizen leader communicates the results of the analysis to the key stakeholders. **Minimum Time Period:** 1 calendar week *from* completion of a verified scope document
Milestone C	Prepare for the Kaizen Event	■ Kaizen leader prepares for the Kaizen event. ▪ Arranges logistics. ▪ Acquires needed business information. ▪ Prepares communications about the event. ▪ Readies the team and stakeholders to participate the event. **Minimum Time Period:** 3 calendar weeks *from* completion of a verified scope document
Milestone D	Perform the Kaizen Event	■ Kaizen leader and team conduct the Kaizen event. ▪ Focus the Kaizen event. ▪ Evaluate the target work process. ▪ Solve the performance issue. ▪ Act to improve the target work process. ▪ Measure results. ▪ Communicate results to stakeholders. **Minimum Time Period:** 1 calendar week *beginning* when preparations are fully complete; some events may need just 3 days to complete
Milestone E	Institutionalize the Process Improvements	■ Kaizen leader follows through to encourage sustained use of improvements, transfer of soft to hard benefits, action on post-event improvements, and replication of benefits to other sites. ■ Kaizen leader extracts learning and uses it to improve Kaizen and his or her performance of Kaizen. ■ Kaizen leader provides a follow-up report on the event. **Minimum Time Period:** 6 months *from* completion of Kaizen event
Full Business Benefits Realized		**End Kaizen Process**

Minimum Time Period, Prior to an Event - 4 Weeks (vertical bracket spanning Milestones A through C)

Exhibit 5. Kaizen - The Essential Ideas

Goal

To: Eliminate waste in a work process

For: The business and target work process, its customers, and all other stakeholders

By: Empowering people to uncover improvement opportunities and make change through the use of Kaizen

So That: Kaizen:

- ✓ Elevates the yield of work processes generating improved top line or bottomline results depending on the precise improvements
- ✓ Increases the abilities of the company's employees, providing the business with a greater capability to grow
- ✓ Provides products and services that better satisfy customer values
- ✓ Provides an opportunity for employees to remove barriers to their success and satisfaction and the tools with which to do it
- ✓ Stimulates new challenges and creates new opportunities for suppliers to learn about and strengthen their relationship with the business

Conditions:
- ✓ Waste exists in the workplace
- ✓ Business leadership and membership are aligned with respect to making improvements that will eliminate waste and benefit all stakeholders inclusively
- ✓ The Kaizen leader possesses the capacity, skills, and proficiency levels needed to interpret and execute the guidance in the *Kaizen Desk Reference Standard*

Standards:
- ✓ Measurable business and work process benefits accomplished as defined in the mission and goals of the event
- ✓ New or improved work standards developed during the Kaizen event applied to the work process (or submitted for approval)
- ✓ Sustained or improved safety
- ✓ Performers elevated in their business participation, ownership, teamwork, confidence in their ability to make change, and capabilities to achieve success
- ✓ New learning about Kaizen, its application, and the Kaizen leader's capabilities generated
- ✓ New opportunities for Kaizen events identified
- ✓ Documentation of the event completed

Continued...

Exhibit 5. Kaizen - The Essential Ideas (continued)

Input	Process	Output
✓ The identity of the business and target work process you will improve ✓ A source for information to define the scope of the event ✓ Authorization to proceed from management	*Kaizen Work Flow* Next Page	✓ Measurable business and work process benefits as defined in the mission and goals of the event ✓ New or improved work standards either applied to the work process or submitted for approval ✓ Sustained or improved safety ✓ Performers elevated in their business participation, ownership, teamwork, confidence in their ability to make change, and capabilities to achieve success ✓ New learning about Kaizen, its application, and the Kaizen leader's capabilities ✓ New opportunities for Kaizen events ✓ Completed documentation of the event

Feedback

1. Measure the results produced by the Kaizen event, including both operating and monetary results
2. Document the results produced by the event
3. Evaluate the achievement of the event's purposes (mission, goals)
4. Evaluate the impact of the event on the team using the Kaizen Participant Feedback Form
5. Mine learning from the completed event

Coordination

✓ Sponsor	✓ Designated representatives of other organizations that must be consulted before modifying the target work process	✓ Maintenance supervisor ✓ Suppliers
✓ Event coordinator		✓ Safety supervisor ✓ Community
✓ Manager of the target work process	✓ Work process performers	✓ Work standards supervisor
✓ Manager of the target work process manager	✓ Union	✓ Customer

Continued...

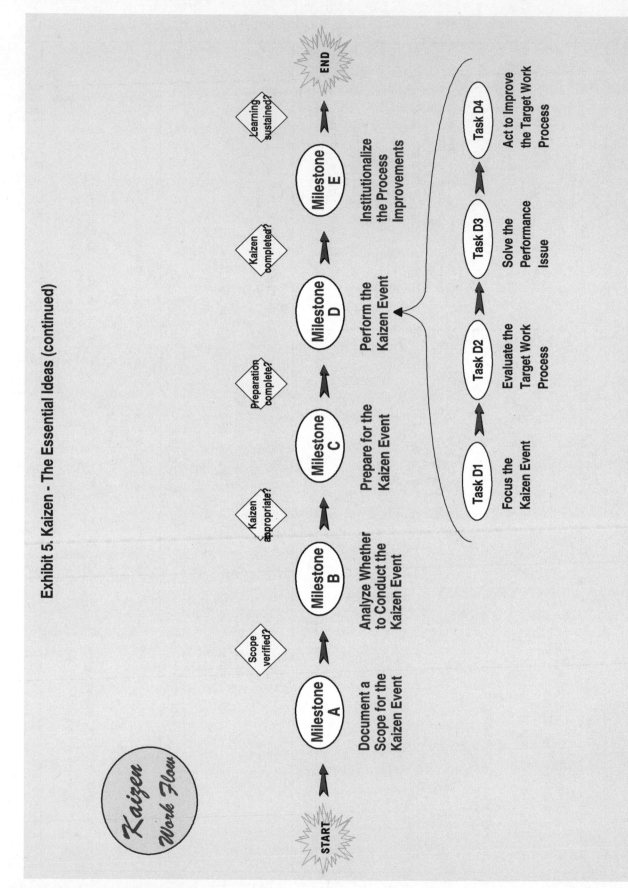

Exhibit 5. Kaizen - The Essential Ideas (continued)

Kaizen in Action

Preview

This section describes an actual Kaizen event conducted according to the *Kaizen Desk Reference Standard*.

Topics

► Understanding What Is Requested

► Getting Ready for the Kaizen Event

► Doing the Event

   ► Day 1 - Focus the Kaizen Event
     Build a Description of the Target Work Process
     Walk Through the Target Work Process
     Build the Mission Statement
     Set Goals for the Kaizen Event
     Define the Do's and Don'ts
     Close Day 1

   ► Day 2 - Evaluate the Target Work Process
     Gather Information
     Analyze the Amounts and Sources of Waste
     Summarize the Results of the Evaluation
     Close Day 2

   ► Day 3 - Solve the Performance Issue
     Generate Improvement Ideas
     Trim Improvement Ideas
     Conduct an Experiment
     Select Improvement Ideas
     Close Day 3

   ► Days 4 and 5 - Act to Improve the Target Work Process
     Create Action Plans
     Execute Improvement Ideas
     Measure Results

► Following Up the Event

   ► Close the Kaizen Event

   ► Communicate Results to All Stakeholders

   ► Mine Learning From the Completed Event

► Postscript

This unit describes a Kaizen event from request through completion. It is based on an actual event; the names of the company, locations, and participants have been changed to honor our confidentiality responsibilities. This example applies Kaizen to a manufacturing business and improves both human and machine performance. (We have also applied Kaizen to office and service-oriented work processes with equal success.) Use this description to help you form a personal experience of Kaizen—what it does and how it does it. If you have already studied the *Overview of Kaizen* unit, look for how the concepts and procedures described there are applied in a real event. If you are beginning here before you have read the *Overview of Kaizen* unit, use this virtual experience of a Kaizen event to formulate your own mental image of this method for improving business performance.

Be forewarned. A Kaizen event requires a great deal of hard work to complete. It may seem overwhelming as you imagine yourself leading such an event. Remember, however, that there is detailed guidance in the *Kaizen Desk Reference Standard* to support you in performing each task described in the following example. There are also tools (e.g., paper and electronic forms, handouts) to make the tasks easier. Finally, be aware that we have trained both shop floor and office workers to lead Kaizen events successfully, many of whom have had no more than a high school education.

Understanding What Is Requested

ABC Gases produces commercial gases for use in the electronics, home healthcare/ MRI, metals finishing, export, and chemical process industries. The company has 109 plants engaged in filling and distributing cylinders, liquid dewars, tube trailers, and other containers of industrial gases and non-electronic specialty gases. These facilities are distributed across the United Sates and Canada. The three largest sites are in Newark, Delaware; Madison, Wisconsin; and Oakland, California. ABC Gases's revenue was $240 million in FY 2001; it employs 1,200 people and has an operating budget of approximately $200 million. The company produces over 100 different flammable and nonflammable gas products including argon, carbon dioxide, helium, hydrogen, nitrogen, oxygen, and neon, and many combinations of these products. ABC customers care most about quality products, on-time deliveries, and price.

Mike Fellows, head of ABC Gases, has requested a Kaizen event for the blending area in the Oakland plant (1234 Industrial Boulevard). The process is done in four ABC plants, but Oakland is the largest site. Mike hopes that improvement there will have the biggest initial impact and then be rolled into the other plants (i.e., Canton, Ohio; Jackson, Florida; and New Orleans, Louisiana) for even greater benefit. In the blending area, workers create custom mixes of gases (e.g., methane-argon mixes, hydrocarbon mixes). Mike is concerned because products are not getting done on time and unit cost is rising. He reports that customers are getting angry about delayed receipt of orders and that profit margins are shrinking. He further reports that the company has this year set reducing cost as its major improvement target. The company's key business driver is to increase profit margins while not increasing prices.

The blending process is done in the flammable and nonflammable fill areas. Mike wants the Kaizen event to focus on the nonflammable area, where approximately 50 different mixes are blended. Mike agreed to have the event focus on the backbone of the work process, meaning those operations that every mix goes through. Forty-three people work in the Oakland plant: 21 fill blended gas orders, and 12 are assigned specifically to the nonflammable blending process. These are full-time employees. The plant operates seven lines that fill blended gases (three nonflammable, four flammable), three shifts a day, five days a week. Mike directed us to contact Sandra Shore, manager of the Oakland plant, to get more information and set up the event.

I, as the Kaizen leader, contacted Sandra the day after talking with Mike. Sandra provided additional details about the blending process. She said that the work is done almost always in a batch of two cylinders, meaning multiple cylinders are produced as one unit of output. "These are highly customized mixes of gases, and multiple orders for exactly the same mix are uncommon." For efficiency's sake, the fill operator interweaves blending and filling different orders so that at any one time there may be eight cylinders hooked up to the manifold and being processed. "It can look like the operator is working on a batch of eight cylinders, but actually he is filling four different orders each of which is at a different point in processing. While one is being purged, for example, another is being filled with its blend of gases."

In talking with Sandra to get a definition of the scope of the proposed event, she shared some details about the blending process. The process uses three pieces of equipment: a manifold, scale, and a rolling machine. The blend booth manifold is a four-sided device with eight filling lines (two per side) to which cylinders can be connected (see Exhibit 1). The manifold executes the vacuum, purge, and fill. It is connected to large liquid gas tanks stationed outside the building from which it draws the gases to be placed in the cylinders. At the base of the manifold, there is a scale on which the cylinders stand. The weight of the cylinder is monitored to ensure that the proper amount of each gas component is filled. The rolling machine (Exhibit 2, next page) is a table-like device which literally rolls the cylinders to mix their contents. The manifold and rolling machines account for the majority of the work process's cycle time (90%) but not much of the product's unit cost (10%).

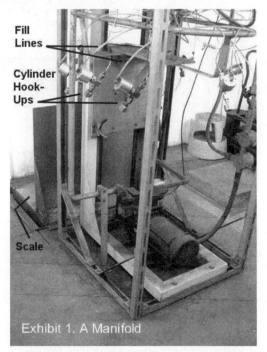

Exhibit 1. A Manifold

Sandra said that the process begins with getting an order and then completing a pre-fill inspection of the manifold and scale. "The operator wants to make sure the manifold lines have no leaks and the scale is properly zeroed out. The pre-fill inspection requires hooking up a cylinder so that the lines and scale can be tested. This is called a 'scale check cylinder.' Then the operator removes the scale check cylinder

Exhibit 2. Rolling Machine

and loads the line with cylinders to be filled. This means placing the cylinders on the scale that sits on each side of the manifold and hooking them up to the fill lines.

"The blend booth itself is an enclosed structure in which the filling process is completed. The upper half of each wall of the blending booth has shatter-proof glass panels which allow viewing into the booth. Its purpose is to protect the workers and work area from hazards. The worker directs the process from a control panel located outside the blend booth. The panel allows the worker to control the fill to each cylinder separately. Once the cylinder is loaded onto the manifold, the worker inspects it, touching up bare spots with paint when needed and making sure damaged labels are replaced. Next, the operator allocates a cylinder to its customer by scanning the bar code on the cylinder (called 'shooting the cylinder') and associating it with the order number it will satisfy. Once the cylinder is allocated, the operator vacuums and purges the cylinder and figures out the weights for each gas that will be blended to satisfy the customer's order (termed 'fixing grams'). Then the operator fills the cylinder with the prescribed mix and, when finished, checks for leaks.

"Next, the operator moves the cylinders from the blend booth to the rolling machine which rolls the order to ensure that the gases are fully mixed. Finally, the operator labels the cylinders, places a protective net over each oylinder to prevent the labels and paint from being rubbed off as cylinders bang against each other in transit, and moves the filled cylinders to the lab for testing. The point of variation occurs before prepping a cylinder. If a cylinder is being filled with a medical mix, then special paperwork must be done before prepping it."

In doing this work, the blending area must relate to a number of other work processes in the total value chain that ultimately delivers a filled cylinder to a customer. The other groups involved are the Maintenance Department, which prepares cylinders for filling; the Mix Identification Group, which approves the mix as safe and assigns an identifying number for each mix so that it may be tracked; the Bulk Product Group, which ensures that the liquid gas tanks are full; and the Lab, which tests the filled cylinders for purity and correctness of mix.

I asked Sandra whether the plant was using takt time to regulate the flow of work through the work process. Takt time is the pace at which customers require a product. It is an essential piece of information in establishing a just-in-time work process. "We don't use takt time. We did set up *kanbans* though." Kanban is a Japanese word which means signal or card. One use of kanbans is to tell an upstream—meaning one that occurs earlier—work process that an output is needed downstream. Sandra did say that the current cycle time of the work process was about an hour and a half for one order, "assuming nothing unusual happens." She continued, "Now remember, we rarely do one order at a time. Our operators work on multiple orders at a time, which gives us a better average cycle time to fill an order. I can't say exactly what that is."

With respect to work process measures, Sandra said that she watches unit cost and on-time delivery. "If we can get the cost down and on-time delivery up, we should be able to meet both our profit and customer satisfaction goals. Right now, our on-time delivery rate is 84%. That leaves too many customers unhappy. Also, if we can free people up as a result of shortening the cycle time, I can redeploy them to the flammable side, where we expect demand to grow. As to when to do the event, we can pretty much accommodate the dates you select."

Sandra indicated that she expected at least a two-to-one return on the cost of the event in hard benefits. Hard benefits are cost reductions or revenue gains that begin to flow as soon as the event ends. She also said that safety is a priority of the company, so improvement in safety is also a desired outcome. "By the way," she added, "you will need some safety equipment while in the workplace. You must wear earplugs, safety glasses, safety shoes (steel toes and metatarsal plates), and gloves." As to the team's authority, she said that it could make decisions about improvements in the blending process as long as there were no negative effects on the other organizations with which blending interacts. If an idea required an adjustment by another department, that department would have to be consulted and agree to it prior to its execution. She also said the event should stay within regular working hours and require no overtime. She offered the names of people to be on the Kaizen team. Three proposed team members were fill operators: two filled blended gases (Reggie B. and Thomas C.), and one filled straight gases (James L.). One team member was a supervisor (Vincent L.), another a maintenance worker (Nathan H.), and the last member was a lab technician (Clarice T.). I also obtained from her a list of stakeholders (Exhibit 3) other than the work process employees. Stakeholder is the term we use to identify any person or group who may either affect the success of an event or be affected by its occurrence.

Exhibit 3. Stakeholders		
Role	**Name**	**Telephone**
Designated event coordinator	Sandra Shore	123-456-7890
Maintenance supervisor	Mike T.	123-456-7891
Manager of target work process	Sandra Shore	123-456-7890
Manager of the target work process's manager/sponsor	Mike Fellows	123-456-7878
Person with whom to coordinate logistics and travel	Sam W.	123-456-7892
Safety supervisor	Rufus W.	123-456-7893
Work standards supervisor (or contact person)	Sandra Shore	123-456-7890

Getting Ready for the Kaizen Event

Every Kaizen event begins with defining a scope and building a strawperson direction. The scope document is developed with the key stakeholders. These are the people who either have authority over whether the Kaizen event happens or whether the changes proposed for the target work process are implemented. The scope document records information that describes the business, the target work process, and what the key stakeholders seek from the Kaizen event. Using the scope information, the Kaizen leader creates a mission for the event, a set of goals, and a statement of the do's and don'ts for the Kaizen team. These components make up the strawperson direction for the event. The mission states the purpose the team will pursue. It always includes the business results the event will produce and the improvement in the performance of the target work process it will make to generate those results. The goals set out the specific areas the team will address. The do's and don'ts tell what the team is empowered to do and what it may not do. Each of these is a "strawperson" because it is based solely on what the scope says. Later, once the event begins, the Kaizen team will rebuild each of these based on the facts in the workplace and reconcile any differences that emerge.

After talking with Sandra, I prepared a scope document and a strawperson direction for the event. I then shared these materials with both Sandra and Mike, the two key stake-holders. Exhibit 4 presents the strawperson mission, goals, and do's and don'ts for this event.

Exhibit 4. Strawperson Direction for ABC Gases Kaizen Event

Mission
To increase profit without increasing price and elevate customer satisfaction with on-time delivery by reducing the cycle time and cost of the nonflammable blending work process for ABC Gases and its stakeholders.

Goals
■ Reduce unit cost. ■ Reduce cycle time. ■ Improve safety.

Do's and Don'ts	
Must or Can Do's	**Can't Do's**
■ Can make decisions about improvements in the blending process as long as there is no negative effect on the other organizations with which blending interfaces. ■ Must get agreement from another department prior to executing a change if the proposed change requires an adjustment by that department in how it operates.	■ No overtime. Event should stay within regular working hours.

Once the scope was verified as correct by Sandra and Mike, my next task was to analyze whether to conduct the Kaizen event. As a professional, I am responsible for ensuring that what my clients seek is in their best interests and that a Kaizen event on the target work processes they are specifying can deliver what they want. My responsibility is not to second guess my customer but to independently verify the customer's thinking so that if a problem exists from my perspective, I can raise it and we can work it through together before resources are expended. In essence, I analyze whether to conduct the event assuming the perspective of the business that is asking for the event and my knowledge of Kaizen. In doing this, I apply five tests. I test whether (1) the focus of the Kaizen event makes sense, (2) the business case for doing the event is reasonable, (3) people will support the event, (4) the setting and resources available to the event are adequate, and (5) the timing of the event will not interfere with business. To complete this analysis, I must estimate the resources needed for the event and talk with prospective team members to get a sense of their thoughts about the work process, its problems, and the prospects of improving them. I also gather more specifics about the work process such as its overall operating cost and factor costs (e.g., labor, machine, raw materials). Once I have brought my thinking to a conclusion, I get back with the key stakeholders and let them know my perspective on the event.

My analysis of the proposed event for ABC Gases indicated that the event could achieve Mike and Sandra's purpose. The focus was to improve a work process that, in talking with team members, was having problems that affected cost and timeliness in fulfilling customer orders. While the amount of cycle time controlled by worker execution (as compared to machine execution) was limited, my conversations suggested that actual cycle time and "official" cycle time were not aligned. In fact, there was a lot more labor going on than management assumed. Even without this discovery, a significant reduction in labor time would accelerate the work process and, most importantly, based on the economics of the work process (90% of unit cost is labor), have an impact on unit cost. Also, this work process was negatively affecting a key customer value—on-time delivery. With respect to blended gases, the on-time delivery rate was only 84%. To increase this rate, the work process would have to be accelerated. My contacts also suggested that both management and workers were on the same page with regard to wanting improvements—even if not for quite the same reasons. Management wanted the cost down, and workers wanted the frustration of the work relieved. From the workers' perspective, the way the work process was currently operating led to a lot of wasted time and effort on their part.

All other factors supported doing the event. Preparation for the event looked quite possible given the resources at the site and the time we had in which to prepare. Also, as Sandra said, the timing of the event would not disrupt any other priority in the work process. She had enough staff to participate in the event and keep the work process rolling. Even if some of these issues had turned out to be problematic, we could have found ways to address them and still do an event. The value of the analysis is in raising the "red flag" early so that any issues can be resolved and success ensured. On the other hand, the analysis has turned up situations where doing an event—even after discussion with all key stakeholders—just made no sense.

With a sound event clearly specified, my next task was arranging logistics (e.g., meeting room, equipment, materials, meals, travel, lodging); gathering any additional business information I needed (e.g., work standards, safety procedures, management of change procedure); preparing communications to stakeholders; and connecting with stakeholders (e.g., the team, workers in the target work process) to prepare them for the event. Connecting with these people up front and staying connected with them throughout the Kaizen process is important to the success of any change effort, especially Kaizen because it is about engaging, energizing, and enabling people and not just about making process improvements. So I prepared a flyer to be posted in the blending area a week before the event, announcing the Kaizen event and asking workers for their ideas and suggestions. I communicated with the team members from the area ahead of time so they would be able to explain the flyer and the event and collect ideas from fellow workers. I also alerted the safety, maintenance, and work standards supervisors about the event and made sure that they would be available to us during the week the event was scheduled so we could get their counsel as needed. Finally, I inquired whether any best practice databases existed that might contain ideas relevant to the work process the event was to improve. If such a database existed, I wanted to be sure we could access it and draw ideas from it. Similarly, I inquired as to whether any other sites had developed improvements to the blending work process that might not yet be implemented at Oakland. Kaizen is about advancing improvement and not reinventing the wheel so if there were improvement ideas already uncovered and in use elsewhere, we wanted to incorporate them and add to their effectiveness and not spend the team's time rediscovering them. In this case, there was a best practice database, but its contents were poorly organized and Its information was deemed of little value. Also, no other site had yet tackled the blending work process. It was this event that management hoped would seed improvements elsewhere.

With preparations complete, I finished the arrangements for my own travel and made sure I arrived sufficiently ahead of time to verify that the meeting room was properly set up and all the materials we needed were in place.

Doing the Event

Day 1 - Focus the Kaizen Event

The event was set to begin at 8 AM, Monday. I arrived early with my co-leader to be sure that our meeting area was still set up correctly and to meet each team member personally as he or she arrived. I had spoken with each team member previously but had not met each person face to face.

Once all the team members arrived, I asked for their attention. I began by reintroducing myself and my co-leader and stating the purpose of the team's getting together. This I shared in a simple summary way: "We are here today to significantly improve the blending of nonflammable gases work process for our business, its customers, and all its stakeholders by applying the Kaizen tool."

Once I confirmed that the team members knew each other, I reviewed administrative issues (e.g., bathrooms, refreshments, etc.) and safety procedures. Next, I told the team that we would begin by doing a warm-up exercise in which we would think about and share with each other what seemed to work well in the target work process and what was problematic. This exercise would give us an opportunity to start thinking about the work process and to uncover the team's concerns and those the team had heard from other employees. We built a list of pluses and minuses with respect to how the work process currently operates; we posted this and used it as a reference during the event. Right away, however, we made a discovery that had a big impact on the event. One team member noted as a minus how long it took to get the filling done. In exploring this, he indicated that it typically took a whole day to finish just six cylinders (three orders). That is two hours longer than we had heard during all previous conversations. In discussing it further, it became clear that the job included a great deal of waiting for empty cylinders; alternatively, fill operators could prepare cylinders themselves. "Nathan and the other maintenance workers just can't get all the cylinders prepared when we need them, so we either wait or help out by getting and prepping the cylinders as part of the blending process," Reggie said. The other fill operators agreed. Nathan added: "You see, we don't just prep cylinders. That's a small amount of our time. We are responsible for unloading cylinders from the trucks and repairing cylinders, among other jobs." So, while management was correct in detecting that blending was taking too long, it was off by not recognizing that a major portion of the time being spent was either waiting for or doing another work process.

It seemed clear that cutting down the blending cycle time required us to extract this preparation work from it. That probably would not completely achieve our mission but would make a significant contribution to it. Tackling two processes—cylinder preparation and blending—as we were about to do, violates our standard approach, which specifies one work process per event. On the other hand, the two processes together involved no more than four hours of actual work once machine time was discounted. Thus, the total time required for both work processes was within the allowable limit of four hours for one event. Also, we had within the team expertise to address both work processes, along with an experienced Kaizen event leader and co-leader. I therefore decided that we could successfully address the two processes. In compliance with our do's and don'ts, I spoke with Mike T., maintenance supervisor, to get his okay about the team's looking into ways to improve the cylinder preparation work process. I had already communicated with Mike prior to the event, so he was both aware of it and on board with its purpose. He said he was happy that we would look into the cylinder preparation process: "It's a bottleneck, no doubt about it. If the guys can help fix that, it's fine with me. You know, the cost of that operation is also booked against the blending work process so it's really all one bundle of money anyway." Mike also said that he was comfortable having Nathan as our contact person for changes and would stand behind any decisions Nathan approved. "He knows the process and our situation in maintenance. He's not going to go for anything stupid."

After we explored the team's sense of the target work process, I reviewed with the team a simple set of communication skills team members had previously learned. These are Working With Others (WWO) skills that enable people to get and give information from and to each other effectively. (WWO skills are delineated by J.S. Byron and P.A. Bierley in *Working With Others*, Hope, ME: Lowrey Press, 2003). We applied these skills throughout the event to maximize the efficiency and effectiveness of our teamwork.

Next, team members built a set of ground rules for how they would work together. These ground rules included items like "say what you think," "what is said in the team stays in the team," and "use your WWO skills." With these details satisfied, I provided a 20-minute presentation about Kaizen and the process we would complete together during the week. I then asked my co-leader to review the strawperson direction for the event and brief the team on how we would accomplish it. He then reviewed the day's agenda with the team. Our Day 1 agenda specified that the team would get through *Task D1. Focus the Kaizen Event* (Exhibit 5).

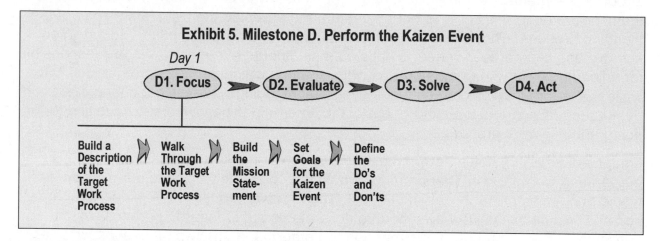

After a short break, the team reassembled to begin the work of Kaizen. *Task D1. Focus the Kaizen Event* specifies that the team's first job is to build a direction for the event based on the facts in the workplace. We build our "fact base" by describing the target work process and doing a walk through of the process. With the information we gather, we redefine the mission, goals, and do's and don'ts of the event, reconciling the new direction with that we inherited from the scope document. This process of focusing the event based on the facts in the workplace offers many rich benefits.

- It enables the team to form a common understanding of what is going on in the work process and ensures that the team works toward the same end. (Remember, the strawperson direction is based only on the ideas of the key stakeholders.)

- It ensures that the end the team aims toward addresses the real problems in the work process.

- It finalizes the team's accountability so that the team can judge its success.
- In the focusing process, the team learns about the concept of waste and how to detect waste in the workplace. Being able to detect waste is essential to applying Kaizen. Learning this skill enables team members to not only uncover improvement opportunities during the event but also prepares them to detect new opportunities as they continue to pursue business improvement efforts after the event.

There are even more benefits from this focusing effort. For example, it provides the team leaders with a reference point for judging whether the demonstration of the work process they observe later in the week properly represents how that process is supposed to be performed. The focusing task is thus a very rich and important activity.

Build a Description of the Target Work Process

We now began to describe the target work process. Our description had two components: an overview that captures the purpose of the work process and certain essentials about it (e.g., inputs, outputs, departments with which it coordinates); and a work process map that shows the sequence of operations that execute it. Given the information I developed prior to the event, I was able to draft both the overview (Exhibit 6) and the work process map (Exhibit 7, page 32) and show them to the team for approval or correction. As to the map, based on what Reggie said, I felt that we needed to map activities occurring in the cylinder preparation work process as well as the blending work process since fill operators were doing both under the name of the blending process. The team agreed and worked swiftly to confirm the overview for the blending process and then the work process map.

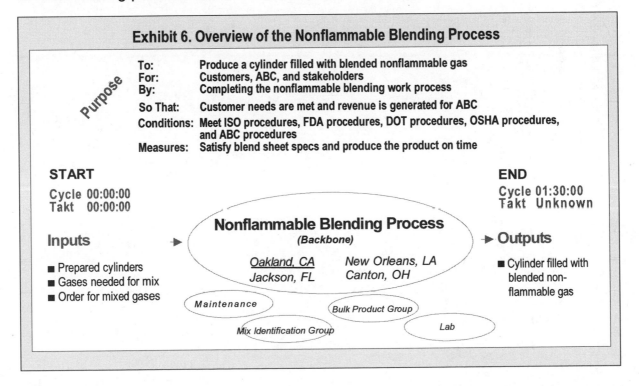

Exhibit 6. Overview of the Nonflammable Blending Process

Purpose

To: Produce a cylinder filled with blended nonflammable gas
For: Customers, ABC, and stakeholders
By: Completing the nonflammable blending work process

So That: Customer needs are met and revenue is generated for ABC
Conditions: Meet ISO procedures, FDA procedures, DOT procedures, OSHA procedures, and ABC procedures
Measures: Satisfy blend sheet specs and produce the product on time

START
Cycle 00:00:00
Takt   00:00:00

END
Cycle 01:30:00
Takt Unknown

Inputs

Nonflammable Blending Process
(Backbone)

Oakland, CA   New Orleans, LA
Jackson, FL   Canton, OH

Outputs

- Prepared cylinders
- Gases needed for mix
- Order for mixed gases

- Cylinder filled with blended non-flammable gas

Maintenance   Bulk Product Group

Mix Identification Group   Lab

Exhibit 7. Work Process Map for the Cylinder Preparation and Nonflammable Blending Processes

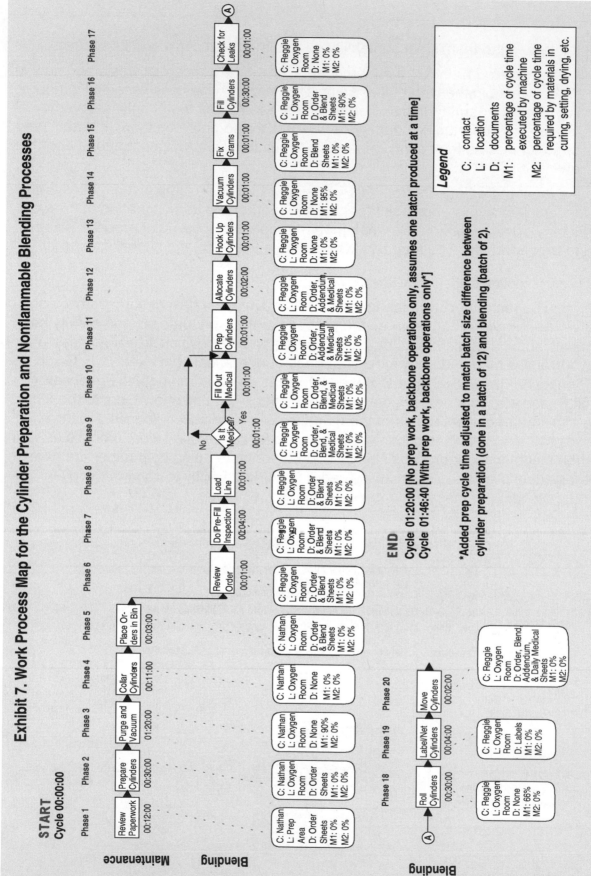

In confirming the work process map, we reached several points where team members disagreed about operations. For example, to what level of vacuum did the cylinders need to be brought? Here, we were guided by the official work standard which I, as the Kaizen leader, had acquired in preparation for the event. Using the standard to resolve the questions that arose had an added value. When the team got into the standard, we found that it specified a range of acceptable vacuum levels rather than a single level. Thus, both our operators were correct. What was not correct was each person's notion that his or her way was the exact right and *only* way. We discovered that many activities that may have been perceived as "required" might well be optional or at least modifiable without violating the current work standard.

The cycle time estimate for the work process varied. When we added together the cycle times for each blending operation we mapped, the total was 1 hour and 20 minutes if cylinders were ready and 1 hour, 46 minutes, and 40 seconds if the fill operator prepared his or her own cylinders. These cycle times are for a batch of two cylinders. The cylinder preparation work process actually produces a batch of 12 cylinders, so we determined its cycle time contribution to producing one batch of cylinders filled with a nonflammable blend by taking one-sixth of it. We used the cycle times for the backbone operations of the blending work process only to compute our time estimates. These cycle times are for a unit of output done on its own. Actual times for per unit production are different because, as Sandra said, orders are not processed on a single piece basis. For example, as one is being filled, another is being readied to fill.

We could begin to see waste in the work process as we mapped its operations. There was much paperwork to complete, several wait periods (even with interweaving the production of different orders), and repeated inspections—all of which might offer opportunities for improvement.

Walk Through the Target Work Process

We next prepared ourselves to complete the walk through. To get the team ready, I explained what a walk through is and why it is done. The purpose of the walk through is to gather more information about the work process, the work areas within which it is performed, and any instances of waste. With this information, the team has the facts needed to define a mission and set goals for the event. Team members literally walk through the process from beginning to end, if time permits, focusing on learning about the work process and detecting instances of waste. The team makes observations, asks questions, and listens to what workers say. After the walk through, the Kaizen event co-leader conducts a separate personal interview of each operator to gather his or her ideas about ways to improve the process. We find a personal interview for gathering worker judgments is better than asking the questions during the walk through, as it provides the worker greater privacy.

In planning the walk through, I saw that we could not observe every operation as it is performed within the one hour allotted for the walk through. Therefore, I made selections and got the team's feedback. We wanted to physically walk through each area in which work is performed so that we could get a sense for distances and the flow of work. At a minimum, we wanted a "talk through" on each activity. Before we began, my co-leader instructed the team in how to detect waste. This instruction is critical as it provides team members with a fresh way to view their work activities and their workplace. This fresh perspective opens their eyes to previously unseen improvement opportunities.

Nathan provided the talk through and demonstrations of the cylinder preparation process. We wanted to see where Nathan got his paper work and unprepared cylinders, how he hooked up a cylinder, where the vacuum and purge equipment were located, and where he moved his prepped cylinders once he was done. This all sounded like a lot of transport activity and setup, both of which are forms of waste in that they do not materially contribute to the final product but do consume resources. Also, we were interested in seeing the start of the vacuum and purge operations and especially how cylinders are hooked up to the manifold. We were concerned about the ergonomics of the activity as well as with safety. Additionally, the vacuum and purge operations ate up a lot of cycle time, so we wanted to see if we could detect any ways to speed machine operations. Before we observed the activities, Nathan told us how he reviewed the paperwork on each cylinder he prepared, then got the cylinders from storage and checked the test dates stamped on them. We observed the hook-up of several cylinders. Afterward, Nathan showed how he placed a collar on the prepped cylinder and told us about the additional paperwork he completed.

Next we observed the fill process. We could observe each operation up to the filling activity itself as, together, they required no more than 14 minutes to perform. We were especially interested in the cylinder prep activity, as this seemed to indicate a repetition of work that maintenance had already completed. We also suspected that the rolling operation after the cylinders were filled might be important to see. We thought that there would be lifting involved which could have safety and ergonomic implications. Reggie led us through the blending process, demonstrating the operations we wanted to see.

The value of the walk through was evident. First, we saw that the prepping activity inside the blending process did not repeat work done in maintenance, but did seem as if it might better belong to that process. This activity involves scraping off old labels (usually four, some of which do not come off easily) and doing touch-up painting of bare spots on the cylinders. While observing the rolling operation, I discovered that the platform on which the cylinders rested while they were rolled rotated to a vertical position so that the movement of the cylinders onto the rolling machine did not require lifting. The cylinders were moved to the platform in its vertical position and placed on a support connected to the rolling platform; the platform was then tilted back to its horizontal position for rolling. The operators moved cylinders from place to place two at a time, tilting them on edge and rotating them in the direction they needed to travel. This avoided the need to lift and carry cylinders. Also during the walk through, Nathan noticed that a vacuum pump with piping was mounted up on a wall, seemingly away from the processing. He asked about it; it turned out to be a spare vacuum not in use. This discovery would play an important role in the solutions generated later in the week.

With the walk through over, the team members regrouped to pool their observations and share whether they had detected instances of waste. The team made 51 non-redundant observations of waste during the walk through. The team categorized this list by type of waste, which involved looking at each observation, deciding what type of waste it represented, and recording it on a flipchart page titled with that type of waste. This activity provided the team an opportunity to practice what it had learned about the different categories of waste prior to the walk through. It also would provide us with a rapid visual assessment of which types of waste were most dominant in the work process. We needed this analysis to build our fact-based direction (i.e., mission, goals, and do's and don'ts).

Travel/transport and setup were the forms of waste with the most examples; the categories of wait, hazard, and interruption were next in order of frequency of observations. With respect to travel/transport, the operator had to travel to get labels, valves, nets, leak soap, wrenches, and orders. Every step used time. Almost all the prepping work process and most of the blending work process was setup. Each involved getting cylinders ready for reuse or preparing them for machine operations (vacuum, purge, vent, and roll). During these machine operations, the operator waited. Workers also waited for orders to be processed and put into the pickup bin. Some of the hazards observed included the operator not wearing a face shield and cryogenic gloves, a cable exposed on the floor (trip hazard), a door stop on the oxygen blend booth that did not work, and the operator not wearing earplugs. The normal processes of prepping and blending were each interrupted by having to sort cylinders, make repairs, deal with power surges, and answer questions about orders. Equipped with our profile of waste in the work process, we were ready to build the mission, goals, and do's and don'ts that would guide us during the remainder of the week.

Build the Mission Statement

Building the mission statement required us to work from the waste we observed to the effects it had on overall performance of the work process. We then took this work process problem and asked ourselves how that affected business success. We came up with this mission: To *expand profit margins and ensure customer satisfaction with on-time delivery by reducing cycle time and the unit cost of blending nonflammable gas mixes for ABC Gases and all its stakeholders.*

To finish our work, we needed to compare this mission based on what we observed in the workplace with the mission developed from the scope document (see Exhibit 4, page 26). They matched, so we went with the language of the scope mission since that was already approved by the key stakeholders. Note that at least 20% of the time, the two versions of the mission statement do *not* match, and the team then needs to reconcile the differences. That is why we make sure that the key stakeholders are available to us during the week of the event.

Set Goals for the Kaizen Event

Setting the goals was even easier than defining the mission. Basically, we took the top five forms of waste we had discovered during the walk through and stated a goal to reduce the presence of each. The goals we set based on the walk through were: reduce travel and transport by 25%, reduce setup by 50%, reduce wait time by 50%, eliminate all hazard items, and reduce interruptions by 50%. The team estimated an amount of reduction based on what it saw and how much change it felt was needed to improve the work process and produce the promised business results. (The precise reduction is not that important at this point. Once we do the process observations during *Task D2. Evaluate the Target Work Process*, we have exact quantitative information with which we can better specify reduction targets.)

We checked the goals set based on the walk through with those set based on the scope. They were consistent—as usual, however, the walk through provided a richer set of goals than had the scope since it built the goals using far more information than is available from the scope document. We accepted the goals based on the walk through and added to them two goals from the strawperson direction that addressed unit cost reduction and cycle time since we felt that the key stakeholders might want to see these goals in the list even though we had already stated them in the mission.

Define the Do's and Don'ts

We had no new information about do's and don'ts from the walk through, so the team adopted those already specified based on the scope. Exhibit 8 (next page) shows our final direction. Compare it to the strawperson direction I developed based on the scope document (Exhibit 4, page 26).

Close Day 1

At the end of each day, the team reviews the day's agenda, noting what it accomplished and completes an exercise that evaluated what went well during the day and what went poorly. This is called a plus/minus exercise. We use it to identify how to improve our process during the next day of the event.

At the end of Day 1, the team indicated that it valued the Kaizen presentation, as it provided an understanding of what team members were being asked to do. They liked the way things were organized, since it allowed the team's work to move along without any hitches. They also liked the mapping activity, which was the first time the operators in the team had seen a visual representation of all the tasks they did in completing their jobs. Another valued experience was the discovery that there is a lot of difference in the way operators worked and that the work standards gave them latitude to change. Previously, each person was operating under the notion that the work had to be done the way he or she was doing it. This discovery excited the team members, because it seemed to say that they could make change. Finally, the team thought that it had gotten a lot done in one day and that team members had followed the ground rules, especially that about using their WWO skills. On the negative side, apart from walking around the plant on the walk through, there was a lot of sitting and talking time which, while productive, was not the team's preferred way to spend time. The team would rather be doing things. Given the Kaizen hands-on approach, I knew that we would correct that problem in the following days.

Exhibit 8. Direction for ABC Gases Kaizen Event Following the Walk Through

Mission
To increase profit without increasing price and elevate customer satisfaction with on-time delivery by reducing the cycle time and cost of the nonflammable blending work process for ABC Gases and its stakeholders.

Goals	
■ Reduce travel and transport by 25%.	■ Reduce interruptions by 50%.
■ Reduce setup by 50%.	■ Reduce unit cost.
■ Reduce wait time by 50%.	■ Reduce cycle time.
■ Eliminate all hazard items.	

Do's and Don'ts	
Must or Can Do's	**Can't Do's**
■ Can make decisions about improvements in the blending process as long as there is no negative effect on the other organizations with which blending interfaces. ■ Must get agreement from another department prior to executing a change if the proposed change requires an adjustment by that department in how it operates.	■ No overtime. Event should stay within regular working hours.

Day 2 - Evaluate the Target Work Process

Once again, the team started at 8 AM. My co-leader and I arrived early to be sure that our meeting area was still set up correctly. Once the team arrived, I began our work with a brief review of the purpose of the event, our approach, and what we had accomplished thus far. I asked the team for any thoughts or comments about our progress to date before we looked at the day's agenda. There were none, so I previewed the day's agenda with the team members and got their feedback.

The focus for Day 2 was *Task D2. Evaluate the Target Work Process* (Exhibit 9, next page). This task provides an exact measure of the types and amounts of waste in the operations of the target work process and a baseline against which to measure the

Kaizen event's achievement of its goals. It also identifies for the team the specific behaviors that, if changed, would eliminate waste. The team had three main activities to complete: (1) gather information about the target work process, (2) analyze the amounts and sources of waste, and (3) summarize the results of the evaluation.

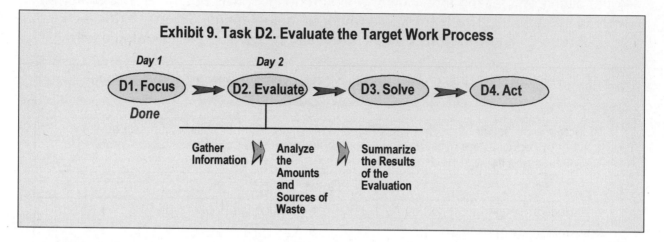

Exhibit 9. Task D2. Evaluate the Target Work Process

Gather Information

The night before, my co-leader and I had reviewed what we knew about the target work process so we could draft a plan for gathering information about it. The plan had to answer five questions: (1) how many observations will the team make of the target work process; (2) what operations will it observe;
(3) which operators; (4) in what order; and (5) who will perform each role (e.g., process observer, timekeeper, distance measurer) in making the observations. We prepared a draft plan to speed our work and ensure that the information we gathered was reliable.

Given the variability in the reports about the cycle time to complete the blending work process and the manner in which it is done (i.e., interweaving the work of different orders), it seemed to us that the team needed to observe multiple cycles— meaning the processing of multiple orders—so it could average the times across these orders to understand the cycle time for one unit of output (i.e., one order or two cylinders). Our plan recommended observing the completion of three orders (six cylinders) since that seemed to provide the team with enough observations to average and still allow it to finish its evaluation by day's end. Our plan included only one observation of the cylinder preparation work process, since that seemed to have a consistent estimate of cycle time and was regularly done in a batch of 12.

According to our plan, the team would make its observations on the day shift. It would focus on the operations performed by workers as opposed to machines since we lacked sufficient time to do both. Nathan would be the operator for preparing cylinders and Reggie for blending gases and filling the cylinders. Our plan had Vincent doing the process observation since he was familiar with both jobs. As process observer, Vincent's job was to record and describe each work activity executed by the operator using the Process Observations Data Sheet. I took the utility role, which includes collecting examples of documents that the workers receive or produce as a part of their jobs. My co-leader assumed the documentor role and would enter the information collected by the team into our electronic forms. We assigned Thomas to the timekeeper role, James to handle distance measurement, and Clarice to do the spaghetti charting. The timekeeper reports the end time for each work activity using a stopwatch so that the cycle time of each work activity can be computed. The distance measurer reports the distance an operator moves while executing his or her job using a distance wheel. Vincent, as the process observer, would call for the time and distance measures and record them along with the identity of each work activity on the Process Observations Data Sheet. The spaghetti charter charts the movements of the operator as he or she transports, travels, and searches in the performance of the job.

When the team met, I shared our plan and got the team's feedback. All agreed that the plan made sense. Before we started implementing it, I gave each team member a description of the role he or she was to perform and had the member read it; we then discussed the roles together as a team. It is important that each person understands what he or she needs to do. My co-leader distributed the materials each team member needed to do his or her assignment and provided Clarice with 12 copies of the workplace layout form I had previously produced. We reviewed safety guidelines and made sure everyone put on their safety gear. We then moved into the workplace to complete our information gathering.

Gathering information took us about five hours. The team made the observations of the cylinder preparation process, then took a break for lunch. After lunch, the team completed observations of the blending process. My co-leader entered information about each process into the forms included in the electronic Kaizen Tool Kit. I brought him the observation sheets as Vincent completed them; the co-leader entered them into our Process Analysis Sheet, a spreadsheet that automatically computes a summary and distribution of value added and waste. This allows the team to move quickly to the analysis activity once it finishes gathering information.

Analyze the Amounts and Sources of Waste

Given our automated spreadsheet, analyzing the amounts and sources of waste requires only that the documentor complete the entry of the process observations (activity, time, distance) and assign each work activity to the category of value added or a category of waste. The spreadsheet is designed to compute the value-added ratio and total time per waste category and to chart the information depicting the distribution of time by value added and waste categories. We built separate spreadsheets for the cylinder preparation process and the blending process so that we could attack each on its own basis.

It took 141 activities to complete the cylinder preparation work process. The process was made up of three types of work: paperwork (getting, reviewing, filling out, filing, organizing, and discarding forms, tags, and orders); readying the cylinders for preparation (locating and getting cylinders, checking the cylinders for damage, hooking cylinders up to the manifold); and prepping the cylinders (venting, vacuuming, and purging their contents). The vent, vacuum, and purge cycle occurs twice as per the work standard. Interspersed through the process is travel, transport, and search for paperwork and cylinders. The worker traverses some 1,255 feet each time he or she does this work process.

The cycle time we observed for preparation of a batch of 12 cylinders was 2 hours 19 minutes, and 30 seconds. None of the activities could be classified as value adding because none materially produce the product the customer seeks—that is, gas of a specific blend. The process takes a used cylinder and refurbishes it for reuse by the company. Cylinder reuse is the standard approach in the industry to providing vessels for transporting the customer's gas and controlling cost. The entire process, however, exists by the choice of the producers. The customer has not specified that he or she wants the blended gas in a used cylinder, for example. We recognized that the customer had indicated that price was an issue and that the *company had decided* that reusing cylinders would help it address that concern. That calculation is the producer's judgment and satisfies the producer's assessment of what it feels it can do. The fact remains that the customer has *not* requested this solution. If a customer *did* specify that the gas he or she receives be delivered in recycled cylinders, then at least some portion of this work process would be value adding.

Exhibit 10 presents the distribution of waste observed in the cylinder preparation work process. The analysis of the cylinder preparation work process showed that 65% of the work time was consumed in waiting for machine operations to finish. These machine-driven operations were vacuuming the cylinders and purging any remnants of old products from them. The team observed that if it could speed up these machine operations, it could greatly reduce waste in the work process. The remainder of the time was used in setup activities (20%), unnecessary processing (8%), travel/transport (6%), and search (1%). Almost all of the unnecessary processing involved transferring information that was already recorded on the order sheet to other documents. This added documentation was not required by the work standard but had evolved in response to the preferences of different individuals, some of whom were no longer at the plant.

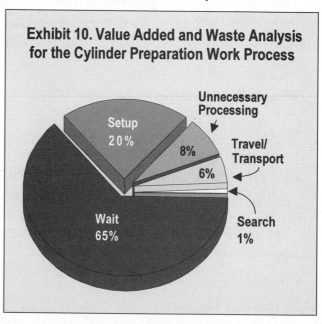

Exhibit 10. Value Added and Waste Analysis for the Cylinder Preparation Work Process

Setup 20%

Unnecessary Processing 8%

Travel/ Transport 6%

Wait 65%

Search 1%

The blending work process was made up of 336 activities to complete three orders (six cylinders). These activities fell into five categories: paperwork (getting, reviewing, filling out, filing forms, etc.); machine setup (testing for leaks, checking the scale, etc.); cylinder preparation (scraping and replacing labels, doing touch-up painting, etc.); blending gases and filling the cylinders; and packaging (labeling, netting, moving cylinders, etc.). The worker traverses some 3,602 feet to complete the process for three orders. The total time to produce the required outputs was 2 hours, 25 minutes, and 14 seconds, resulting in an average cycle time of 48 minutes and 25 seconds per unit of output (one batch of two cylinders)—assuming that the blending operator does not need to do the cylinder preparation work process.

Exhibit 11 presents the distribution of waste observed in the blending work process. The analysis showed that 8% of cycle time was used in performing value-added work. This was the percentage of cycle time during which the blending and filling occurs. The remainder of the time was waste, including 28% setup, 22% travel/transport, 19% wait, and 18% unnecessary processing. Most of the unnecessary processing involved paperwork: for example, the operator recorded the results from testing the scale used in the blending booth. Discussion with the team revealed that no one ever uses that information and no one could recall the reason for its being collected. Nathan observed: "That scale is checked and maintained by its manufacturer on a monthly basis. I have been here 15 years. The scale has never failed a test. Even if it did fail, I would need to fix it immediately. I could not continue the blending process. I have never referenced that log book, nor has anyone else." "Shooting the cylinder" was also cited as unnecessary. This involves reading the bar code on the cylinder and associating it with an order. It seems important, but, as it turned out, the information is not used. Vincent, a supervisor, offered: "The cylinder has a label on it that says what is in it. There is an order form that goes with the cylinder. It has an order number and specifies the blend that should be in the cylinder. No one uses the bar code. Everyone uses the label and the order."

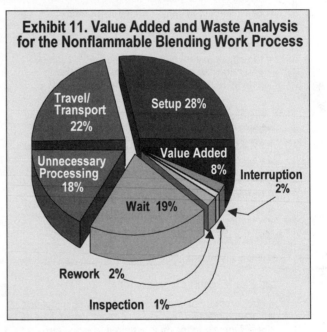

Exhibit 11. Value Added and Waste Analysis for the Nonflammable Blending Work Process

Summarize the Results of the Evaluation

As my co-leader completed the analyses of the work processes, Clarice prepared a visual display of operator movements during cylinder preparation and blending. She selected up to five sheets of the spaghetti chart of operator movement for each work process, copying them onto overhead transparencies. She then produced a single overlaid visual display of movements for each work process. This gave the team a good way to judge the orderliness of movement in each process.

The team reviewed the printed reports of the process observations including the pie charts depicting the distribution of work by value added or category of waste. It viewed the spaghetti charting for each work process and pooled its observations of safety issues. The team then prepared a summary of findings for each work process (see Exhibits 12 and 13).

Exhibit 12. Findings for the Cylinder Preparation Work Process	**Exhibit 13. Findings for the Nonflammable Blending Work Process**
Findings	**Findings**
Movement	**Movement**
▪ 1,255 feet of distance per batch	▪ 3,602 feet of distance (600 feet per unit of output)
▪ Great amount of distance in travel/transport	▪ Great amount of distance in travel/transport
▪ More orderly than chaotic	▪ Somewhat orderly
▪ A great deal of motion	▪ Little motion obseved
▪ Repetitive motion on hooking pigtails to cylinders and removing cylinder caps; each hook-up activity required a lot of hand movement	
Status of Human Operations	**Status of Human Operations**
▪ 02:19:30 cycle time	▪ 02:25:14 total time—0:24:12 cycle time
▪ 0% value-added ratio	▪ 8% value-added ratio
▪ Wait (65% of cycle time)	▪ Setup (28% of cycle time)
▪ Setup (20% of cycle time)	▪ Travel/transport (22% of cycle time)
▪ Unnecessary processing (8% of cycle time)	▪ Wait (19% of cycle time)
▪ Travel/transport (6% of cycle time)	▪ Unnecessary processing (18% of cycle time)
Status of Inventory	**Status of Inventory**
▪ Not a significant issue at this time	▪ Not a significant issue at this time
Status of Machine Operations	**Status of Machine Operations**
▪ Measurement of machine operations not completed	▪ Measurement of machine operations not completed
▪ Vacuum machine was old and underpowered for its job, increasing the time required to reach target vacuum levels	▪ Uses same vacuum pump as cylinder prep—same problem
Status of Workplace/Work Process Hazards	**Status of Workplace/Work Process Hazards**
▪ Repetitive motion on hooking pigtails to cylinders and removing cylinder caps	▪ Operator not wearing face shield and cryogenic gloves
▪ Operator not wearing earplugs	▪ Door stop not working on oxygen booth
	▪ Operator not wearing earplugs

Before we could call our evaluation complete, we needed to determine whether there were any differences between the goals currently defined for the event and those suggested by the results of the process observations. There was one difference. The degree to which interruptions detracted from the performance of the blending work process was less striking when time was considered and not as significant as unnecessary processing. We therefore replaced our goal for reducing interruption with a new goal for reducing unnecessary processing, as we were looking for the maximum benefit from our efforts. The team also felt it needed to separate out a set of goals for each of the work processes. Finally, the team adjusted the reduction targets for four of the goals based on the measurements it made during the evaluation but verified that the new targets would still accomplish the event's mission. Exhibit 14 presents the final direction for the Kaizen event.

Exhibit 14. Final Direction for ABC Gases Kaizen Event

Mission

To increase profit without increasing price and elevate customer satisfaction with on-time delivery by reducing the cycle time and cost of the nonflammable blending work process for ABC Gases and its stakeholders.

Goals

Cylinder Preparation

- Reduce wait time by 25%.
- Reduce setup by 20%.
- Reduce travel/transport by 25%.
- Eliminate all hazard items.

Nonflammable Blending

- Reduce setup by 20%.
- Reduce travel/transport by 25%.
- Reduce wait time by 50%.
- Reduce unnecessary processing by 50%.
- Eliminate all hazard items.
- Reduce unit cost.
- Reduce cycle time.

Do's and Don'ts

Must or Can Do's	Can't Do's
■ Can make decisions about improvements in the blending process as long as there is no negative effect on the other organizations with which blending interfaces. ■ Must get agreement from another department prior to executing a change if the proposed change requires an adjustment by that department in how it operates.	■ No overtime. Event should stay within regular working hours.

Close Day 2

Once we finished the evaluation, we completed our close-of-day activities. First I reviewed the day's agenda and noted what we had achieved. Next, we completed our plus-minus exercise. The team felt that one plus for the day was its use of the WWO skills which helped keep the team working together on issues. Team members also liked the process observation activity because it provided hard evidence about how much they do in their jobs and how real the waste is that frustrates them. They also were excited about the possible fixes that began to emerge and just how much real improvement those fixes could make. They had no minuses for Day 2. Before we finished for the day, I alerted the team as to tomorrow's focus.

Day 3 - Solve the Performance Issue

The team started at 8 AM. As usual, my co-leader and I arrived early to be sure that our meeting area was still set up correctly. Once the team arrived, I began the session with a brief review of the purpose of the event, our approach, and what we had accomplished thus far. I asked the team for any thoughts or comments about our progress to date before we looked at the day's agenda. There were none, so I previewed the day's agenda with the team and got its feedback.

The priority focus for Day 3 was *Task D3. Solve the Performance Issue* (Exhibit 15). In this task, the team conceives and selects the best ways to achieve the Kaizen event's goals and elevate the performance of the target work process. The team had four main activities to complete: (1) generate improvement ideas, (2) trim improvement ideas, (3) conduct an experiment, and (4) select improvement ideas. The team would only conduct an experiment if it needed to test whether an idea would be effective in eliminating waste.

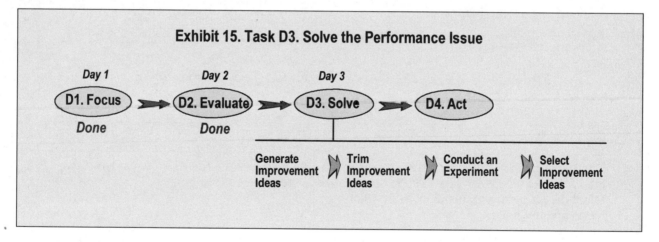

Exhibit 15. Task D3. Solve the Performance Issue

Generate Improvement Ideas

There are two main techniques a team uses to generate improvement ideas: brainstorming and "ask an expert." In brainstorming, team members voice whatever ideas come to mind as ways to eliminate a form of waste. In ask an expert, the team uses the input of other employees in the work process; this input is collected in response to the pre-event flyer and in the course of the personal interviews done during the walk through. When available, the team also uses the improvements stored in best practice databases and improvements already in use at other work sites. Our pre-event preparation indicated that neither of these latter resources were available in this case.

The team brainstormed improvement ideas to each work process separately, since each work process had a separate set of goals and process observations. We began with cylinder preparation. In our Kaizen method, we first build brainstorming sheets as a focusing aid. Each sheet is a flipchart page on which a separate goal is recorded. Below the goal, the team lists examples of the waste targeted by the goal. These examples are taken from the Process Analysis Sheet. The examples listed on each brainstorming sheet are the most resource-consuming instances of the waste the team observed during its process observation. Exhibit 16 presents the brainstorming sheets for the cylinder preparation goals.

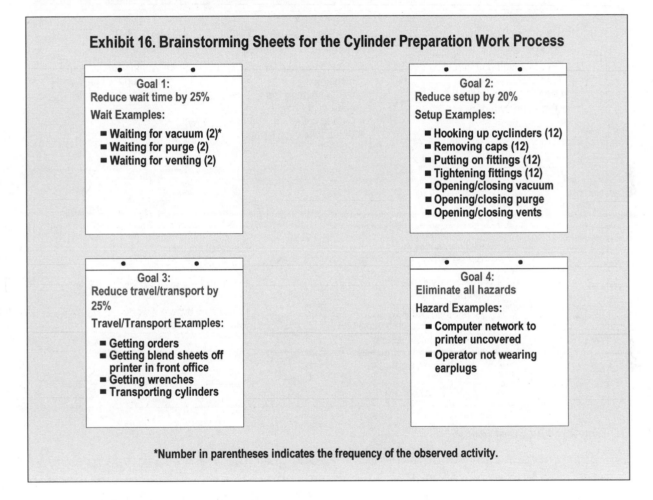

Exhibit 16. Brainstorming Sheets for the Cylinder Preparation Work Process

Goal 1:
Reduce wait time by 25%

Wait Examples:

- Waiting for vacuum (2)*
- Waiting for purge (2)
- Waiting for venting (2)

Goal 2:
Reduce setup by 20%

Setup Examples:

- Hooking up cyclinders (12)
- Removing caps (12)
- Putting on fittings (12)
- Tightening fittings (12)
- Opening/closing vacuum
- Opening/closing purge
- Opening/closing vents

Goal 3:
Reduce travel/transport by 25%

Travel/Transport Examples:

- Getting orders
- Getting blend sheets off printer in front office
- Getting wrenches
- Transporting cylinders

Goal 4:
Eliminate all hazards

Hazard Examples:

- Computer network to printer uncovered
- Operator not wearing earplugs

*Number in parentheses indicates the frequency of the observed activity.

We split building the sheets among the team members so it took only 10 minutes to prepare them. We next proceeded to generate improvement ideas. We worked on one goal at a time, with a time limit of 10 minutes for brainstorming solutions. The team read over the examples as a way to focus brainstorming. I stood at the easel and recorded the ideas as team members offered them. In brainstorming, any idea is accepted and listed. Our rules are simple: (1) one speaker at a time, (2) say whatever comes into your head, (3) no one judges any ideas during brainstorming, and (4) keep generating ideas until time is up. After the team finished brainstorming ideas for all the goals, we returned to each goal and looked at the input other employees had provided about how to improve the work process. We added those ideas to our lists if they were not already included.

Once the team finished generating improvement ideas for the cylinder preparation work process, we built brainstorming sheets for the blending work process (Exhibit 17) and repeated the brainstorming procedure.

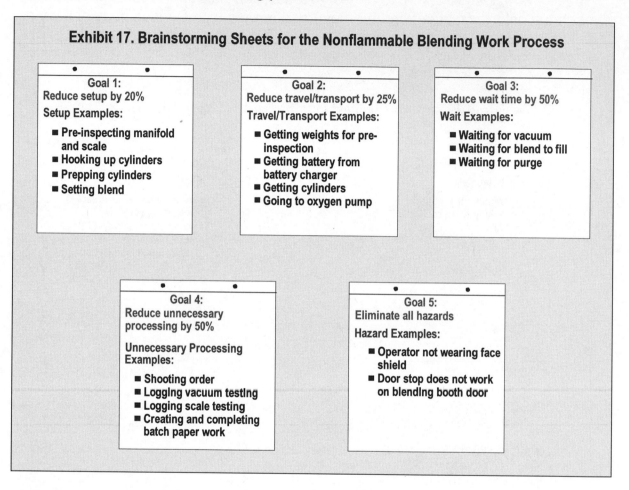

Exhibit 17. Brainstorming Sheets for the Nonflammable Blending Work Process

Goal 1:
Reduce setup by 20%

Setup Examples:
- Pre-inspecting manifold and scale
- Hooking up cylinders
- Prepping cylinders
- Setting blend

Goal 2:
Reduce travel/transport by 25%

Travel/Transport Examples:
- Getting weights for pre-inspection
- Getting battery from battery charger
- Getting cylinders
- Going to oxygen pump

Goal 3:
Reduce wait time by 50%

Wait Examples:
- Waiting for vacuum
- Waiting for blend to fill
- Waiting for purge

Goal 4:
Reduce unnecessary processing by 50%

Unnecessary Processing Examples:
- Shooting order
- Logging vacuum testing
- Logging scale testing
- Creating and completing batch paper work

Goal 5:
Eliminate all hazards

Hazard Examples:
- Operator not wearing face shield
- Door stop does not work on blending booth door

Trim Improvement Ideas

After generating improvement ideas for each goal, the team's task was to review each idea and explore whether it was worth pursuing further. This meant that, for a given idea, the sense of the team was that doing the improvement would not be prohibitively costly, would be effective in advancing the achievement of the goal, and would not harm safety. If an idea satisfied these concerns, it was retained. If it did not, it was dropped from further consideration. If the team was uncertain about the idea, we did an experiment to test the question about which we were unsure. The key to this trimming process is having the team thoroughly explore each idea with the person who offered it so that everyone understands just how it would work. Frequently, team members have very different notions of what an improvement idea as recorded on the list really means. The use of WWO skills is critical in drawing out the meaning of each idea. This benefits the team later when it proceeds to execute the improvements.

After discussing each idea for improving the cylinder preparation process, the team voted whether each was worth pursuing. All the ideas passed the "worth pursuing" test. The team next explored the improvement ideas it generated for the blending work process. Here, three ideas raised concerns; the remaining ideas passed the team's "worth pursuing" test. The first idea raising concern was moving the label scraping operation from the blending work process to the cylinder preparation process. Nathan was not happy with the notion of adding work to the cylinder preparation process. He understood that it made sense in terms of the type of work it was, but reminded us that he currently did not have the time to get the process done as it stood. He asked, "How am I going to get it done by adding still another operation to it?" The team took the concern seriously. Without Nathan's sign-off, this improvement would not be made. Through discussion, the team worked out with Nathan what the likely time savings would be on the cylinder preparation process when we made all the proposed improvements. We then struck a deal with him. Reggie, speaking for the team, offered: "If we don't get down to this cycle time for cylinder prep, then we will put the label removal and painting operation back into the blending work process." Nathan agreed with the offer. Reggie added that he would show Nathan a technique the fill operators used to remove labels that seemed to work well.

The next idea that raised concerns involved eliminating the vacuuming, purging, and venting operations in the blending work process. Vincent summed up the feeling of those who supported the idea: "We are just duplicating what has already been done in cylinder preparation. We never see any benefits from it." But other team members felt that eliminating this operation was a risky step and needed to be tested before it could be pursued. The team decided to do an experiment on this idea.

The last idea raising concern involved reducing the rolling time for filled cylinders from 10 minutes to 5. The rationale was that the added time was unneeded. Reggie said: "We had to do this [reducing rolling time] a few times last year to get products out to customers who were screaming for them because they were so delayed. Our backs were to the wall. We did it, and we had no problems. Maybe we can do it regularly?" On the other hand, some team members worried whether we could reach the mixture levels of the blended gases that we promised our customers by rolling cylinders for just five minutes. Again, the team felt an experiment was needed.

Conduct an Experiment

An experiment tests the effectiveness of an improvement idea. It provides the information needed to rate the value of an idea in eliminating waste so that the team can make the most intelligent selection of improvement ideas. We structure an experiment by using a template that guides the team in defining the question it is exploring, the method it will use to develop information about the question, and the test it will apply to judge what the answer to the question is. This experiment protocol is also useful when the team must submit a formal request for a change in a work standard. We add to the protocol the findings of the experiment and attach it to the submission as evidence supporting the request.

The team developed and then executed protocols for each experiment. The protocol for the rolling experiment is presented in Exhibit 18, along with the results found. The reduced rolling time proved effective in ensuring the proper mixing of the blended gases. Eliminating the added vacuuming of the cylinder in the blending process also proved effective, as it did not result in added impurities in the cylinder. The experiments took an hour and a half to complete. Clarice, Reggie, and Vincent did the experiments, while the remainder of the team moved to the next task.

Exhibit 18. Experiment: Testing the Effects of Reduced Rolling Time

Purpose	Determine whether reducing the current standard rolling time cylinders from 10 minutes to 5 will produce an adequate mixing of gases.
Conducted By	Clarice T., Reggie B., and Vincent L.
Total Time	30 minutes
Hypothesis	If we compare the mix achieved after rolling a sample of three cylinders of the most complicated nonflammable blend for 5 minutes with the mix realized after rolling for 10 minutes, then we will observe no difference.
Resources	Three B-size cylinders each with a blend of 10% N_2/He. This blend of gases is the most difficult for which to achieve a proper mix.
Measure	Analyze gas to determine mix.
Decision Rule	If we find that the mix of the N_2/He gases analyzes at 10% for each cylinder after 5 minutes of rolling, then we will conclude that rolling for 5 minutes is effective.
Description	A 10% N_2/He mix was blended in three B-size cylinders. The N_2 (the heavier component) was added first; the He was added second. Three cylinders were rolled on a cylinder rolling device for 5 minutes. The cylinders were analyzed, and the level of mix achieved was compared to the target level (10%).
Results	The mix in each cylinder analyzed at 10% after 5 minutes of rolling, the same result achieved by rolling for 10 minutes.
Conclusion	Five minutes is sufficient to allow mixing of gas components when the heavier gas is added first and the lighter gas second.
Learning	No additional learning.

Select Improvement Ideas

The team members not involved in conducting the experiments reviewed the list of ideas for improving the cylinder preparation work process to determine their priority for execution in the event. We used a voting method to rank the ideas, placing at the top the ideas that were most effective, least costly, and most "doable" within the confines of the event. The team then performed the same voting activity for the list of ideas for improving the nonflammable blending work process and included the two ideas under study simply because removing them, should they fail, would be easier than adding them. The team then decided which of the ideas on each list—beginning with the highest priority ideas—it could implement in the event. Any remaining ideas were placed on a follow-up action list to be pursued after the event. One idea placed on the follow-up action list involved installing a switch in the blending booth for the oxygen pump. This would not have been costly (estimated at $200) but would have greatly reduced travel/transport, as the oxygen pump was some 100 feet from the blending booth and had to be accessed repeatedly. When discussed by the team, there was enthusiastic support for the idea but a firm conviction that it would take a great deal of conversation with the Engineering Group which would have to approve the action—and which was against such an idea. On this basis, we put the idea on our follow-up action list.

The team listed the improvement ideas selected for execution in the event on a separate flipchart page (Exhibit 19, next page). When Clarice, Reggie, and Vincent finished the experiments, they returned and reported the results to the team. Both experiments proved the effectiveness of the improvements tested, so the list of ideas for implementation in the event did not need to be adjusted.

Close Day 3

Once we finished listing the improvement ideas we would implement in the event, we completed our close-of-day activities. I reviewed the day's agenda and what we had achieved. Then we completed our plus-minus exercise. The team again felt that one of the pluses for the day was its use of WWO skills, which helped especially when it explored the different improvement ideas brainstormed. The other big plus was the brainstorming exercise because, team members said, they could get all their ideas out and no one stopped them short. They had no minuses on Day 3. Before we finished for the day, I alerted the team as to the focus for the remaining two days.

Days 4 and 5 - Act to Improve the Target Work Process

As usual, the team started at 8 AM and my co-leader and I arrived early to be sure that our meeting area was still set up correctly. Once the team arrived, I began our work with a brief statement of the purpose of the event, our approach, and what we had accomplished thus far. I asked the team for any thoughts or comments about our progress to date before we looked at the day's agenda. There were none, so I previewed the day's agenda with the team members and got their feedback.

Exhibit 19. List of Selected Improvement Ideas

Improvement Idea	Goal Affected
Cylinder Preparation Process	
Establish a lower minimum purge pressure.	1
Reduce the level to which cylinders need to be vacuumed (now 200 psig).	1
Hook unused vacuum pump in tandem to current vacuum pump to speed vacuum and purge operations.	1
Install hand wheels on pigtails of the prep manifold to speed hook-up of cylinders.[1]	1
Have storage bins for each type of cylinder valve adapter mounted on manifold.[1]	2, 3
Replace wrenches used in hook-up operations and have a separate set for prep area.[1]	2, 3
Organize cylinders in storage area by expiration date (soonest in front).[1]	2
Shift preparation of 296 Ar/O_2 to blending area.[2]	2
Place trip protector over exposed line from computer network to printer.	4
Counsel worker on use of earplugs.	4
Nonflammable Blending Process	
Eliminate vacuum, purge, and vent in blending area.	3
Move painting and scraping of labels to cylinder preparation process.	1
Replace wrenches and locate in blending area.	1, 2
Install a battery charger in blending area.	2
Place prepped cylinder storage area closer to blending area.	2
Have nets stored at blending workstation.	2
Reduce rolling time.	3
Eliminate allocation of cylinders.	4
Eliminate logging of scale testing data.	4
Use only one card per batch; use sticker on card.	4
Do scale check once a week.	4
Print lab addendum from bar code machine.	4
Eliminate recording pressures and weights on fill orders.	4
Fix door stop on blending booth.	5
Counsel worker on use of face shield.	5

[1]Worker input obtained from either the personal interview conducted during the walk through or in response to the pre-event flyer.
[2]This blend is always filled using a cylinder that previously contained the same gas. The cylinder only needs to be vented, not vacuumed and purged—therefore, the most time-consuming operations completed in the cylinder preparation work process are not necessary.

The priority focus for Days 4 and 5 was *Task D4. Act to Improve the Target Work Process* (Exhibit 20). This task makes the changes in the work process and workplace that eliminate waste and produce business benefits. This is always the most satisfying part of a Kaizen event for team members as they see their efforts translated into results. The task has three main activities: (1) create action plans, (2) execute improvement ideas, and (3) measure results.

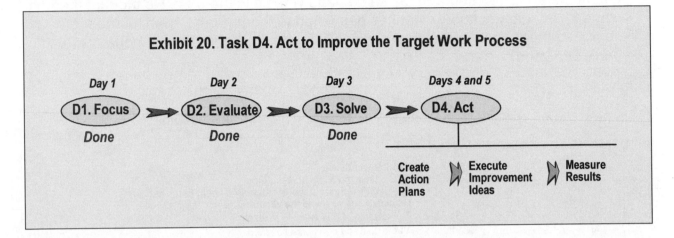

Exhibit 20. Task D4. Act to Improve the Target Work Process

The night before, my co-leader and I had prepared a "What, Who, When" chart that detailed our image of which team members would work on the different improvement actions. Splitting up the team to execute different actions would allow us to get changes made faster. We set a goal for each improvement idea as a guide for the team members who would execute it. Before we began making changes, I shared the chart with the team and got its feedback. We then made a few adjustments to better match people and assignments.

Create Action Plans

Before making changes, the team reviewed each improvement idea to identify any that seemed either complicated or potentially risky in that a mistake in implementation might have a significant consequence with respect to cost, time, or impact on the work. For these ideas, my co-leader and I worked with the team members to complete an action plan to guide their execution of the improvement. An action plan ensures that you have the resources you need and understand the steps you must take to execute the process improvement successfully. The only change idea the team felt needed an action plan was deploying the unused vacuum pump in tandem with the current vacuum pump to speed the vacuum and purge operations in the cylinder preparation work process. Exhibit 21 (next page) presents the action plan for this improvement idea.

Execute Improvement Ideas

The excitement of Kaizen team members peaks when the opportunity arrives to execute their improvement ideas. It is at this point in the event when they experience the satisfaction of actually making improvements in the work process and work setting. Before we begin, we once again review safety procedures and ensure that everyone is wearing safety gear. At this event, the execution of most of the improvement ideas went smoothly. Some items required extra effort. We had trouble locating a supplier for the hand wheels we wanted to place on the pigtails of the cylinder prep manifold. These wheels allow hand tightening and speed cylinder hook-up. When we thought we would have to give up on this change, Nathan remembered that he had ordered some of the same hand wheels in the past. He thought they had come in, but did not know what had happened to them. Some team members searched the maintenance area and finally found the hand wheels, none of which had been used.

Exhibit 21. Action Plan for Deploying the Unused Vacuum Pump

Goal

To:	Reduce wait time by 35%
For:	ABC Gases and all its stakeholders
By:	Hooking the unused vacuum pump in tandem to the current vacuum pump to speed the vacuum and purge operations
So That:	The mission of this event is realized
Conditions:	All the do's and don'ts are satisfied
Standards:	1. Change idea executed as planned
	2. Waste reduction accomplished

Plan

Getting Ready Steps

1. Obtain work permit.
2. Obtain vacuum line blueprints.
3. Obtain work safety procedures.
4. Gather safety equipment.
5. Aoquire a ladder.
6. Acquire wrenches.
7. Gather pipe fittings.
8. Gather pipe threader, solder, and torch.

Doing Steps

1. Test spare vacuum pump to make sure it operates.
2. Service the pump (perform basic maintenance).
3. Trace the pipeline to find best tie-in location.
4. Connect the two vacuum lines together.

Following Up Steps

1. Verify that the system works.

Resources

People

Nathan H., Maintenance
James L., Fill Operator
Thomas C., Fill Operator

Resources (cont'd)

Information

- Vacuum line blueprints
- Work safety procedures

Equipment, Materials, Etc.

■ Ladders	■ Pipe fittings	■ Solder
■ Wrenches	■ Torch	■ Pipe threader

Problems/Solutions

Possible Problem	Fix
Vacuum pump does not operate	Troubleshoot and repair

Fallback

If you can't get the idle pump to work, the team's fallback plan is to purchase a replacement pump for the unit currently in use. The pump is 25 years old and is grossly underpowered for its current workload. The team has found that we could obtain a new vacuum pump that could pump three times the cubic feet per minute of the current unit for a cost of $2,800. The team has checked this with the plant manager, and he is willing to purchase the new pump if the team can't get the idle pump to work.

One of the blending process improvements raised some concerns. The process observations showed a great deal of unnecessary processing associated with writing information tags for each cylinder. On the tag, the operator recorded the type of blend, the weight of the mix, bar code numbers, order numbers, and other information. Creating these tags was not part of the work standard, but something that the lab desired and was added to the process informally. Executing the improvement idea to eliminate these tags meant convincing the lab technicians that the handwritten tags were not needed. Clarice reported that the lab technicians had grown accustomed to the tags and would not agree to their elimination.

To address this concern, Clarice and the team assigned to making this improvement prepared a presentation for the other lab technicians. The presentation showed the technicians how much waste was associated with writing the tags and how the same information that appears on the tag was already easily available. (The information appears both on the order that accompanies the cylinders and in a database that the lab uses.) She included in the presentation a demonstration of how the information could be printed from the computer onto the lab addendum, a form used by the lab. The presentation worked, and the team was able to execute the improvement. Clarice felt that the key to success was showing an understanding at the start for how the lab technicians used these tags and why they felt they were necessary. In her words: "We needed to show that we were including their needs in our solution and not just satisfying our needs."

Measure Results

With the improvement ideas executed, the team turned its efforts to measuring results. This step detects and quantifies the work process and business benefits produced by the Kaizen event. It provides the information needed to verify whether the event achieved its mission and goals. Our Kaizen process measures both operating improvements and monetary benefits. The team measured the operating improvements by repeating its process observations of each work process doing a similar batch of work but now executed in a manner that incorporated the improvements made by the team. Measuring monetary benefits translates the operating and non-operating changes into dollar savings or revenue gains, adjusting for the cost associated with implementing any of the changes. We computed both hard and soft monetary benefits. Hard monetary benefits are savings or revenue gains that begin to flow as soon as the event ends. Soft monetary benefits require an additional management action before they can be realized. In this event, hard monetary benefits were realized for the two work processes the team modified. The soft benefits would flow from the replication of the improvements to the flammable fill side of the Oakland plant and then to the nonflammable and flammable blending fill operations at the three remaining plants producing blended gases. These replication benefits are judged "soft" because the managers at these sites will need to authorize the changes before the improvements can be made.

Operating Improvements

Computation of operating improvements is facilitated by a spreadsheet contained in the Kaizen Tool Kit. Exhibit 22, next page, presents the operating improvement realized for the cylinder preparation work process; Exhibit 23 (page 56) presents the operating improvements achieved for the nonflammable blending work process.

The cylinder preparation work process went from requiring 141 steps to just 92 steps after implementation of the team's improvements. This reduction in the number of required operations is even more striking given that the work accomplished by this process was increased to absorb scraping labels and touch-up painting of cylinders—tasks previously done in the blending work process.

The cycle time of the cylinder preparation work process was reduced by 35%. This shrinking of the work while expanding its outputs was largely due to installing a second vacuum pump which accelerated the preparation process and by eliminating unnecessary paperwork. The addition of the scrapping and painting activities did not add to cycle time because the activities are accomplished concurrent with the vacuuming, purging, and venting operations. In this way, wait time is transformed into productive activity. Indeed, wait time was completely eliminated (reduced 100%).

The other significant improvement was in unnecessary processing, which was reduced 22%. An unwanted byproduct of moving the scrapping and touch-up painting of cylinders into the cylinder preparation work process was an increase in setup activities, as scrapping and painting are entirely setup in nature—that is, these work activities prepare cylinders to be filled but do not accomplish the filling. Nonetheless, the improvement resulted in a 55% increase in labor productivity. The team also felt that a follow-up Kaizen event focusing on setup would reduce its presence in the cylinder preparation work process.

The improvements reduced nonflammable blending process activities from 336 steps to 227. The major benefits were in cycle time (reduced 31%), value-added ratio (increased 98%), wait (reduced 96%), setup (reduced 23%), and travel/transport (reduced 20% in time and 18% in distance). These improvements were largely due to reducing rolling time; eliminating the vacuum, purge, and vent operations; transferring cylinder prep activities to the cylinder preparation work process; installing the battery charger and nets in the blending area; and eliminating unneeded paperwork. The value-added ratio was increased by trimming down these elements of waste. Overall, the improvements elevated labor productivity by 45% and increased throughput capability by 80%. One anomalous finding in the post-observation was a spike in rework (almost four minutes). This was due to three problems that were not observed earlier: a faulty safety valve, a improperly purged cylinder, and a blending sheet with the incorrect mix specified. Clearly, rework should be an area looked into in future events.

Exhibit 22. Summary of Operating Improvements for Cylinder Preparation Work Process

Work Process Element	Original Finding	Post-Change Finding	Improvement
Human Operations			
■ Distance (in feet)	1,255	875	30%
■ Cycle time	02:19:30	01:30:14	35%
■ Value-added ratio	0.00	0.00	0
■ Travel/transport	00:08:28	00:08:06	4%
■ Motion	00:00:00	00:00:00	
■ Wait	01:29:45	00:00:00	100%
■ Interruption	00:00:00	00:00:00	
■ Search	00:01:20	00:00:00	100%
■ Inspect	00:00:00	00:00:00	
■ Rework	00:00:28	00:00:25	11%
■ Setup	00:28:29	01:13:09	-157%
■ Unnecessary processing	00:11:00	00:08:34	22%
■ Hazard	2 found	2 removed	100%
Machine Operations			
■ Accelerated vent, vacuum, and purge operations			
Other Operating Improvements			
■ Inventory	No effect	No effect	No effect
■ Materials or supplies	No effect	No effect	No effect
■ Energy or other utilities[1]	No effect	No effect	No effect
■ Equipment or tools[2]	No effect	No effect	No effect
■ Facility (square feet needed)	No effect	No effect	No effect
■ Scrap or waste	No effect	No effect	No effect
■ Contracted services	No effect	No effect	No effect
■ Labor productivity (cylinders per person/hour)	5.16	7.98	55%
■ Throughput (batches per line/shift/week)	17.20	26.60	55%

[1]Any added energy consumption due to using a second vacuum pump was estimated to be offset by reduced total pumping time.
[2]See Exhibit 24 for reporting of the cost associated with buying new hand tools and a battery charger.

Exhibit 23. Summary of Operating Improvements for Nonflammable Blending Work Process

Work Process Element	Original Finding	Post-Change Finding	Improvement
Human Operations			
▪ Distance (in feet)	3,602	2,937	18%
▪ Cycle time	02:25:14	01:40:15	31%
▪ Value-added ratio	0.08	0.22	175%
▪ Travel/transport	00:31:40	00:25:20	20%
▪ Motion	00:00:00	00:00:00	
▪ Wait	00:27:23	00:01:05	96%
▪ Interruption	00:02:39	00:00:20	87%
▪ Search	00:00:24	00:00:05	79%
▪ Inspect	00:01:55	00:01:13	37%
▪ Rework	00:02:23	00:06:10	-159%
▪ Setup	00:42:08	00:32:35	23%
▪ Unnecessary processing	00:25:26	00:11:06	56%
▪ Hazard	2 found	2 removed	100%
Machine Operations			
▪ Accelerated vent, vacuum, and purge operations			
Other Operating Improvements			
▪ Inventory	No effect	No effect	No effect
▪ Materials or supplies	No effect	No effect	No effect
▪ Energy or other utilities	No effect	No effect	No effect
▪ Equipment or tools[1]	No effect	No effect	No effect
▪ Facility (square feet needed)	No effect	No effect	No effect
▪ Scrap or waste	No effect	No effect	No effect
▪ Contracted services	No effect	No effect	No effect
▪ Labor productivity (cylinders per person/hour)	2.48	3.59	45%
▪ Throughput (batches per line/shift/week)[2]	20.00	35.90	80%

[1]See Exhibit 24 for reporting of the cost associated with buying new hand tools and a battery charger.
[2]Actual throughput was four orders (eight cylinders) per day prior to changes because the blending fill operator needed to prepare cylinders to fill or wait for cylinders. The improvements in the cylinder preparation work process eliminated this problem.

Monetary Benefits

Computation of monetary benefits is also facilitated by a spreadsheet contained in the Kaizen Tool Kit. Before using the spreadsheet, the Kaizen co-leader calculates the dollar value of labor time savings and then calculates the dollar value of non-labor savings. Examples of non-labor savings include inventory, materials or supplies, energy or other utilities, equipment or tools, facility space, scrap or waste, and contracted services. Once the computations are made, the benefits are designated as either hard or soft based on whether they flow immediately following the Kaizen event or require additional management action. Exhibit 24 presents the information the team developed to enable it to compute the monetary benefits produced by the event. The information was obtained from the scope document and the team's process observations and was supplemented by input from the site manager.

Exhibit 24. Information Used to Compute Monetary Benefits Produced by the Kaizen Event

Information	Cylinder Preparation	Nonflammable Blending
Number of lines operating per shift per day	2	3
Number of shifts per day	1	3
Number of days operating per year	250.00	250.00
Work process cycles per line per day (average)	3.44	4.00
Labor time per cycle - before event (in seconds)	8,370.00	2,904.70
Labor time per cycle - after event (in seconds)	5,414.00	2,005.00
Time savings per cycle (in seconds)	2,956.00	899.70
Loaded labor rate per hour	$22.50	$22.50
1 year labor savings (lines x shifts x 250 days)	$31,777.00	$50,608.13
Additional Benefits		
Flammable blending process at Oakland		
▪ 1 year labor savings (4 lines x 3 shifts x 250 days)		$67,477.50
Replications at Canton, Jackson, and New Orleans		
▪ Blending process (2 lines x 1 shift x 250 days/site)		$33,738.75
▪ Cylinder preparation process (1 line x 1 shift x 250 days/site)		$31,777.00
Cost of Improvements		
Battery chargers (7 at Oakland, 6 for other sites @ $50 each)	$650.00	
Tools (7 sets at Oakland, 6 sets for other sites @ $20 each)	$260.00	
Vacuum pumps (3 for other sites @ $2,500 each)	$8,400.00	

The team determined that all monetary savings at Oakland associated with the non-flammable blending process and cylinder preparation were hard savings as the changes needed to realize them were done in the event and the labor freed was re-deployed to the flammable blending side. These savings amounted to $82,385.13 for the first year of operation. From this amount, the cost of the tools and battery chargers for the three nonflammable blend booths was deducted to achieve a first year savings of $82,175.13. Exhibit 25 summarizes the final monetary benefits from the Kaizen event.

Exhibit 25. Summary of First Year Monetary Benefits From the Oakland Kaizen Event

Monetary Benefit	Total Value	Hard	Soft
Labor Dollar Savings			
■ Oakland blending work process (3 nonflammable fill lines; 4 flammable fill lines)	$118,085.63	$50,608.13	$67,477.50
■ Oakland cylinder preparation work process (2 lines)	$31,777.00	$31,777.00	$0.00
■ Replication of blending work process improvements at remaining ABC sites (6 lines)	$33,738.75	$0.00	$33,738.75
■ Replication of cylinder preparation work process improvements at remaining ABC sites (3 lines)	$31,777.00	$0.00	$31,777.00
Subtotals	$215,378.38	$82,385.13	$132,993.25
Savings From Other Operating Improvements			
■ None			
Less New Expenses			
■ Battery chargers	$650.00	$150.00	$500.00
■ Tools	$260.00	$60.00	$200.00
■ Vacuum pumps	$8,400.00	$0.00	$8,400.00
Total expenses	$9,310.00	$210.00	$9,100.00
Summary			
Net benefits	$206,068.38	$82,175.13	$123,893.25

The benefits produced on the flammable side at Oakland required that the team continue its change implementation past the week. With Sandra's support, this was a certainty—but we abided by the rule that if a change is not achieved during the event and requires additional action, it is counted as soft *until that action is taken*. The soft savings at Oakland amounted to $67,477.50 for the first year, less the costs of improvements. With the replication of the process improvements to the re-maining three plants producing nonflammable blended gases, the first year soft sav-ings would rise by $31,777.00 for the cylinder preparation work processes and $33,738.75 for the blending processes.

By Friday noon, we had completed *Task D4. Act to Improve the Target Work Process*. We were ready to address the tasks that end a Kaizen event.

Following Up the Event

As I have said, the Kaizen event is not just about process improvement, it is about engaging, energizing, and enabling people. Therefore, my co-leader and I ended the event by consolidating the experiences of the team and informing all stakeholders about what happened in the event and what it produced. Finally, I mined the learning from my experience in leading the event.

Close the Kaizen Event

The first task in closing the event is to complete the documentation of the Kaizen event. This produces the information we need to lead the close-out meeting with the team and brief the stakeholders about the results. A helpful tool in this regard is the Kaizen Summary. This document, which is contained in the Kaizen Tool Kit, summarizes the essentials of the event—namely, its focus, direction, results, and follow-up actions. The Kaizen Summary for this event is presented in Exhibit 26 (next page). The team uses this information plus the photographs taken during the pre- and post-process observations to prepare a storyboard. This storyboard is approximately three by five feet in size and includes the mission, goals, and do's and don'ts for the event; before, during, and after photos; a team photo with names; and a copy of the Kaizen Summary. While the team prepared the storyboard, I prepared certificates of recognition for the team members.

I then led the team in its close-out meeting. I began by summarizing for the team what it had accomplished. I returned us to the scope request and covered the mission and goals undertaken by the team. I summarized how the team members worked together to uncover the sources of waste in the workplace, generated ideas for improvement, and made those improvements. I briefly reviewed the results the team achieved. At this point, I sought the team's perspective about the critical factors that produced success; the barriers, if any, encountered during the work; and what the team members learned from this experience. The key success factors for the team were everyone working toward the same goals and the excitement and satisfaction of being able to make change and see its results.

The key worry of the team was sustaining some of the changes, since these required that people change their habits. The lab technicians and the maintenance workers especially needed to incorporate new ways of doing their work, and they would need support and encouragement to adhere to the new approach. A big plus was that representatives of these departments participated in making the changes and saw for themselves that the changes were effective.

Exhibit 26. Kaizen Summary

Kaizen Team Members
Joseph V., Kaizen leader
Mark G., Kaizen co-leader
Reggie B., Fill Operator
Thomas C., Fill Operator
Vincent L., Supervisor
Nathan H., Maintenance
James L., Fill Operator
Clarice T., Lab Technician

Mission Statement

To increase profit without increasing price and elevate customer satisfaction with on-time delivery by reducing the cycle time and cost of the nonflammable blending work process for ABC Gases and its stakeholders.

Operating Measure	Cylinder Preparation		Nonflammable Blending		Monetary Measure	Result
	Pre-Event	Post-Event	Pre-Event	Post-Event		
Cycle Time	02:19:30	01:30:14	02:25:14	01:40:15	Labor Savings	$215,378.38
Value-Added Ratio	0.00	0.00	0.08	0.22	Non-Labor Savings	$0.00
Labor Productivity	5.16	7.98	2.48	3.59	Dollar Gains	$0.00
Throughput	17.20	26.60	20.00	35.90	Less New Costs	$9,310.00
					Total Dollar Benefits	$206,068.38

Charge #: 20-2001   Dates of Event: 8/06-8/10   Total Cost of Event: $14,500

	Goal	Result	Action Item	Who	Date Due	Status
Cylinder Preparation Process						
1	Reduce wait time by 25%	Down 100%	None			
2	Reduce setup by 20%	Up 157%	Do a follow-up Kaizen event focusing on travel/transport and setup	Team	10/15/01	Open
3	Reduce travel/transport by 25%	Down 4%				
4	Eliminate all hazard items	Eliminated	None			
Nonflammable Blending Process						
5	Reduce setup by 20%	Down 23%	None			
6	Reduce travel/transport by 25%	Down 20%	Install oxygen pump switch in the blending booth	Reggie	9/15/01	Open
7	Reduce wait time by 50%	Down 96%	None			
8	Reduce unnecessary processing by 50%	Down 56%	None			
9	Eliminate all hazard items	Eliminated	None			
10	Reduce unit cost	Down 28%	None			
11	Reduce cycle time	Down 31%	None			

The team developed three basic learnings: (1) the company has, in its people, the intelligence it needs to continuously improve its competitiveness; (2) using a systematic approach that guides people in applying their intelligence—such as Kaizen—turns that potential into a reality; and (3) given the way most companies still operate, it takes someone in management to understand and act on these first two learnings if a company is to benefit from the people within it.

Once we concluded our discussion, I asked the team to complete the Kaizen Participant Feedback Form. This evaluation provides quantitative information about how the team experienced the event. The evaluation is completed anonymously, and the results computed after the event is finished.

With the evaluation done, my co-leader and I recognized the performance of individual team members and distributed their certificates of recognition. At this point, we also distribute a token gift from management to each team member for his or her efforts and contributions to advancing business success. In this event, each team member received a department store gift certificate for $10—not much, but appreciated nonetheless.

Our last order of business was to prepare for the briefing of the stakeholders. As usual, each team member assumed responsibility for covering some element of the presentation.

Communicate Results to All Stakeholders

The meeting of the stakeholders was arranged prior to the beginning of the Kaizen event so that we could be assured of a place for the gathering and presence of the employees, supervisors, and managers. We held the meeting on the loading dock, which had sufficient room to accommodate us all. The team used flipcharts and the storyboard to help with its presentation. Reggie reviewed the scope of the event and ended with the mission and goals for the event. Vincent picked up by reviewing what waste is and sharing examples of waste observed during the event. Clarice and Nathan reviewed the brainstorming ideas the team came up with, crediting to the employees the ideas the team got from them. Finally, Thomas and James reviewed the results achieved by the event, using the Kaizen Summary as an aid. The team then opened up the discussion to the group for questions.

We expected that people would focus immediately on the spike in setup time that occurred in the cylinder preparation work process as a result of our work. They did not. Instead, they focused on the change ideas they heard, recognizing the ones they had contributed. They credited the common sense in the changes made—such as having the battery charger in the blending areas; dropping out the unnecessary vacuum, purge, and vent cycle in blending; and moving the cylinder prep activities in the blending process into cylinder preparation.

Once discussion of the changes and their results was done, the group quickly identified the need to transfer these improvements to the flammable blending process;

management endorsed this action. Sandra assumed responsibility for contacting Mike Fellows and sharing with him the results of the event and proposed transfer of the improvements to the remaining three plants producing blended gases. She also said she would make sure that the work standards for both the cylinder preparation and blending work processes were modified to incorporate the improvement ideas.

Our last order of business was to discuss "leave-behind" measures that the workers could monitor to verify that their improvements were sustained. For each work process, cycle time was the agreed-on measure. For the blending work process, we added on-time delivery. Sandra said that since she was already checking these measures, she would provide the Kaizen team weekly updates on each. We suggested posting the measures and current status in the work area so that everyone could participate in monitoring the work process's performance and feel good about its improved performance. The Kaizen team members also agreed to get together each Monday and check where they stood with respect to each measure and, if problems existed, discuss ways to resolve them. Sandra committed to be available to the team should it need her support.

We concluded the event by the close of business Friday, five very busy days from when we began.

Mine Learning From the Completed Event

After the event, I had one more task to complete: to extract my learning from having led the event. For this, I used the targets against which we evaluate our performance of Kaizen (Exhibit 27) and applied the SRLD[SM] (Status, Reason, Learning, Direction) method. This method is delineated in R.L. Vitalo and P.A. Bierley *Mining Learning From Performance* (Hope, ME: Lowrey Press, 2003).

Exhibit 27. Targets Used to Evaluate the Performance of a Kaizen Event

Task: To eliminate waste in a work process by empowering people to use Kaizen to uncover improvement opportunities and make changes

Targets:

1. Documentation of the event completed

2. Measurable business and work process benefits accomplished as defined in the mission and goals of the event

3. New learning about the Kaizen tool, its application, and the Kaizen leader's capabilities generated

4. New opportunities for Kaizen events identified

5. New or improved work standards developed during the Kaizen event applied to work process (or submitted for approval)

6. Performers elevated in their business participation, ownership, teamwork, confidence in their ability to make change, and capabilities to achieve success

7. Sustained or improved safety

Status of Achievement

The results of the event indicated that the team had achieved its mission as specified. Specifically, it improved the nonflammable blending work process by reducing the cycle time and unit cost for ABC Gases and its stakeholders. As a consequence, the team enabled the business to increase its profit without increasing price and elevate customer satisfaction with better on-time delivery. At the time I completed the SRLD[SM], I did not have the final information about on-time delivery, but the reduced cycle time and increased throughput clearly positioned the business to achieve it. With respect to the goals of the event, the team met or exceeded 8 out of 11 goals (Exhibit 28). This is less than expected. The team did comply with the do's and don'ts of the event, produced new work standards for each work process, and elevated the safety in both work processes. Both the level of participation exhibited by the Kaizen team and the results of the Kaizen participants' feedback indicated that team members were engaged, energized, and enabled in contributing to the improvement of the business by the event. Every team member indicated learning from the event, and the team overall rated the event an 8.5 out of 9.0 with respect to its collective satisfaction. One new opportunity for a Kaizen event was identified. This is a follow-up event on the cylinder preparation work process that focuses on reducing travel/transport and setup. Both of these types of waste offer significant opportunities for additional improvement. In summary, I judged six out of the seven targets listed in Exhibit 27 achieved at or above expectation. The first target was achieved below expectation, as we failed to accomplish every goal.

Exhibit 28. Summary of Goal Achievement		
Goals	**Result**	**Status[1]**
Cylinder Preparation Process		
1 Reduce wait time by 25%	Down 100%	Exceeded
2 Reduce setup by 20%	Up 157%	Not met
3 Reduce travel/transport by 25%	Down 4%	Not met
4 Eliminate all hazard items	Eliminated	Met
Nonflammable Blending Process		
5 Reduce setup by 20%	Down 23%	Exceeded
6 Reduce travel/transport by 25%	Down 20%	Not met
7 Reduce wait time by 50%	Down 96%	Exceeded
8 Reduce unnecessary processing by 50%	Down 56%	Exceeded
9 Eliminate all hazard items	Eliminated	Met
10 Reduce unit cost	Down 28%	Met
11 Reduce cycle time	Down 31%	Met

[1]Status may be met, not met, or exceeded.

Reasons for Results

The factors that enabled the success we experienced seemed to be the following: (1) we followed the Kaizen process; (2) we took time to explore and understand the work processes we were trying to improve; (3) the team was open to challenging the way things had been done and to using ideas developed by employees not on the team; and (4) the team was ready to let the facts drive their decisions, not their biases. One factor that hindered achieving even greater success than we experienced was my failure to identify the Engineering Group as a stakeholder to the event and to ensure that its personnel were informed and on board with the event. As a result, a change that would have significantly reduced travel/transport in the blending work process (installing a switch for the oxygen pump in the blending booth) could not be made.

Learning

Two key learnings emerged for me, each of which reinforced current guidelines. The first is the importance of getting the work standards for the target work process *prior* to the event and having it available during the event. Once again, we saw that practice had acquired a necessity that was more folklore than fact when we were able to check the work standard and see precisely what was required behavior. The second learning was the importance of understanding who the stakeholders are and connecting with them up front so that they are aware of and aligned with the purposes of the event.

Direction

My direction coming out of this event was to reinforce my execution of the guidance in the *Kaizen Desk Reference Standard* and to devise an approach to inquiring about stakeholders that would better uncover all who exist with respect to a given event. One idea is to add a question during my interview with the event coordinator prior to the event that focuses on decisions in the workplace, asking who would have to comment on each or approve. I could structure the decisions around people; operations; physical layout; modification of infrastructure (e.g., utilities, wiring); and types of tools and equipment used.

Postscript

During the two months following the event, I kept in touch with the team to stay abreast of the status of the changes we had made and to offer any support the team might need in sustaining improvements. The team reported that the changes were sustaining at Oakland and the improvements were being realized. A conversation with Sandra confirmed this information. She was especially pleased that the on-time delivery rates for blended gases had gone up from the pre-event level of 84% to 98% given the same volume of demand. She reported that both Mike and she felt that the event was a big success. However, getting the results replicated in the remaining plants, she reported, was still under discussion. "We are solid here, and I am eager to see what we can do as a next event. But we have had a culture in this business where managers have had the latitude to run their shops their way. Mike hasn't wanted to take that culture on. Maybe seeing what it is costing us will trigger some action. I can't say." In the end, as the team said, given the way most companies still operate, it takes someone in management to understand and act if a company is to benefit from the people within it.

Milestone A. Document a Scope for the Kaizen Event

Preview

This milestone gathers and verifies information that defines the focus, boundaries, and expectations for performing a Kaizen event. It ensures that you have the information needed to:

- understand what process and business level benefits are expected from the proposed Kaizen event,

- verify that all stakeholders are aligned with the proposed purposes of the event,

- evaluate whether a Kaizen event can accomplish the results desired from the event, and

- prepare for leading the Kaizen event.

Getting Ready Tasks

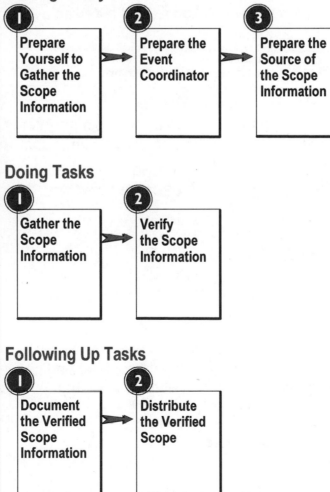

1 Prepare Yourself to Gather the Scope Information

2 Prepare the Event Coordinator

3 Prepare the Source of the Scope Information

Doing Tasks

1 Gather the Scope Information

2 Verify the Scope Information

Following Up Tasks

1 Document the Verified Scope Information

2 Distribute the Verified Scope

Purpose

To gather information that defines the focus, boundaries, and expectations for performing a Kaizen event.

Benefit

Ensures that you have the information needed to:

- understand what process and business level benefits are expected from the proposed Kaizen event,

- verify that all stakeholders are aligned with the proposed purposes of the event,

- evaluate whether a Kaizen event can accomplish the results desired from the event, and

- prepare for leading the Kaizen event.

Application

Use this knowledge when you are asked to lead a Kaizen event and before you commit to doing the event.

Performer

Kaizen leader. The performer must be proficient in clarifying, confirming, constructively criticizing, and hitchhiking, and be able to perform simple inferencing—that is, use the guidance of a rule to determine what action or decision is appropriate in a given circumstance.

Resources

People

- Sponsor of the event

Information, Knowledge, and Training

- *Task A1. Understand the Scope Document*

- *Working With Others* (J.S. Byron and P.A. Bierley, Hope, ME: Lowrey Press, 2003) - teaches how to get (clarify and confirm) and give (constructive criticism and hitchhiking) ideas and information in ways that build collaboration and elevate results

Materials, Tools, and Other Resources

- Kaizen Tool Kit
  - Guide: The Event Coordinator Role

- Guide: The Role of Providing Scope Information
- Kaizen Scope Document
- Scope Statement Checklist

Output

- Complete, consistent, and verified scope document
- Paper and electronic folders established for the proposed event

Method

Getting Ready Tasks

1. Prepare yourself to gather the scope information.

    a. Understand the scope document.

    Tip: Master the purpose, importance, and contents of the scope document. Ready yourself to explain the document and the information it requires to the person with whom you will work to complete it. Also ready yourself to test the internal and external consistency of information you are provided. For detailed guidance, see *Task A1. Understand the Scope Document* (beginning on page 91).

    b. Create a folder for the requested event.

    Tip: Establish both a paper and an electronic folder for the event since materials will be received in both formats. Use these folders to centralize all materials related to the event. Use the location of the event and its proposed date as the folders' name (e.g., Oakland 12-01-02).

    c. Learn about the business requesting the Kaizen event.

    Tip: Learn about the business from Internet sources including the business's website, business research sites, and online newspapers. Learn about the business from print materials including its annual report, product brochures, other public communications, and library reference materials. Build a picture of basic information about the business including where it operates; its industry group; its size with respect to employees, revenues, and expenses; its products or services; and its major competitors. Also learn about the company's purpose, values, and vision, and anything available on its current business strategy.

2. Prepare the event coordinator.

    a. Identify who is designated as the event coordinator.

    Tip: From the person requesting the Kaizen event, obtain the name of the person with whom you should coordinate activities associated with planning and performing the Kaizen event. This person will be your designated event coordinator. Also obtain the event coordinator's mailing address, e-mail address, and telephone number. Finally, determine when the person may be first contacted. This contact should not occur before the individual knows about his or her designation as the event coordinator.

b. Establish a working relationship with the event coordinator.

1) Contact the event coordinator.

2) Introduce yourself and your task.

   Tip: Say your name and company affiliation. Identify your assignment as leading a Kaizen event and who asked you to do the event. Name the work process that the event will improve.

   a) Establish whether the person knows what a Kaizen event is, how it is used, and what types of benefits it can produce.

   b) As required, provide knowledge about what a Kaizen event is, how it is implemented, and what types of benefits it can produce (see Guide: Explaining What Kaizen Is, pages 79 and 80).

3) Orient the event coordinator to his or her role.

   Tip: Tell the event coordinator about his or her role (see Guide: The Event Coordinator Role, page 81). Emphasize that it is your responsibility to prepare for and conduct the event but that you cannot succeed without the event coordinator's guidance and support.

4) Determine who will be the source for defining the scope of the event.

   Tip: Orient the event coordinator to the task of defining the scope of the event. Tell the event coordinator that defining the scope is the first task in doing a Kaizen event. The scope describes the focus and boundaries of the event and makes clear what key stakeholders expect from it. Ask whether the event coordinator will be providing the information needed or if someone else will be the source. If another person is the source for scope information, obtain that person's name, telephone number, and mailing and e-mail addresses, and identify when you may first contact him or her.

   If the event coordinator is the source of the scope information, tell him or her that you will use telephone conversations to gather the scope information (if you cannot easily arrange a face-to-face meeting). Alert the event coordinator that, typically, it takes about three conversations to complete this task. There will be two conversations to gather the information. Then you will draft the scope document, send it to the event coordinator, and recontact him or her to confirm or correct it.

   Reaffirm the importance of defining the scope of the event: without a proper scope statement, the Kaizen event is unlikely to produce the business benefits sought, and resources will therefore be wasted. Tell the event coordinator that you will also provide him or her with a description of what is involved in supplying the scope information. Send the event coordinator a copy of the Guide: The Role of Providing Scope Information (page 82). An electronic copy of this document is in the Kaizen Tool Kit.

5) Close the first meeting.

Tip: Ask for and answer any questions the event coordinator may have about the topics discussed or any other issue related to planning and conducting the Kaizen event. Thank the person for the opportunity to talk with him or her. If the event coordinator is not the source of the scope information, state that you will be recontacting him or her once you have a draft of the scope document so that he or she can provide feedback on its contents. Also inform the event coordinator that you will give him or her periodic updates on progress in setting up the event. Be sure to send the event coordinator a copy of the Guide: The Event Coordinator Role. An electronic copy of this document is in the Kaizen Tool Kit.

3. Prepare the source of the scope information.

Tip: If the event coordinator is the source of the scope information, skip this task since you have already addressed it.

a. Contact the source of the scope information.

b. Introduce yourself and your task.

Tip: Say your name and company affiliation. Identify your assignment as leading a Kaizen event and who asked you to do the event. Name the work process that the event will improve. Name the event coordinator and state that he or she identified the person with whom you are speaking as the contact for defining the scope of the event.

1) Establish whether the person knows what a Kaizen event is, how it is used, and what types of benefits it can produce.

2) As required, provide knowledge about what a Kaizen event is, how it is implemented, and what types of benefits it can produce (see Guide: Explaining What Kaizen Is, pages 79 and 80).

c. Orient the source to what a scope is and how it is defined.

Tip: Inform the source that defining the scope is the first task in doing a Kaizen event. The scope describes the focus and boundaries of the event and makes clear what key stakeholders expect from it. Tell the source that you will use telephone conversations to gather the scope information (if you cannot easily arrange a face-to-face meeting). Alert the source that, typically, it takes about three conversations to complete the task. There will be two conversations to gather the information. Then you will draft the scope document, send it to the person with whom you are speaking, and recontact him or her to confirm or correct it. Reaffirm the importance of defining the scope of the event: without a proper scope statement the Kaizen event is unlikely to produce the business benefits sought, and resources will therefore be wasted. Inform the person that you will be sending him or her a guide explaining the role of providing scope information (Guide: The Role of Providing Scope Information, page 82).

d. Close the first meeting.

Tip: Ask for and answer any questions the person may have about providing scope information or any other issue related to the Kaizen event. Set the time for your first conversation to define the scope of the proposed event. Thank the person for the opportunity to talk with him or her. As a follow up to the conversation, be sure to send the source a copy of the Guide: The Role of Providing Scope Information.

Doing Tasks

1. Gather the scope information.

a. Contact the source of the scope information as arranged.

b. Obtain the basic business information.

1) Ask clarifying questions to obtain each item of information contained in the basic business information section of the scope document.

Tip: Use the knowledge provided in section A. Basic Business Information of the Guide: Why Each Scope Information Item Is Needed (see *Task A1. Understand the Scope Document*, page 101) to help the source understand why you are asking for this information.

2) Confirm the answers you receive.

3) Verify that the answers provide the information required.

Tip: Check that the information offered responds to the needs of the item. You need to understand the meaning of each term in the scope so that you can detect whether the information provided by the source is responsive. Also you need to check what you hear from the source against the information you gathered through your own research. If the information received is not what you need, credit the value of the information offered, then clarify more precisely what you need. For example, "You shared with me some of the discussion leadership had as it considered what direction to emphasize across the business this year, and this gives me a good sense as to how leadership is thinking. But I need to know what they finally decided on as the business driver for this year." If the person offers you information inconsistent with what you have learned from prior research, you need to resolve the conflict to ensure that the facts you record in the scope document are correct.

4) Record the information you confirmed.

   Tip: Write out the information. Also check off the items on the Scope Statement Checklist (pages 83 and 84) corresponding to the information gathered.

c. Obtain the target work process information.

1) Ask clarifying questions to obtain each item of information contained in the target work process information section of the scope document.

   Tip: Use the knowledge provided in section B. Target Work Process Information of the Guide: Why Each Scope Information Item Is Needed (see *Task A1. Understand the Scope Document*, page 102) to help the source understand why you are asking for this information.

2) Confirm the answers you receive.

3) Verify that the answers provide the information required.

   Tip: Check that the information offered responds to the needs of the item. You need to understand the meaning of each term in the scope so that you can detect whether the information provided by the source is responsive. Also you must check what you hear from the source about the work process against the information you previously gathered. If the information received is not what you need, credit the value of what the source offered you, then clarify more precisely what you need. If the person offers information inconsistent with what you have learned from prior research or from what the source previously stated, you need to resolve the conflict to ensure that the facts you record in the scope document are correct.

4) Record the information you confirmed.

   Tip: Write out the information. Also check off the items on the Scope Statement Checklist (pages 83 and 84) corresponding to the information gathered.

d. Learn the expectations of the Kaizen event.

1) Ask clarifying questions to obtain each item of information contained in the expectations for the Kaizen event section of the scope document.

   Tip: Use the knowledge provided in section C. Expectations for the Kaizen Event of the Guide: Why Each Scope Information Item Is Needed (see *Task A1. Understand the Scope Document*, page 105) to help the source understand why you are asking for this information. Be ready to work with the source to guide him or her in providing the needed information, especially with respect to the information about estimated benefits and costs. You will need to explain the concepts of soft and hard benefits and help the person estimate each. Also you will need to work with the source to estimate the cost of the event (Exhibit 1). Review each possible element of cost with the source and get his or her sense of whether it is relevant and, if it is, what its dollar value will likely be.

Exhibit 1. Estimated Costs and Benefits	
Item	**Meaning**
Cost of a Kaizen event	In general, the cost of an event is computed by calculating participant salaries for the week of their participation, consultant costs, travel and accommodation expenses, and any special expenses (e.g., equipment rentals, meals).
Hard savings or dollar gains	The yearly cost reductions or revenue increases that flow immediately after the Kaizen event concludes and require no additional actions beyond the event to be realized. These are also referred to as *hard benefits*.
Soft savings or dollar gains	The yearly cost reductions or revenue increases that require some additional action beyond the Kaizen event to realize (e.g., redeployment of workers to other productive tasks, review and approval of a new work standard, additional sales to benefit from greater throughput). These are also referred to as *soft benefits*.

2) Confirm the answers you receive.

3) Verify that the answers provide the information required.

   Tip: Check that the information offered responds to the needs of the item. You need to understand the meaning of each term in the scope so that you can detect whether the information provided by the source is responsive. Also you must check what you hear from the source regarding expectations against the information the source previously supplied. If the information received is not what you need, credit the value of what the source offered you, then clarify more precisely what you need. If the person offers information inconsistent with what he or she previously stated, you need to resolve the conflict to ensure that the facts you record in the scope document are correct.

4) Record the information you confirmed.

   Tip: Write out the information. Also check off the items on the Scope Statement Checklist (pages 83 and 84) for which information was gathered.

e. Confirm with the source that the documented scope is accurate.

1) Draft the scope document using the information obtained from the source.

   a) Confirm the completeness of the scope information.

   Tip: Review your Scope Statement Checklist (pages 83 and 84) to confirm that all information has been gathered. Return to any missing item and either obtain it from the source or identify with the source how you may get the information you need.

   b) Confirm the consistency of the scope information.

   Tip: Use the Guide: Checking Consistency of Scope Information (*Task A1. Understand the Scope Document*, pages 106 and 107) to assist you in uncovering inconsistencies. Resolve any inconsistencies before continuing.

   c) Prepare the scope document for review.

2) Submit the draft scope document to the source of the scope information.

3) Confirm that the document accurately reflects the information he or she supplied; correct the document as needed.

4) Repeat Steps 1) through 3) until the source verifies that the document accurately captures the information he or she supplied.

5) Orient the source to the next step in documenting the scope.

   Tip: Inform the source that now you are ready to share the draft scope document with each key stakeholder to ensure that it represents a consensus perspective. Emphasize that sharing this information with the key stakeholders for their approval does not imply any lack of trust in the source, but is an effort to ensure that all parties have a complete picture of the proposed event and do not feel in anyway blind-sided.

2. Verify the scope information.

   Tip: You must verify the scope of the Kaizen event with key stakeholders. Stakeholders are individuals or groups that may either affect the success of an event or be affected by its occurrence. Key stakeholders are the subset of all stakeholders who have authority either over whether the event happens or whether the changes proposed for the target work process get implemented.

   a. Coordinate the verification process with the event coordinator.

      1) Alert the event coordinator that a draft scope document exists.

      2) Orient the event coordinator to the next step in documenting the scope.

         Tip: Inform the event coordinator that you are now ready to share the draft scope document with each key stakeholder to ensure that it represents a consensus perspective. Be sure to remind the event coordinator that he or she is one of the people with whom you need to verify that the draft scope accurately captures the focus, boundaries, and expectations for the Kaizen event.

3) Confirm who the key stakeholders are.

Tip: The key stakeholders to an event usually include, at a minimum, the sponsor of the event (if he or she is not one of the following individuals), the manager of the target work process and that person's manager, and the head or his or her designee of each organization outside the target work process who must be consulted before that process may be modified. The sponsor is the person who originally requested the event.

a) Explain the concept of "key stakeholders" to the event coordinator.

b) Learn who the key stakeholders in the proposed event are.

Tip: Obtain each person's name, mailing address, e-mail address, and telephone number.

c) Ask the event coordinator to inform each key stakeholder that the Kaizen event leader will be contacting him or her to discuss the scope of the proposed Kaizen event.

b. Confirm the accuracy of the draft scope document with each stakeholder.

1) Prepare the key stakeholders.

Tip: Send each stakeholder a copy of the draft scope document. Attach a cover letter introducing yourself and your task and ask the person to review the scope document and determine whether he or she feels that it accurately represents the focus the Kaizen event should have, the boundaries it needs to stay within, and the results it should produce. Alert the person that you will be contacting him or her by phone to verify that the scope document is accurate. If possible, identify a date and time when you will contact the person.

2) Contact each key stakeholder to obtain his or her feedback.

Tip: You need to interact with each stakeholder, so a telephone call or a face-to-face meeting is required. Confirm that the stakeholder knows what a Kaizen event is, how it is used, and what types of benefits it can produce. Provide knowledge about Kaizen as required. Ask for and answer any questions the stakeholder has about the task at hand. Get the stakeholder to verify that he or she has read the scope document. This is critical, as any discussion beyond this point only has value if the party has read the document. If the person has not read the document, reschedule the contact.

3) Confirm the basic business information contained in the scope.

Tip: Get the stakeholder's verification or modification of the information. Be sure to confirm whatever the stakeholder shares. Also be sure to evaluate the information to ensure that the changes proposed by the person do not create any inconsistencies. If the changes do create inconsistencies, resolve them immediately with the stakeholder before proceeding.

4) Confirm the target work process information.

Tip: Get the stakeholder's verification or modification of the information. Include feedback on the work process map (referred to in Item B5 of the scope document), if one exists, for the target work process Kaizen is to improve. Be sure to confirm whatever the stakeholder shares. Also be sure to evaluate the information to ensure that the changes proposed by the person do not create any inconsistencies. If the changes do create inconsistencies, resolve them immediately with the stakeholder before proceeding.

5) Confirm the expectations for the Kaizen event.

Tip: Get the stakeholder's verification or modification of the information. Be sure to confirm whatever the stakeholder shares. Also be sure to evaluate the information to ensure that the changes proposed by the person do not create any inconsistencies. If the changes do create inconsistencies, resolve them immediately with the stakeholder before proceeding.

6) Repeat Steps 2) through 5) with each key stakeholder.

7) Resolve any differences among the key stakeholders.

Tip: Review the feedback from all stakeholders. If any stakeholder has modified the document, you need to pass the modification by each other stakeholder and the event coordinator to confirm their acceptance.

c. Judge whether you have verified the scope document.

Tip: Use the Guide: Deciding Whether the Scope Document Is Verified (page 85) to judge whether you have verified the scope document with the key stakeholders. You cannot proceed with the Kaizen process until a verified scope is documented.

Following Up Tasks

1. Document the verified scope information.

   Tip: Update the electronic scope document with the verified changes and save the file in the computer folder you established for the proposed event.

2. Distribute the verified scope.

   Tip: Print and send a copy of the verified scope to each key stakeholder, the event coordinator, and the source of the scope information.

Check Steps

Use the following checklist to verify that the milestone was achieved.

Benchmark	√
Getting Ready Tasks	
1. Prepared yourself to gather the scope information.	☐
2. Prepared the event coordinator.	☐
3. Prepared the source of the scope information.	☐
Doing Tasks	
1. Gathered the scope information.	☐
2. Verified the scope information.	☐
Following Up Tasks	
1. Documented the verified scope information.	☐
2. Distributed the verified scope.	☐

Tips

- Assume nothing. Do not assume that the person you have been told is the source of scope information is knowledgeable. Do not assume that management below or above the person sponsoring the event is aligned with the purposes of the event. Do not assume that someone has verified that it makes good business sense to do the event either on its own terms or when judged against other possible points of focus.

- When in doubt, check it out. If any content seems inconsistent or simply leaves you uncertain, explore the issue with the source of the scope information. Trust your instincts. In the end, if it does not make sense to you, you will not be able to use the information to guide your performance or support anyone else's performance.

- To develop proficiency in documenting a scope, practice preparing a scope document for the ABC Gases Kaizen event using the information presented in the beginning of the *Kaizen in Action* unit (especially pages 22 through 25). Check your answer against the solution provided beginning on page 86 of this unit.

Guide:
Explaining What Kaizen Is

Purpose of Kaizen

Kaizen (pronounced *ki-zen*) is the Japanese word for continuous improvement. As we use the term, it is a method that strives toward perfection by eliminating waste. It eliminates waste by empowering people with tools and a methodology for uncovering improvement opportunities and making change. Kaizen understands waste to be any activity that is not value-adding from the perspective of the customer. By value-adding, we mean any work done right the first time that materially changes a product or service in ways for which a well-informed and reasonable customer is willing to pay.

Benefits

A Kaizen event benefits the business and its customers, employees, and suppliers.

For the business itself, Kaizen:

- produces improved top-line (e.g., revenues and profits) or bottomline (e.g., cost reduction) results depending on the precise improvements made; and
- elevates the abilities of the business's employees, providing the company with a greater capability to grow.

For customers, Kaizen:

- provides products and services that better satisfy their values.

For employees, Kaizen:

- provides an opportunity to remove barriers to job success and satisfaction and the tools with which to do it.

For suppliers, Kaizen:

- can stimulate new challenges and create new opportunities to learn and strengthen their relationships with the business sponsoring the Kaizen events.

How Kaizen Is Performed

Our Kaizen process is accomplished through a set of milestones (see Exhibit 1, next page). Three milestones, performed in sequence, guide us in getting ready to do a Kaizen event. One milestone completes the event, and one milestone follows up to ensure that the changes made in the event produce continued benefits for the stakeholders.

Continued...

Guide:
Explaining What Kaizen Is (continued)

Exhibit 1. The Kaizen Process

	Milestone
Getting Ready	Milestone A. Document a Scope for the Kaizen Event Milestone B. Analyze Whether to Conduct the Kaizen Event Milestone C. Prepare for the Kaizen Event
Doing	Milestone D. Perform the Kaizen Event
Following Up	Milestone E. Institutionalize the Process Improvements

Milestone D. Perform the Kaizen Event is the heart of the Kaizen process. It encompasses the activities the team of employees executes during the week the Kaizen event occurs. The team defines a focus for its improvement efforts, evaluates the target work process by measuring current performance, solves performance issues identified during the evaluation, makes changes to the work process, and measures and reports on the results produced.

Guide:
The Event Coordinator Role

Task

To be the point of contact for information about the business and arrangements for planning, executing, and following up on the Kaizen event.

Steps

1. Provide the information needed to define the scope of the Kaizen event or designate a person who can.

   Tip: The scope of the Kaizen event defines where it should focus and what results it should produce for the business. It also provides information needed to plan the Kaizen event and execute it in a manner that is received positively by all stakeholders.

2. Handle on-site logistics and assist with travel arrangements or designate a person to do these tasks.

3. Assist with communication tasks associated with the Kaizen event.

   Tip: Prior to the event, you need to act as the local contact able to respond to questions from employees about the event and prompt team members to be available and on time for the event. Following the event, you need to carry forward communication about what was done by the employees during the event and what results they produced.

4. Select and arrange for an appropriate gift (e.g., ball cap, coffee mug, T-shirt, department store gift card) to be given to team members.

5. Provide input and feedback on decisions related to preparing for and conducting the event and ensuring the effective follow through on its results.

6. Follow up on action items coming out of the Kaizen event, as required.

Tips

- You can speed the time to the event by being available to the Kaizen leader and providing timely turnaround on requests for information, ideas, and feedback.

- If you are not familiar with the target work process or work setting, quickly notify the Kaizen leader of someone who is. Recommend someone who is both knowledgeable of the target work process and respected by the other employees so that they view the preparations for the event as credible.

Guide:
The Role of Providing Scope Information

Task

To supply the information needed to define the focus, boundaries, and reason for conducting the Kaizen event.

Steps

1. Provide the information needed to describe the business.

    Tip: Knowing about the business helps the Kaizen leader ensure that decisions made with respect to the Kaizen event and the target work process are consistent with the business's direction and welfare. The information you supply includes the type, size, and geographical scope of the business; the current business intent and drivers; and the key customer expectations for the products and service outcomes the business produces.

2. Provide the information needed to describe the target work process.

    Tip: This information describes the target work process, the perceived problem with its current operation, and how that problem affects business success. It helps in planning the Kaizen event (e.g., by identifying required safety gear and procedures for visiting the workplace).

3. Provide the information needed to describe the expectations for what the Kaizen event should achieve.

    Tip: This information tells how stakeholders will measure the effects of the Kaizen event, the size benefits the business expects to reap, who should be engaged in the event, and other details critical to preparing for the event (e.g., names and contact information of proposed Kaizen team members).

4. Provide feedback on the draft scope document to ensure that it correctly captures the information you supplied.

Tips

- If you are not personally familiar with the target work process or work setting, or with the expectations stakeholders have for the Kaizen event, promptly inform the person who selected you and recommend someone who can provide the information needed to define a scope for the proposed Kaizen event. Recommend someone who is both knowledgeable of the target work process and respected by the other employees so that they view the preparations for the event as credible.

Scope Statement Checklist

A. Basic Business Information

1. Name of business	☐
2. Locations at which business operates (three largest sites and total number of sites)	☐
3. Industry group to which business belongs	☐
4. Size of business including number of employees and yearly operating budget and revenues	☐
5. Product or service outcomes produced (list all if possible, or just the main products and identify the total number of products produced)	☐
6. The three to five key customer concerns about the product or service output the Kaizen event will affect	☐
7. Business level end-to-end work flow map for the product or service output the Kaizen event will affect	☐
8. Statement of the company's purpose, values, and vision	☐
9. Description of the company's current business driver and key performance improvement targets	☐

B. Target Work Process Information

1. Name of target work process and its product or service output	☐
2. Locations at which target work process is performed (city, state)	☐
3. Location at which event is to be held (complete address)	☐
4. Name of the on-site manager of the target work process	☐
5. Target work process map (if available) beginning with the inputs and ending with the product or service output	☐
6. Status of the target work process as a just-in-time production system	☐
a. Takt time for target work process (if just-in-time is implemented)	☐
b. Whether unit of output is a batch and, if so, how many units in the batch	☐
c. Cycle time for the target work process	☐
7. Number of employees (full and part time)	☐
8. Number of lines and shifts (if any)	☐
9. Number of variations in work flow to accommodate different product or service outputs	☐
a. If mixed model, where the Kaizen event should focus: backbone or name of model	☐
10. Number of locations in the work site (e.g., workshop, administrative office, storage room) where target work process operations are performed	☐

Continued...

Scope Statement Checklist (continued)

B. Target Work Process Information (continued)	
11. Presence of machinery in the target work process ☐ Yes ☐ No If yes, then complete items 11a through 11d	☐
a. Number of machines	☐
b. Percentage of cycle time executed by machines	☐
c. Contribution to unit cost	☐
d. Special characteristics, if any (e.g., sensitive to temperature change)	☐
12. Perceived problem with the target work process (e.g., cycle time too long, defects too many, throughput too low, excess inventory, unit cost too high, product not delivered when needed)	☐
13. Perceived impact of the work process problem on the business (e.g., lost sales, shrinking profit due to low margins, customer dissatisfaction)	☐
14. Other work processes or departments with which the target work process interfaces (i.e., from which it gets something or gives something or uses something in common)	☐
a. Interface organizations that must be consulted before the target work process may be modified (if any)	☐
15. Safety guidelines related to the target work process or work area (attach list or record "none exist")	☐
a. Any personal protective equipment or clothing a person must wear while visiting this workplace	☐
C. Expectations for the Kaizen Event	
1. Measures the Kaizen event should affect	☐
2. Desired start and completion dates for the Kaizen event	☐
3. Annual dollar benefits expected from the Kaizen event	
a. Annual hard benefits expected from the event	☐
b. Annual soft benefits expected from the event	☐
4. Other benefits expected from the Kaizen event	☐
5. Estimated cost of the event (including cost of employee time, lost production, travel)	☐
6. Kaizen team's authority and restrictions to make change	☐
7. Employees the customer wants to include on the team (names, e-mail addresses, and telephone numbers)	☐
8. Stakeholders to the event (names and telephone numbers)	☐
9. Person with whom to coordinate logistics and travel (name, e-mail address, and telephone number)	☐

Guide:
Deciding Whether the Scope Document Is Verified

Instructions: The scope statement must be complete and consistent before testing whether the key stakeholders agree with its contents. If all questions listed below are answered "Yes," then the scope document can be considered *verified*.

	Question	Yes	No
Sponsor	Has read the completed scope statement?	☐	☐
	Agrees with the contents of the completed scope statement?	☐	☐
Event Coordinator	Has read the completed scope statement?	☐	☐
	Agrees with the contents of the completed scope statement?	☐	☐
Manager of the Target Work Process	Has read the completed scope statement?	☐	☐
	Agrees with the contents of the completed scope statement?	☐	☐
Manager of the Target Work Process Manager	Has read the completed scope statement?	☐	☐
	Agrees with the contents of the completed scope statement?	☐	☐
Designated Representatives	The designated representative of each organization outside the target work process who must be consulted before the target work process may be modified:		
	Has read the completed scope statement?	☐	☐
	Agrees with the contents of the completed scope statement?	☐	☐

Example:

ABC Gases Kaizen Event Scope Document

A. Basic Business Information

1. Name of business

ABC Gases

2. Locations at which business operates (if many locations, list the three largest and indicate how many sites there are in total)

■ Newark, DE	■ Oakland, CA	Total: 109 locations
■ Madison, WI		

3. Business industry group

Specialty Gases Industry

4. Size of business

Number of employees: 1,200

Yearly operating budget: ~$200 million	Yearly revenue: $240 million

5. Product or service outcomes produced

Cylinders of gas: argon, carbon dioxide, helium, hydrogen, nitrogen, oxygen, neon, and many combinations of these products. In all, over 100 different flammable and nonflammable gas products

6. The three to five key customer concerns about the product or service output the Kaizen event will affect

- ■ Quality of product
- ■ On-time delivery
- ■ Price

7. Business level end-to-end work flow map for the product or service output the Kaizen event will affect

☐ Attached	☒ None exists

8. Statement of the company's purpose, values, and vision

☐ Attached	☒ None exists

9. Description of the company's current business driver and key performance improvement targets

To increase profit margins while not increasing prices

Key performance targets:

1. Reduce cost. Also concerned about on-time delivery and shrinking profit margins.

Continued...

Example:

ABC Gases Kaizen Event Scope Document (continued)

B. Target Work Process Information

1. Name of target work process and its product or service outputs

Nonflammable blending process; produces cylinders filled with mixed nonflammable gases

2. Locations at which target work process is performed (If many locations, list the four largest and indicate how many additional sites there are in total)

▪ Oakland, CA	▪ Canton, OH	Total: 4
▪ New Orleans, LA	▪ Jackson, FL	

3. Location at which event is to be held (complete address)

1234 Industrial Boulevard, Oakland, CA

4. Name of the on-site manager of the target work process

Sandra Shore

5. Target work process map

☐ Attached	☒ None exists

6. A just-in-time production system has been implemented for this work process or its parent work process

☐ Yes If yes, please provide both takt and cycle time ☒ No If no, provide cycle time

6a. Takt time for target work process	6b. Unit of output is a batch	6c. Current cycle time for the target work process
Not known. Kanbans are used but not all elements of a just-in-time production system.	☒ Yes ☐ No If yes, how many units in a batch? 2	1 hour 30 min.

7. Number of employees

Full time: 12   Part time: 0

8. Number of lines and shifts

Lines: 3   Shifts per 24 hours: 3   Shifts per week: 15 (3 x 5 days)

9. Number of variations in work flow to accommodate different product or service outputs

Approximately 50 based on the type of nonflammable gas blend produced

9a. If mixed model, where the Kaizen should event focus

☒ Backbone or ☐ (name model)

10. Number of locations in the work site where target work process operations are performed

☒ One location	☐ Multiple locations If multiple locations, record the number

Continued...

Example:
ABC Gases Kaizen Event Scope Document (continued)

B. Target Work Process Information (continued)

11. Is machinery used in the target work process

☐ Yes ☐ No If yes, then complete items 11a through 11d

11a. Number of machines	11b. Percentage of cycle time executed by machines	11c. Contribution of machinery to unit cost
2 (Blend booth manifold; rolling machine)	90%	10% out of total 100%

11d. Special characteristics (e.g., sensitive to temperature change)

None identified

12. Perceived problem with the target work process (e.g., cycle time too long, defects too many, throughput too low, excess inventory, unit cost too high, product not delivered when needed)

Cost too high; cycle time too long, hindering on-time delivery

13. Perceived impact of the problem on the business (e.g., lost sales, shrinking profit due to low margins, customer dissatisfaction)

Reduced profits; customer dissatisfaction with on-time delivery

14. Other work processes or departments with which the target work process interfaces

- Maintenance
- Lab
- Mix Identification Group
- Bulk Product Group

14a. Organizations that must be consulted before the target work process may be modified

- Maintenance
- Lab
- Mix Identification Group
- Bulk Product Group *only if* the change *requires* a change in the way any of these departments operate

15. Safety guidelines related to the target work process or work area

☒ Attached ☐ None exist

15a. Any personal protective equipment or clothing a person must wear while visiting this workplace

- Earplugs
- Safety glasses
- Safety shoes (steel toes and metatarsal plates)
- Safety gloves

Continued...

Example:

ABC Gases Kaizen Event Scope Document (continued)

C. Expectations for the Kaizen Event

1. Measures the Kaizen event should affect (e.g., unit cost, throughput, first-time quality)
■ Unit cost ■ On-time delivery

2. Desired start and completion dates for the Kaizen event	
Start date: Open	End date: Open

3. Annual dollar benefits expected from the Kaizen event	
Annual hard benefits: At least 2 times the cost of the event	Annual soft benefits: None specified

4. Other benefits expected from the Kaizen event (e.g., safety)
■ Current safety level improved

5. Estimated cost of the event (including cost of employee time, lost production, travel)
$14,500

6. Kaizen team's authority and restrictions to make change	
Do's	**Don'ts**
■ Can make decisions about improvements in the blending process as long as there is no negative effect on the other organizations with which blending interfaces ■ Must get agreement from another department prior to executing a change if the proposed change requires an adjustment by that department in how it operates	■ No overtime. Event should stay within regular working hours.

7. Employees the customer wants to include on the Kaizen team		
Name	**E-mail**	**Telephone**
Reggie B., Fill Operator, Blended Gases	rb@abc.com	123-456-7894
Thomas C., Fill Operator, Blended Gases	tc@abc.com	123-456-7895
Vincent L., Supervisor	vl@abc.com	123-456-7896
Nathan H., Maintenance	nh@abc.com	123-456-7897
James L., Fill Operator, Straight Gases	jl@abc.com	123-456-7898
Clarice T., Lab Technician	ct@abc.com	123-456-7899

Continued...

Example:

ABC Gases Kaizen Event Scope Document (continued)

C. Expectations for the Kaizen Event (continued)

8. Stakeholders to this event

Stakeholder	Name	Telephone
Event coordinator	Sandra Shore	123-456-7890
Maintenance supervisor	Mike T.	123-456-7891
Manager of target work process	Sandra Shore	(same as above)
Manager of the target work process's manager	Mike Fellows	123-456-7878
Safety supervisor	Rufus W.	123-456-7893
Site manager	Sandra S.	(same as above)
Sponsor	Mike Fellows	(same as above)
Work standards supervisor (or contact person)	Sandra Shore	(same as above)
Other person(s) you feel need to be involved	None	

9. Person with whom to coordinate logistics and travel

Name	E-mail	Telephone
Sam W.	Unknown	123-456-7892

Task A1. Understand the Scope Document

Preview

This task helps you master the purpose, structure, and contents of the scope document and the rationale underlying the importance of each. It ensures that you can:

- explain the scope document and its contents to stakeholders and guide them through the process of describing the scope of a proposed Kaizen event; and

- efficiently detect whether the information you gathered is sufficient to document the focus, boundaries, and reasons for the proposed Kaizen event, analyze its appropriateness, and prepare to perform it.

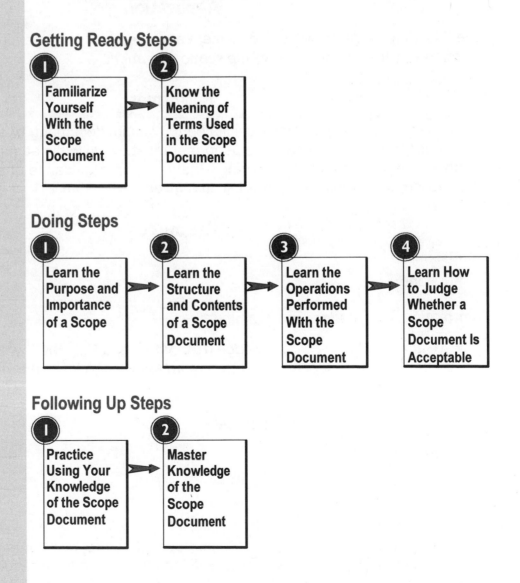

Getting Ready Steps

1 Familiarize Yourself With the Scope Document

2 Know the Meaning of Terms Used in the Scope Document

Doing Steps

1 Learn the Purpose and Importance of a Scope

2 Learn the Structure and Contents of a Scope Document

3 Learn the Operations Performed With the Scope Document

4 Learn How to Judge Whether a Scope Document Is Acceptable

Following Up Steps

1 Practice Using Your Knowledge of the Scope Document

2 Master Knowledge of the Scope Document

Purpose

To master the purpose, structure, and contents of the scope document and the rationale underlying the importance of each.

Benefit

- Prepares you to explain the scope document and its contents to stakeholders and guide them through the process of describing the scope of a proposed Kaizen event.

- Enables you to detect efficiently whether the information you gathered is sufficient to document the focus, boundaries, and reasons for the proposed Kaizen event; analyze its appropriateness; and prepare to perform it.

Application

Use this knowledge before you document a scope for a Kaizen event either to acquire or refresh your understanding of the scope document.

Performer

Kaizen leader and any person designated to explain, document, or analyze the scope for a proposed Kaizen event. The performer must be skilled in acquiring knowledge and be able to perform simple inferencing—that is, use the guidance of a rule to determine what action or decision is appropriate in a given circumstance.

Resources

People

- None

Information, Knowledge, and Training

- *Gathering Practical Knowledge* (R.L. Vitalo and P.A. Bierley, Hope, ME: Lowrey Press, 2003) - teaches how to acquire knowledge for performing procedures and describing things

Materials, Tools, and Other Resources

- Kaizen Tool Kit
  - Kaizen Scope Document

Output

- A person who understands the purpose, structure, and contents of the scope document and the rationale underlying the importance of each

Method

Getting Ready Steps

1. Familiarize yourself with the scope document.

    a. Print a copy of a blank scope document.
        Tip: The Kaizen Tool Kit contains an electronic copy of the scope document.

    b. Note the structure of the scope document.
        Tip: The document is divided into three sections: business information, target work process information, and expectations for the Kaizen event.

    c. Note the contents of the scope document.
        Tip: Each section of the scope document contains information elements that build a picture of the topic of the section (i.e., the business, the target work process, and expectations for the Kaizen event).

2. Know the meaning of terms used in the scope document.

    a. Identify any terms used in the document that are unfamiliar.

    b. Study the definitions of these terms to learn their meaning.
        Tip: Terms used in the scope document are defined in the *Glossary*.

Doing Steps

1. Learn the purpose and importance of a scope.

    a. Learn the purpose of having a scope defined for a Kaizen event.
        Tip: Use the Guide: Understanding Scope (page 99). Read the purpose of a scope definition. Confirm what it communicates by restating the purpose in your own words. Try hitchhiking on the ideas expressed. Test your understanding of the purpose with someone who has already mastered the meaning of a scope definition. If this is not possible, review how the scope information assisted the Kaizen leader in responding to the request to conduct a Kaizen event for ABC Gases as described in the *Kaizen in Action* unit. Use this example to test your learning.

    b. Learn the benefits provided by a defined scope.
        Tip: Use the Guide: Understanding Scope (page 99). Read the benefits of having a scope definition. Confirm what it communicates by restating the purpose in your own words. Try hitchhiking on the ideas expressed. Test your thoughts about this material with someone who has already mastered the meaning of a scope definition. If this is not possible, review how the scope

information benefited the Kaizen leader in conducting the Kaizen event for ABC Gases as described in the *Kaizen in Action* unit. Use this example to test your learning.

c. Learn the special benefits provided by the scope document itself.

Tip: The scope document provides a single repository for all scope information. It allows everyone associated with the Kaizen event to find *in one place* all the information that focuses and bounds the Kaizen event and justifies its performance. It also guarantees that everyone sees exactly the same information, thereby providing everyone with the same opportunity to ensure that the event reflects his or her thinking.

2. Learn the structure and contents of a scope document.

a. Learn the structure of a scope document and the purpose and importance of each section.

Tip: Use the Guide: Understanding Scope (pages 99-100). Read the description of the structure of a scope definition and the type of information each component contains. Compare each description with what you detected during your inspection of the scope document.

b. Learn the information that each element requires and the reason why each element is needed.

Tip: Test whether you can define each element of information the scope document requires. Check your definitions against those provided in the *Glossary*. Next, read the Guide: Why Each Scope Information Item Is Needed (beginning on page 101). Try covering the right-hand column of the guide and generating the answer to the following questions for each information item listed in the left-hand column: Why is this information needed? How will it contribute to conducting a better event? Check your answer against that provided in the guide. If the rationale for an item seems unclear, check with someone who has already mastered the meaning of a scope definition. If this is not possible, review how the information was used in the Kaizen event for ABC Gases as described in the *Kaizen in Action* unit.

3. Learn the operations performed with the scope document.

Tip: There are three operations you will perform with a scope: (1) explain it to the event sponsor, the key stakeholders to the event, and the Kaizen team; (2) document it for each Kaizen event; and (3) analyze whether it describes an event that is likely to produce the benefits sought by the company sponsoring it. Read about these operations in Guide: Understanding Scope (page 100).

4. Learn how to judge whether a scope document is acceptable.

   Tip: A scope document is judged acceptable if it is complete, consistent, and verified as accurate by the key stakeholders. Read about these criteria in the Guide: Understanding Scope (page 100). In preparation for judging a scope document, you need to master how to check consistency of the scope information. Study the Guide: Checking Consistency of Scope Information (beginning on page 106). It lists the elements of a scope document that must logically interrelate. You need to know these relationships between information elements within a scope document well enough that, when you gather scope information, you can detect inconsistencies in the information a source provides and act immediately to resolve them through discussion with the source.

Following Up Steps

1. Practice using your knowledge of the scope document.

   Tip: Create an opportunity where you can role play to explain the scope document. Ask one or more co-workers to give you 40 minutes to explain to them the concept of a scope. Ask them to assume the role of someone who will be asked to provide scope information for a proposed event. Set up a meeting area where you can have privacy. Have a copy of a sample scope document for each person. Do the following steps, observing whether people show signs of understanding what you are saying. If they seem puzzled, make note of this and explore with them why they are puzzled by the item. At the end, get their feedback about how well they feel they understand what a scope is, why it is important, and how it is used.

   a. Greet the participants.

   b. State the purpose of the meeting.

      Tip: Say: "The purpose of this meeting is to provide you with an understanding of the scope document so that we can work together to build the information needed to ensure a successful Kaizen event."

   c. Provide an introductory experience to communicate the importance of having a scope document.

      Tip: A scope document is an instance of understanding a customer's requirements. Use an example of what can happen when you fail to get an accurate picture of what someone seeks from you before you go about providing it. Consider using the Let's Build a Swing: Introductory Learning Experience (pages 108 and 109).

   d. Provide an overview of the scope document.

      1) Tell the definition and importance of the scope document.

2) Distribute a sample scope document to the participants.

Tip: Use a completed scope document that will be understandable to the audience members so they can recognize each example of the information sought.

3) Explain the structure of the document.

Tip: Point out that the document is divided into three sections: A. Basic Business Information, B. Target Work Process Information, and C. Expectations for the Kaizen Event.

4) Describe what is done with the scope information.

Tip: Tell them that three operations are performed on the scope information: (1) it is explained to participants; (2) it is documented for the proposed event; and (3) it is analyzed to determine whether the event, as defined, is likely to produce the benefits the business seeks. Briefly explain each of these operations to the audience.

5) Ask for and answer any questions the participants may have about the definition and importance of a scope, the structure of the scope document, and what is done with it.

e. Explain the basic business information section to the participants.

Tip: Say: "This section provides a description of the business so that the people conducting the Kaizen event can understand the larger enterprise to which their efforts are intended to contribute. The information it records includes the type, size, and geographical scope of the business; the current business intent (i.e., purpose, values, and vision) and drivers; and the key customer expectations for product and service outcomes. This information ensures that decisions made with respect to the Kaizen event and the target work process are consistent with the overall business direction and welfare."

1) Review each information item in the section and tell the reason why the information is needed.

2) As an exercise, build with the participants the basic business information for their organization.

Tip: Point out that, once built, this information is reusable for every Kaizen event done within the organization until or unless the basic business information changes.

3) Ask for and answer any questions the participants may have about the section.

f. Explain the target work process section to the participants.

Tip: Say: "This section provides a description of the target work process—that is, the work process on which Kaizen is to be conducted. It records information one needs to understand the target work process, the perceived problem with its current operation, and how that problem affects business success. It also helps in preparing for the Kaizen event (e.g., identifying required safety gear and procedures for visiting the workplace)."

1) Review each information item in the section and tell the reason why the information is needed.

2) As an exercise, build with the participants the target work process information for a work process with which they are familiar.

   Tip: If there is no work process with which all participants are familiar, build a narrative about a fictitious work process that contains within it the information needed to complete Sections B and C of the scope document. Consider using the example of the Kaizen event detailed in the *Kaizen in Action* unit. Distribute the first four pages of this narrative to the participants and have them read it, then walk them through completing the target work process information for the work process described.

3) Ask for and answer any questions the participants may have about the section.

g. Explain the expectations for the Kaizen event section to the participants.

   Tip: Say: "This section records how the effects of the Kaizen event will be measured, the size benefits the customer expects to reap, who should be engaged in the event, and other information critical to preparing for the event (e.g., names and contact information of people designated to participate in the event)."

1) Review each information item in the section and tell the reason why the information is needed.

2) As an exercise, build with the participants the expectations for the Kaizen event for the work process they described.

3) Ask for and answer any questions the participants may have about the section.

h. Ask the participants for feedback on your presentation.

   Tip: Ask them to comment on what they learned, what elements of your presentation seemed effective, what elements were problematic, and what you might do to improve your communication of knowledge about scope.

2. Master knowledge of the scope document.

   Tip: Recycle your study of scope and the scope document until you are able to explain it to others successfully.

Check Steps

Use the following checklist to verify that the task was done correctly.

Benchmark	√
Getting Ready Steps	
1. Familiarized yourself with the scope document.	☐
2. Know the meaning of terms used in the scope document.	☐
Doing Steps	
1. Learned the purpose and importance of a scope.	☐
2. Learned the structure and contents of a scope document.	☐
3. Learned the operations performed with the scope document.	☐
4. Learned how to judge whether a scope document is acceptable.	☐
Following Up Steps	
1. Practiced using your knowledge of the scope document.	☐
2. Mastered knowledge of the scope document.	☐

Tips

- Think about the work done by audience members. Look for information they may use in their jobs that is similar to the contents or purpose of a scope document. Use this connection to help the audience recognize what a scope document is. Also, look for experiences audience members may have had in which the absence of a clear definition of what they were supposed to do led to their being frustrated in succeeding in their purposes. Use this connection to help the audience recognize why a scope document is important.

Guide:
Understanding Scope

Purpose

A scope defines the focus of the Kaizen event and the reasons for performing it. It is a statement of customer requirements, where the people managing the business are the "customer" of the Kaizen event in that they request and authorize its occurrence. The scope tells you which work process management seeks to improve and why. It also provides you with the information you need to evaluate your customer's request and respond to it in a way that will meet his or her needs.

Benefits

As a Kaizen leader, you are responsible for conducting a Kaizen event that satisfies your customer's expectations. The scope describes the information you need to:

- define a tentative focus for the Kaizen event,

- allow all stakeholders to see a common description of the proposed Kaizen event so that they can judge whether they agree and support the event as proposed,

- make a judgment of whether a Kaizen event is appropriate to hold so that resources are not wasted in events that do not yield adequate business benefits, and

- prepare for the event so that you can ensure that all the resources needed to produce a successful process improvement are in place.

The scope description also lets the customer confirm that the Kaizen leader correctly understands what the customer is seeking prior to the event.

Structure

The scope document is divided into three sections:

- **A. Basic Business Information** - Provides a description of the business so that the people conducting the Kaizen event can understand the larger enterprise to which their efforts are intended to contribute. The information it records includes the type, size, and geographical scope of the business; the current business intent and drivers; and the key customer expectations for the product and service outcomes it produces. This information ensures that decisions made with respect to the Kaizen event and the target work process are consistent with the overall business direction and welfare.

Continued...

Guide:
Understanding Scope (continued)

- **B. Target Work Process Information** - Provides a description of the target work process—that is, the work process on which Kaizen is to be conducted. It records information needed to understand the target work process, the perceived problem with its current operation, and how that problem affects business success. It also helps in planning for the Kaizen event (e.g., required safety gear and procedures for visiting the workplace).

- **C. Expectations for the Kaizen Event** - Records how stakeholders will measure the effects of the Kaizen event, the size benefits the business expects to reap, who should be engaged in the event, and other information critical to preparing for the event (e.g., names and contact information of people designated to participate in the event).

Key Operations

As a Kaizen leader, there are three operations you will need to perform on the scope.

- The *first* is to explain it to your customer, the key stakeholders to the event, and the Kaizen team. This operation enables another person to understand what a scope is, why it is recorded in a document, what information the document contains, how it is used, and the benefits it can produce.

- The *second* operation is to document the scope for a proposed event. This operation gathers and records the information needed to define the scope of an event from a person designated by the customer. This operation also requires you to ensure that the information is complete, internally and externally consistent, and verified by all stakeholders.

- The *third* operation is to analyze the scope as verified by the customer. This operation allows you to judge whether holding the Kaizen event is likely to produce the business benefits sought by the people requesting it.

Judging Whether a Scope Document Is Acceptable

A scope document is judged acceptable when it is:

- **complete**—it contains all required information,

- **consistent**—information reported for one item makes sense given the information reported in another related item, and

- **verified by all key stakeholders**—it is agreed to by all the key stakeholders.

Guide:
Why Each Scope Information Item Is Needed

Information Item	Reason for Inclusion
A. Basic Business Information	
1. Name of business	To know the revenue center in whose service you will be seeking to make improvements. This may or may not be the company per se, since large companies are typically made up of many "businesses," each of which targets a different product or service to specific customers.
2. Locations at which business operates	To help understand the size and geographical scope of the enterprise with which you will be working.
3. Business industry group	To anticipate (1) the kinds of processes the business might employ, (2) the kinds of problems or challenges it might face, (3) the degree to which the business is labor versus machine intensive, and (4) where to locate possible sources of information and ideas that might help you make process improvements.

4. Size of business
  • Number of employees
  • Yearly operating budget
  • Yearly revenues
	To complete your understanding of the size of the business with which you will be working and to help you build a sense of the labor contribution to the cost of operating the business.

5. Product or service outcomes	To help you visualize the variety of work processes executed by the business and the possible Interactions among processes.
6. The three to five key customer concerns about the product or service outcome the Kaizen event will affect	To help you detect what is value adding and what is not in the product and process you seek to improve.
7. Business level end-to-end work flow map for the product or service the Kaizen event will affect	To ensure sensitivity to the needs and expectations of the other components with which the target work process interacts and thereby avoid unintended consequences that a process change might create.
8. Statement of the company's purpose, values, and vision	To understand the business intent to which the Kaizen event should contribute including the core values it should reflect.
9. Description of the company's current business driver and key performance improvement targets	To understand the company's strategy to improve its competitiveness and the measures (both operating and monetary) it is monitoring to determine whether it is executing this strategy.

Guide:
Why Each Scope Information Item Is Needed (continued)

Information Item	Reason for Inclusion
B. Target Work Process Information	
1. Name of target work process and its product or service output	To ensure that you improve the right work process and understand what it produces.
2. Locations at which target work process is performed	To anticipate where your improvement ideas might be replicated so that they add more value to the business and from where you might get improvement ideas.
3. Location at which event is to be held	To know where to go to do the Kaizen event.
4. Name of the on-site manager of the target work process	To know whom to contact to (1) learn about the work process, (2) check out expectations about what the event should accomplish, and (3) understand any limitations (do's and don'ts) the event should observe.
5. Target work process map	To understand how the work process is currently structured so that you can (1) verify that you understand what operations are included in the process and how they are sequenced, (2) plan the walk through, and (3) plan the evaluation of the work process.
6. Status of the target work process or its parent work process as a just-in-time production system	To know whether takt time exists.
6a. Takt time for target work process	To determine whether there is a gap between cycle time and takt time. In a work process where a just-in-time production system has been implemented, the elimination of such a gap would normally be a priority focus for a Kaizen event.
6b. Whether unit of output is a batch and, if so, how many are in a batch	To be able to compute the number of items produced by a single run of the work process when the unit of output for the work process is a batch and not a single item.
6c. Cycle time for the target work process	To determine whether you can improve the work process within the five days of the Kaizen event.
7. Number of employees	To anticipate (1) all the people who may need to be informed about the event both before and after it is completed, (2) the size of the pool of people available for participation in the event, and (3) the degree to which the event might be disruptive to production (e.g., if only a few people implement the process, the Kaizen event is likely to have a big impact on production since those people are needed in the event).

Guide:
Why Each Scope Information Item Is Needed (continued)

Information Item	Reason for Inclusion
B. Target Work Process Information (continued)	
8. Number of lines and shifts	To alert you to the need to select workstations for observation from different lines and shifts.
9. Number of variations in work flow to accommodate different product or service outcomes	To detect whether you are dealing with a mixed model work process and, if the work process is a mixed model, to isolate where you should focus the Kaizen event. The focus will be on the backbone (the sequence of operations that every model goes through in exactly the same way) or a variation of the work process that produces a single model.
9a. If mixed model, where the Kaizen event should focus: backbone or name of model	
10. Number of locations in the work site (e.g., workshop, administrative office, storage room) where target work process operations are performed	To anticipate any time needed to travel between locations during the Kaizen walk through and evaluation activities. The travel time may require focusing on a smaller work process segment so that all the work can be done within the five days of the event.
11. Whether machinery is used in the target work process	To plan for including machine observations in the evaluation process and properly understand the effort required to observe both human and machine performance. A heavy presence of machines will suggest an extra focus on certain issues (e.g., setup, wait, interruption due to machine breakdowns) and allow you to evaluate whether expectations for the event make sense.
11a. Number of machines	
11b. Percentage of cycle time executed by machines	
11c. Contribution to unit cost	
11d. Special characteristics	
12. Perceived problem with the target work process	To ensure that you address the work process problem that the people requesting the event seek to eliminate and to measure the benefits of the Kaizen event in terms of its affect on the work process problem.
13. Perceived impact of the work process problem on the business	To understand the significance of the perceived work process problem for the business and evaluate whether expectations for the event and the customer's construction of how the work process problem is affecting business performance make sense. For example, if the work process problem is excess cost, it does not make sense that the resulting business impact is lost sales due to the availability of product. It would make sense if the business impact is lost profit or lost sales due to noncompetitive pricing. Finally, to measure the benefits of the Kaizen event in terms of its affect on the business problem.

Continued...

Guide:

Why Each Scope Information Item Is Needed (continued)

Information Item	Reason for Inclusion
B. Target Work Process Information (continued)	
14. Other work processes or departments with which the target work process interfaces	To ensure that you know whom you must consider as you evaluate possible work improvements in the target work process. An effective improvement elevates the performance of the target work process while not detracting from the performance of other interfacing work processes.
14a. Organizations that must be consulted before the target work process may be modified	To ensure that you know whom you must consult in preparing for, and making decisions about, the Kaizen event.
15. Safety guidelines related to the target work process or work area	To prepare yourself and the Kaizen team to bring any safety gear needed and to abide by any safety procedures required of people at the work site.
15a. Personal protective equipment or clothing a person must wear while visiting this workplace	
C. Expectations for the Kaizen Event	
1. Measures the Kaizen event should affect	To understand how improvement in the work process will be judged (e.g., by whether it reduces unit cost, increases throughput, improves first-time quality).
2. Desired start and completion dates for the Kaizen event	To analyze whether the Kaizen event makes sense and to plan the event should the expected dates be achievable.
3. Annual dollar benefits expected from the Kaizen event	To be aware of the amount and types of dollar benefits stakeholders expect and be able to provide feedback as to whether the event, as proposed, could satisfy those expectations.
3a. Annual hard benefits	
3b. Annual soft benefits	
4. Other benefits expected from the Kaizen event	To be aware of other types of results stakeholders expect you to produce through the Kaizen event.
5. Estimated cost of the event	To evaluate whether the return on investment justifies conducting the event.
6. Kaizen team's authority and restrictions to make change	To know what decisions and actions the team can take on its own and which are not allowed or require the team to obtain prior approval or consultation.

Continued...

Guide:

Why Each Scope Information Item Is Needed (continued)

Information Item	Reason for Inclusion
C. Expectations for the Kaizen Event (continued)	
7. Employees the customer wants to include on the Kaizen team	To allow you to contact the proposed team members prior to the event.
8. Stakeholders to the event	To allow you to contact stakeholders so you can properly involve them in the Kaizen event. Some stakeholders will be contacted to verify the scope statement; others will be contacted to coordinate issues that fall under their authority.
9. Person with whom to coordinate logistics and travel	To allow you to arrange logistics and travel for the event.

Guide:

Checking Consistency of Scope Information

Compare...	To...	Apply Rule...
Section B, Item 6	■ Section B, Item 6A	If a work process is said to be a just-in-time production system, then takt time must exist. If not, *there is an inconsistency*.
Section B, Item 11c	■ Section B, Item 12 ■ Section C, Item 3 ■ Section A, Item 4	If a work process has a large degree of machine presence (e.g., machine contribution to unit cost is greater than 75%; Section B, Item 11c) and the perceived problem is reported to be excess labor cost (Section B, Item 12), then the amount of expected savings (Section C, Item 3) relative to total budget (Section A, Item 4) must be small. If not, *there is an inconsistency*.
Section B, Item 12	■ Section B, Item 13	If the perceived problem with the target work process (Section B, Item 12) is not likely to cause the identified business impact (Section B, Item 13), *there is an inconsistency*. For example, a perceived problem of "cycle time is too long" does not match with a business impact reported as "customer dissatisfaction with product quality."
Section B, Item 13	■ Section A, Item 9	If the perceived impact of the work process problem on the business (Section B, Item 13) does not connect to the description of the company's current business driver (Section A, Item 9), *there is an inconsistency*. For example, a perceived business impact reported as "oustomer dissatisfaotion with produot quality" does not match a business driver that emphasizes inadequate profit margins.

Guide:
Checking Consistency of Scope Information (continued)

Compare...	To...	Apply Rule...
Section C, Item 1	■ Section A, Item 9	If the measures that the Kaizen event should affect (Section C, Item 1) do not match measures implied by the company's key performance improvement targets (Section A, Item 9), *there is an inconsistency.*
Section C, Item 1	■ Section B, Item 12	If the measures that the Kaizen event should affect (Section C, Item 1) do not seem to relate to the perceived problem with the work process (Section B, Item 12), *there is an inconsistency.* For example, if the measure was reduction in cycle time but the perceived problem with the target work process was safety hazards, these statements would not be consistent.
Section C, Item 3	■ Section A, Item 9	If the dollar benefits expected from the event (Section C, Item 3) are not consistent with the company's key performance improvement targets (Section A, Item 9) when averaged across all Kaizen events scheduled for the year, *there is an inconsistency.* Find out the total number of Kaizen events to be held in the current planning year and divide the dollar value of key performance improvement targets by that number. The estimated dollar benefits expected from a single event should roughly equal this number, assuming that no other actions to improve monetary performance are planned.
Section C, Item 4	■ Section A, Item 8 ■ Section A, Item 9	If the other benefits expected from the event (Section C, Item 4) do not address any of the core values of the company (Section A, Item 8) or its business driver and its key performance targets (Section A, Item 9), *there is an inconsistency.*

Note: Any inconsistencies detected should be resolved before proceeding with the Kaizen process.

Let's Build a Swing: Introductory Learning Experience

1. Share the following observations:
   - "Often a cartoon captures a truth more succinctly and powerfully than words."
   - "Let's look at one such example that relates to our topic of goals."

2. Conduct the learning experience.

   a. Distribute the handout *Let's Build a Swing!* (next page).

   b. Ask participants to read the captions. Give them a couple of minutes to complete the task.

   c. Ask participants: "What is the problem here? Why?"
   Response:
      - "Everyone involved in the project had a different image of the product the customer wanted."

   d. Ask participants: "Who among the parties involved in building this swing do you imagine is satisfied with its outcome?"
   Response:
      - "No one is satisfied."

3. Conclude the activity by making these points:
   - "A good set of information up front focuses the efforts of multiple people in the same direction by defining for all what must be done, where, and why."
   - "The Kaizen scope document gathers this information in one place so that every stakeholder to the proposed Kaizen event can see it and judge whether it makes sense to them as proposed."

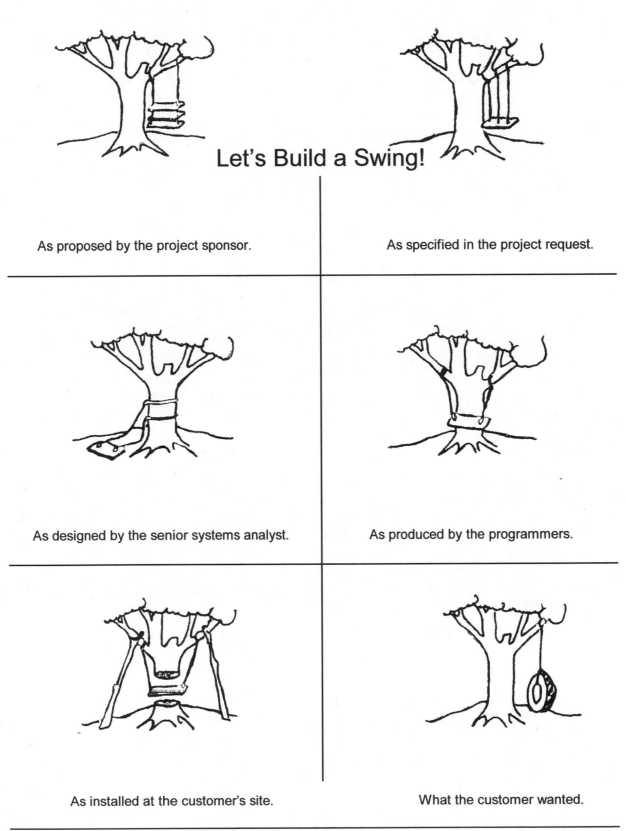

Let's Build a Swing!

As proposed by the project sponsor.

As specified in the project request.

As designed by the senior systems analyst.

As produced by the programmers.

As installed at the customer's site.

What the customer wanted.

From the University of London *Computer Center News* No. 53, March 1973.

Milestone B. Analyze Whether to Conduct the Kaizen Event

Preview

This milestone judges whether holding the Kaizen event is likely to produce the business benefits sought by the people requesting the event. Executing this milestone:

- avoids wasting company resources, and
- ensures that the people who participate in the Kaizen event have a positive and rewarding experience.

Getting Ready Tasks

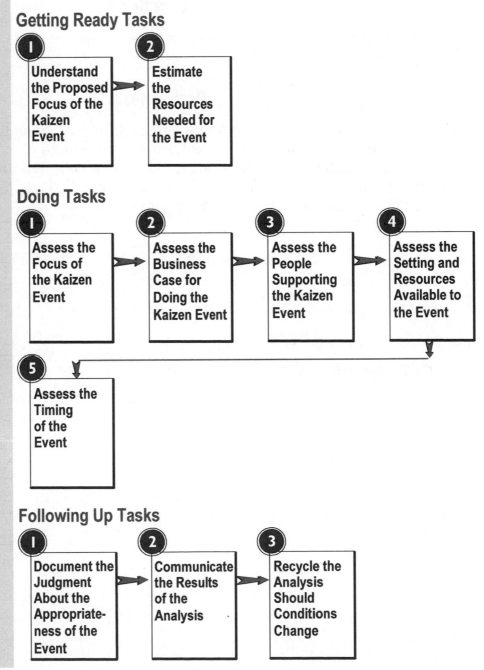

1 Understand the Proposed Focus of the Kaizen Event

2 Estimate the Resources Needed for the Event

Doing Tasks

1 Assess the Focus of the Kaizen Event

2 Assess the Business Case for Doing the Kaizen Event

3 Assess the People Supporting the Kaizen Event

4 Assess the Setting and Resources Available to the Event

5 Assess the Timing of the Event

Following Up Tasks

1 Document the Judgment About the Appropriate-ness of the Event

2 Communicate the Results of the Analysis

3 Recycle the Analysis Should Conditions Change

Purpose

To judge whether holding the Kaizen event is likely to produce the business benefits sought by the people requesting the event.

Benefit

- Avoids waste of company resources.
- Ensures that the people who participate in the Kaizen event have a positive and rewarding experience.

Application

Use this knowledge when you have a documented scope and before you commit to conducting the Kaizen event.

Performer

Kaizen leader or designee. The performer must fully comprehend the purpose, structure, and contents of the scope document. He or she must be proficient in clarifying, confirming, constructively criticizing, and hitchhiking. Finally, the person must be able to perform simple inferencing—that is, use the guidance of a rule to determine what action or decision is appropriate in a given circumstance.

Resources

People

- None

Information, Knowledge, and Training

- Complete, consistent, and verified scope document
- *Task A1. Understand the Scope Document*
- *Working With Others* (J.S. Byron and P.A. Bierley, Hope, ME: Lowrey Press, 2003) - teaches how to get (clarify and confirm) and give (constructive criticism and hitchhiking) ideas and information in ways that build collaboration and elevate results

Materials, Tools, and Other Resources

- Kaizen Tool Kit
  - Logistics Checklist
  - Results of Judging the Appropriateness of Doing the Kaizen Event
  - Strawperson Direction for the Proposed Event

Output

- Strawperson direction for the proposed event (i.e., a tentative statement of the mission, goals, and do's and don'ts for the event)

- Judgment as to whether the Kaizen event is likely to produce the business benefits sought by the people requesting the event

Method

Getting Ready Tasks

1. Understand the proposed focus of the Kaizen event.

   Tip: To understand the focus for the Kaizen event, you must build a strawperson direction for it—that is, a tentative statement of the mission and goals that the Kaizen team must accomplish and the do's and don'ts with which the team must comply as it does its work. We treat this direction as tentative because it is based on the scope document, which is in turn derived from the perspectives of the key stakeholders. Later, when you lead the Kaizen event, the team will construct a final direction based on facts in the workplace, reconciling any discrepancies between these facts and stakeholder perspectives.

   Rule:

IF	you cannot draft a strawperson direction for the event (i.e., a mission, statement of goals, and list of do's and don'ts)
THEN	do not continue the analysis of whether to conduct the Kaizen event
and	identify and remove the barriers preventing you from completing the strawperson mission, goals, and do's and don'ts
and	restart *Milestone B. Analyze Whether to Conduct the Kaizen Event* after the barriers are removed.

   a. Draft a strawperson mission statement for the event based on the scope document.

   Tip: A mission statement has three components: a "to" component that states the business result your event should produce, a "by" component that tells the work process improvement your event will make, and a "for" component that says for whom you are generating these benefits (Exhibit 1).

Exhibit 1. Components of a Mission Statement		
To	**By**	**For**
Improve a business result	Making a work process improvement	The person(s) or group(s) you seek to benefit

Here is an example: "*to* increase profit margins [business result] *by* reducing the cost of fabricating pipe spools for cooling columns [work process improvement] *for* XYZ Manufacturing and all our stakeholders."

1) Build the "to" component of the mission statement.

   Tip: The *to* portion of a mission statement states the improvement of a business result—for example: "to increase market share," "to widen profit margins," "to increase sales," or "to improve shareholder return on equity." Locate Item B13 (Perceived impact of the problem on the business) in the scope document for the event. Flip the contents of Item B13 from a negative to a positive statement, and use this statement as the *to* component. For example, B13 of the scope document for ABC Gases (page 88) states: "Reduced profits; customer dissatisfaction with on-time delivery." Flip this content to form the *to* component: "to increase profits and elevate customer satisfaction with on-time delivery."

2) Build the "by" component of the mission statement.

   Tip: The *by* component tells the work process improvement that will be made to create the business improvement. It should include the name of the work process you will improve—for example, "by lowering the cost of the trailer preventive maintenance process" or "by reducing the frequency with which we fail to respond to customer queries." Locate Item B12 (Perceived problem with the target work process) in the scope statement for the event. Flip the contents of Item B12 from a negative to a positive statement, and use this statement as the *by* component. For example, Item B12 of the scope document for ABC Gases (page 88) states: "Cost too high; cycle time too long, hindering on-time delivery." Flip this content to form the *by* component: "by lowering the cost and reducing the cycle time of the nonflammable blending process."

3) Specify the "for" component of the mission statement.

   Tip: The *for* component of the mission statement identifies for whom the team is trying to make this improvement. The *for* will always be one or more of the following: the company, its customers, its employees, its shareholders, its suppliers, or the community. As a default, consider using "[name of host company] and all its stakeholders."

4) Document the complete mission statement.

   Tip: Put the *to*, *by*, and *for* components together to form a complete mission statement. Record it in the Strawperson Direction for the Proposed Event (Kaizen Tool Kit). For example:

   - To increase profits and elevate customer satisfaction with on-time delivery by lowering the cost and reducing the cycle time of the nonflammable blending process for ABC Gases and all its stakeholders.

- To elevate customer satisfaction with the quality of our products by increasing the accuracy of the TEOS purity testing process for Tempe Chemicals, Inc., and all its stakeholders.
- To elevate customer satisfaction with our response to questions by reducing the frequency with which we fail to respond to customer queries for Customer Services, Inc., and all its stakeholders.

b. Draft a strawperson statement of goals for the event based on the scope document.

Tip: Here are some examples of event goals derived from scope documents:

- Reduce unit cost by 20%.
- Reduce cycle time by 40%.
- Improve safety.

1) Identify the waste in the work process as presented in the scope document.

Tip: Ultimately, the goals for the Kaizen event will each target a type of waste that is causing the work process problem specified in the mission statement. The common types of waste are hazard, inspect, interruption, motion, rework, search, setup, travel/transport, unnecessary processing, and wait. (See Guide: Understanding the Forms of Waste, page 138.) It is unlikely that key stakeholders will specifically express what they wish the event to work on in these terms. At this point in the Kaizen process, the best sources for defining goals are Items C1 and C4 of the scope document. Item C1 records the measures the Kaizen event should affect; Item C4 lists the other benefits expected from the Kaizen event. Use the contents of these items to formulate answers to Steps 2) and 3) below.

2) Build the "what" component of each goal.

Tip: Review Items C1 and C4 of the scope document. You will build one goal statement for each measure identified (Item C1) and for each type of "other benefit" (Item C4) the event is expected to produce. The *what* component simply asserts that you will reduce or elevate a measure, depending on how the measure is expressed, or produce some other benefit. For example, Item C1 of the scope document for ABC Gases (page 89) states: "Unit cost; on-time delivery." Add to each measure the appropriate action to form the *what* component of each goal. Do the same for the contents of Item C4 ("Current safety level improved"). Here are the resulting statements:

- Reduce unit cost...
- Elevate on-time delivery...
- Improve safety...

3) State "how much or how well" each goal will be accomplished.

Tip: Your final statement of event goals will have a quantitative target for achievement (e.g., a percentage reduction or an absolute number; see examples in Step 1b, above). The key stakeholders who provide the scope information frequently cannot state such a target, and so Items C1 and C4 may not have this information. In that case, do not assign a quantitative target for the goal(s).

4) Document the goals.

Tip: Put the *what* and *how much or how well* components together to form complete goals. Record the goals in the Strawperson Direction for the Proposed Event (Kaizen Tool Kit). Here are examples with and without quantitative targets.

- Reduce unit cost by 20%.
- Elevate on-time delivery to 98%.
- Improve safety by eliminating all hazards detected in the workplace.
- Reduce cycle time.

c. Draft a strawperson list of the do's and don'ts for the event.

Tip: Item C6 of the scope document records the authority of the team to act and the constraints with which it must comply. Add these to your strawperson direction; record them in the Strawperson Direction for the Proposed Event (Kaizen Tool Kit). Exhibit 2 (next page) presents an example of a complete strawperson direction.

2. Estimate the resources needed for the event.

a. Estimate your needs for rooms, tables, and chairs.

Tip: You will need a meeting area for the full team, a meeting area for the final report to all stakeholders, and wall space sufficient to post materials (approximately 20 linear feet). You may also need small group meeting areas for subteam discussions. Should a team member have special needs, all areas might have to be wheelchair accessible. Remember that you need this space (except the area used for the final report to stakeholders) for the entire five days of the event. You also need access to the main meeting space one day prior to the event's start so that you can set up for the event. Use the Logistics Checklist to record your needs for rooms, tables, and chairs (beginning on page 139; an electronic copy is available in the Kaizen Tool Kit).

b. Estimate information and material needs.

Tip: Consider the nature of the target work process and the type of problems identified as existing in it to anticipate what information and materials you will need to conduct the proposed Kaizen event. Use the Logistics Checklist to assist you in identifying what may be required.

1) Determine the performance information (e.g., customer demand for products, product unit cost, cycle times for components of the work process) you need prior to the event.

2) Determine what equipment, supplies, food, gifts, and other resources are needed for the event.

   Tip: The Logistics Checklist identifies the materials typically needed for an event. Review the list and mark those items you anticipate needing. Add any required items not listed. Check with team members to determine whether anyone has special mobility or dietary needs. With regard to gifts, shirts or caps with a company logo, coffee mugs, or a gift certificate are usually offered as a statement of appreciation by the company to the Kaizen team. The site decides on the gift since it will pay for the items and has a better sense of what the local participants might enjoy. Blank certificates of recognition can be purchased at local stationary stores. The Kaizen Tool Kit also contains a certificate you could use. Be sure to have a gift and certificate of recognition for each team member. We also like to have one dinner during the week as a team, preferably on Thursday of

Exhibit 2. Strawperson Direction for ABC Gases Kaizen Event	
Mission	
To Increase profit without increasing price and elevate customer satisfaction with on-time delivery by reducing the cycle time and cost of the nonflammable blending work process for ABC Gases and its stakeholders.	
Goals	
■ Reduce unit cost. ■ Reduce cycle time. ■ Improve safety.	
Do's and Don'ts	
Must or Can Do's	**Can't Do's**
■ Can make decisions about improvements in the blending process as long as there is no negative effect on the other organizations with which blending interfaces. ■ Must get agreement from another department prior to executing a change if the proposed change requires an adjustment by that department in how it operates.	■ No overtime. Event should stay within regular working hours.

the event. We recommend that the business fund a dinner out for the team as an added recognition of its contribution.

Doing Tasks

1. Assess the focus of the Kaizen event.

   a. Test whether the strawperson direction makes sense.

   Tip: Test the mission, goals, and "do's and don'ts" statements against each other. The statements make sense together if the goals you wrote would accomplish the mission and the "do's and don'ts" give you and the team the latitude to get the goals done. Ask yourself: "If we were to achieve these goals, is it reasonable to believe that we would also accomplish this mission?" Note your answer. Next ask: "If we abide by the do's and don'ts as specified, is it reasonable to believe that we would have the latitude we need to get the goals done?" Note your answer, then apply the following rule.

   Rule:

IF	I conclude that accomplishing the goals defined in the strawperson direction would also accomplish the mission as stated in the strawperson direction
and	I conclude that the team would have the latitude it needs to get the goals done if it abides by the do's and don'ts as specified in the strawperson direction
THEN	the strawperson direction for the event makes sense
ELSE	the strawperson direction for the event does not makes sense.

   b. Determine whether the selection of the target work process makes sense.

      1) Determine whether the work process is standardized.

      Tip: Verify that a work standard for the target process exists and that there is an official policy requiring that performers comply with the standard. If *either* is *not* true, then conclude that the work process is not standardized. If there is no work standard, you cannot do a Kaizen event because Kaizen improves a baseline work process and, without a standard process, no baseline exists. In this case, use the guidance provided in the unit *Customizing the Kaizen Process* (pages 398–99) to address the needs of a business that lacks a standard for its target work process. If there is a standard but no evidence that the business expects compliance with it, then the business cannot benefit from a Kaizen event because an improved work process that is not used consistently will produce little to no benefits.

2) Determine whether reengineering of the work process is likely to occur.

Tip: In general, it makes little sense to improve the performance of a target work process when it, or the larger work process in which it exists, is being reengineered, since reengineering may result in the elimination of the target work process or its drastic redesign. Use Exhibit 3 to assist you in making your judgment. Work with the managers of the target and parent work processes to answer the questions listed.

Exhibit 3. Guide for Judging Whether Reengineering Is Likely to Occur		
Statement	**Yes**	**No**
1. Neither the target work process nor the parent work process is scheduled for reengineering.	☐	☐
2. No one is raising questions about the appropriateness of any of the operations that constitute the target work process or the parent work process.	☐	☐
3. No one is raising questions about the sequence of the operations in the target work process or the parent work process.	☐	☐
4. No one is raising questions about the current use of machinery in the target work process or the parent work process.	☐	☐
5. No one is recommending the introduction of different machinery in the target work process or the parent work process.	☐	☐
6. No one is planning to introduce new software systems or modify the existing software systems that support the target work process or the parent work process.	☐	☐

Instructions: Answer each question. Treat "unknown" as a "no" in this decision aid. If you respond "yes" to all statements, then conclude that the parent work process is *not* likely to be reengineered and proceed to Step 4), page 120. If you respond "no" to any statement, conclude that the parent work process is likely to be reengineered and go to Step 3), below.

3) Decide whether improving the target work process makes sense despite its possible reengineering.

Tip: It may still make sense to improve the target work process despite the judgment that it or its parent work process may change. You need to determine whether the target work process is likely to remain intact even if the parent work process is modified. You also need to evaluate whether improvements to the target work process now would generate sufficient benefits prior to the reengineering to justify the cost of a Kaizen event. Work with the manager of the target work process to discover these facts, then apply the following rules:

Rule 1:

IF   the target work process is likely to be reengineered

and   both the manager of the target work process and the manager of the parent work process affirm that the reengineering will not occur within the next 12 months

THEN   improving the target work process at this time makes sense.

Rule 2:

IF   the target work process is likely to be reengineered

and   the target work process is a segment of the parent work process that is likely to remain intact

or   the elimination of the problem in the target work process is likely to return sufficient value to justify the cost of the Kaizen event prior to the reengineering

THEN   improving the target work process at this time makes sense.

Rule 3:

IF   the parent work process is likely to be reengineered

and   the target work process is a segment of the parent work process that is not likely to remain intact

and   the elimination of the problem in the target work process is not likely to return sufficient value to justify the cost of the Kaizen event prior to the reengineering

THEN   improving the target work process at this time does not make sense.

4) Determine whether the likely source of the work process problem is within the target work process.

Tip: Explore with the source of the scope information, proposed Kaizen team members, and the manager of the target work process likely causes for the problems with the target work process. Use what you learned in your discussions to decide whether the source of the problem lies within the target work process. For example, we were once asked to address a problem of throughput for a loading area. The current work process was not getting product out the door on time. With a little investigation, we learned that the loading area *did not have* the product to ship. The throughput problem was precipitated by a bottleneck in the final finishing work process, namely painting. Here, the work process problem was caused by operating issues belonging to another work process not under the control of that targeted for the Kaizen event.

5) Conclude whether the selection of the target work process makes sense.

   Tip: Apply the following rules:

   ### Rule 1:

IF	the work process is standardized
and	neither the target work process nor its parent work process is likely to be reengineered
and	the likely source of the work process problem is within the target work process
THEN	the selection of the target work process makes sense.

   ### Rule 2:

IF	the work process is standardized
and	either the target work process or its parent work process is likely to be reengineered
and	despite the reengineering, improving the target work process at this time makes sense
and	the likely source of the work process problem is within the target work process
THEN	the selection of the target work process makes sense.

   ### Rule 3:

IF	the work process is not standardized
or	improving the target work process at this time does not make sense
or	the likely source of the work process problem is not within the target work process
THEN	the selection of the target work process does not make sense.

c. Decide whether the work process problem is something Kaizen can remedy.

   Tip: Kaizen is an extremely robust improvement method. It has elevated work process performance by remedying workplace disorganization, issues of machine use and tool design, and waste due to the content and sequence of human operations, among other factors that detract from safe, efficient, and effective performance. However, you still need to ask yourself whether Kaizen is the right tool to apply to the situation described in the scope document. Two sources of problems for which we do not advise a Kaizen process are problematic software systems and inadequate training.

Regarding the former, we were once asked to reduce excess cost and cycle time for tracking the status of customer orders. Conversations with employees during the analysis phase quickly revealed that there were excessive delays and rework due to a poorly designed and largely out-of-date software system. The system required repeated entry of the same information and did not trap errors well. Consequently, errors built up in the system, and, at the end of the work process, the operator was required to correct them prior to declaring the output of the work process ready. In this case, work process efficiency was constrained by the software system supporting it. That system required a redesign, and the redesign of software requires a special process which is not part of Kaizen (i.e., software engineering). The second source of performance problems not especially appropriate to Kaizen is inadequate training of employees. Here, people are not executing the work process as specified because of either the type or amount of training they receive. It is understood that if they were, then the work process would not exhibit the problem management wants corrected. While Kaizen events may uncover problems caused by problematic software or inadequate training, correcting them requires expertise in other specialty areas (i.e., software engineering and instructional technology).

d. Confirm that the target work process begins with a single set of inputs and produces only one version of output or is the backbone of a mixed model.

Tip: Here, you simply need to confirm that what you were told by the key stakeholders in completing Item B9 of the scope document is correct. This confirmation is necessary because, in our experience, people typically do not grasp the concept of mixed model work processes the first time around. Therefore, you need to ask additional questions of people knowledgeable of the target work process. If you have been told that the target work process is *not* a mixed model, you must confirm that there is only one version of inputs and one version of output. With respect to inputs, this means one set of materials and information, delivered by one means, from one source. Any variation in these features of an input typically requires variation in handling.

For example, processing customer orders may seem like a single model work process, especially if you are told that every order is handled the same way. The order is received, verified, and logged into the customer order system, after which ship and bill orders are issued. In reality, however, orders are received from different sources: phone, e-commerce, fax, and mail. Typically, each of these methods of receipt requires different handling, at least initially. Frequently, they are handled by different groups of people in different locations.

With respect to output, be careful of the shorthand way in which people refer to their product or service outputs. As someone not familiar with the setting, you may not understand what information is hidden in the shorthand. Confirm *explicitly* that the output has a single configuration, content, function, and finish. Any variation in these features of an output typically requires variation in processing.

If you have been told that the work process is a mixed model and the set of operations you will improve is the backbone of the mixed model, identify the variations in inputs and outputs for the target work process and confirm that the work proceeding from all the variations in inputs and resulting in all the variations in outputs goes through the specified work operations in *exactly the same way*. If it does, you are truly dealing with a backbone work process.

e. Determine whether the team can observe the operation of the target work process within the time available during a Kaizen event.

Tip: The Kaizen team needs to complete at least two observations of the target work process—one when the team evaluates the process and a second when the team measures the effects of its improvements. In our experience, a target work process taking more than four hours is too long to allow the team to do these observations and complete the rest of its Kaizen work within the five-day time period of an event.

1) Confirm your understanding of the time characteristics of the target work process.

Tip: Connect with a source for the information on how long it takes to complete the target work process. It is best to talk with the team members who execute the work process—and preferably to talk with more than one, since reports can vary from one person to another. Review with each person the sequence of operations that accomplish the work process. Ask the person to talk you through the process. Keep notes, then read back to the person the sequence of steps you recorded to confirm whether you heard correctly. Make sure you can imagine the activities a person performs at each step. You do not need to "deep drill" what is done at each step; just be sure you grasp the type of work done. Confirm that the description you have represents the way the work is to be performed *according to the work standard*. Then have the person provide you with his or her estimate of the time it *typically* takes to do *each step*. (By typical, we mean a cycle time that is *not* exceeded 8 out of 10 times the work process is performed.) Finally, determine whether the work process is performed intermittently—this means that it starts and then stops *between* operations, usually until a worker is free to complete the next operation. If there is intermittence, identify where it occurs and how long the typical interruption is. (Intermittence is most common in office work processes where, for example, information to be processed remains in someone's in-basket until he or she is free to attend to it.)

2) Confirm that the cycle time for the operations the team must observe does not exceed four hours.

Tip: Once you have an image of the work process and the time it takes to execute each step, compute the cycle time by adding the times to complete each step. Check this against the cycle time reported in the scope document. If there is a discrepancy between the two times, you need to clarify which is the typical time. If the work process is intermittent, add to the cycle time computed from the steps the period of time the work process stops prior to completion. This may resolve the discrepancy.

Once you have a good estimate of the typical cycle time for the work process, verify that it is four hours or less. If it is greater than four hours, check whether there is more than four hours of manual or machine operations in the cycle time that you must observe. Operations that do not need to be observed—for example, unattended machine time, time required for materials to cure or dry, or work stoppage due to the absence of a worker to perform the operation—are not counted in judging whether the process exceeds the four-hour limit.

3) Confirm that the way the process is performed does not prevent the team from observing the entire process.

Tip: A work process is usually performed in a uniform manner. Each piece of like work is handled in the same way. Occasionally, a work process deviates from the uniform treatment of like work. For example, some pieces of work may be passed from one shift to another with the same operation being repeatedly started and then halted prior to completion while other pieces of the same type flow through the work process without passing from one shift to another. If each piece of the same type of output is not processed in a uniform manner, decide whether the team needs to follow a single piece of work through the entire process in order to obtain reasonable measurements. Although it is often possible to observe a different piece of work at each step and still get good measurements, this is not always true.

For example, imagine a work process that fills an order from inventory. In executing the work process, a worker receives the order, gets a forklift, goes to the storage area, locates and pulls the product, and transports it to shipping. In discussing the process with workers, you learn that frequently the worker gets the order, goes to the storage area, gets a forklift, and starts searching for the product only to give up after 15 minutes because he or she cannot locate it. The worker returns the order to the bin and pulls another order. This experience may occur 6 out of 10 times orders are filled. Those orders the person returns are left for the next shift to handle. On the next shift, the same pattern may be repeated. A particular order may carry over for three shifts before it is filled. One order may have multiple executions of the same steps, and the time to complete the "locates and pulls" step is the sum of all the times it is started and not finished plus the one time it is started and finished. In this case, you would have to follow one piece across all the shifts it travels, measuring all the labor time put into filling it to get proper measurements of the work process. Simply observing the execution of the process for orders where the requested product is located within 15 minutes will distort your measurements.

4) Decide whether the team can observe the operation of the target work process within the time available during a Kaizen event.

Tip: Apply the following rule:

Rule:

IF	the cycle time for the operations the team must observe does not exceed four hours
and	the way the process is performed does not prevent the team from observing the entire process
THEN	the team can observe the operation of the target work process within the time available during a Kaizen event
ELSE	the team cannot observe the operation of the target work process within the time available during a Kaizen event.

f. Conclude whether the focus of the Kaizen event is appropriate.

Tip: Use the decision aid in Exhibit 4 to assist you in concluding whether the focus of the Kaizen event is appropriate.

Exhibit 4. Guide for Concluding Whether the Focus of the Kaizen Event Is Appropriate		
Statement	**Yes**	**No**
1. The strawperson direction for the event makes sense.	☐	☐
2. The selection of the target work process makes sense.	☐	☐
3. The likely source of the work process problem is something Kaizen can remedy.	☐	☐
4. The target work process begins with a single set of inputs and produces only one version of output OR is the backbone of a mixed model.	☐	☐
5. The team can observe the operation of the target work process within the time available during a Kaizen event.	☐	☐
Instructions: Respond to each statement. Treat "unknown" as a "no" in this decision aid. If you respond "yes" to all statements, the focus of the Kaizen event is appropriate; otherwise, the focus of the Kaizen event is not appropriate.		

2. Assess the business case for doing the Kaizen event.

Tip: In assessing the business case, you are deciding whether doing the event is likely to produce the right benefits for the company at a level that is cost beneficial within the time period required. You have already established that the benefits sought from the event are consistent with the company's current business driver, key performance improvement targets, and core values. You also confirmed that the size of the monetary benefits sought by the company from the event would, if realized, materially advance its progress toward the goals it set for itself. Additionally, when you evaluated whether the strawperson direction for the event made sense, you determined that the event, as defined, can accomplish its mission—namely, produce the desired business result and make the intended work process improvement. Now you will build on this foundation to complete the assessment of the business case for conducting the Kaizen event. You must evaluate whether the target work process could yield the monetary benefits the company seeks, whether those benefits would exceed the cost expended to realize them, and whether the event can produce benefits quickly enough to meet the company's needs.

a. Determine whether the target work process can yield the monetary benefits the company seeks.

1) Determine the likely amount of savings from improving the target work process.

Tip: You can devise a rough, conservative estimate of the likely savings a Kaizen event will produce by using the labor cost of the target work process. It is a conservative estimate because it does not account for improvements made in machine operations, and, even with respect to human operations, it typically underestimates the savings the actual event produces. Nonetheless, it provides a reference for judging whether the target work process can yield the monetary benefits the company seeks. First, determine the labor cost of the work process by multiplying the number of employees by the sum of the average salary and fringe benefit employees receive. Any manager should be able to provide the number of full-time-equivalent employees, average salary, and average fringe benefit paid. Now you have an estimate of the labor component of cost. Next, multiply the labor cost of operating the target work process by 0.3 to get your savings estimate. For example, if a nickel-plating work process had 16 full-time-equivalent workers and the average salary plus fringe benefits they received was $44,000, the labor cost of operating the work process is $704,000 annually (16 x $44,000). The estimate of the likely savings from the Kaizen event is $211,200 ($704,000 x 0.3). Remember to add to the labor cost whatever is paid annually to contract workers. Remember too that this is a "go-by" estimate, not a guaranteed result.

Caution

Do not assume that determining the likely savings from the proposed event is unnecessary. We have had a number of occasions where the designated target work process could not possibly yield the amount of dollars required from a Kaizen event simply because the work process itself consumed too few dollars to begin with. We would not have understood this fact based simply on the statements from the people requesting the event; it became clear only when we did the math.

Also be sure to check for any special costs due to poor performance. Ask whether there are any cost consequences to the business due to the current performance of the target work process. For example, the business may be paying penalty fees for untimely performance or extra shipping fees for expedited service in order to avoid penalties or waste due to quality problems. Add these costs to your estimate of potential savings from a Kaizen event.

---

2) Determine the amount of unrealized revenue associated with a target work process.

   Tip: In addition to realizing benefits by reducing cost, Kaizen events can produce revenue gains by increasing throughput. For these gains to be counted as monetary benefits from an event, there must be unrealized opportunities for sales. Therefore, you must uncover whether there is unmet market demand for the product or service outputs of the target work process. If there is unmet demand, you need three pieces of information to estimate the unrealized revenues the Kaizen event could generate: (1) the current annual volume of output of the product the event will affect, (2) an estimate of the number of units that could be sold above the current volume if throughput over the same lines was elevated, and (3) the price of each unit. To compute your estimate, multiply the current annual volume of output by 0.2 to determine the likely number of additional units of output the event will enable the work process to produce. Check the likely increase in output against the estimate of the number of units that could be sold above the current volume. If the estimated additional output enabled by the event is greater than the number of units that could be sold above the current volume, use the latter number for the remaining computations; otherwise, use the former. Multiply the number by the price per unit to obtain the estimated amount of unrealized revenue the Kaizen event will produce. Exhibit 5 (next page) provides an example of calculating unrealized revenue.

3) Estimate the replication benefits the event may yield.

   Tip: The replication benefits are the extended savings or revenue gains that may be realized by transferring improvements made in the target work process at the site designated for the Kaizen event to other sites executing the same work process. Multiply the benefits expected from the Kaizen event, including both savings and revenue gains, by the number of sites where the improvements will be replicated. Adjust for differences in size of sites, volume of unmet demand, and other relevant factors as needed.

Exhibit 5. Example of Calculating Unrealized Revenue

Let's assume that the unmet demand for the product resulting from the nickel-plating work process is 10,000 units per year and that each unit sells for $35. The current annual volume of the work process is 60,000 units. By multiplying 60,000 units by 0.2, we estimate the likely number of additional units of output the event will enable the work process to produce (12,000). When we check the added production capability (12,000) against the unmet demand (10,000), we see that it is larger. We use 10,000 as the number that is likely to be sold. Next, we multiply the 10,000 units by $35; the result ($350,000) is the estimate of unrealized revenue the event will produce.

---

4) Allocate the potential benefits as either hard or soft.

Tip: If the cost savings or dollar gains will flow immediately after the Kaizen event concludes and require no additional actions past the event to be realized, then count them as hard benefits. For dollar gains to flow immediately following an event, a company needs to have unfulfilled orders that, without the event, it is unable to fill within the current accounting period. If the cost savings or dollar gains require some additional action beyond the Kaizen event to realize (e.g., redeployment of workers to other productive tasks, review and approval of a new work standard, additional sales), then count the benefits as soft. Always count the benefits the company expects from replicating the improvements generated by the Kaizen event as soft benefits.

5) Decide whether the type of monetary benefits the event is likely to produce meet the company's needs.

Tip: Apply the following rule:

Rule:

IF   the amount of savings and revenue gains from the event matches or exceeds the monetary benefits the company expects from the event

and   the distribution of monetary benefits as hard and soft meets the distribution required by the business

THEN   the target work process can yield the monetary benefits the company seeks

ELSE   the target work process cannot yield the monetary benefits the company seeks.

b. Evaluate whether the event will be cost beneficial over the period of time required by the company.

1) Determine the proper time period to use in calculating the cost-benefit ratio.

   Tip: The default payback period for computing cost-benefit ratios is five years in relatively stable industries and three years in moderately fast-changing work settings. A company may need a faster payback period for its investment in the Kaizen event, however. Ask the event coordinator or the manager of the target work process what payback period you should use in estimating the cost-benefit ratio for the event.

2) Calculate the total hard benefits for the cost-benefit payback period.

3) Calculate the cost for conducting the Kaizen event.

   Tip: The expected cost of the event is reported in the scope document (Item C5).

4) Compute the cost-benefit ratio.

   Tip: Divide the event's estimated hard benefits over the payback period by the total cost of the event. A result greater than 2 is preferred, although any ratio greater than 1 is positive. A ratio of 1 is a neutral finding; a ratio of less than 1 is a negative finding. For any finding of 1 or greater, compare it to the ratio desired by the company to decide whether to characterize it as cost beneficial. If the company has no criterion, then accept a ratio greater than 1 as cost beneficial. A finding of 1 or less is never cost beneficial.

c. Conclude whether the business case supports doing the Kaizen event.

   Tip: Use Exhibit 6 (next page) to assist you. Note that while statements 1 and 2 are critical elements in a full consideration of the business case for conducting a Kaizen event, each of these statements has already been judged to be true because you addressed and resolved any issues related to them when you tested the consistency of the scope information.

3. Assess the people supporting the Kaizen event.

   Tip: For the Kaizen event to succeed, the people associated with it as team members and in-house advisors or approvers of team actions (e.g., safety supervisor, work standards supervisor) must understand the performance issues of the target work process and be available to the Kaizen team throughout the event. Also, all parties, including those who must adopt and promote the improvements the event produces, must be aligned with the purposes of the event and the company it is serving.

   a. Decide if the "right" people have been selected for the Kaizen team.

      1) Form an image of who needs to be on the Kaizen team.

         Tip: Consider who should be on the team as a first step in deciding whether you have the right people. A Kaizen team is generally made up of six to eight members not including the leader and co-leader. The team always includes people who operate the work process being improved, both experienced and new employees. Be certain that the proposed team has people who are knowledgeable about the machines and software systems used in the target work process if the event is likely to involve these. The team should also include a representative of every organization directly involved in the problem and every organization that must be consulted before the target work process may be modified (see Item B14a of the scope document). The team should include a customer representative when the event may have an immediate impact on the customer or is taking place at the customer's site. Similarly, the team should include a supplier representative when the event may affect products or services requested from the supplier. Finally, reflect on the likely sources of the work process problem that the Kaizen event is expected to fix. Use this information to determine whether there are other people with expertise relevant to the problem whom you need on the Kaizen team so that it can successfully accomplish its work.

Exhibit 6. Guide for Judging Whether the Business Case Supports Doing the Kaizen Event		
Statement	**Yes**	**No**
1. The type of benefits sought from the event are consistent with the company's current business drivers, key performance improvement targets, and core values.	☒	☐
2. The size of the monetary benefits sought by the company would materially advance its progress toward the goals it set for itself.	☒	☐
3. The target work process can yield the monetary benefits the company seeks.	☐	☐
4. The event will be cost beneficial over the period of time required by the company.	☐	☐
Instructions: Statements 1 and 2 are included for clarity; each is true. Respond to statements 3 and 4. In using this decision aid, treat "unknown" as a "no." If you respond "yes" to all statements, conclude that the business case supports doing the Kaizen event; otherwise, the business case does not support doing the Kaizen event.		

2) Get additional nominations to the proposed team, if needed.

   Tip: Contact the event coordinator and explain the problem with the proposed membership of the Kaizen team. Describe the type of person who is missing from and needed on the team. Share your rationale. Determine who might meet these needs and whether the site is open to changing the membership of the team. Address any concerns the event coordinator may have. Adjust the membership of the team, if permitted. Be sure to get the names, telephone numbers, and e-mail addresses of each new proposed member. Verify the acceptance of the new proposed team roster with the event's sponsor.

3) Gather information about each proposed team member.

   Tip: Talk with each proposed team member. Try to understand what each knows about the event and provide information to close any gaps in the person's understanding of the event's purpose and nature. Also find out how the work process problem affects the proposed team member. Explore what in general is important to the person about his or her job and workplace and what the person's expectations are for the event. Explain that this will help you understand where each team member's thinking is so you can better relate what happens in the event to the team member's interests. If a proposed team member is not available to speak with, check with others who may know the person or have worked with him or her. Be sure to ask each proposed team member whether he or she can be present for the entire event.

4) Assess the proposed team membership against the needs of the event.

   Tip: Use the decision aid in Exhibit 7 to evaluate whether the proposed team membership fits the needs for conducting the event.

Exhibit 7. Guide for Judging Whether the Right People to Execute the Event Have Been Selected

Statement	Yes	No	NA
1. Each proposed team member is able to attend the event for its entire duration.	☐	☐	
2. The proposed team members represent the variety of roles that execute the target work process.	☐	☐	
3. The proposed team has people who are knowledgeable about the machines and software systems used in the target work process.	☐	☐	☐
4. The proposed team members include a representative of every organization directly involved in the problem and every organization that must be consulted before the target work process may be modified.	☐	☐	☐
5. The proposed team includes suppliers.	☐	☐	☐
6. The proposed team includes customers.	☐	☐	☐
7. Most of the proposed team members have a positive attitude toward the event.	☐	☐	

Instructions: Respond to each statement. If the statement does not apply to the proposed event, check "NA." Treat "unknown" as a "no." If you respond "yes" to all applicable statements, conclude that the right people have been selected for the Kaizen team; otherwise, the right people have not been selected.

b. Determine whether the people needed to advise the team or authorize its actions (e.g., manager of the target work process, safety supervisor, work standards supervisor, maintenance supervisor) will be available during the time the event is to be held.

c. Determine the alignment among leaders and members with respect to supporting the Kaizen event.

   Tip: Alignment among leaders and members is a powerful factor in determining the likelihood of success—and especially the likelihood that a company will realize extended benefits from an event. Ask the event coordinator for background on the alignment of leaders and members with respect to implementing the proposed Kaizen event. Find out, for example, whether the members of the organization are aware that a problem exists and that a Kaizen event has been requested. Discover whether other efforts to improve the target work process have been undertaken and how these efforts were received. Obtain information about the status of follow through by leadership and members on performance improvements previously uncovered. If replication of improvements at other company sites is an important element of the benefits the sponsor seeks from the Kaizen event, ask about the readiness of leadership at those sites to adopt and implement process improvements. Use the information you uncover to judge the degree of alignment within the setting of the Kaizen event and across the sites where replicated benefits are sought.

d. Determine whether there is alignment with respect to supporting the purpose of the event among all organizations that interface with, and have veto authority over whether changes are made in, the target work process.

   Tip: Ask the event coordinator for background on how the leadership of the organizations feel about the proposed Kaizen event. Find out whether they are aware that a problem exists and that a Kaizen event has been requested. Discover whether they are receptive to efforts to improve the target work process and open to adjusting the operations of their own organizations should a solution beneficial to the company require it.

e. Conclude whether the status of the people involved with the event supports doing the Kaizen event.

   Tip: Use the decision aid in Exhibit 8 (next page) to evaluate whether the status of the people connected with the event supports doing the Kaizen event.

Exhibit 8. Guide for Concluding Whether the Status of the People Involved With the Event Supports Doing the Kaizen Event		
Statement	**Yes**	**No**
1. The "right" people have been selected for the Kaizen team.	☐	☐
2. The people needed to support the event (e.g., manager of the target work process, safety supervisor, work standards supervisor, maintenance supervisor) will be available throughout the time the event is to be held.	☐	☐
3. Leaders and members of the organization are aligned with respect to supporting the Kaizen event and following through on the improvements it produces.	☐	☐
4. All organizations with veto authority over changes that may be made to the target work process are aligned with the purpose of the event.	☐	☐
Instructions: Respond to each statement. Treat "unknown" as a "no." If you respond "yes" to all statements, conclude that the status of the people involved with the event supports doing the Kaizen event; otherwise, the status of the people involved with the event does not support doing the Kaizen event.		

4. Assess the setting and resources available to the event.

   a. Decide whether the projected location of the event and its key characteristics support doing the event.

   Tip: Ask the person with whom you are to coordinate logistics where the team would work during the week and where the meeting with stakeholders would be held. Use your description of the space you need (estimated in Getting Ready Task 2, page 16) to prompt your clarifying questions about the characteristics of these spaces. Get information on the size of the meeting areas, proximity to the work process, lighting, accessibility, available wall space, and availability during the entire event. Note any discrepancies between the actual characteristics of the space that will be available and the desired characteristics. Use the decision aid in Exhibit 9 (next page) to evaluate whether the projected location of the event and its key characteristics support doing the event.

   b. Decide whether the materials and information resources needed for the event are likely to be available.

   Tip: Ask the person with whom you are to coordinate logistics which of the resources you specified when you completed Getting Ready Task 2, page 16, will be available for the event. Use the Logistics Checklist (pages 139–41) to assist you in determining the availability of the materials you require. Ask only about the materials that the site must supply, not those that you will provide. Also list the performance information you need to prepare for the event and verify with the person coordinating the logistics that the information items will be available to you prior to the event. Once you have determined the availability of materials and information, use the decision aid in Exhibit 10 (next page) to evaluate whether the materials and information resources that will be available for the event support doing the event.

Exhibit 9. Guide for Concluding Whether the Location of the Event and Its Key Characteristics Support Doing the Kaizen Event

Statement	Yes	No	NA
1. A single meeting area in which the team will gather and work is available every day of the proposed event.	☐	☐	
2. The team meeting area is proximate to the area where the target work process is performed.	☐	☐	
3. A meeting area of adequate size for the final report to all stakeholders is available.	☐	☐	
4. Multiple small group meeting areas are available.	☐	☐	☐
5. All areas are wheelchair accessible.	☐	☐	☐
6. There is wall space adequate for hanging storyboards and materials.	☐	☐	

Instructions: Respond to each statement. If the statement does not apply to the proposed event, check "NA." Treat "unknown" as a "no" in this decision aid. If you respond "yes" to all applicable statements, conclude that the projected location of the event and its key characteristics support doing the event; otherwise, the projected location of the event and its key characteristics do not support doing the event.

---

c. Conclude whether the setting and resources support doing the Kaizen event.

   Tip: Apply the following rule:

   Rule:

   IF the projected location of the event and its key characteristics support doing the event

   and the materials and information resources available to the event support doing the event

   THEN the setting and resources support doing the Kaizen event

   ELSE the setting and resources do not support doing the Kaizen event.

Exhibit 10. Guide for Concluding Whether the Available Materials and Information Resources Support Doing the Kaizen Event			
Statement	**Yes**	**No**	**NA**
1. General equipment (e.g., display, recording, and communications equipment) needed for the event will be available.	☐	☐	☐
2. Safety equipment needed for the event will be available.	☐	☐	☐
3. Supplies (e.g., pads, pencils, tape) needed for the event will be available.	☐	☐	☐
4. Food needed for the event will be available.	☐	☐	☐
5. Recognition and awards including certificates, gifts, and dinner as a team one evening during the event will be available.	☐	☐	☐
6. Performance information needed for the event will be available.	☐	☐	☐
Instructions: Respond to each statement. If the statement does not apply to the proposed event, check "NA." Treat "unknown" as a "no." If you respond "yes" to all applicable statements, conclude that the available materials and information resources support doing the Kaizen event; otherwise, conclude that they do not.			

5. Assess the timing of the event.

   a. Verify with the manager of the target work process that the projected timing of the event is acceptable from the perspective of operating concerns.

   b. Check whether the dates requested for the event as recorded in the scope document are reasonable.

   Tip: A reasonable date for the first event in any workplace is not sooner than three weeks from the completion of this analysis.

   c. Conclude whether the timing of the event supports doing the event.

   Tip: Apply the following rule:

   Rule:

   IF the projected timing of the event is acceptable from the perspective of operating concerns

   and the dates requested for the event as recorded in the scope document are reasonable

   THEN the timing of the event supports doing the Kaizen event

   ELSE the timing of the event does not support doing the Kaizen event.

Following Up Tasks

1. Document the judgment about the appropriateness of the event.

   Tip: Use the Guide: Judging the Appropriateness of Doing the Kaizen Event (pages 142–43) to document the outcome of your reasoning. An electronic version of the document is available in the Kaizen Tool Kit.

2. Communicate the results of the analysis.

   Tip: If the analysis concludes that the event is appropriate to conduct, then the communication to the event coordinator and the key stakeholders simply informs them about the purpose of the analysis, why it was done, and its finding. If the analysis concludes that the event is *not* appropriate to conduct, complete the following steps.

   a. Brief the event coordinator and the key stakeholders.

      Tip: Review with the event coordinator and the key stakeholders the purpose for your analysis and why it was done. The purpose of the analysis is to judge whether holding the Kaizen event is likely to produce the business benefits sought by the people requesting the event. The Kaizen leader does the analysis to fulfill his or her responsibility for ensuring that he or she avoids wasting company resources and that the people who participate in the Kaizen event have a positive and rewarding experience. Emphasize that the analysis is not intended to second guess the customer but to independently verify his or her thinking so that if a problem exists with the proposed event, it can be raised and worked through before resources are expended. Once the purpose and rationale for the analysis are understood, explain the factors you assess in making your judgment and why each is important. Share the results of your analysis and how you arrived at these results.

   b. Get feedback on your analysis from the event coordinator and key stakeholders.

      Tip: Observe the reactions of the event coordinator and key stakeholders and respond to their issues and concerns. Gather from each person any information that might change your conclusion about whether holding the Kaizen event is likely to produce the business benefits sought by the company.

   c. Resolve differences in perspective as to whether the Kaizen event is appropriate to hold.

      Tip: First, ensure that you and the other parties agree that the driving factor in deciding whether to do the event is if it is likely to produce the business benefits sought by the company. If there is not agreement on this purpose, there will be no chance to resolve the discrepancies in perspective since you are professionally bound to ensure that what you do delivers the benefits requested by the company. If there *is* alignment with this purpose, verify that you and the other parties agree on the facts used in the analysis. If there is disagreement on facts, reconcile them; the final arbiter of facts is empirical information. Once there is alignment on purpose and facts as used in the analysis, there must be agreement on judgment since you have applied the knowledge specific to the Kaizen process. At this point, explore whether problematic conditions can be changed so that a different conclusion can be reached.

3. Recycle the analysis should conditions change.

    Tip: Recycle the analysis any time the facts underpinning the judgment are modified.

Check Steps

Use the following checklist to verify that the milestone was accomplished.

Benchmark	√
Getting Ready Tasks	
1. Understand the proposed focus of the Kaizen event.	☐
2. Estimated the resources needed for the event.	☐
Doing Tasks	
1. Assessed the focus of the Kaizen event.	☐
2. Assessed the business case for doing the Kaizen event.	☐
3. Assessed the people supporting the Kaizen event.	☐
4. Assessed the setting and resources available to the event.	☐
5. Assessed the timing of the event.	☐
Following Up Tasks	
1. Documented the judgment about the appropriateness of the event.	☐
2. Communicated the results of the analysis.	☐
3. Recycled the analysis as conditions changed.	☐

Tips

- Always complete the assessment of all factors affecting the decision of whether to conduct the Kaizen event so that you have a complete picture of the strengths and problems associated with the proposed event and can share that picture with the key stakeholders.

Guide:
Understanding the Forms of Waste

1. **Hazard** - Any observed workplace conditions or worker behaviors that could result in harm.

2. **Inspect** - Checking for error in a component, product, or activity. It is waste because production cost is added.

3. **Interruption** - Stoppage during work activity due to some external factor (e.g., machine breakdown, request for information). It is waste because production time is lost during the period of interruption.

4. **Motion** - Changes in position by the performer (e.g., turning, bending, lifting) while he or she is at the workstation. It is waste because production time is lost during movement.

5. **Rework** - Behavior required to reprocess a product or product component to salvage a defective unit or part. It is waste because production cost is added.

6. **Search** - Behavior required to locate some needed resource (e.g., a person, tool, part, or piece of information). It is waste because production time is lost during the search.

7. **Setup** - Labor required to ready a performer or machine to execute a task. Setup is waste because production time is lost during the preparation period.

8. **Travel/transport** - Movement by a performer from his or her workstation to another place. If the performer is moving parts, materials, and information around the workplace, it is called transport; otherwise, it is travel. Both are waste because production time is lost during travel or transport around the plant.

9. **Unnecessary processing** - Work done that is not needed to produce the product or service as required by the customer. Such processing may be done at the discretion of the performer or required by the work instruction. It may even modify the output, but it will do so in a way that a well-informed and reasonable customer does not value. It is waste because production cost is added unnecessarily.

10. **Wait** - Delay in work activity until some needed resource becomes available or authority to proceed is received. It is waste because production time is lost during the waiting period.

Logistics Checklist

Need	How Much/ How Many?	Got It?
Room/Tables/Chairs		
■ Chairs		☐
■ Meeting area for the full team available every day		☐
■ Meeting area for the final report to all stakeholders		☐
■ Multiple small group meeting areas		☐
■ Tables		☐
■ Wheelchair-accessible areas		☐
■ Wheelchair-accessible tables		☐
■ Wall space for hanging storyboards and materials	20 feet	☐
Equipment - General		
■ Calculators		☐
■ Computer printer or access to one		☐
■ Copier or access to one		☐
■ Digital camera		☐
■ Flipchart easels or hangers		☐
■ Foam board 3'x5' (1/4")	4	☐
■ Label maker		☐
■ Laminator		☐
■ Laptop computer with Microsoft Office 2000® and Adobe Acrobat Reader® 4.0 or higher		☐
■ LCD computer projector		☐
■ Overhead projector		☐
■ Projection screen		☐
■ Stopwatches		☐
■ Tape measures		☐
■ Telephone for conferencing		☐
■ Wheels for measuring travel distances		☐

Continued...

Logistics Checklist (continued)

Need	How Much/ How Many?	Got It?
Equipment - Safety		
▪ Clothing		☐
▪ Earplugs		☐
▪ Gloves		☐
▪ Hard-hats		☐
▪ Safety glasses		☐
▪ Safety shoes		☐
Supplies		
▪ Clear tape		☐
▪ Clipboards		☐
▪ Colored tape		☐
▪ Double-sided tape		☐
▪ Erasers		☐
▪ Flashlights		☐
▪ Flipchart pads		☐
▪ Flipchart markers		☐
▪ Flow pens		☐
▪ Graph paper		☐
▪ Kaizen Tool Kit		☐
▪ Laminating sheets		☐
▪ Magnifying glasses		☐
▪ Masking tape		☐
▪ Multicolored Post-its® - 3"x5"		☐
▪ Wheels for measuring travel distances		☐
▪ Name tags		☐
▪ Notebooks		☐
▪ Pens and pencils		☐
▪ Printer paper (white and colored)		☐

Continued...

Logistics Checklist (continued)

Need	How Much/ How Many?	Got It?
Supplies (continued)		
▪ Roll of white paper (34"x44")		☐
▪ Ruler		☐
▪ Scissors		☐
▪ Small tool kit (screwdriver, pliers, wrench)		☐
▪ Transparency film (for a copier)		☐
▪ Utility knife		☐
Food		
▪ Lunch		☐
▪ Morning and afternoon snacks		☐
▪ Special dietary needs (e.g., kosher food, low salt)		☐
Recognition/Awards		
▪ Certificates of recognition		☐
▪ Dinner as a team one evening during the event		☐
▪ Gifts to recognize team contributions		☐

Guide:
Judging the Appropriateness of Doing the Kaizen Event

Instructions: Respond to each statement. Treat "unknown" as a "no." If you respond "yes" to all statements, then conclude that the Kaizen event is appropriate to conduct; otherwise, the Kaizen event is not appropriate to conduct.

Statement	Yes	No
A. Focus of Event Is Appropriate		
1. The strawperson direction for the event makes sense.	☐	☐
2. The selection of the target work process makes sense.	☐	☐
3. The work process problem is something Kaizen can remedy.	☐	☐
4. The target work process begins with a single set of inputs and produces only one version of output *OR* is the backbone of a mixed model.	☐	☐
5. The team can observe the operation of the target work process within the time available during a Kaizen event.	☐	☐
B. Business Case Supports Doing the Kaizen Event		
1. The type of benefits sought from the event are consistent with the company's current business drivers, key performance improvement targets, and core values.	☒	☐
2. The size of the monetary benefits sought by the company would materially advance its progress toward the goals it set for itself.	☒	☐
3. The target work process can yield the monetary benefits the company seeks.	☐	☐
4. The event will be cost beneficial over the period of time required by the company.	☐	☐
C. The Status of People Involved With the Event Supports Doing the Kaizen Event		
1. The "right" people have been selected for the Kaizen team.	☐	☐
2. The people needed to support the event (e.g., manager of the target work process, safety supervisor, work standards supervisor, maintenance supervisor) will be available throughout the time the event is to be held.	☐	☐
3. Leaders and members of the organization are aligned with respect to supporting the Kaizen event and following through on the improvements it produces.	☐	☐
4. All organizations with veto authority over changes that may be made to the target work process are aligned with the purpose of the event.	☐	☐

Continued...

Guide:
Judging the Appropriateness of Doing the Kaizen Event (continued)

Statement	Yes	No
D. Setting and Resources Support Doing the Kaizen Event		
1. The projected location of the event and its key characteristics support doing the Kaizen event.	☐	☐
2. The available materials and information resources support doing the Kaizen event.	☐	☐
E. Timing of the Event Supports Doing the Kaizen Event		
1. The projected timing of the event is acceptable from the perspective of operating concerns.	☐	☐
2. The dates requested for the event as recorded in the scope document are reasonable.	☐	☐

Milestone C. Prepare for the Kaizen Event

Preview

This milestone advances the success of the Kaizen event by readying the people, setting, and resources needed to conduct it. It increases the likelihood that the event will achieve its purpose by:

- preparing people to participate in the event, and
- preventing problems (e.g., missing information or materials, wrong equipment) from detracting from the flow of the event.

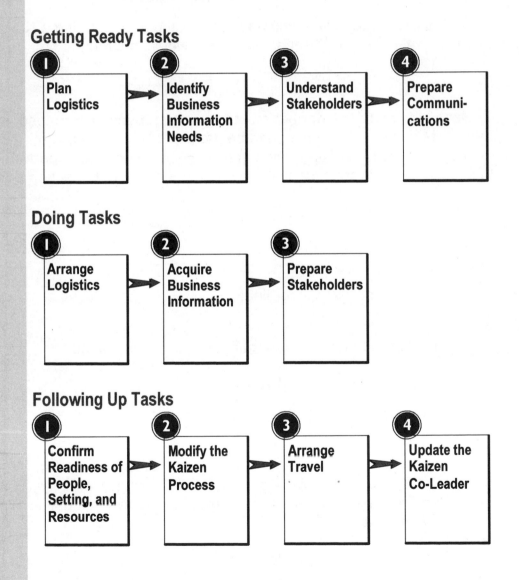

Getting Ready Tasks

1 Plan Logistics → **2** Identify Business Information Needs → **3** Understand Stakeholders → **4** Prepare Communications

Doing Tasks

1 Arrange Logistics → **2** Acquire Business Information → **3** Prepare Stakeholders

Following Up Tasks

1 Confirm Readiness of People, Setting, and Resources → **2** Modify the Kaizen Process → **3** Arrange Travel → **4** Update the Kaizen Co-Leader

Purpose

To advance the success of the Kaizen event by readying the people, setting, and resources needed to conduct it.

Benefit

Increases the likelihood that the event will achieve its purpose by preparing people to participate in the event and preventing problems (e.g., missing information or materials, wrong equipment) from detracting from the flow of the event.

Application

Use this knowledge when you have committed to performing a Kaizen event. Begin preparing for the Kaizen event *at least* three weeks prior to the first day of the event.

Performer

Kaizen leader. The performer must fully comprehend the purpose, structure, and contents of the scope document and be proficient in clarifying, confirming, constructively criticizing, and hitchhiking. The person must also be able to perform simple inferencing—that is, use the guidance of a rule to determine what action or decision is appropriate in a given circumstance.

Resources

People

- Designated event coordinator
- Kaizen team
- Person with whom to coordinate logistics and travel

Information, Knowledge, and Training

- Complete, consistent, and verified scope document
- Strawperson direction for the proposed event
- *Working With Others* (J.S. Byron and P.A. Bierley, Hope, ME: Lowrey Press, 2003) - teaches how to get (clarify and confirm) and give (constructive criticism and hitchhiking) ideas and information in ways that build collaboration and elevate results

Materials, Tools, and Other Resources

- Kaizen Tool Kit
  - Guide: Explaining What Kaizen Is

- Guide: Judging Readiness for the Event
- Kaizen News - Day 1
- Kaizen Post-Event Flyer
- Kaizen Pre-Event Flyer
- Logistics Checklist
- Stakeholder Perspective
- Travel and Shipping Arrangements Job Aid

Output

- Business information acquired
- Communications developed
- Kaizen team prepared
- Logistics completed
- Stakeholders prepared

Method

Getting Ready Tasks

1. Plan logistics.

   Tip: Consider any new information about the nature of the work process and the likely sources of its problems to determine any changes in the space or materials you will require. Update the Logistics Checklist (pages 139–41) prepared in *Milestone B. Analyze Whether to Conduct the Kaizen Event*, adjusting the space and materials needed to complete the event.

2. Identify business information needs.

   Tip: In *Milestone B. Analyze Whether to Conduct the Kaizen Event*, you determined the performance information you needed prior to the event (page 117). Consider now any new information you may have about the work process or the likely sources of its problems and revise the information you need prior to the event. Be sure to add the following items to your list of information needs:

   - any existing work flow diagrams of the target work process;
   - contractual agreements (e.g., with customers, unions) that constrain how the target work process may operate;
   - government regulations (e.g., from the Occupational, Safety, and Health Administration) applicable to the target work process;
   - names of the best practice databases that store improvement ideas that apply to the target work process and the procedure for accessing each;

- names of "go-to" people at other work sites who may have addressed and solved problems like the ones experienced in the target work process;
- procedure for auditing compliance of work process operations to work standards;
- procedure for modifying work process procedures or workplace layout;
- safety rules; and
- work standards (e.g., ISO-9000, Quality Management System) for the target work process.

Recognize that some of these information products may be large. Be sure to narrow your specification to the portions of each that apply to the target work process. Also, access to some items may be restricted, so a briefing on relevant sections may need to replace a physical copy of the product and you may need to sign a nondisclosure agreement.

3. Understand stakeholders.

   Tip: Build a snapshot image of information important to constructively involving stakeholders in the event. Having this information allows you to appreciate what communication you need to have with each stakeholder and what information each is likely to find valuable.

   a. List the stakeholders to the Kaizen event.

      Tip: Begin with the list of stakeholders provided in the scope document (Item C8). Add to this list the performers of the target work process, as a group; be sure that the list includes the union, should one be involved in the target work process.

   b. Learn the perspective of each stakeholder.

      Tip: Work with the event coordinator, members of the Kaizen team, or each stakeholder directly to understand to what extent the stakeholder is aware of the planned event, what his or her key concerns might be with respect to the event, what expectations he or she may have concerning involvement and communication about the event (see Exhibit 1). Use the electronic form, Stakeholder Perspective, in the Kaizen Tool Kit to record your learning.

Exhibit 1. Stakeholder Perspective			
Stakeholder	**Awareness**	**Concerns**	**Expectations**
Manager of target work process	Fully informed	Anxious to see improvements; a major customer may switch supplier if the business can't do better.	Solve the problem. Keep her informed of progress. Tell her immediately if you encounter any road blocks.
Etc.			

4. Prepare communications.

a. Create the Kaizen News for Day 1.

Tip: The Kaizen News is the daily agenda and progress report you will produce for the team and performers of the target work process. This communication identifies each task scheduled to occur on a given day, the team action required, who is responsible to lead the task, the time it is to occur, and the results the team produced. The tasks listed in each Kaizen News reflect the major activities the team completes in performing the Kaizen event. A Day 1 version of the Kaizen News is contained in the Kaizen Tool Kit. (This form may be modified for use as the Kaizen News for Days two through five.) The Day 1 news is sent to the Kaizen team before the event begins. Each morning, the day's news is posted in the workplace where the target work process is performed. During the day, the results column is updated from "open" to "done" as agenda items are completed, to provide a running description of the team's progress in accomplishing its mandate as defined in the mission and goals of the event.

Exhibit 2. Kaizen News Format				
Date:	Area: [name of site and target work process]			
Task	Team Action	Responsibility	Time	Results
Open the event	Participate	Kaizen leader	0800	Open
Administrative issues/Safety	Review	Kaizen leader	0815	Open
Etc.				

b. Prepare the communication to the Kaizen team.

Tip: Kaizen team members need the following information to prepare for the event:

- a brief explanation of what a Kaizen event is (you could include the Guide: Explaining What Kaizen Is—see the electronic version in the Kaizen Tool Kit);

- the name of the work process the event will improve;

- the strawperson direction for the event (this was prepared in *Milestone B. Analyze Whether to Conduct the Kaizen Event*);

- the date, time, and place where the team will meet;

- a list of the Kaizen team members (this is supplied in Item C7 of the scope document);

- the Kaizen News for the first day of the event;

- information about any personal protective equipment that must be brought to the site (this is supplied in Item B15 of the scope document);

- a copy of the Kaizen Pre-Event Flyer (use the template provided in the Kaizen Tool Kit and see the example on pages 156–57);
- travel guidance for participants coming from outside the site; and
- other information that may be necessary given the nature of a particular event.

Do not send the scope document itself, as it contains more information than the team needs.

c. Prepare the communication to performers of the target work process.

Tip: Members of the target work process workforce need the following information in order to prepare for the Kaizen event and participate in it:

- a brief explanation of what a Kaizen event is (you could include the Guide: Explaining What Kaizen Is—see the electronic version in the Kaizen Tool Kit),
- the strawperson direction for the event (this was prepared in *Milestone B. Analyze Whether to Conduct the Kaizen Event*),
- the Kaizen Pre-Event Flyer (use the template provided in the Kaizen Tool Kit and see the example on pages 156–57), and
- the Kaizen Post-Event Flyer (use the template provided in the Kaizen Tool Kit and see the example on page 158).

These materials will be posted in the workplace where the target work process is performed, with the Pre-Event Flyer serving as the display's focal point. Learn from the Kaizen team members where the materials should be posted for best viewing by the work process employees. Identify a team member to be responsible for displaying these materials; if this is not possible, arrange to have the event coordinator post the materials. All materials except the Kaizen Post-Event Flyer should be displayed at least one week prior to the event. The Post-Event Flyer should be displayed at the end of the first day of the event.

d. Prepare the communication to other stakeholders.

Tip: Every stakeholder needs the following minimum set of information about the Kaizen event in order to support it:

- a brief explanation of what a Kaizen event is;
- the name of the target work process;
- the strawperson direction for the event;
- when the event will occur;
- who will participate in the event;
- the requested involvement of the stakeholder in supporting the event (e.g., provide advice during the event, attend the post-event meeting);

- the significance of the stakeholder's involvement for the success of the event; and
- the name of a contact person from whom additional information can be obtained and to whom ideas may be offered.

1) Decide on the content of the communication to each stakeholder.

   Tip: The content listed above is the minimum set of information a stakeholder needs to participate in a Kaizen event. Be sure to use your understanding of each stakeholder's perspective to tailor the communication by adding content that shows recognition for his or her concerns and indicates how the event will address any expectations the stakeholder has.

2) Decide on the method of communication.

   Tip: Choose among e-mail, telephone conversation, or face-to-face meeting. Also decide whether you can delegate the communication to the event coordinator or must complete it yourself. The more critical the stakeholder is to the success of the event and the more uncertain or negative the stakeholder's attitude toward the event is, the more important that the content of the communication address the stakeholder's concerns and expectations and that the method of communication be a face-to-face contact or, at a minimum, a telephone conversation with the Kaizen leader.

3) Construct the communication for each stakeholder.

   Tip: Use the same materials you prepared for the team and the performers of the target work process to construct your basic communication.

Doing Tasks

1. Arrange logistics.

   a. Arrange for the space and materials needed to complete the Kaizen event.

      Tip: Speak with the person assigned to coordinate logistics and travel to learn how to arrange for logistics. Abide by these guidelines to avoid creating any friction that might detract from a positive attitude by site personnel.

   b. Ensure that logistics are arranged.

      Tip: You must ensure that every item you need for the event is obtained. Use the Logistics Checklist (pages 139–41) to monitor the arrangement of logistics. As space and materials are confirmed, place checkmarks (√) in the "Got It?" column. Stay in touch with the person with whom you coordinate logistics so that you can intervene early should there be problems in acquiring the resources you need. If a problem emerges, get a clear description of what it is, understand its cause, and consider options for resolving it. Perhaps a substitute for the materials is possible, or you can arrange for the materials and bill the site, or you can adjust the process to accommodate the absence of whatever materials are not available. The solution, however, must enable the team to perform its work in a manner that will accomplish the goals of the event.

   c. Ship materials you will be supplying for the event to the site.

      1) Get travel and shipping information.

        Tip: Acquire travel and shipping guidance from the person coordinating logistics and travel. The information you need includes recommendations about the best airport at which to arrive, best location to stay, and directions to the work site from the airport and hotel. Use the Travel and Shipping Arrangements Job Aid (see pages 159–60) to assist you in gathering this information. An electronic copy of this form is in the Kaizen Tool Kit. Supply the document to your contact person and ask him or her to complete it.

      2) Send materials.

        Tip: Be sure to send materials sufficiently early that they arrive before the event.

2. Acquire business information.

   a. Request business information.

   Tip: Provide a list of the information you need to the event coordinator. Be sure that the event coordinator understands why each item is needed.

   b. Resolve problems in acquiring business information.

   Tip: The most likely problems you will encounter are:

- no measurement information about the work process's current performance is available, or the available information is suspect;

- no unit cost or factor cost information for the output of the target work process is available; and

- access to certain materials is restricted or denied.

With respect to performance information, be sure that you learn about any company methods for gathering or computing operating statistics, even if they are not employed. Do this because you may need to gather these metrics, and you must use the method approved by the company in doing so.

With respect to missing cost information, use the estimate of the labor contribution to cost developed in *Milestone B. Analyze Whether to Conduct the Kaizen Event.* You can estimate the total cost of operations from the labor cost by acquiring an estimate of the percentage of total cost labor contributes. Capital-intensive industries will have a low percentage of total cost that labor contributes (perhaps as little as 10% or less). Service-intensive industries have a high percentage of total cost labor contributes (perhaps 70% or higher). Whichever it is for the company you are serving, take the percentage of total cost labor contributes and divide it into your estimate of the labor cost of operation. For example, a power-generating work process may have a 4% labor cost of operation. If you estimate the labor cost at $180,000 for this work process, the total operating cost of the work process is $4.5 million ($180,000 ÷ 0.04 = $4,500,000).

With respect to information denied to you, see if signing a nondisclosure agreement will allow you access. If this is not successful, check whether someone knowledgeable of the information will be participating in the event. Otherwise, request a briefing so you can take this information into consideration as you lead the event. Be sure that your contact for business information understands that you need either access in the event to a person knowledgeable of the information or access to the information itself—otherwise, the event cannot be performed.

c. Ensure receipt of business information.

Tip: Monitor the receipt of the business information you requested. Detect and resolve any problem in getting information. Follow the guidance for resolving problems in acquiring business information (see Task 2b, above).

3. Prepare stakeholders.

a. Prepare the Kaizen team to participate in the event.

Tip: Transmit the communication you prepared to the Kaizen team at least two weeks before the event. Be sure to include a note introducing yourself and the materials you are sending and requesting the person to review the materials prior to the event. Complete an initial follow-up contact by e-mail or telephone to verify that each team member has received the materials. Complete a second follow-up contact by e-mail or telephone to verify that each team member has read the materials and to solicit any questions the team members may have. Respond to questions as needed.

b. Prepare performers of the target work process to participate in the Kaizen event.

Tip: Ship the communication materials you prepared for the performers of the target work process to the person who will display them two weeks prior to the event. Follow up to ensure that the materials were received and are posted *at least* one week before the event begins.

c. Prepare other stakeholders to participate in the event.

Tip: Provide each remaining stakeholder with the communication you prepared. Follow up to ensure that the materials were received and to elicit and respond to any questions the stakeholder may have.

Following Up Tasks

1. Confirm readiness of people, setting, and resources.

   Tip: Verify that people are prepared, logistics are in place, and needed business information is in hand. Use the Guide: Judging Readiness for the Event (page 161) to assist you. The electronic form of this guide is in the Kaizen Tool Kit. Update stakeholders about any readiness issues for the event. Resolve any problems related to readiness in a timely manner. If readiness issues remain unresolved and they prevent you from conducting the Kaizen event, the event must be canceled.

2. Modify the Kaizen process.

   Tip: Study the information you gathered from the customer. Detect any facts that suggest a change in the process you will execute in this event. Adjust the Kaizen process as appropriate. The most common information source that causes a modification in the process is the company's procedures for approving a change to a work standard. Sometimes these procedures require that an experiment be performed to prove the effectiveness of a new idea, or that a pilot be done to prove that it can be implemented successfully in the work process, or that some specific measurement be done and included in the application for change in a work standard. Modify the Kaizen process to address these requirements for obtaining official approval of a work process or workplace change.

3. Arrange travel.

   Tip: Complete travel arrangements to the site for you and your co-leader. Use the information you obtained from the Travel and Shipping Arrangements Job Aid (pages 159–60) to assist you. Be sure to arrange travel to the location, ground transportation while at the location, and hotel accommodations.

4. Update the Kaizen co-leader.

   Tip: Provide the Kaizen co-leader with the information he or she needs to prepare for the event. Be sure to discuss the information with the co-leader prior to the event and decide how you will divide responsibilities for conducting the event.

Check Steps

Use the following checklist to verify that the milestone was accomplished.

Benchmark	√
Getting Ready Tasks	
1. Planned logistics.	☐
2. Identified business information needs.	☐
3. Understand stakeholders.	☐
4. Prepared communications.	☐
Doing Tasks	
1. Arranged logistics.	☐
2. Acquired business information.	☐
3. Prepared stakeholders.	☐
Following Up Tasks	
1. Confirmed readiness of people, setting, and resources.	☐
2. Modified the Kaizen process (if required).	☐
3. Arranged travel.	☐
4. Updated the Kaizen co-leader.	☐

Tips

- Appreciate the importance of proper preparation for the Kaizen event. At every event, you will encounter circumstances you could not predict. To maximize your flexibility in addressing these unknowns, you need time, energy, and the good-will of the team. You create time and ensure that you have both energy and good will when you address all the issues you can predict in your preparations.

- Begin preparations early and assume that nothing is done until it is verified.

Coming Soon!

Kaizen Event

Date: June 17-21, 2002   Time: 8:00 AM

Sponsored by the
Nonflammable Blending Team

Members of your work area will be using the Kaizen process to discover and make improvements to this area.

WE ARE LOOKING FOR YOUR INPUT!

Read the mission and goals posted with this notice to learn what the Kaizen event is trying to do.

If you have any suggestions for improvements to this area or work process, please share them with a member of the Kaizen team so that your ideas become part of the event.

Questions? Contact: Sandra Shore at 123-456-7890

Kaizen Event Mission

To increase profit without increasing price and elevate customer satisfaction with on-time delivery by reducing the cycle time and cost of the nonflammable blending work process for ABC Gases and its stakeholders.

Goals

- Reduce unit cost
- Reduce cycle time
- Improve safety

Kaizen Team

Reggie B., Fill Operator, Blended Gases

Thomas C., Fill Operator, Blended Gases

Nathan H., Maintenance

Vincent L., Supervisor

James L., Fill Operator, Straight Gases

Clarice T., Lab Technician

Mark Your Calendars!

You Are Invited to the Report-Out Session for the Kaizen Event

Sponsored by the Nonflammable Blending Team

When: June 21, 2002

Where: 3:00 PM

Come to this session to find out what was done and what results were produced.

Support Your Team!

Travel and Shipping Arrangements Job Aid

Work Site Information

Site name:	**Contact person:**
Address:	**Telephone:**
	E-mail:
	Fax:

Shipping Information

Receiving person:	**Location where Kaizen leader picks up materials:**
Ship-to address:	**Person with whom to arrange pick-up:**
	Name:
	Telephone:

Travel Information

Accommodations

Recommended hotel	Recommended alternative hotel
Name:	**Name:**
Address:	**Address:**
Telephone:	**Telephone:**
Fax:	**Fax:**
Possible restaurants:	

Air Travel

Recommended airport:

Continued...

Travel and Shipping Arrangements Job Aid (continued)

Travel Information (continued)	
Ground Travel	
Directions from airport to hotel: Approximate time: Approximate distance:	**Directions from airport to alternative hotel:** Approximate time: Approximate distance:
Directions from airport to site of the Kaizen event: Approximate time:	Approximate distance:
Directions from hotel to Kaizen site: Approximate time: Approximate distance:	**Directions from alternative hotel to Kaizen site:** Approximate time: Approximate distance:

Guide:

Judging Readiness for the Event

Instructions: Respond to each statement. Treat "unknown" as "no." If you respond "yes" to all statements, you are ready for the event; otherwise, you are not ready.

Item	Yes	No
A. Logistics Arranged		
1. The space needed for the Kaizen event is arranged (team meeting areas and the post-event stakeholder meeting area).	☐	☐
2. The seating and work surfaces are arranged.	☐	☐
3. The safety equipment needed for the event is arranged.	☐	☐
4. The other equipment (e.g., display, recording, and communications equipment) needed for the event is arranged.	☐	☐
5. The supplies needed for the event are arranged.	☐	☐
6. The food needed for the event is arranged.	☐	☐
7. The gifts needed for the event are arranged.	☐	☐
B. Business Information Acquired		
1. The key performance measures for the target work process are known, and baseline information on each is either in hand or verified as not existing.	☐	☐
2. Safety rules for the target work area are known, and a copy is in hand or an expert is immediately available to the team.	☐	☐
3. Government regulations applicable to the target work process are identified, and a copy is in hand or an expert is immediately available to the team.	☐	☐
4. Work standards applicable to the target work process are identified, and a copy is in hand or an expert is immediately available to the team.	☐	☐
5. Contractual agreements (e.g., with customers, unions) that apply to the target work process are identified, and a copy is in hand or an expert is immediately available to the team.	☐	☐
C. People Prepared		
1. The Kaizen team is prepared to participate in the event.	☐	☐
2. The performers of the target work process are prepared to participate in the event.	☐	☐
3. Other stakeholders are prepared to participate in the event.	☐	☐
4. Stakeholders are prepared to attend the post-event briefing on the results of the Kaizen event.	☐	☐

Milestone D. Perform the Kaizen Event

Preview

This milestone uncovers and eliminates waste in a work process in a manner that accomplishes the business's purposes. It:

- improves the operation of the target work process;
- elevates the involvement, energy, and skills of employees to make future work process improvements;
- improves the company's business results; and
- enables opportunities for new business growth.

Getting Ready Tasks

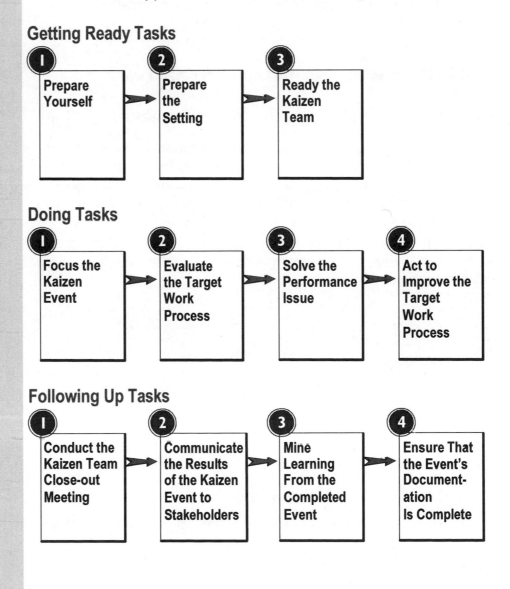

| **1** Prepare Yourself | **2** Prepare the Setting | **3** Ready the Kaizen Team |

Doing Tasks

| **1** Focus the Kaizen Event | **2** Evaluate the Target Work Process | **3** Solve the Performance Issue | **4** Act to Improve the Target Work Process |

Following Up Tasks

| **1** Conduct the Kaizen Team Close-out Meeting | **2** Communicate the Results of the Kaizen Event to Stakeholders | **3** Mine Learning From the Completed Event | **4** Ensure That the Event's Documentation Is Complete |

Purpose

To uncover and eliminate waste in a work process in a manner that accomplishes the business's purposes.

Benefit

- Improves the operation of the target work process.
- Elevates the involvement, energy, and skills of employees to make future work process improvements.
- Improves the company's business results.
- Enables opportunities for new business growth.

Application

Use this knowledge when you perform a Kaizen event.

Performer

Kaizen leader, co-leader, and team. The leader must be fully qualified in doing every task required during the execution of a Kaizen event. He or she must be skilled in leading a team and managing stakeholders. The highly interactive nature of executing Kaizen also requires that the leader and co-leader be proficient in the skills of attending, greeting, clarifying, confirming, constructively criticizing, and hitchhiking. They will need to be able to detect waste in the workplace, extract learning from prior performance, and perform simple inferencing—that is, use the guidance of a rule to determine what action or decision is appropriate in a given circumstance.

Resources

People

- Designated event coordinator
- Performers of the target work process
- Kaizen team
- Maintenance supervisor
- Manager of the target work process
- Person with whom to arrange pick-up of materials shipped to site
- Person with whom to coordinate logistics and travel
- Safety supervisor
- Work standards supervisor

Information, Knowledge, and Training

- Complete, consistent, and verified scope document
- Contractual agreements (e.g., with customers, unions) that affect the target work process
- Government regulations applicable to the target work process
- Kaizen News - Day 1
- Logistics Checklist
- Names of "go-to" people at other work sites who may have solved problems like the ones experienced in the target work process
- Names of, and information for accessing, the best practice databases that store improvement ideas that apply to the target work process
- Procedure for auditing compliance of work process operations to work standards
- Procedure for modifying work process or workplace layout standards
- Safety rules
- *Mining Learning From Performance* (R.L. Vitalo and P.A. Bierley, Hope, ME: Lowrey Press, 2003) - teaches how to use prior performance to improve one's next performance
- Strawperson direction for the event
- Work flow diagrams of the target work process
- Work standards for the target work process
- *Working With Others* (J.S. Byron and P.A. Bierley, Hope, ME: Lowrey Press, 2003) - teaches how to get (clarify and confirm) and give (constructive criticism and hitchhiking) ideas and information in ways that build collaboration and elevate results

Materials, Tools, and Other Resources

- Space, equipment, and supplies to support the team's work

Room/Tables/Chairs

- Chairs
- Meeting area for the final report to all stakeholders
- Meeting area for the full team available every day
- Multiple small group meeting areas

- Tables
- Wall space for hanging storyboards and materials
- Wheelchair-accessible areas
- Wheelchair-accessible tables

Equipment - General

- Calculators
- Computer printer or access to one
- Copier or access to one
- Digital camera
- Flipchart easels or hangers

- Foam board 3'x5' (1/4")
- Label maker
- Laminator
- Laptop computer with Microsoft Office 2000® and Adobe Acrobat Reader® 4.0 or higher
- LCD computer projector
- Overhead projector
- Projection screen
- Stopwatches
- Tape measures
- Telephone for conferencing
- Wheels for measuring travel distances

Equipment - Safety

- Clothing
- Earplugs
- Gloves
- Hard-hats
- Safety glasses
- Safety shoes

Supplies

- Clear tape
- Clipboards
- Colored tape
- Double-sided tape
- Erasers
- Flashlights
- Flipchart markers
- Flipchart pads
- Flow pens
- Graph paper
- Laminating sheets
- Magnifying glasses
- Masking tape
- Multicolored Post-its® - 3"x5"
- Name tags
- Notebooks
- Pens and pencils
- Printer paper (white and colored)
- Roll of white paper (34"x44")
- Ruler
- Scissors
- Small tool kit (screwdriver, pliers, wrench)
- Transparency film (for a copier)
- Utility knife

Food

- Lunch
- Morning and afternoon snacks
- Special dietary needs (e.g., kosher food, low salt)

Recognition/Awards

- Certificates of recognition
- Dinner as a team one evening during the event
- Gifts to recognize team contributions

- Kaizen Tool Kit
  - Checklist for Preparing the Setting
  - Certificate of Recognition
  - Kaizen Participant Feedback Form
  - Kaizen Summary
  - Kaizen Participant Feedback Summary Form
  - Parking Lot Issues
  - Working With Others 10-Minute Review

Output

- Documentation of the event
- Measurable business and work process benefits as defined in the event's mission and goals

- New learning about the Kaizen tool, its application, and the Kaizen leader's capabilities
- New opportunities for Kaizen events
- New or improved standards that apply to the work process
- Performers elevated in their business participation, ownership, teamwork, confidence in their ability to make change, and capabilities to achieve success
- Sustained or improved safety

Method

Getting Ready Tasks

1. Prepare yourself.

   a. Review the process for completing *Milestone D. Perform the Kaizen Event*.

   b. Study the scope document and the strawperson direction for the event.

   c. Review the business information gathered prior to the event.

   Tip: Be familiar with the safety procedures, the work standards that apply to the target work process, and any constraints placed on the work process by government regulations or contractual agreements. Also, be sure you understand the procedure for modifying the target work process's work standards or workplace layout and identify what you may need to add to the event to ensure compliance with the procedure.

   d. Draft a description of the target work process.

   Tip: Using the guidance in *Step D1-S1. Build a Description of the Target Work Process* (beginning on page 197) and the information you collected prior to the event, draft a work process overview. The overview should include the work process name and purpose and its inputs, outputs, locations of performance, cycle time, takt time, and the names of other work processes or departments with which the target work process interrelates (see example on page 212). Next, draft a work process map for the target work process. Use any existing work flow diagrams you collected to assist you. Leave blank any items for which you do not have information and put a question mark next to any information about which you are unsure. This draft description will speed the work of the team during the first day of the event.

2. Prepare the setting.

   Tip: Contact the person with whom to arrange pick-up of materials shipped to the site upon your arrival. Confirm that all shipped materials are at the event site. Get access to the team's meeting area on a day prior to the event. Set up the equipment and organize your materials. Distribute participant materials to each member's seating location. Use the Checklist for Preparing the Setting (page 179) to ensure that you perform all the tasks required to ready the setting for the team and the event. An electronic version of the checklist is contained in the Kaizen Tool Kit. Note that some tasks need to be done prior to the beginning of the event and some need to be completed the morning of the event. Use the Guide: Arranging the Main Meeting Room (page 180) as an aid in arranging the table, chairs, and equipment so that people can attend to you and your presentation as well as to each other and so you can attend to them. Prepare a flipchart page depicting the major tasks to be accomplished during the Kaizen event. Use Exhibit 1 as a guide. Prepare a second flipchart page recording the strawperson direction for the event and a third page listing the key customer values as recorded in the scope document (Item A6). Position these pages so that the team can view them when you reference them during your opening presentation.

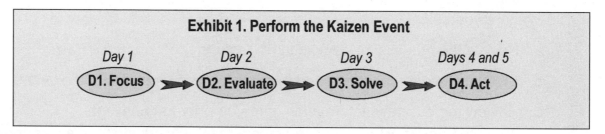

Exhibit 1. Perform the Kaizen Event

3. Ready the Kaizen team.

   a. Meet each team member as he or she arrives.

   1) Attend to the team member as he or she enters the meeting room.

   Tip: Attending means to focus both physically and mentally on another person or on a team. It signals your readiness to relate to and work with the individual or team, places you in a position to observe and listen to the individual or team, and triggers reciprocal attending from the individual or team.

   2) Greet the team member.

   Tip: Maintain your focus on the team member. Extend your hand to greet the person and say "hi" or "hello" or something similar and the team member's name (if you know it). Introduce yourself and your role. For example, "My name is..., and I will be leading the Kaizen event." Ask the team member's name (if you do not know it). Make a welcoming comment—for example, "I am pleased to meet you" or "I look forward to working with you." Ask the person to fill out a name tag and invite him or her to enjoy the morning snack and take a seat when he or she is ready.

   b. Open the Kaizen event.

   1) Announce the opening of the meeting.

   Tip: Attend to the team as a whole. Ask the team members for their attention. Then say loudly, "Let's begin. Good morning, I am [name].

Welcome to the Kaizen event for the [name the target work process]. I am the Kaizen leader for this event. And, [name] is my co-leader."

2) Summarize why the participants have come together.

   Tip: Use a simple "to, for, by" format to summarize the purpose. For example, "We are here today *to* significantly improve the preventive maintenance work process *for* our business, its customers, and all its stakeholders *by* applying the Kaizen tool." You will define, with the team, the specific mission of the event later. (Note that the "by" segment is always the same: "by applying the Kaizen tool.")

3) Ensure that the team members know each other.

   Tip: Find out how many of the team members already know each other. Apply the following rule to guide you in having the team members introduce themselves.

   Rule:

IF	30% or more of the participants do not work with each other regularly
THEN	ask each person to stand and say his or her name, job, where he or she currently works, and why he or she came to the Kaizen event
ELSE	ask each person new to the majority of participants to stand and say his or her name, job, where he or she currently works, and why he or she came to the Kaizen event.

   Once the team finishes its introductions, use your confirming skills to summarize the major themes expressed by team members as to why they came to the event. Connect the reasons for their coming to the event with the purpose and benefits Kaizen can deliver. Do this in one or two sentences at most. Then tell the participants that before you begin the event you want to address administrative issues and safety procedures.

4) Review administrative issues.

   Tip: Tell the participants where to locate bathrooms, refreshments, phones, and messages. Give lunch and break information (time and location).

5) Review safety rules (e.g., emergency evacuation procedures, safety equipment to be used in the workplace).

   Tip: Have someone expert in the safety requirements of the workplace review requirements with the team. If safety equipment is needed, have its use demonstrated and have the team practice its use.

6) Review the Kaizen News.

Tip: Prepare an overhead transparency of the Kaizen News - Day 1 and display it to the team. Direct team members to look at the transparency or the copy of the Kaizen News - Day 1 they received prior to the event. Tell them that the Kaizen News is the daily agenda you will produce for the team and performers of the target work process. It identifies each task scheduled to occur on a given day, the team action required, who is responsible to lead the task, the time it is to occur, and the results the team produced. Share with them that each morning, the day's news is posted in the workplace where employees can view it. During the day, the results column is updated from "open" to "done" as agenda items are completed, to provide a running description of the team's progress. Review today's Kaizen News with the team. Ask for and answer any questions the team has about the day's agenda.

c. Build the Kaizen team.

1) Make the team comfortable.

Tip: Have the team perform an icebreaker. Select an icebreaker that builds your understanding of each team member's expectations and concerns with respect to the Kaizen event (see Expectations and Concerns Icebreaker, page 181). If you already have an understanding of each team member's expectations and concerns, use an icebreaker that has them share their perspectives about the strengths and weaknesses of the target work process (see Strengths and Weaknesses Icebreaker, page 182). If you use the Strengths and Weaknesses Icebreaker, remember that you still must show understanding for the team's expectations and concerns with respect to the Kaizen event prior to beginning the first task of the event.

2) Review Working With Others skills.

Tip: If team members have been trained in Working With Others skills, encourage them to use these communication skills and complete a brief review of them. Using getting and giving skills ensures that team members share their ideas and information effectively and build better ideas together as they implement Kaizen. These skills are delineated in *Working With Others* by J.S. Byron and P.A. Bierley. A slide presentation (Working With Others 10-Minute Review) is provided in the Kaizen Tool Kit to assist you with the review as well as guidance in how to lead the review.

3) Establish ground rules for how the team will work together.

Tip: Use the Guide: Building Ground Rules (page 183) to assist you.

d. Prepare the team to conduct the event.

1) Provide an overview of Kaizen.

   Tip: Use the Guide: Explaining What Kaizen Is (pages 79–80) which you provided to the team in your pre-event communication to refresh participants about the basics of Kaizen. Refer to the chart showing the tasks to be performed (Exhibit 1, page 168). You prepared this earlier, and it should be displayed on the wall (see Getting Ready Task 2). Tell the purpose and benefits of each task and the major Doing Steps that execute each. Ask for and answer any questions the team may have about Kaizen.

2) Review the strawperson direction for the event.

   Tip: Point to the display of the strawperson direction you prepared. Review the contents of the strawperson direction. Ask for and answer any questions the team may have about the strawperson direction for the event.

3) Review customer values.

   Tip: Point to the display of customer values you prepared and explain to the team why these values are the key reference point for all decision-making about improvements within a Kaizen event. Ask for and answer any questions the team may have the role of customer values.

Doing Tasks

1. Focus the Kaizen event.

   Tip: For detailed guidance, see *Task D1. Focus the Kaizen Event* (beginning on page 189).

2. Evaluate the target work process.

   Tip: For detailed guidance, see *Task D2. Evaluate the Target Work Process* (beginning on page 267).

3. Solve the performance issue.

   Tip: For detailed guidance, see *Task D3. Solve the Performance Issue* (beginning on page 311).

4. Act to improve the target work process.

   Tip: For detailed guidance, see *Task D4. Act to Improve the Target Work Process* (beginning on page 333).

Following Up Tasks

1. Conduct the Kaizen team close-out meeting.

   a. Prepare for the team close-out meeting.

1) Build the storyboard.

Tip: A storyboard is a visual display that presents information about the direction, participants, and results of a Kaizen event. It is constructed from three panels of 1/4-inch foam board each 3'x5'. The boards are formed into a triptych by taping each long side of the center board to the long side of one of the remaining boards. The display is intended to stand on a table but may be mounted on a wall. The storyboard presents the mission, goals, and do's and don'ts of the event; before, during, and after photos of the target work process; a team photo with names; and the Kaizen Summary (see example on page 184; an electronic form is contained in the Kaizen Tool Kit). Laminate the items placed on the storyboard so that they maintain a good appearance over time, as you will be leaving the storyboard behind.

2) Prepare certificates of recognition for team members.

Tip: Certificates should have been purchased by the site in preparation for the event. Make a certificate for each team member. The Kaizen Tool Kit includes a blank certificate which you may use if printed certificates are not available (see page 185).

b. Lead the team close-out meeting.

1) Orient the team to the purpose of the close-out meeting.

Tip: The purpose of the close-out meeting is to consolidate the team's learning from the event and recognize its achievements.

2) Summarize what was accomplished.

Tip: Use the storyboard to assist you in summarizing what was accomplished by the team.

a) Review the mission of the event.

b) Review the goals of the event.

c) Review the problems identified in the target work process.

d) Review the improvement ideas selected for implementation (from the Prioritized List of Process and Workplace Improvement Ideas).

e) Review the results produced.

3) Review with the team how the results were accomplished.

a) Have the team generate the critical factors that produced success (i.e., success enablers).

b) Have the team identify any barriers to achievement it encountered.

c) Have the team extract learning that can be used to improve future events.

d) Document the success enablers, barriers, and learning on a flipchart page.

4) Revisit the team's expectations and concerns and verify that the event met their expectations and resolved their concerns.

5) Ready the team to monitor follow through on work process improvements.

   Tip: Sustaining the benefits of the Kaizen event requires vigilance by the performers of the target work process to ensure that the improvements introduced in the event continue to be practiced. The use of a leave-behind measure and regular progress review meetings are essential to achieving sustained benefits.

   a) Review the leave-behind measure developed in *D4. Act to Improve the Target Work Process.*

   b) Orient the team to the idea of regular progress review meetings.

   c) Discuss the agenda for such meetings.

   d) Discuss how to report the results of these meetings using the leave-behind measure display and how to seek assistance if needed.

   e) Set up a schedule for the progress review meetings.

6) Recognize team performance.

   a) Recognize the contribution of each team member verbally.

   b) Distribute certificates and gifts to express appreciation for the team's efforts.

7) Have the team evaluate the event using the Kaizen Participant Feedback Form.

   Tip: An electronic version of this form is available in the Kaizen Tool Kit; a printed version begins on page 186.

   a) Distribute the forms.

   b) Ask the team to complete the forms.

      Tip: Tell the team members that they do not have to put their names on the form if they don't want to.

   c) Collect the forms.

2. Communicate the results of the Kaizen event to stakeholders.

   Tip: Presenting the results of the Kaizen event to stakeholders is important in gaining support for the improvements made and ensuring that the improvements are sustained. On the last day of the event, the team should prepare and deliver a formal presentation of results to all stakeholders.

   a. Prepare a presentation to communicate the results of the event.

      Tip: Build the presentation around the storyboard. Everyone on the team should participate in preparing and delivering the presentation. Display the storyboard where attendees can view it before the beginning of the meeting and where the team can easily reference it during the presentation. Print enough copies of the Kaizen Summary to distribute to participants. Display the leave-behind measure and the list of actions needed to transform soft into hard benefits so that the team can introduce them also. Assign each team member a portion of the information to communicate.

b. Make the presentation of results with the team.

Tip: Whenever possible, have the team lead the presentation and not just participate in it. Assign yourself a support role, keeping the presentation on track and providing additional clarification when needed.

1) Introduce the team members.

2) Identify the target work process.

3) State the event's mission and goals (from the Kaizen Summary).

4) Review the four tasks accomplished during the week (Exhibit 1, page 168).

5) Present the pre-event observations of the work process's performance.

Tip: Use the Summary of Findings and the charts developed in *Task D2. Evaluate the Target Work Process* as appropriate.

6) Present the improvement ideas developed and implemented by the team (from the Prioritized List of Process and Workplace Improvement Ideas).

7) List results for each goal (from the Kaizen Summary).

8) Identify outstanding action items, including owners and due dates (from the Kaizen Summary).

c. Review the follow-through plan.

1) Introduce the leave-behind measure.

Tip: The use of a leave-behind measure supports the continued use of and benefit from the Kaizen improvements. Review the leave-behind measure and its purpose. Show the visual control display. Discuss the team's continuous improvement meetings to track and further advance the improvements created by the event.

2) Review the plan for obtaining changes to the work standards.

3) State the team's recommendations for leveraging the improvement ideas generated by the event.

a) Review the opportunities for replication of the Kaizen improvements at other sites implementing the same work process.

b) Review the list of actions needed to change soft to hard benefits.

c) Identify improvements designated by the team for execution after the event.

    d. Acknowledge the contribution of people outside the team who helped make the event a success.

    e. Close the meeting.

      Tip: Ask for any remaining comments or feedback. On behalf of yourself and your co-leader, thank the meeting participants, the host business, and the team for the opportunity to perform the Kaizen event.

3. Mine learning from the completed event.

   Tip: This task is performed by the Kaizen event leader, preferably with the co-leader, after the event is complete. The information used is the documentation of the event, the insights and learning produced by the team at its close-out meeting, the results of the Kaizen Participant Feedback Forms, and observations made by the leader and co-leader. Keep the learning generated by this task and refer to it before beginning each new Kaizen assignment so that your expertise and success grow.

    a. Summarize the participant feedback contained in the Kaizen Participant Feedback Forms.

      Tip: Use a blank electronic copy of the Kaizen Participant Feedback Form to record your summary of participant feedback. An electronic form for recording a summary of the results is provided in the Kaizen Tool Kit (Kaizen Participant Summary Feedback Form).

      1) Compute the mean score for each question asking participants to respond by assigning a numerical rating.

        Tip: The mean is computed across participants. For Questions 1 and 3, compute the average rating assigned by participants for each item separately. For the remaining numerically answered questions, just compute the average for the question. In each case, sum the ratings participants assigned the item and divide by the number of ratings summed. Blanks do not count. Where a person circled more than one number, average the numbers the person circled and use that as the score to sum.

      2) Record the mean rating alongside each item in the electronic summary of participant feedback.

        Tip: For Question 1, the form computes the percent change in proficiency for each knowledge and skill automatically.

      3) List all the comments offered in the electronic summary of participant feedback.

        Tip: List the comments verbatim under the question to which they respond. Do not correct or otherwise modify the comment as recorded by the participant. Again, use an electronic version of the form so you can maintain and share the results electronically. If a portion of a written comment is illegible, record what you can read and insert the phrase "[word(s) illegible]" for the portion you cannot read. If the entire comment is not legible, record: "comment illegible."

b. Extract learning from the event.

Tip: Judge the results produced by the event against the targets established for every Kaizen (Exhibit 2) and the unique expectations defined for this event. Analyze the sources of its results. Determine what can be learned from the achievements that were realized and the reasons that produced them. Consider completing an SRLD[SM] (Status, Reason, Learning, Direction) analysis for the event. SRLD[SM] is the Vital Enterprises method for mining learning from performance (see *Mining Learning From Performance* R.L. Vitalo and P.A. Bierley, Hope, ME: Lowrey Press, 2003). Use the information in Exhibit 2 to anchor your analysis.

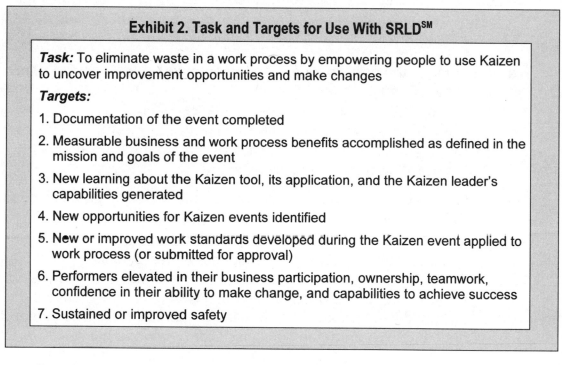

Exhibit 2. Task and Targets for Use With SRLD[SM]

Task: To eliminate waste in a work process by empowering people to use Kaizen to uncover improvement opportunities and make changes

Targets:

1. Documentation of the event completed

2. Measurable business and work process benefits accomplished as defined in the mission and goals of the event

3. New learning about the Kaizen tool, its application, and the Kaizen leader's capabilities generated

4. New opportunities for Kaizen events identified

5. New or improved work standards developed during the Kaizen event applied to work process (or submitted for approval)

6. Performers elevated in their business participation, ownership, teamwork, confidence in their ability to make change, and capabilities to achieve success

7. Sustained or improved safety

4. Ensure that the event's documentation is complete.

Tip: Typically, the Kaizen co-leader completes the documentation. Exhibit 3 lists the records included in a complete documentation of a Kaizen event. You should have documented the event as it was being performed using paper records, electronic forms provided in the Kaizen Tool Kit, and/or your own electronic forms. Check to be sure your documentation is complete. Add any missing documents. Note that not every event requires each of the documents listed in Exhibit 3 (next page). For example, if machine observations are not made, you will not produce Machine Analysis Sheets.

Exhibit 3. Required Documentation for a Kaizen Event

1. Scope
2. Description of Target Work Process
3. Waste Observed During Walk Through Categorized by Type
4. Direction for the Kaizen Event (includes Mission Statement, Goals for the Event, and Do's and Don'ts)
5. Process Analysis Sheet - Pre
6. Machine Analysis Sheet - Pre
7. Summary of Findings
8. Prioritized List of Process and Workplace Improvement Ideas
9. Experiment (include both the Design and Results of the Experiment)
10. Pilot (include both Design and Results of the Pilot)
11. Process Analysis Sheet - Post
12. Machine Analysis Sheet - Post
13. Summary of Operating Improvements
14. Summary of Monetary Benefits
15. Leave-Behind Measure
16. Kaizen Summary
17. Parking Lot Issues
18. Summary of Kaizen Participant Feedback
19. Learning From the Event

Check Steps

Use the following checklist to verify that the milestone was achieved.

Benchmark	√
Getting Ready Tasks	
1. Prepared yourself.	☐
2. Prepared the setting.	☐
3. Readied the Kaizen team.	☐
Doing Tasks	
1. Focused the Kaizen event.	☐
2. Evaluated the target work process.	☐
3. Solved the performance issue.	☐
4. Acted to improve the target work process.	☐
Following Up Tasks	
1. Conducted the Kaizen team close-out meeting.	☐
2. Communicated the results of the Kaizen event to stakeholders.	☐
3. Mined learning from the completed event.	☐
4. Ensured that the event's documentation is complete.	☐

Tips

- Keep the team and the stakeholders connected to the event before, during, and after so that they experience ownership for its ideas and results. Such ownership ensures the continued support and use of the improvements the event produces.

Checklist for Preparing the Setting

What to Do	
Before the First Day of the Event	**Done**
■ Confirm presence of participant materials	☐
■ Confirm presence of equipment needed for the event	☐
■ Set up equipment (see Guide: Arranging the Main Meeting Room, page 180)	☐
▪ Table	
▪ Chairs	
▪ Overhead or LCD projector	
▪ Flipchart easels, paper, and markers	
▪ Other equipment	
■ Test equipment to make sure that it works	☐
■ Verify that participants can see you, the display media, and each other	☐
■ Organize your materials	
▪ Handouts	☐
▪ Transparencies	
▪ Job aids	
■ Distribute participant materials to each member's seating location	
▪ Name tags	☐
▪ Pencils	
▪ Paper	
■ Create and position flipchart displays	
▪ Prepare a chart depicting the major tasks for executing *Milestone D. Perform the Kaizen Event* (see Exhibit 1, page 168)	☐
▪ Prepare a flipchart page recording the strawperson direction for the event	☐
▪ Prepare a flipchart page recording the customer values reported in the scope document	☐
First Day of the Event	
■ Arrive early	☐
■ Check room lighting and temperature	☐
■ Ensure that the coffee and morning snack are present	☐
■ Ensure that lunch and an afternoon snack are arranged	☐

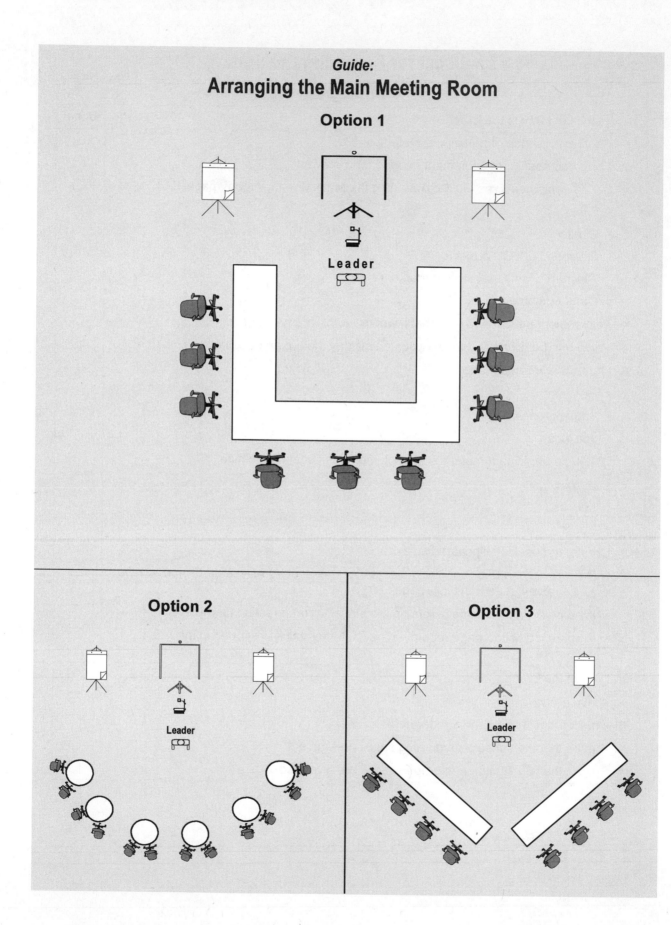

Expectations and Concerns Icebreaker

Instructions

1. Have each team member work at his or her seat.

2. Explain to the team members that you want to understand what their expectations are for the event so you can ensure that they are satisfied by the event.

3. Ask the Kaizen co-leader to create two flipchart pages, one for "Expectations" and one for "Concerns."

4. Ask each member to take a moment to reflect on what he or she hopes to get from participating in the Kaizen event and what concerns, if any, he or she may have about the event. Give participants five minutes to complete this task, then ask the team members to share their expectations and concerns. Go around the room and get each member's expectations and concerns. Confirm what each team member says.

5. Have the co-leader record your confirmation of what team members say about their expectations and concerns on the appropriate flipchart page.

6. When you have gone around the entire team, review the "Expectations" of the team and summarize the major themes. Discuss how, when, and where the event will address these expectations.

7. Next, review the "Concerns" of the team and summarize the major themes. Discuss how, when, and where the event will address these concerns.

Strengths and Weaknesses Icebreaker

Instructions

1. Divide participants into subteams of two, three, or four members.

2. Tell each group to choose a recorder.

3. As you give the following instructions, demonstrate what will be done.

   a. Each group will go to a blank piece of flipchart paper posted on the walls of the training room.

   Tip: Ensure that enough sheets of blank flipchart paper are on the walls prior to training.

   b. The recorders will draw a line down the center of the page and head the left side "Strengths" and the right side "Weaknesses."

   c. Each person in the group will brainstorm three to four features of the target work process he or she sees as working well. Features may include people, work process design, quality of machinery or tools, or procedures. Tell the team that working well means operating efficiently and effectively from the customer's perspective. Tell the participants to write down their ideas and share them when asked.

   Tip: Tell the group members that if they do not have direct knowledge of the customer, they should imagine themselves as the customer buying their product and use this viewpoint as their guide.

   d. Next, each person in the group will brainstorm three to four features of the target work process he or she sees as weaknesses. A weakness is some feature of the work process that makes it inefficient or ineffective from the customer's perspective. Tell the participants to write down their ideas and share them when asked.

   e. After a few minutes, the recorders should gather the strengths and weaknesses from their group and list them in the appropriate column, eliminating redundancies.

4. Give the groups 10 minutes to complete these tasks, then go around the room and ask each recorder to present his or her group's ideas.

5. Clarify and confirm the meaning of each item.

6. Summarize the major strengths and weaknesses of the work process as viewed by the entire team. Make the point that the team will be working during the Kaizen event to reduce the weaknesses and boost the strengths of the target work process.

Guide:
Building Ground Rules

Task

To establish rules that will guide how we work together during the Kaizen event so that we understand each other's expectations and agree on a common set of behaviors we can all endorse.

Steps

1. Explain the importance of setting ground rules. Point out that ground rules:

    - express the team members' expectations regarding how everyone will behave during the meeting;
    - minimize problem behaviors; and
    - keep everyone focused, and the environment positive.

2. Involve all team members in setting the ground rules.

    Tip: Use one or more of the following typical ground rules to trigger the team's thinking, if necessary.

    - Start and end on time.
    - One speaker at a time.
    - Respect the opinions of others.
    - Use clarifying, confirming, constructive criticism, and hitchhiking skills.
    - Eliminate side conversations.
    - Encourage full participation.
    - What is said in the room stays in the room.

3. Ask: "What ground rules do we need to guide how we work together this week?"

4. Record responses on flipchart paper.

5. Ensure that everyone agrees to abide by the ground rules.

6. Post the ground rules where everyone can see them during the meeting.

7. Elicit everyone's commitment in enforcing the ground rules.

Tips

- Ground rules that are not enforced have no value. Review the ground rules at the beginning and end of each day. Also at the end of each day, have the team rate how well members abided by the ground rules during the day. Use this exercise to uncover ways to improve compliance with the team's ground rules.

Example:

Kaizen Summary

Kaizen Team Members

Joseph V., Kaizen leader
Mark G., Kaizen co-leader
Reggie B., Fill Operator
Thomas C., Fill Operator
Vincent L., Supervisor
Nathan H., Maintenance
James L., Fill Operator
Clarice T., Lab Technician

Mission Statement

To increase profit without increasing price and elevate customer satisfaction with on-time delivery by reducing the cycle time and cost of the nonflammable blending work process for ABC Gases and its stakeholders.

Operating Measure	Cylinder Preparation		Nonflammable Blending		Monetary Measure	Result
	Pre-Event	Post-Event	Pre-Event	Post-Event		
Cycle Time	02:19:30	01:30:14	02:25:14	01:40:15	Labor Savings	$215,378.38
Value-Added Ratio	0.00	0.00	0.08	0.22	Non-Labor Savings	$0.00
Labor Productivity	5.16	7.98	2.48	3.59	Dollar Gains	$0.00
Throughput	17.20	26.60	20.00	35.90	Less New Costs	$9,310.00
					Total Dollar Benefits	$206,068.38

Charge #: 20-2001 | Dates of Event: 8/06-8/10 | Total Cost of Event: $14,500

	Goal	Result	Action Item	Who	Date Due	Status
Cylinder Preparation Process						
1	Reduce wait time by 25%	Down 100%	None			
2	Reduce setup by 20%	Up 157%	Do a follow-up Kaizen event focusing on travel/transport and setup	Team	10/15/01	Open
3	Reduce travel/transport by 25%	Down 4%	None			
4	Eliminate all hazard items	Eliminated	None			
Nonflammable Blending Process						
5	Reduce setup by 20%	Down 23%	None			
6	Reduce travel/transport by 25%	Down 20%	Install oxygen pump switch in the blending booth	Reggie	9/15/01	Open
7	Reduce wait time by 50%	Down 96%	None			
8	Reduce unnecessary processing by 50%	Down 56%	None			
9	Eliminate all hazard items	Eliminated	None			
10	Reduce unit cost	Down 28%	None			
11	Reduce cycle time	Down 31%	None			

Certificate of Recognition

For the dedication and extra effort applied during the Kaizen event held [Date] at [Site]

Awarded to

[Name]

World Class Contributor!

[Signature above]

Kaizen Participant Feedback Form

Name (Optional): _____ Date: _____

1. For each knowledge and skill, indicate how proficient you were **before** participating in the Kaizen event and how proficient you are **now**. Assign a rating of 0 to 9 using the scale below. Write your answers in the boxes provided.

0	**1 2 3**	**4 5 6**	**7 8 9**
No proficiency	Little proficiency	Moderate proficiency	High proficiency

Knowledge and Skills	**Before Event**	**After Event**
Rate your mastery of the following topics:		
a. The purpose of Kaizen		
b. The importance of Kaizen events		
c. The process of doing Kaizen		
d. The forms of waste as depicted in Kaizen		
Rate your proficiency in each of the following skills		
e. Detecting waste in a work process		
f. Brainstorming improvement ideas		
g. Prioritizing improvement ideas		
h. Planning a work process improvement		
i. Executing a work process improvement		
j. Communicating the results of an improvement to stakeholders		

2. Overall, how satisfied are you with the Kaizen event? Circle the number that best shows your reaction.

0	**1 2 3**	**4 5 6**	**7 8 9**
Not satisfied at all	Somewhat satisfied	Satisfied	Completely satisfied

3. Provide your assessment of the facilitators of the event. Read each of the statements below and circle the number that represents how much you agree or disagree with it.

Statement	Strongly Disagree	Disagree	Agree & Disagree	Agree	Strongly Agree	Don't Know
a. The event leaders made it clear what was to be done and why.	1	2	3	4	5	DK
b. The event was well organized.	1	2	3	4	5	DK
c. The event leaders made adequate use of practice as a way to prepare the team to perform its roles.	1	2	3	4	5	DK
d. The event leaders included an opportunity to ask questions about the tasks the team was asked to perform.	1	2	3	4	5	DK
e. The event leaders included opportunities to discuss what was being done and to elicit the team's issues and concerns.	1	2	3	4	5	DK
f. The event leaders displayed energy throughout the event.	1	2	3	4	5	DK
g. The event leaders displayed understanding for the team's issues and concerns.	1	2	3	4	5	DK
h. The event leaders were able to develop a team spirit among the participants.	1	2	3	4	5	DK
i. The event leaders displayed respectful attitudes throughout the event.	1	2	3	4	5	DK

4. What were the strengths of this event?

5. What could be done to improve the Kaizen event?

6. Overall, how much benefit do you judge the event produced *for the target work process?* Circle the number that best shows your reaction.

0	1 2 3	4 5 6	7 8 9
Not benefited at all	Somewhat benefited	Benefited	Greatly benefited

7. Overall, how much benefit do you feel the event produced *for you?* Circle the number that best shows your reaction.

0	1 2 3	4 5 6	7 8 9
Not benefited at all	Somewhat benefited	Benefited	Greatly benefited

Task D1. Focus the Kaizen Event

Preview

This task defines the direction the Kaizen event will pursue based on the facts in the workplace. It:

- establishes the accountability of the Kaizen event, and
- ensures that all participants drive toward the same and correct end.

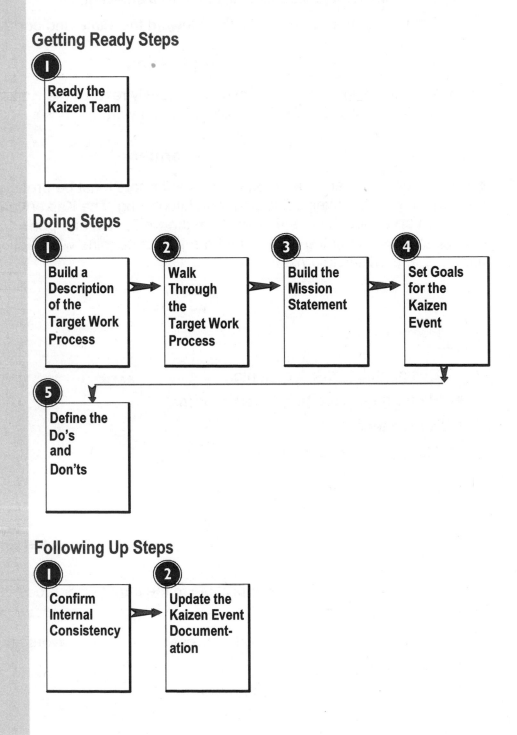

Getting Ready Steps

1 Ready the Kaizen Team

Doing Steps

1 Build a Description of the Target Work Process

2 Walk Through the Target Work Process

3 Build the Mission Statement

4 Set Goals for the Kaizen Event

5 Define the Do's and Don'ts

Following Up Steps

1 Confirm Internal Consistency

2 Update the Kaizen Event Document-ation

Purpose

To define the direction the Kaizen event will pursue based on the facts in the workplace.

Benefit

- Establishes the accountability of the Kaizen event.
- Ensures that all participants drive toward the same and correct end.

Application

Apply this knowledge when you have successfully readied the Kaizen team to begin the event and before you complete any other Kaizen work.

Performer

Kaizen leader, co-leader, and team. The performers must be proficient in clarifying, confirming, constructively criticizing, and hitchhiking. The Kaizen leader and co-leader must also be skilled in detecting waste in the workplace and performing simple inferencing—that is, using the guidance of a rule to determine what action or decision is appropriate in a given circumstance.

Resources

People

- Designated event coordinator
- Performers of the target work process
- Kaizen team
- Manager of the target work process

Information, Knowledge, and Training

- Complete, consistent, and verified scope document
- Contractual agreements (e.g., with customers, unions) that affect the target work process
- Government regulations applicable to the target work process
- Kaizen News - Day 1
- Procedure for modifying work process or workplace layout standards
- Safety rules
- Strawperson direction for the event

- Work flow diagrams of the target work process
- Work standards for the target work process
- *Working With Others* (J.S. Byron and P.A. Bierley, Hope, ME: Lowrey Press, 2003) - teaches how to get (clarify and confirm) and give (constructive criticism and hitchhiking) ideas and information in ways that build collaboration and elevate results

Materials, Tools, and Other Resources

- Space, equipment, and supplies to support the team's work

Room/Tables/Chairs

- Chairs
- Meeting area for the full team
- Tables
- Wall space for hanging storyboards and materials
- Wheelchair-accessible areas
- Wheelchair-accessible tables

Equipment - General

- Computer printer or access to one
- Copier or access to one
- Flipchart easels or hangers
- Laptop computer with Microsoft Office

2000® and Adobe Acrobat Reader® 4.0 or higher
- LCD computer projector
- Overhead projector
- Projection screen

Equipment - Safety

- Clothing
- Earplugs
- Gloves
- Hard-hats
- Safety glasses
- Safety shoes

Supplies

- Clipboards
- Flipchart markers
- Flipchart pads
- Masking tape

- Multicolored Post-its® - 3"x5"
- Name tags
- Notebooks
- Pens and pencils
- Printer paper (white and colored)
- Roll of white paper (34"x44")
- Ruler
- Scissors
- Transparency film (for a copier)

Food

- Lunch
- Morning and afternoon snacks
- Special dietary needs (e.g., kosher food, low salt)

- Kaizen Tool Kit
  - Detecting Value-Added Work and the Forms of Waste Exercise
  - Direction for the Kaizen Event (includes mission statement, goals for the event, and do's and don'ts)
  - Guide: Understanding the Forms of Waste
  - Questions That Could Be Asked During the Walk Through
  - Questions That Could Be Asked During the Personal Interview

- Guide: Observe First
- Waste Observed During Walk Through Categorized by Type

Output

- Waste observed during walk through categorized by type
- Description of the target work process
- Direction for the Kaizen event
  - Mission statement
  - Goals for the event
  - Do's and don'ts
- Integrated list of improvement ideas obtained from the workers in the target work process
- Kaizen team able to detect waste
- Updated documentation of the Kaizen event

Method

Getting Ready Steps

1. Ready the Kaizen team.

   Tip: Before readying the team, prepare a flipchart page showing the Doing Steps that accomplish *Task D1. Focus the Kaizen Event*. Use Exhibit 1 (next page) as a guide. Position this page next to the chart you previously created depicting the tasks that implement *Milestone D. Perform the Kaizen Event* (see page 168).

   a. Remind the team of the four tasks that perform the Kaizen event.

      Tip: Use the chart you previously created depicting the tasks that implement *Milestone D. Perform the Kaizen Event*.

   b. Tell the team that it will now complete *Task D1. Focus the Kaizen Event*.

   c. Briefly explain Task D1.

      Tip: Refer to the chart showing the steps that complete Task D1 (Exhibit 1, next page). You prepared this before you began and it should be displayed on the wall. Tell the purpose and benefits of each step and the major activity completed in each. Ask for and answer any questions the team may have about Kaizen.

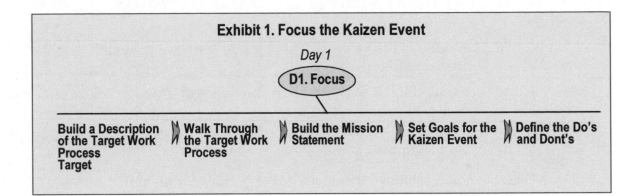

Exhibit 1. Focus the Kaizen Event

Doing Steps

1. Build a description of the target work process.

   Tip: For detailed guidance, see *Step D1-S1. Build a Description of the Target Work Process* (beginning on page 197).

2. Walk through the target work process.

   Tip: For detailed guidance, see *Step D1-S2. Walk Through the Target Work Process* (beginning on page 215).

3. Build the mission statement.

   Tip: For detailed guidance, see *Step D1-S3. Build the Mission Statement* (beginning on page 241).

4. Set goals for the Kaizen event.

   Tip: For detailed guidance, see *Step D1-S4. Set Goals for the Kaizen Event* (beginning on page 253).

5. Define the do's and don'ts.

   Tip: For detailed guidance, see *Step D1-S5. Define the Do's and Don'ts* (beginning on page 261).

Following Up Steps

1. Confirm internal consistency.

   Tip: As a final check, apply the rule stated below to confirm that the direction the team produced is internally consistent. If the direction defined by the team is not internally consistent, you must resolve the inconsistencies with the team. Before you proceed with the event, the team must have a set of goals that accomplish the mission and are achievable within the constraints defined in the do's and don'ts for the event. If you modify the team-defined direction, be sure that it remains consistent with the strawperson direction. If it does not, resolve the inconsistencies with the event coordinator.

Rule:

	IF	achieving the goals would produce the results specified in the mission statement
	and	the goals of the event attack the major sources of waste observed during the walk through
	and	the do's and don'ts would permit the team the latitude it needs to achieve the goals
	THEN	the direction for the event is internally consistent
	ELSE	the direction for the event is not internally consistent
	and	the Kaizen leader must resolve the inconsistencies.

2. Update the Kaizen event documentation.

   Tip: If you modify the direction of the event in Following Up Step 1, you need to update the event documentation. Update each element of the direction for the event you modified (i.e., the mission, goals, and or do's and don'ts).

Check Steps

Use the following checklist to verify that the task was done correctly.

Benchmark	√
Getting Ready Steps	
1. Readied the Kaizen team.	☐
Doing Steps	
1. Built a description of the target work process.	☐
2. Walked through the target work process.	☐
3. Built the mission statement.	☐
4. Set goals for the Kaizen event.	☐
5. Defined the do's and don'ts.	☐
Following Up Steps	
1. Confirmed internal consistency.	☐
2. Updated the Kaizen event documentation.	☐

Tips

- Build the direction for the Kaizen event on what you directly observe and what people executing the work process share. Follow through to check the consistency of the direction built from the facts in the workplace against what the scope statement specified. Do not proceed until you resolve any discrepancies between the focus you define in the event and the strawperson direction you received prior to the event.

Step D1-S1. Build a Description of the Target Work Process

Preview

This step equips the team with a common image of the target work process to guide its information gathering and process improvement efforts. It:

- educates team members not familiar with the target work process about how it operates,

- uncovers and resolves inconsistencies in how the target work process is perceived by the people who perform it,

- allows the Kaizen leader to verify his or her understanding of the work process, and

- provides the Kaizen leader information he or she needs to plan the walk through.

Getting Ready Substeps

① Draft the Description of the Target Work Process

Doing Substeps

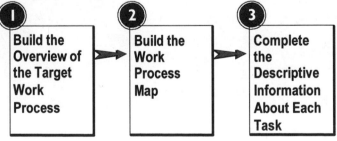

① Build the Overview of the Target Work Process

② Build the Work Process Map

③ Complete the Descriptive Information About Each Task

Following Up Substeps

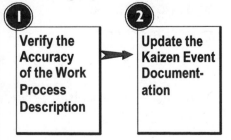

① Verify the Accuracy of the Work Process Description

② Update the Kaizen Event Documentation

Purpose

To equip the team with a common image of the target work process to guide its information gathering and process improvement efforts.

Benefit

- Educates team members not familiar with the target work process about how it operates.

- Uncovers and resolves inconsistencies in how the target work process is perceived by the people who perform it.

- Allows the Kaizen leader to verify his or her understanding of the work process.

- Provides the Kaizen leader information he or she needs to plan the walk through.

Application

Use this knowledge immediately after preparing the team to focus the Kaizen event and before conducting the walk through of the target work process.

Performer

Kaizen leader, co-leader, and team. The performers must be proficient in clarifying, confirming, constructively criticizing, and hitchhiking.

Resources

People

- Designated event coordinator
- Kaizen team
- Manager of the target work process
- Work standards supervisor

Information, Knowledge, and Training

- Complete, consistent, and verified scope document
- Work flow diagrams of the target work process
- Work standards for the target work process
- *Working With Others* (J.S. Byron and P.A. Bierley, Hope, ME: Lowrey Press, 2003) - teaches how to get (clarify and confirm) and give (constructive criticism and hitchhiking) ideas and information in ways that build collaboration and elevate results

Materials, Tools, and Other Resources

■ Space, equipment, and supplies to support the team's work

Room/Tables/Chairs

- Chairs
- Meeting area for the full team
- Tables
- Wall space for hanging storyboards and materials
- Wheelchair-accessible areas
- Wheelchair-accessible tables

Equipment - General

- Computer printer or access to one
- Copier or access to one

■ Flipchart easels or hangers

■ Laptop computer with Microsoft Office 2000® and Adobe Acrobat Reader® 4.0 or higher

■ LCD computer projector

■ Overhead projector

■ Projection screen

Equipment - Safety

- Clothing
- Earplugs
- Gloves
- Hard-hats
- Safety glasses
- Safety shoes

Supplies

- Flipchart markers
- Flipchart pads
- Masking tape
- Multicolored Post-its® - 3"x5"
- Name tags
- Notebooks
- Pens and pencils
- Printer paper (white and colored)
- Roll of white paper (34"x44")
- Ruler
- Scissors
- Transparency film (for a copier)

Output

■ Description of the target work process

■ Updated Kaizen event documentation

Method

Getting Ready Substeps

1. Draft the description of the target work process.

   Tip: A work process description has two components: (1) an overview that documents the purpose of the work process and the essential components that define it (see example on page 212) and (2) a work process map (see example on page 213). You should always be able to draft at least a partial description of the target work process using the information supplied in the scope document, your conversations with the event coordinator, the work standards for the target work process, and any existing work flow diagrams of the process. You will confirm your draft description and complete missing elements of it by executing the Doing Substeps.

a. Draft the overview information.

Tip: The overview information includes the name of the target work process and its purpose; its inputs, outputs, locations of performance, cycle time, and takt time; and the names of the other work processes or departments with which the target work process interrelates. Exhibit 1 presents an example of an overview. Exhibit 2, next page, identifies where you can obtain the information you need to draft this overview prior to meeting with the team. Use the guidance provided in Doing Substep 1 to help you create the overview.

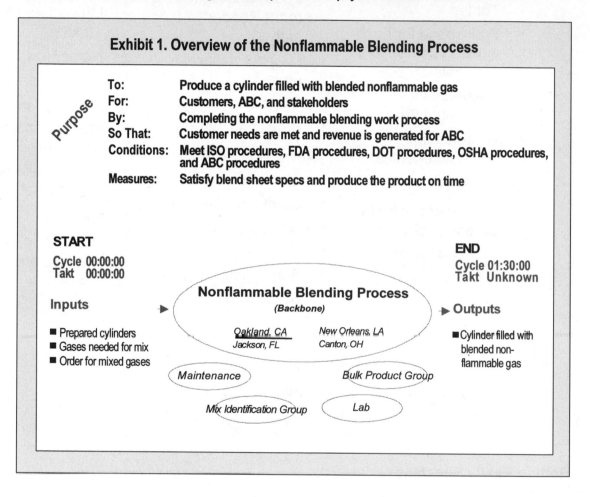

Exhibit 1. Overview of the Nonflammable Blending Process

Purpose

To:	Produce a cylinder filled with blended nonflammable gas
For:	Customers, ABC, and stakeholders
By:	Completing the nonflammable blending work process
So That:	Customer needs are met and revenue is generated for ABC
Conditions:	Meet ISO procedures, FDA procedures, DOT procedures, OSHA procedures, and ABC procedures
Measures:	Satisfy blend sheet specs and produce the product on time

START
Cycle 00:00:00
Takt 00:00:00

END
Cycle 01:30:00
Takt Unknown

Inputs

- Prepared cylinders
- Gases needed for mix
- Order for mixed gases

Nonflammable Blending Process
(Backbone)

Oakland, CA   New Orleans, LA
Jackson, FL   Canton, OH

Maintenance   Bulk Product Group

Mix Identification Group   Lab

Outputs

- Cylinder filled with blended non-flammable gas

b. Draft the work process map.

Tip: The work process map includes the name of the target work process, its cycle time and takt time, the name and cycle time of each operation that executes the work process and its position within the sequence of work, the role or department responsible for doing each operation, and other descriptive information. Exhibit 3 (page 202) presents an example of a work process map. Exhibit 2, next page, identifies where you can obtain the information you need to draft this diagram prior to meeting with the team. Use the guidance provided in Doing Substeps 2 and 3 to help you draft the work process map.

Exhibit 2. Work Process Description Information and Its Source	
Overview Information	**Source**
Name of the target work process	■ Scope document - Item B1
Purpose: ■ *To* - name of product or service output produced	■ Scope document - Item B1
■ *For* - names of the persons or groups for whom the process is done	■ Event coordinator[1]
■ *By* - name of the work process	■ Scope document - Item B1
■ *So That* - list of the benefits the work process should deliver	■ Event coordinator ■ Work standard
■ *Conditions* - list of the constraints under which the work process must operate	■ Event coordinator ■ Work standard
■ *Measures* - list of the measures management uses to determine how well the work process is performing	■ Event coordinator ■ Work standard
Start time	■ Always 00:00:00
End time - cycle time	■ Scope document - Item B6c
End time - takt time	■ Scope document - Item B6a
Inputs	■ Work standard
Outputs	■ Scope document - Item B1
Location(s) of execution	■ Scope document - Item B2
Interfaces	■ Scope document - Item B14
Work Process Map Information	**Source**
Name of the target work process	■ Scope document - Item B1
Start time	■ Always 00:00:00
End time - cycle time	■ Scope document - Item B6c
End time - takt time	■ Scope document - Item B6a
Operations: ■ **Name** ■ Cycle time ■ Role performing it ■ Position in the sequence of work	■ Event coordinator ■ Work standard
Descriptive information (contact, location, documents, machine/materials time)	■ Event coordinator ■ Work standard

[1]Either the event coordinator or whomever he or she identifies as knowledgeable about the target work process.

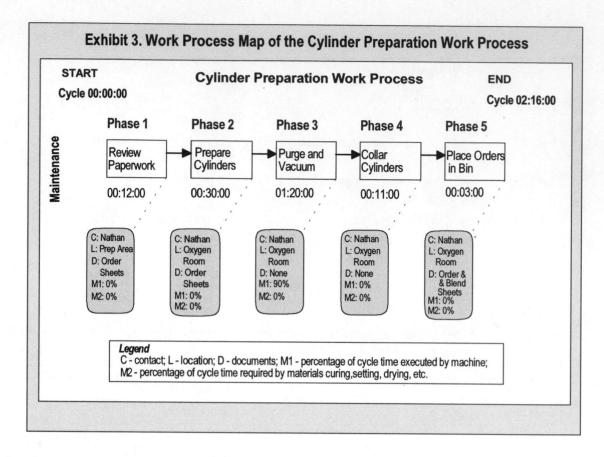

Doing Substeps

1. Build the overview of the target work process.

   Tip: Begin with your draft overview. Complete any missing information with the team. If you were unable to draft an overview, build it with the team in the meeting.

   a. Draw the overview template.

   Tip: Exhibit 4 (next page) presents the template you should draw. Begin by drawing an ellipse at the center of a blank flipchart page. Outside the ellipse and to the left, print "Inputs." Above it, print "START," and between START and Inputs, print the words "Cycle 00:00:00" and "Takt 00:00:00," placing Cycle above Takt (see Exhibit 4). To the right of the ellipse, print "Outputs." Above Outputs, print "END," and between END and Outputs, print the words "Cycle" and "Takt," placing Cycle above Takt. Above the large ellipse, print: "To:," "For:," "By:," "So That:," "Conditions:," and "Measures:" as in Exhibit 4 . Place the label "Purpose" to the left of this list. Later, you will place, below the large ellipse, smaller ellipses in which you will print the names of other work processes with which the target work process interacts.

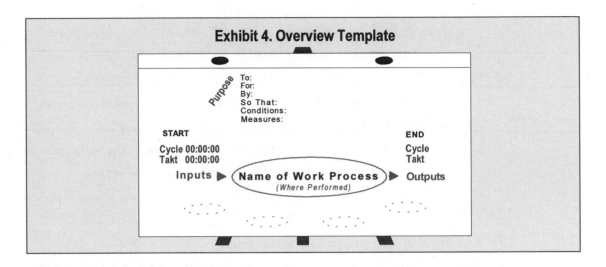

Exhibit 4. Overview Template

b. Name the target work process.

   Tip: Print the name of the target work process inside the ellipse at the center of the template. Be sure to include a model identification as part of the name if the work process is a mixed model and your description applies to one model only. If the work process you are describing is the backbone of a mixed model, then write "Backbone" below its name.

c. Name the inputs.

   Tip: Inputs are the information or materials that trigger the work process (e.g., customer order); control its execution (e.g., work instructions, product design); or are used to form the final output of the process (e.g., empty cylinders, customer specifications, customer complaint, purchase order).

d. Name the outputs.

   Tip: Outputs are the information, materials, or service outcomes that are the expected final results of executing the work process (e.g., an updated database, a trailer loaded with product, a customer satisfied with the resolution of his or her complaint).

e. Complete the purpose section.

   1) Record the "to, for, by, so that" information.

      Tip: The *to* component tells the primary product or service output generated by the work process—for example, "To produce an answer to a customer query" or "complete a door assembly." The *for* component identifies for whom this product or service output is produced. In general, this will be the external customer or the next work process segment to which the target work process passes its output. The *by* component records how the output is produced. It is stated: "By: executing [name of work process]." The *so that* component lists the benefits the work process is trying to provide for the recipient of its output and the company.

Exhibit 5. Example of "To, For, By, So That" Information

To: Produce trailers ready for road service

For: The Shipping Department, our drivers, and customers

By: Performing the trailer preventive maintenance work process

So That:
- The safety of drivers and community members is protected
- Disruptions in service due to trailer breakdowns are minimized
- Our fleet of trailers operates most cost effectively

2) Record the "Conditions" information.

   Tip: List the conditions under which the work process operates. Conditions are the limits on resources or approach with which the work process must comply (e.g., no overtime; exhaust inventory before ordering new parts; resolve complaints on a first-in, first-out basis). See example in Exhibit 6.

3) Record the "Measures" information.

   Tip: List the key performance measures applied to the work process (e.g., impurities must be less than 0.0001 ppm). With regard to measures, get both what is measured (e.g., impurities) and what target defines successful performance (e.g., less than 0.0001 ppm). Limit yourself to five key measures only, as there may be many measures monitored by management.

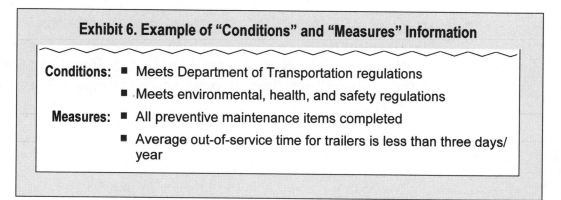

Exhibit 6. Example of "Conditions" and "Measures" Information

Conditions:
- Meets Department of Transportation regulations
- Meets environmental, health, and safety regulations

Measures:
- All preventive maintenance items completed
- Average out-of-service time for trailers is less than three days/year

f. Name the locations of execution.

   Tip: Inside the large ellipse below the name of the target work process, list up to four locations where the target work process is performed. Include the location where the Kaizen event is occurring, indicating it by underlining its name. Also identify the total number of locations where the target process is performed should that be greater than four.

g. Name the other work processes and departments with which the target work process interrelates.

Tip: Each work process and department the target work process gives something to (e.g., information, products); gets something from; or shares some resource in common with must be listed below the large ellipse. Draw a smaller ellipse around each name. See Exhibit 1, page 200, for an example.

h. Record the cycle time and takt time.

Tip: All time is represented using hours, minutes, and seconds (00:00:00). The start times, both cycle and takt, are 00:00:00. The cycle time recorded under the label "END" is the rate at which a product or service output exits the work process. For example, if one unit of output exits the work process every 3.5 hours, then record the cycle time as 03:30:00. Be sure that the cycle time is the typical rate of output when the process is executed according to the approved work standard. The takt time recorded under the label "END" is the rate at which output *must* exit the work process to meet customer demand. If the work process does not have a takt time computed, print "Unknown" next to the "Takt" label.

i. Verify that the work process overview is complete.

Tip: Check your overview against the example on page 212. Make sure it has each of the elements of information depicted in the example.

2. Build the work process map.

a. Prepare a flipchart page for mapping the work process.

Tip: Reproduce the layout depicted in Exhibit 7. Name the work process being mapped at the top of the chart.

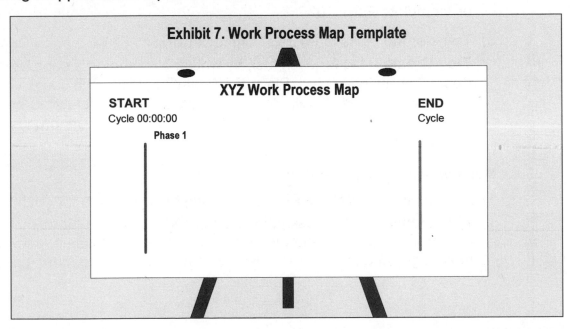

Exhibit 7. Work Process Map Template

b. Build a list of tasks that accomplish the work process.

Tip: Identify the major tasks that complete the work process. These are the 5 to 10 chunks of work that transform an initial input into a final output. If this is a mixed model work process and you are mapping the backbone operations, focus the team on the set of tasks through which every model of the final product or service output must pass in *exactly the same way*. Use the information you gathered prior to the event to create a draft list. Otherwise, build the list with the team in the meeting.

1) List the major tasks that complete this work process on a blank flipchart page.

Tip: Ask the team to name the 5 to 10 major tasks that complete this work process. List the tasks the team identifies on a blank flipchart page. Do not press the team for any arbitrary number of activities, assuming that there must be 10, for example, or that there cannot be more than 10. If the work process is performed by one person and has a short cycle time, it may not have more than three to five major tasks. Try to keep the maximum number of tasks listed to less than 15. Focus on the notion that you want the "big" activities. Remind the team that you are building a top-level view of the work process, not a list of all the detailed activities a worker performs.

2) Refine the task list.

Tip: Once the list is recorded, use your clarifying and confirming skills to make sure that each item is unique and that you understand the nature of the work the task completes. Have the offeror of each task tell some of the steps that execute the task. Name tasks using a verb plus object construction—for example, "load truck," "verify the customer's identification," or "complete Form 102."

3) Transfer the tasks to Post-its® or index cards.

Tip: Create a tag for each task by writing its name on a separate 3"x5" Post-it® or an index card. Place the Post-it® or tack each card to a blank flipchart page or to a wall. You will be taking these Post-its® or cards from this temporary storage area to build your map of the work process in the next step.

c. Map the tasks to time periods.

1) Assign start-up tasks to Phase 1, adding the cycle time for each task.

Tip: Identify the first task performed of all tasks listed. Move the name tag for the first task performed into the area below Phase 1 (see Exhibit 8, next page) and place an asterisk (*) on the name tag to mark it as the first started task in the time period.[1] Next, place under Phase 1 all the other tasks that start up *before* the first performed task ends. Identify the typical time it takes to complete each task when executed according to the current work standard (cycle time). Record this time on the task's name tag in hours, minutes, and seconds (00:00:00). Finally, draw a vertical line after the set of tasks you placed under Phase 1 to mark the end of the phase.

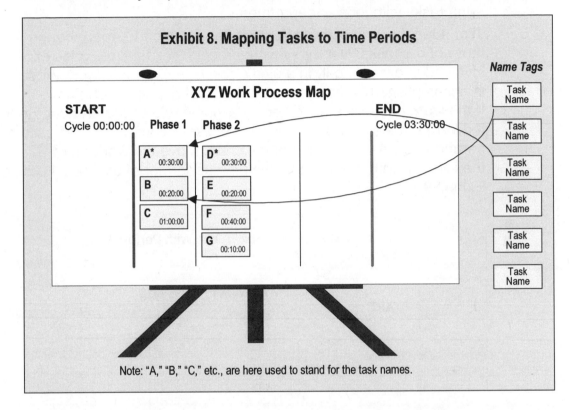

Exhibit 8. Mapping Tasks to Time Periods

Note: "A," "B," "C," etc., are here used to stand for the task names.

2) Assign the remaining tasks to subsequent phases, adding the cycle time for each.

   a) Create a new column to the right of the last column. Place the label "Phase n" at the top of this new column. On your chart, replace the "n" with the next number in the sequence of time periods.

   b) Identify the first task that is started in the new time period. That task is the first activity to begin after the first task identified in the prior time period ends. Move the task's name tag into the column. Place an asterisk (*) on the card to mark it as the first started task in the time period.

   c) Place in the column all the other tasks that start up before the first task of this time period ends.

---

[1] If more than one task starts the period simultaneously, move each tag to the time period. Place the asterisk (*) on the task that has the *longest* period of execution (cycle time). For example, if two tasks, X and Y, started in the same period and the end time for Task X is 00:01:10 and the end time for Task Y is 00:02:05, place the asterisk on Task Y's name tag.

d) Identify the cycle time in hours, minutes, and seconds (00:00:00) for each task in this period and record it on the task's name tag.

e) Draw a vertical line after the set of tasks to mark the end of Phase n.

f) Repeat a) through e) until all tasks are posted under a column heading.

d. Align tasks with jobs or departments.

Tip: Identify each of the different roles (or departments) that performs one or more of the tasks. Not every work process has multiple roles or departments involved in executing it. In a single role or department work process, all work is accomplished by one person or by a set of people who have the same job. If the work process is executed by a single role or department, go to e, below. If different roles execute the work process, list the names of each role or department down the left side of the chart. Move the work tasks up or down so they line up with the row on which the performer of that task is listed. (See Exhibit 9.)

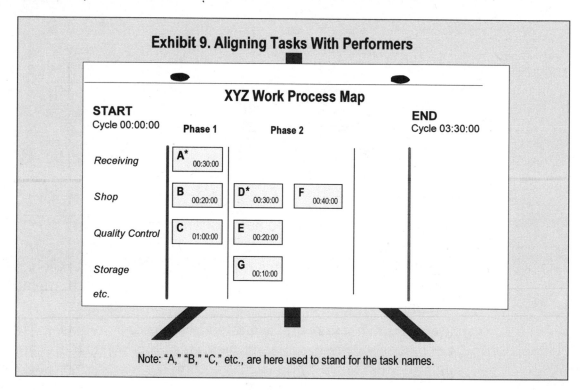

Exhibit 9. Aligning Tasks With Performers

Note: "A," "B," "C," etc., are here used to stand for the task names.

e. Connect tasks in sequence.

Tip: In this activity, you are depicting the flow of work from one task to another. See Exhibit 10 (next page) for an example of the product you will produce. Begin with the first started work activity. In the example in Exhibit 10, it is labeled "A." Draw an arrow from it to every other activity to which it gives something. Then draw an arrow to this from every activity that gives it something. Repeat these actions for every other task identified in the work process. In Exhibit 10, the flow of work is in one direction. This is the simplest and most common flow.

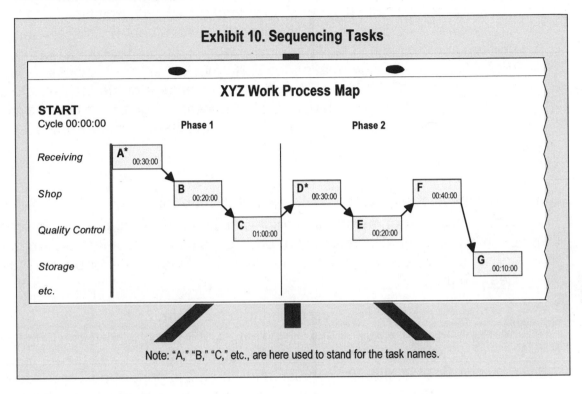

Exhibit 10. Sequencing Tasks

XYZ Work Process Map

START
Cycle 00:00:00   Phase 1   Phase 2

Receiving   A* 00:30:00

Shop   B 00:20:00   D* 00:30:00   F 00:40:00

Quality Control   C 01:00:00   E 00:20:00

Storage   G 00:10:00

etc.

Note: "A," "B," "C," etc., are here used to stand for the task names.

f. Determine when there are delays between operations.

   Tip: Ask the team whether the work process is performed intermittently—this means that it starts and then stops *between* operations, usually until a worker is free to complete the next operation. If there is intermittence, identify where it occurs and how long the typical interruption is; record the delay on the map where it occurs. (Intermittence is most common in office work processes where, for example, information to be processed remains in someone's in-basket until he or she is free to attend to it.)

g. Record the cycle time for the work process on the work process map.

   Tip: Compute the cycle time for the work process by adding together the cycle times for each operation and the delays between operations. If an operation is done more than once, be sure to add its cycle time to the total for as many times as it is repeated. For example, if tightening a clamp takes 10 seconds and it is repeated seven times, then add 70 seconds for this operation to the work process's cycle time. Record the cycle time under the label "END." If the cycle time in the overview differs from the cycle time computed from the work process map, explore why it does with the team. This may lead to new information about the work process. Afterwards, correct the erroneous cycle time(s).

3. Complete the descriptive information about each task.

Tip: Create an information tag for each task, place it on the map, and link it with a line to the task it describes (see example in Exhibit 3, page 202). The tag has five items of information: contact, location, documents, machine, and materials. *Contact* names a performer of the task from whom you may obtain added information. *Location* identifies where in the workplace the task is performed. *Documents* identifies the information the performer of the task receives as input or produces as output. *Machine* reports the percentage of the task's cycle time that is machine executed. *Materials* reports the percentage of the task's cycle time due to material requirements (e.g., time to dry, cure, harden, separate).

Following Up Substeps

1. Verify the accuracy of the work process description.

Tip: Ask the team members familiar with the target work process to confirm that the work process description you recorded is correct. Confirm also that the description matches the current work standard. Resolve any errors or discrepancies you uncover.

a. Confirm the overview description with the team.

Tip: Present the overview description element by element, confirming each one or correcting it before you proceed further. Start with the name of the work process, then its purpose and where it is performed. Next, review the inputs to the work process and its outputs. Then confirm the work process's cycle time and takt time. Finally, confirm the names of the other departments or work processes with which the target work process interrelates. Modify the overview as required based on team feedback.

b. Confirm the work process map with the team.

Tip: Talk through the work process, naming each task, briefly describing the work done and who does it, and telling the added descriptive information. Ask the team members to confirm that the information and sequence of work are correct. Modify the map as required based on team feedback.

c. Confirm that the work process description is consistent with the official work standard.

Tip: Check the work process description against the official work standard. Split the task with you reading the work standard section by section, and the team reviewing the work process description to determine whether its information matches the standard. If there are any discrepancies, you must resolve them before proceeding. Check with the work standards supervisor or the manager of the target work process as to whether the standard is current, for example, and whether it is a formal standard—meaning that it must be followed—or a "go-by" reference from which the work may deviate. In the end, if the work standard is current and formal, then the work process description must align with it and the work process you observe and evaluate must be performed as described in the standard.

2. Update the Kaizen event documentation.

   Tip: Record the description of the target work process and store it with the remaining documentation of the Kaizen event.

Check Steps

Use the following checklist to verify that the step was done correctly.

Benchmark	√
Getting Ready Substeps	
1. Drafted the description of the target work process.	☐
Doing Substeps	
1. Built the overview of the target work process.	☐
2. Built the work process map.	☐
3. Completed the descriptive information about each task.	☐
Following Up Substeps	
1. Verified the accuracy of the work process description.	☐
2. Updated the Kaizen event documentation.	☐

Tips

- Approach this task with fresh eyes. Assume you know nothing about the work process. Use your clarifying skills to ask about the meaning of terms and to explore what activities are done in each task. Strive to be able to imagine each task including the materials it uses and the outputs it generates.

- Do not shortchange performing this step. Our experience is that team members value the opportunity to share what they do and find it helpful to see it depicted visually in the work process description. Also, they frequently make discoveries themselves. One common discovery is how much discretion they really have in determining how a work process is executed and how much difference exists among workers in how they execute tasks.

Example:

Overview of the Nonflammable Blending Process

Purpose

To: Produce a cylinder filled with blended nonflammable gas

For: Customers, ABC, and stakeholders

By: Completing the nonflammable blending work process

So That: Customer needs are met and revenue is generated for ABC

Conditions: Meet ISO procedures, FDA procedures, DOT procedures, OSHA procedures, and ABC procedures

Measures: Satisfy blend sheet specs and produce the product on time

START

Cycle 00:00:00
Takt 00:00:00

Inputs

■ Prepared cylinders
■ Gases needed for mix
■ Order for mixed gases

Nonflammable Blending Process
(Backbone)

Oakland, CA   New Orleans, LA
Jackson, FL   Canton, OH

Maintenance

Mix Identification Group

Bulk Product Group

Lab

END

Cycle 01:30:00
Takt Unknown

Outputs

■ Cylinder filled with blended non-flammable gas

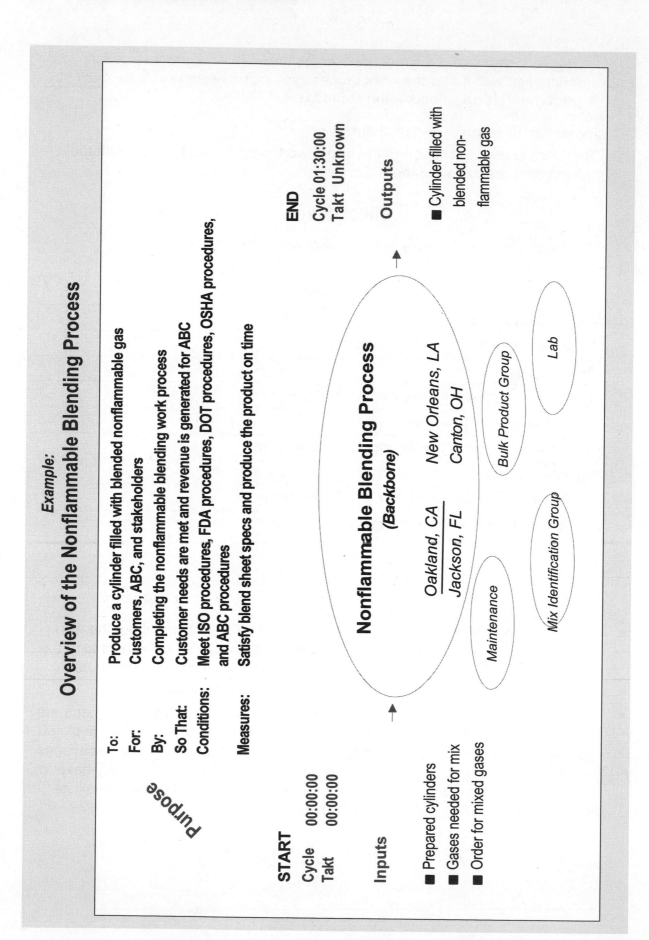

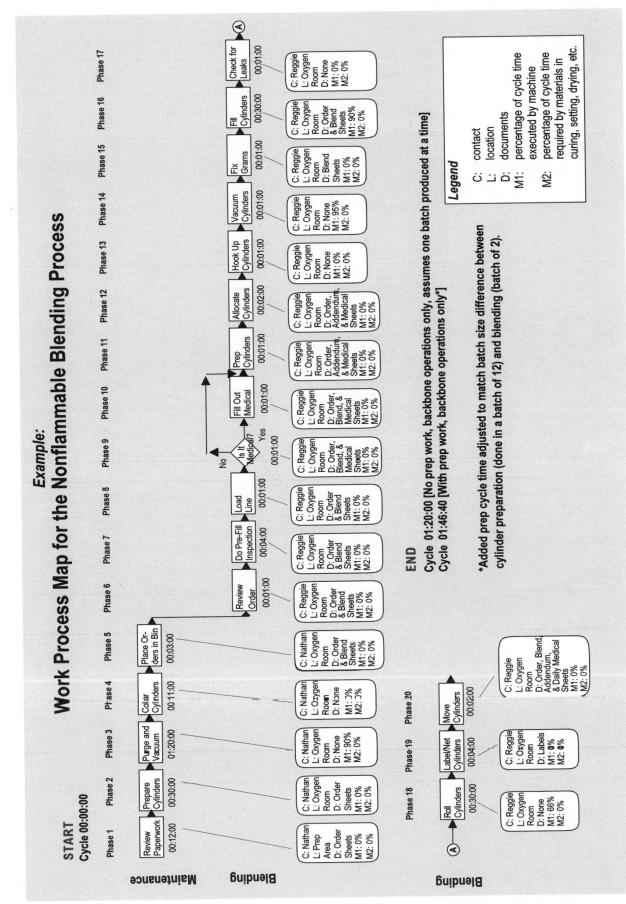

Example:

Work Process Map for the Nonflammable Blending Process

Step D1-S2. Walk Through the Target Work Process

Preview

This step gathers information about the work process and any instances of waste within it. The walk through:

- deepens the team's understanding of the work process and the concept of waste,
- uncovers opportunities for improvement,
- ensures that the mission and goals for the event are based on facts derived by direct observation of the workplace, and
- builds relationships with the performers of the target work process.

Getting Ready Substeps

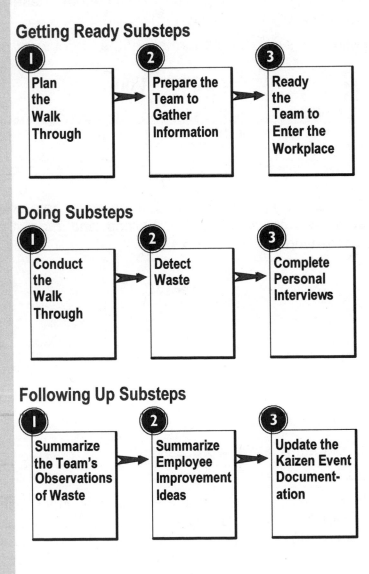

1 Plan the Walk Through

2 Prepare the Team to Gather Information

3 Ready the Team to Enter the Workplace

Doing Substeps

1 Conduct the Walk Through

2 Detect Waste

3 Complete Personal Interviews

Following Up Substeps

1 Summarize the Team's Observations of Waste

2 Summarize Employee Improvement Ideas

3 Update the Kaizen Event Documentation

Purpose

To gather information about the work process and any instances of waste within it so that you can define a mission and set goals for the event. The team literally walks through the process from beginning to end, if time permits, making observations, asking questions, and listening to what is said, all the while seeking to detect instances of waste and gather employee ideas about ways to improve the process.

Benefit

- Deepens the team's understanding of the work process and the concept of waste.

- Uncovers opportunities for improvement.

- Ensures that the mission and goals for the event are based on facts derived by direct observation of the workplace.

- Builds relationships with the performers of the target work process.

Application

Use this knowledge after building a description of the target work process and before forming the mission and goals for the event. The walk through must not exceed one hour.

Performer

Kaizen leader, co-leader, and team. The performers must be proficient in clarifying, confirming, constructively criticizing, and hitchhiking, and in detecting and recalling features of people and settings (observation skills).

Resources

People

- Kaizen team
- Performers of the target work process

Information, Knowledge, and Training

- Description of the target work process
- Safety rules
- *Working With Others* (J.S. Byron and P.A. Bierley, Hope, ME: Lowrey Press, 2003) - teaches how to get (clarify and confirm) and give (constructive criticism and hitchhiking) ideas and information in ways that build collaboration and elevate results

Materials, Tools, and Other Resources

- Space, equipment, and supplies to support the team's work

Room/Tables/Chairs

- Chairs
- Meeting area for the full team
- Tables
- Wall space for hanging storyboards and materials
- Wheelchair-accessible areas
- Wheelchair-accessible tables

Equipment - General

- Computer printer or access to one
- Copier or access to one

- Flipchart easels or hangers
- Laptop computer with Microsoft Office 2000® and Adobe Acrobat Reader® 4.0 or higher
- LCD computer projector
- Overhead projector
- Projection screen

Equipment - Safety

- Clothing
- Earplugs
- Gloves
- Hard-hats
- Safety glasses

- Safety shoes

Supplies

- Clipboards
- Flipchart markers
- Flipchart pads
- Masking tape
- Multicolored Post-its® - 3"x5"
- Name tags
- Notebooks
- Pens and pencils
- Printer paper (white and colored)
- Scissors
- Transparency film (for a copier)

- Kaizen Tool Kit
    - Detecting Value-Added Work and the Forms of Waste Exercise
    - Guide: Observe First
    - Guide: Understanding the Forms of Waste
    - Guide: Questions That Could Be Asked During the Personal Interview
    - Guide: Questions That Could Be Asked During the Walk Through
    - Waste Observed During Walk Through Categorized by Type

Output

- Integrated list of improvement ideas obtained from workers in the target work process
- Kaizen team able to detect waste
- Updated Kaizen event documentation
- Waste observed during walk through categorized by type

Method

Getting Ready Substeps

1. Plan the walk through.

   Tip: Prepare a plan to guide the team in completing its walk through of the target work process. Draft the plan on your own while the team is on a break. Use a flipchart page to record the plan (see example in Exhibit 1). Later, you will brief the team on the plan, get its feedback, and use that feedback to adjust the plan, if required. If you lack information you need to complete the plan, ask one of the team members to stay behind and assist you.

Exhibit 1. Walk Through Plan for the Cylinder Preparation Work Process			
Operation	**Worker**	**Method**	**Time**
1. Review paper work	Nathan	Observe	All of activity
2. Prepare cylinders	Nathan	Observe	All of activity
3. Purge and vacuum	Nathan	Observe hook up of two cylinders and listen to description of how rest of task is done	20 minutes
4. Collar cylinders	Nathan	Observe	All of activity
5. Place orders in bin	Nathan	Observe	All of activity

   a. Decide which work process operations to observe.

      Tip: If the total cycle time of the work process is less than one hour, observe all operations to completion. Otherwise, decide which operations to observe or, if you still desire to observe all operations, how much time to spend observing each. In making your selections, be sure to observe any operation that seems complex, unclear to the team, or otherwise stands out as especially important. If you need to limit the time you spend at each operation, then apportion the one hour you have to complete the walk through according to how much of the total cycle time each operation uses. Obtain the cycle time information from the map of the target work process. Use only the non-machine and non-materials portion of the cycle time of each operation in your computations.

   b. Identify the sequence in which operations will be observed.

      Tip: Typically, the sequence follows the flow of input to output just as it is depicted in the work process map. Record the sequence on a flipchart page. Occasionally, you will need to observe a work operation out of sequence. For example, if an operation uses equipment that requires scheduled access, your visit to that operation may or may not conform to where it logically occurs in the work process.

   c. Select the worker to observe.

     Tip: If a work activity is performed in parallel by multiple performers, select a performer to observe who is competent, motivated, and performs the work at a typical pace. Consider first the contact person listed in the additional descriptive material about each operation that you collected when you mapped the work process. Record your selection on the flipchart page by indicating the name of the worker the team will observe next to the operation he or she will perform. If observing and talking with performers while performing their jobs will seriously disrupt production, consider observing the work as demonstrated by a team member off-line and talking with him or her about each operation. Remember that the Kaizen team will include people who execute the work process being improved.

2. Prepare the team to gather information.

   a. Orient the team to what the walk through is and why it is done.

     Tip: Explain to the team that the purpose of the walk through is to gather more information about the work process, the work areas in which it is performed, and any instances of waste. With this information, the team can define a mission and set goals for the event *based on the facts in the workplace*. Tell the team that it literally walks through the process from beginning to end, if time permits, focusing on learning about each operation and detecting instances of waste. Before doing the walk through, the team will learn about the forms of waste and how to detect each. During the walk through, the team makes observations, asks questions, and listens to what workers say. After the walk through, the team pools its observations and determines which forms of waste are most prevalent in the work process. In parallel, the Kaizen co-leader completes a personal interview of each performer, separately, to gather his or her ideas about ways to improve the process.

   b. Teach the team to detect waste.

     1) Explain value-added work and waste.

       Tip: Tell the definitions of value-added work and waste. Be sure to reference the list of customer values you posted before beginning the event as you explain what value-added work is (e.g., "Customers pay for what they value. Here is the list your customers' values"). Ask team members to say what they think is the same and different about these value-added work and waste. Use a flipchart page to record the ideas team members offer. Use the answers in Exhibit 2 (next page) to confirm and credit the team's answers, correct them, or add to them. Ask for and answer any questions the team has about the differences between value-added work and waste.

| Exhibit 2. Comparison of Value-Adding Work and Waste ||
Similarities	Differences
■ Both are work.	■ Value-added work always materially changes the product or service output. Waste may not.
■ Both may be earnestly executed.	■ Value-added work is always rewarded by a well-informed and reasonable customer. Waste is never rewarded by a well-informed and reasonable customer.
■ Both use resources (i.e., human, intellectual, and material).	■ Value-added work leverages resources into profit; waste consumes resources.
■ Both may be established as the required method of operation.	■ Value-added work fulfills every employee's fiduciary responsibility—namely, to contribute to the success of the company; waste does not.

2) Explain the forms of waste.

Tip: Distribute to the team the Guide: Understanding the Forms of Waste (pages 227–28). An electronic version of this document is in the Kaizen Tool Kit. Ask the team to read it. Once the team is finished, review the forms of waste, one at a time. Say what each is, and ask the team members for examples from their own experience. Be sure that the team hears both a shop and office example of each type of waste. If the team cannot supply an example from its experience, then provide an example or refer the team to page 228 for an example. Ask for and answer any questions the team may have on the forms of waste.

3) Ensure that the team can detect value-added work and the forms of waste.

Tip: Conduct a paper and pencil exercise to help the team consolidate its understanding of the forms of waste and its ability to detect value-added work and waste. Follow the instructions provided in Detecting Value-Added Work and the Forms of Waste Exercise (pages 229–31).

c. Instruct the team to adopt an "observe first" strategy when walking through the work area.

Tip: Explain that benefiting from the walk through depends on making observations. Instruct the team members to begin observing as soon as they enter the work area. This is the "observe first strategy." Tell the team members that, as they proceed through the walk through, they each should be making notes about what they see, hear, and smell. Review with the team suggestions for how to observe first (see Guide: Observe First, page 232; an electronic copy of this guide is in the Kaizen Tool Kit). Explain the look, listen, and smell approach. Look for clutter, machines idle, people waiting, inventory, materials being transported, people traveling to get or place materials, people searching for materials, and unsafe work practices. Look at the workstation itself. See how it is laid out. See what equipment, tools, and materials are present. Note what, if anything, is displayed in the work area (e.g., safety rules, checklist, procedure guide). Check lighting and sound. Listen for noise, machine vibration, and what people have to say. Smell for burning materials, gas, or other troubling odors.

d. Prepare a checklist to guide asking questions.

Tip: Caution the team about asking only *factual questions* during the walk through. Factual questions seek information about how the work is done and *not* judgments about the work or workplace. Use the Guide: Questions That Could Be Asked During the Walk Through (pages 233–34) to help the team understand what you mean by factual questions. Produce one checklist per workstation to be observed. Check off the questions you select on the form. Have team members use the checklist to prompt them in asking questions at the workstation and to track whether they obtained answers.

e. Make assignments.

Tip: Consider having more than one team member ask questions. Break up the responsibility by topic, with one person taking responsibility for asking questions about inputs, outputs, and measures; another person taking responsibility for process questions; and still another taking responsibility for asking the remaining factual questions. Be sure to have all the team members take notes so that they remain attentive during the asking and answering of questions. Set up a standard sequence for asking questions so that people do not compete to get their questions in. Caution the team members that they must allow the worker to show what he or she does before they ask questions, as the worker's demonstration and comments will provide at least some of the answers the team seeks.

3. Ready the team to enter the workplace.

a. Review the walk through plan with the team.

Tip: Tell the team that you have drafted a plan to guide the walk through based on the information developed while building the work process description. Share the details of the plan with the team. Ask for feedback and adjust the plan as required.

b. Ready the team to relate with the work process performers.

1) Review the importance of greeting each worker.

   Tip: Remind the team members that they should see themselves as guests in someone else's work area, and, as guests, it is especially important to communicate respect. Greeting people as you meet them is one important way to communicate respect. Review with the team the steps of greeting, i.e.: (1) establish eye contact, (2) close distance to the worker, (3) extend hand to greet, (4) say "hi" or "hello" or something similar, (5) introduce self, (6) say where you are from, and (7) ask the worker's name. Explain that, as the Kaizen leader, you will greet the worker first using all the steps. Each team member should do steps 1 through 6. You will also orient the worker to what the team is doing and why it is visiting.

2) Review how the team will present its role to the worker.

   Tip: Share with the team that you will explain to each performer that the team has the job of making the work process more effective, is at this workstation to benefit from the knowledge of the performer, and seeks to learn from him or her about the work and how it can be improved. Ask each team member to remember this explanation of what the team is doing and why it is visiting each workstation so that if anyone asks these questions, he or she can offer the same explanation.

3) Underscore the importance of valuing what the worker does.

   Tip: Share with the team that properly greeting each worker and explaining your role is part of showing respect. Underscore that it is also important that we respect the work people are doing even if it is not value adding as they most often are doing the job as specified. We can alienate people and undermine our efforts to make change if we communicate disrespect in any form, especially if we assume a dismissive attitude about people's work. For example, making statements like "Well this is silly, why would you be doing this? It is totally unnecessary" will immediate alienate any worker.

c. Ready the team to abide by safety rules and procedures.

   1) Ensure that the team understands the safety requirements for moving about the workplace.

      Tip: Have someone expert in the safety requirements of the workplace review them with the team and confirm that team members understand the safety rules. Ask and answer any final questions about the rules.

   2) Have the team don required safety gear and gather recording materials.

      Tip: After team members don their safety gear, check to ensure that the gear has been put on correctly and, once again, remind the team to abide by safety rules. Have the team members gather their notepads and pens.

Doing Substeps

1. Conduct the walk through.

   Tip: As you conduct the work through, you have a double responsibility. First, you must observe the work area and learn about the work performed. Second, you must coach the team in doing these same tasks and in using good skills as they meet with and learn from workers.

   a. Lead the team to each workstation in the order specified in the walk through plan.

   b. Ensure that team members are making observations as they approach the workstation.

   Tip: For example, look to see if they are making notes of observations. If you do not see any note-taking, gather the team between workstations and check to see what observations members have made; check these against the observations you have made. Provide the team members with feedback and encourage them to continue to make observations.

   c. Greet each workstation performer.

   Tip: Use the guidance provided in Getting Ready Substep 3b to greet workers. Be sure that after you complete your greeting responsibilities, each team member greets the worker as well.

   d. Orient each worker to your task.

   Tip: Tell the purpose of the visit. Ask for the worker's assistance and say why providing assistance is important. Before beginning to learn about the work, confirm whether it is a good time for you and the team to visit; if it is not, find out when you can return.

   e. Ensure that the team asks its questions and takes notes.

   Tip: Make sure the team gives the worker an opportunity to show his or her job. Then, ensure that the team completes the checklist questions it planned to ask. Encourage the team to use clarifying and confirming skills by modeling their use. Keep the team's questioning to *factual issues* and ensure that team members avoid asking for judgments and opinions. At the end of the visit, thank the worker for his or her assistance.

2. Detect waste.

   Tip: Again, you have a double responsibility in completing this step. You must make observations of waste and coach the team in making its own observations. Periodically, as you walk through the work process, identify and record the work activities you observe. Note your judgment as to whether each activity is value adding or a specific form of waste. Check to see if team members are making notes about waste. Stop between workstations if needed and verify with the team that it is detecting waste. Once the walk through is completed, give team members 10 minutes to organize their observations of the work and categorize the activities they observed as value adding or a specific form of waste. Remind them to use the Guide: Understanding the Forms of Waste (pages 227–28) to assist them in categorizing work activities.

3. Complete personal interviews.

   Tip: The personal interviews are completed by the Kaizen co-leader after the team has completed its walk through and while the team is integrating its observations and doing the Following Up Substeps. The co-leader should use the Guide: Questions That Could Be Asked During the Personal Interview (pages 235–36) as a guide.

   a. Orient each worker to the interview.

      Tip: The co-leader should approach each workstation, orient the worker to the additional questions to be asked, assure the performer that the conversation they will have will be kept in confidence and that the worker's ideas will be used without attributing their source unless the worker wishes otherwise.

   b. Gather evaluative information.

      Tip: Ask each worker about typical performance on measures applied to the workstation; output quality problems and improvement ideas; the presence of movement; the adequacy of resourcing for the worker's job; the use of storage; and any organization, layout, and inventory issues the worker has noted. Thank the performer for his or her assistance at the conclusion of the interview.

Following Up Substeps

1. Summarize the team's observations of waste.

   Tip: Build a nonredundant list of observations for each category of waste. Do this activity with the team in a large group.

   a. Label 10 flipchart sheets, one for each form of waste.

      Tip: Place the name of the form of waste at the top of the sheet.

   b. Select one of the forms of waste.

      Tip: Consider beginning with the form of waste the team finds easiest to detect.

   c. List the team's observations of waste for the selected category.

      Tip: Ask team members for any observations of work that they judged as representing the identified type of waste. Clarify and confirm the information team members offer. Correct their judgments about the relationship between the work they observed and their categorization of it as needed. Build with the team a complete list of the waste it observed, ensuring that each work activity is only listed once.

d. Repeat b and c above until all observations are categorized.

Tip: This will produce the output Waste Observed During Walk Through Categorized by Type. See an example of this output on pages 237–38. Be sure to document this output because you will use it to build your goals for the event.

e. Add to the appropriate list any waste identified by the workers during the walk through or offered by employees in response to the pre-event flyer.

2. Summarize employee improvement ideas.

Tip: The Kaizen co-leader completes this task once he or she has finished the personal interviews. The task is done away from the team while it is compiling and categorizing its observations of waste.

a. List improvement ideas offered by the workers.

Tip: Gather the improvement ideas offered by employees in response to the pre-event flyer. Add to this list the ideas provided by workers during personal interviews. Eliminate repetition from the list.

b. Relate the improvement ideas to the forms of waste each corrects.

Tip: The Kaizen co-leader goes through the list of improvement ideas from workers and tags each with the form of waste it eliminates.

c. Document employee improvement ideas organized by category of waste.

Tip: See page 239 for an example of the document the co-leader should produce. Be sure to retain this document, as it will be used by the team during its efforts to solve the work process's performance issues.

3. Update the Kaizen event documentation.

Tip: Document the waste observed during the walk through categorized by type. Use the form Waste Observed During Walk Through Categorized by Type (example on pages 237–38). An electronic version of this form is contained in the Kaizen Tool Kit. Also record the improvement ideas produced by workers. Use your word processor to produce a document like the one depicted on page 239.

Check Steps

Use the following checklist to verify that the step was done correctly.

Benchmark	√
Getting Ready Substeps	
1. Planned the walk through.	☐
2. Prepared the team to gather information.	☐
3. Readied the team to enter the workplace.	☐
Doing Substeps	
1. Conducted the walk through.	☐
2. Detected waste.	☐
3. Completed personal interviews.	☐
Following Up Substeps	
1. Summarized the team's observations of waste.	☐
2. Summarized employee improvement ideas.	☐
3. Updated the Kaizen event documentation.	☐

Tips

- Recognize that you are in someone else's work area. Behave in a respectful and polite manner. Use your Working With Others skills to guide your interaction with people and be sensitive to how people are reacting to your questions. Be patient; do not pressure.

- Address any concerns workers have about the Kaizen event. Do not ignore their negative feelings, as they will just grow stronger and disrupt the Kaizen process. Respond to them. Understand their source. Adjust your behavior as appropriate. If the person refuses to cooperate, remind the person of the task the team is performing, why it is important, and for whom the team is doing this. If the individual continues to resist, ask for assistance from the manager of the target work process.

- If you do not get all the information you need the first time, revisit the person to obtain the missing information.

Guide:
Understanding the Forms of Waste

1. **Hazard** - Any observed workplace conditions or worker behaviors that could result in harm.

2. **Inspect** - Checking for error in a component, product, or activity. It is waste because production cost is added.

3. **Interruption** - Stoppage during work activity due to some external factor (e.g., machine breakdown, request for information). It is waste because production time is lost during the period of interruption.

4. **Motion** - Changes in position by the performer (e.g., turning, bending, lifting) while he or she is at the workstation. It is waste because production time is lost during movement.

5. **Rework** - Behavior required to reprocess a product or product component to salvage a defective unit or part. It is waste because production cost is added.

6. **Search** - Behavior required to locate some needed resource (e.g., a person, tool, part, or piece of information). It is waste because production time is lost during the search.

7. **Setup** - Labor required to ready a performer or machine to execute a task. Setup is waste because production time is lost during the preparation period.

8. **Travel/transport** - Movement by a performer from his or her workstation to another place. If the performer is moving parts, materials, and information around the workplace, it is called transport; otherwise, it is travel. Both are waste because production time is lost during travel or transport around the plant.

9. **Unnecessary processing** - Work done that is not needed to produce the product or service as required by the customer. Such processing may be done at the discretion of the performer or required by the work instruction. It may even modify the output, but it will do so in a way that a well-informed and reasonable customer does not value. It is waste because production cost is added unnecessarily.

10. **Wait** - Delay in work activity until some needed resource becomes available or authority to proceed is received. It is waste because production time is lost during the waiting period.

Continued...

Guide:
Understanding the Forms of Waste (continued)

Waste	Shop Example	Office Example
Hazard	Machine left operating while operator leaves his or her workstation	Extension cords powering a printer run across the floor without a trip guard
Inspect	Operator measures the diameter of holes punched into a plate	Office worker reviews letter for errors
Interruption	Power outage interrupts machine operation	Supervisor pulls employee off task to answer question
Motion	Operator bends to reach clamp needed to hold pipe	Office worker reaches into lower desk drawer to retrieve stapler
Rework	Operator replaces faulty resistor	Office worker redrafts plan rejected because it failed to accomplish the project by the required completion date
Search	Operator searches for 0.5 mm washers in the parts carton	Office worker searches for replacement ink cartridge in the supply room
Setup	Operator places bit in drill prior to drilling holes	Office worker places transparencies in copier paper tray
Travel/Transport	Operator walks to tool crib to obtain wrench	Office worker goes to supply room to obtain flipchart pad replacement
Unnecessary Processing	Operator cleans drill bit after each plate is drilled because he or she prefers it	Office worker recalculates mileage manually to verify spreadsheet's computation because he or she feels more secure doing that Salesperson must review each customer order but does not provide input to any decisions made about processing that order nor collect or use any information from the order
Wait	Operator waits as machine drills holes in plate	Office workers waits while copier copies and collates reports

Detecting Value-Added Work and the Forms of Waste Exercise

Instructions

1. Distribute to the team the Detecting Value-Added Work and the Forms of Waste Worksheet.

   Tip: The Worksheet appears on page 230. An electronic version of it is contained in the Kaizen Tool Kit.

2. Explain the exercise.

   "This exercise is to confirm that we are seeing the forms of waste in the same way. That is important so that we have consistency in how we interpret our observations of the work we see. Your task is to look at each of the activities listed in the Detecting Value-Added Work and the Forms of Waste Worksheet and write next to it either 'VA' for value adding or the number (1, 2, 3, etc.) identifying the form of waste the activity represents. Use the numbering that appears in the Guide: Understanding the Forms of Waste. You have five minutes to complete the task."

   Tip: Be sure that each team member has a copy of the Guide: Understanding the Forms of Waste. An electronic copy of the guide is in the Kaizen Tool Kit.

3. Ask for and answer any questions the participants have about the exercise.

   Tip: After five minutes, go through each example on the worksheet and ask team members for their answers. Detect whether the team members categorized the item consistently or inconsistently and correctly or incorrectly. Credit correct performance. If the team is inconsistent in its assignment or incorrectly classifies an example, explore why and offer additional coaching to ensure that team members can categorize work consistently and correctly.

   Tip: Answers to the Detecting Value-Added Work and the Forms of Waste Exercise appear on page 231.

4. Summarize what was learned about value-adding work and waste.

   Tip: Tell the team members that they are now ready to complete their preparation for conducting the walk through of the target work process.

Continued...

Detecting Value-Added Work and the Forms of Waste Worksheet

Work Activity	Answer
1 Worker pushes cart containing 12 modules over to band saw.	
2 Worker adjusts saw to accommodate module size.	
3 Worker picks up module to load into machine.	
4 Saw cuts module end to customer specifications.	
5 Worker watches saw as it cuts.	
6 Fitter inserts tungsten tip in weld machine.	
7 Fitter connects sander and router from her tool box to the air lines.	
8 Worker turns off saw when module end has been cut off.	
9 Worker washes cylinders because he prefers them to be clean.	
10 Worker removes module.	
11 Worker flips module around.	
12 Technician torques each hand wheel with a wrench as she prefers.	
13 Worker stops work to answer question from supervisor.	
14 Technician returns camera to equipment locker.	
15 Technician places finished subassembly on table for pick-up by next worker.	
16 Carpenter re-sands edge of cabinet to remove burrs that had not been detected on first pass.	
17 Supervisor checks to see if drilled holes are within tolerances.	
18 Worker looks for correct form in pile of forms.	
19 Worker goes to office.	
20 Worker leaves machine operating as he gets a new order.	

Detecting Value-Added Work and the Forms of Waste Exercise Answers

	Work Activity	Answer
1	Worker pushes cart containing 12 modules over to band saw.	[8] transport
2	Worker adjusts saw to accommodate module size.	[7] setup
3	Worker picks up module to load into machine.	[4] motion[1]
4	Saw cuts module end to customer specifications.	VA
5	Worker watches saw as it cuts.	[10] wait
6	Fitter inserts tungsten tip in weld machine.	[7] setup
7	Fitter connects sander and router from her tool box to the air lines.	[7] setup
8	Worker turns off saw when module end has been cut off.	[7] setup
9	Worker washes cylinders because he prefers them to be clean.	[9] unnecessary processing
10	Worker removes module.	[7] setup
11	Worker flips module around.	[4] motion[1]
12	Technician torques each hand wheel with a wrench as she prefers.	[9] unnecessary processing
13	Worker stops work to answer question from supervisor.	[3] interruption
14	Technician returns camera to equipment locker.	[8] transport
15	Technician places finished subassembly on table for pick-up by next worker.	[7] setup[2]
16	Carpenter re-sands edge of cabinet to remove burrs that had not been detected on first pass.	[5] rework
17	Supervisor checks to see if drilled holes are within tolerances.	[2] inspect
18	Worker looks for correct form in pile of forms.	[6] Search
19	Worker goes to office.	[8] Travel
20	Worker leaves machine operating as he gets a new order.	[1] Hazard

[1]Given no other information, motion is the only possible categorization.
[2]Setup because the action prepares the next worker to do his or her job. Transport [8] is another alternative but is less accurate, as the main purpose of the action is to ready the next worker.

Guide:
Observe First

Look for...

- Clutter
- Machines idle
- People waiting
- Inventory
- Materials being transported
- People traveling to get or place materials
- People searching for materials
- Unsafe work practices

Listen for...

- Excessive noise
- Machine vibration noises
- Complaints, concerns, ideas

Smell for...

- Burning
- Gas
- Unusual odor

Guide:
Questions That Could Be Asked During the Walk Through

Workstation:			
Location:	Operator:		

Question	Ask	Answered
About the Basics		
1. What is the name and job title of the performer?	☑	☐
2. What is the name of the work activity he or she performs?	☑	☐
About Outputs		
1. What product does this workstation produce?	☐	☐
2. How many units must the workstation make a day (expected output)?	☐	☐
3. How many units does the typical workstation produce (actual output)?	☐	☐
About Inputs		
1. What do you start with?	☐	☐
■ What documents do you need?	☐	☐
■ What materials do you need?	☐	☐
2. From where do you get the information, documents, and materials you need?	☐	☐
3. What is your batch size?	☐	☐
About Process		
1. Is there a written procedure for your job?	☐	☐
2. Tell us about what you do.	☐	☐
■ What kicks off your work? Is it a constant flow or do you require a work order or some document to begin processing?	☐	☐
■ What are the steps you perform?	☐	☐
■ How much of the work is done by machinery and how much do you do manually?	☐	☐
■ What is the maximum load this workstation can handle?	☐	☐
■ What is the typical load this type of workstation handles per shift?	☐	☐

Continued...

Guide:
Questions That Could Be Asked During the Walk Through (continued)

Question	Ask	Answered
About Measurement		
1. How does management measure performance of this workstation?	☐	☐
2. How do you measure performance of the workstation?	☐	☐
3. On these measures, what is the typical performance people achieve?	☐	☐
About Movement		
1. Do you travel for documents, parts, tools, advice, other information, or materials?	☐	☐
▪ If you travel, where do you travel to?	☐	☐
2. Do you do sorting, repairing, restacking, etc.?	☐	☐
3. Do you have to search for materials or tools?	☐	☐
4. Do you count parts in doing the job?	☐	☐
5. Do you have to handle parts more than once?	☐	☐
6. How long does it take to set up your equipment? (If machinery is used.)	☐	☐
About Delays		
1. Does work wait at this workstation for anything (e.g., inspection, materials, instructions, equipment)?	☐	☐
2. Is work ever interrupted by stoppages (e.g., machine breakdowns, special requests to do other tasks)?	☐	☐
▪ If yes, how often and why?	☐	☐
3. What do you do when the machine is running? (If machinery is used.)	☐	☐
About Storage/Organization/Layout/Inventory		
1. Do you have inventory of any sort (e.g., parts, work in progress)?	☐	☐
2. Does the work produce any scrap?	☐	☐

Guide:
Questions That Could Be Asked During the Personal Interview

Workstation:			Location:		

Question	Ask	Answered
About Outputs		
1. Are you running into any quality problems?	☐	☐
▪ If so, what types of defects do you run into?	☐	☐
About Measurement		
1. On the measures applied to this workstation, what is the typical performance people achieve?	☐	☐
About Improvement Ideas		
1. What seems to be good about the process you use?	☐	☐
▪ What supports good quality, efficient work, timely execution, least cost operation, and worker safety?	☐	☐
2. What seems to be problematic about the process you use?	☐	☐
▪ What hurts quality, efficiency, timeliness, or safety or adds cost unnecessarily?	☐	☐
3. How would you change your workstation to improve quality, efficiency, timeliness, or safety or to reduce cost?	☐	☐
▪ What changes in the work activities, output design or variations, or inputs would help?	☐	☐
▪ Could you use a template, jig, or fixture to assist you?	☐	☐
▪ What tools or equipment could help improve your job?	☐	☐
▪ How could setup time be shortened? (If setup is observed.)	☐	☐
4. Do you have any problems with your machine? (If machinery is used and the person has not already addressed this question.)	☐	☐
About Movement		
1. Why are you traveling for parts? (If observed.)	☐	☐
2. Why are you doing sorting, repairing, restacking, etc.? (If observed.)	☐	☐
3. Why do you need to search for [state what]? (If observed or reported.)	☐	☐
4. Why do you need to count parts? (If observed or reported.)	☐	☐
5. Why do you need to handle parts more than once? (If observed or reported.)	☐	☐
6. How long does it take to set up your equipment and why?	☐	☐

Continued...

Guide:
Questions That Could Be Asked During the Personal Interview (continued)

Question	Ask	Answered
About Resources		
1. Do you have all the tools you need to do your job?	☐	☐
2. Do you have all the materials you need to do your job?	☐	☐
3. What information or training does someone doing your work need?	☐	☐
4. How are the ergonomics and safety of the workplace?	☐	☐
5. Is there a profile of potential hazards and solutions for this workstation?	☐	☐
About Storage/Organization/Layout/Inventory		
1. Why is the workplace so crowded? (Ask only if the workplace seems to be crowded.)	☐	☐
2. Is there a place for everything, and is everything kept in its place?	☐	☐
3. Why do you have inventory? (Possible answers include buffer, machine breakdown, long setup time, defects, unanticipated customer demand, overproduction.)	☐	☐

Example:

Waste Observed During the Walk Through Categorized by Type - ABC Gases

1. Hazard

- Cable laying across walk path uncovered.
- Not wearing cryogenic gloves.
- Operator not wearing earplugs.
- Operator not wearing face shield.
- Pallet left in walkway.

2. Inspect

- Checks labels and test dates on cylinders.

3. Interruption

- Breaks from task to sort cylinders so he can find ones for his order.
- Interrupts work to answer a question about a prior order.
- Replaced faulty safety on valve.
- Breaks work to deal with power surge problem.

4. Motion

- Stretches up to read gauges, which are difficult to read. (Gauges are up high in a poorly lit area.)
- Leans over and twists to read labels on cylinders. (Labels are small.)

5. Rework

- Replaced replacement safety on valve, which was also faulty.
- Repeatedly applies the pigtail to make hookup as it slips off.

6. Search

- Searches for paperwork.
- Searches for right cylinders to fit order.

7. Setup

- Allocates cylinders to orders.
- Changes labels.
- Removes district tape on caps.
- Hooks up cylinders (12 cylinders for prepping).
- Touches up bare spots with paint.
- Purges cylinders (12 cylinders for prepping).
- Reads bar code.

Continued...

Example:
Waste Observed During the Walk Through Categorized by Type - ABC Gases (continued)

7. Setup (continued)

- Reads gauges on cylinders.
- Removes caps from cylinders.
- Scrapes cylinders.
- Takes caps off and hooks up cylinders to manifold.
- Vents cylinders (12 cylinders for prepping).

8. Travel/Transport

- Gets cylinders from storage.
- Gets weights from other blending area for pretest.
- Goes back to storage to get a second new safety for valve.
- Goes to crib to get tools.
- Goes to office to get blend sheet from printer.
- Goes to shipping area to get nets.
- Goes to storage to get new safety for valve.
- Goes to yard to look for other product to finish out the batch.
- Moves cylinders to rolling machine.
- Moves cylinders from storage bin to fill line.
- Travel involved in allocating cylinders for an order.
- Travels to look for empty cylinders with which to fill order.
- Travels to medical cabinet to get labels for cylinder.
- Walks to battery charger to get battery.
- Walks to engineering area to turn on oxygen pump.
- Walks to inventory area to get leak soap.

9. Unnecessary Processing

- Moves cylinders to reach one of the size he needs. (Different cylinder sizes are grouped in same production bin.)

10. Wait

- Waits on vacuum.
- Waits for blend to fill cylinder.
- Waits for order.
- Waits for purge to finish.
- Waits for rolling machine to finish.
- Waits for venting to finish.

Example:

Integrated List of Improvement Ideas Obtained From Workers in the Target Work Process - ABC Gases

Waste	Employee Idea
Travel	
The location of paperwork causes travel. All paperwork is kept in the office.	Use clipboard at station to hold paperwork.
Motion	
Gauges are difficult to read; they are up high in a poorly lit area.	Angle gauges for easier viewing or provide better lighting.
Setup	
The time to hook up cylinders with the present fitting causes increased setup time.	Change fitting to permit quicker hookup.
Unnecessary Processing	
Different cylinder sizes grouped in same production bin requires moving cylinders to get to what you need.	Sort and separate cylinders by size.

Step D1-S3. Build the Mission Statement

Preview

This step uses the results of the walk through to identify the business benefits the event should produce and the work process improvement that will produce them. The mission:

- drives the Kaizen event's accountability to the business's bottomline, and
- provides a reference for evaluating the strawperson mission statement derived from the scope document.

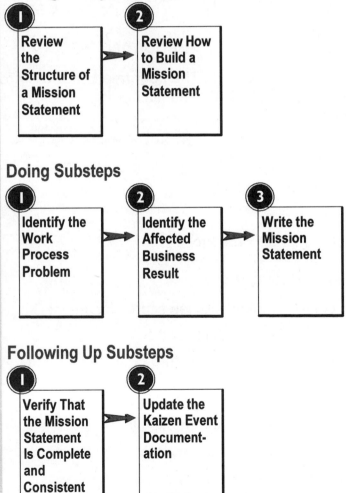

Getting Ready Substeps

1 Review the Structure of a Mission Statement

2 Review How to Build a Mission Statement

Doing Substeps

1 Identify the Work Process Problem

2 Identify the Affected Business Result

3 Write the Mission Statement

Following Up Substeps

1 Verify That the Mission Statement Is Complete and Consistent

2 Update the Kaizen Event Documentation

Purpose

To identify the business results the event should produce and the work process improvement that will produce them using the results of the walk through.

Benefit

- Drives the Kaizen event's accountability to the business's bottomline.
- Provides a reference for evaluating the strawperson mission statement derived from the scope document.

Application

Use this knowledge after completing the walk through of the target work process and before setting the goals for the event.

Performer

Kaizen leader, co-leader, and team. The performers must be proficient in clarifying, confirming, constructively criticizing, and hitchhiking.

Resources

People

- Designated event coordinator
- Kaizen team
- Manager of the target work process

Information, Knowledge, and Training

- Complete, consistent, and verified scope document
- Strawperson direction for the event
- Waste observed during the walk through categorized by type
- *Working With Others* (J.S. Byron and P.A. Bierley, Hope, ME: Lowrey Press, 2003) - teaches how to get (clarify and confirm) and give (constructive criticism and hitchhiking) ideas and information in ways that build collaboration and elevate results

Materials, Tools, and Other Resources

- Space, equipment, and supplies to support the team's work

  Room/Tables/Chairs
  - Chairs

  - Meeting area for the full team
  - Tables

  - Wall space for hanging storyboards and materials

- Wheelchair-accessible areas
- Wheelchair-accessible tables

Equipment - General

- Computer printer or access to one
- Copier or access to one
- Flipchart easels or hangers
- Laptop computer with Microsoft Office 2000® and Adobe Acrobat Reader® 4.0 or higher

- LCD computer projector
- Overhead projector
- Projection screen

Equipment - Safety

- Clothing
- Earplugs
- Gloves
- Hard-hats
- Safety glasses
- Safety shoes

Supplies

- Flipchart markers
- Flipchart pads

- Masking tape
- Multicolored Post-its® - 3"x5"
- Name tags
- Notebooks
- Pens and pencils
- Printer paper (white and colored)
- Scissors
- Transparency film (for a copier)

- Kaizen Tool Kit
  - Direction for the Kaizen Event (includes mission statement, goals for the event, and do's and don'ts)

Output

- Mission statement
- Updated Kaizen event documentation

Method

Getting Ready Substeps

1. Review the structure of a mission statement.

   Tip: A mission statement has three components: a "to" component that states the business result your event should produce, a "by" component that tells the work process improvement your event will make, and a "for" component that says for whom you are generating these benefits (Exhibit 1).

Exhibit 1. Components of a Mission Statement		
To	**By**	**For**
Improve a business result	Making a work process improvement	The person(s) or group(s) you seek to benefit

Here are two examples:

- *"To increase profit margins [business result] by reducing the cost of fabricating pipe spools for cooling columns [work process improvement] for XYZ Manufacturing and all its stakeholders."*

- *"To elevate customer satisfaction with our responses to their questions [business result] by reducing the frequency with which we fail to answer customer queries [work process improvement] for Customer Services, Inc., and all our stakeholders."*

2. Review how to build a mission statement.

   Tip: During the event, build the mission statement from the facts in the workplace. The waste you observed in the work process is your starting point. By thinking about how the waste you observed affects the work process's performance, you will uncover the work process problem you will fix. Eliminating or reducing the work process problem is the *by* part of the mission. Once you have defined the work process problem, ask yourself how this problem hurts business results. Improving the business result is the *to* part of the mission. Finally, ask yourself for whom these improvements are being made. The answer to this question gives you the *for* part of a mission statement.

Doing Substeps

1. Identify the work process problem.

   Tip: The work process problem is the shortcoming in performance of the target work process caused by the waste within it.

   a. Review the types of work process problems waste can produce.

      Tip: Waste may diminish safety, limit the quantity of output, reduce product or service quality, slow the speed of performance, increase cost, or compromise efficiency. Think of an example of each of these problems drawing on your past experience. Use the examples of each of these types of work process problems presented in Exhibit 2 (next page) to assist you.

   b. Identify the five major sources of waste uncovered during the walk through.

      Tip: Use the categorized list of observations of waste constructed at the end of the walk through. The five types of waste with the highest number of observations are the major sources of waste in the work process.

   c. Decide how the major sources of waste in the target work process are hurting its performance.

      Tip: Ask yourself how the waste you observed is hurting the target work process's performance. If you think it is creating a cost problem, identify the particular cost problem waste is causing (see Exhibit 2 for suggestions). Note your answer. The waste you observed may cause multiple work process problems (e.g., elevated unit cost from the cost list and increased cycle time from the speed list). Use your knowledge about the current performance of the target work process and information from the employees on the team to eliminate any problems from your list that do not make sense.

Exhibit 2. How Waste Detracts From Work Process Execution and Results

Waste	Work Process Problem

1. Hazard
2. Inspect
3. Interruption
4. Motion
5. Rework
6. Search
7. Setup
8. Travel/Transport
9. Unnecessary Processing
10. Wait
	Safety
	  • Increased accidents
	  • Increased incidents
	Quantity
	  • Reduced throughput
	Quality
	  • Raised defect rates
	Speed
	  • Increased cycle time
	  • Poor timeliness of delivery
	Cost
	  • Elevated unit cost
	  • Increased factor costs
	Efficiency
	  • Lowered productivity
	  • Need for inventory

---

2. Identify the affected business result.

    Tip: A work process problem negatively affects one or more of the following key measures of business results: customer reaction, financial results, employee reaction, shareholder benefits, or company esteem.

   a. Review the types of shortcomings in business results that the work process problem can produce.

      Tip: See Exhibit 3 (next page) for examples of business results that a work process problem can compromise.

   b. Decide how the work process problem is hurting business results.

      Tip: Ask yourself how the work process problem is hurting business results. Note your answer. This is the business result the Kaizen event will improve. If you judge that the work process problem undermines more than one business result, note all the results you think may be affected.

Exhibit 3. How a Work Process Problem May Negatively Affect Business Results

Work Process Problem	→	Business Result
Safety Problem • Increased accidents • Increased incidents **Quality Problem** • Raised defect rates **Speed Problem** • Increased cycle time • Poor timeliness of delivery **Cost Problem** • Elevated unit cost • Increased factor costs **Efficiency Problem** • Lowered productivity • Need for inventory • Reduced throughput		**Customer Reaction** • Lowers satisfaction • Lowers inclination to buy again • Reduces market share **Financial Results** • Lowers sales or revenues • Narrows profit margin (gross or net) • Restricts opportunity for growth in sales and revenues **Employee Reaction** • Lowers morale • Increases turnover when other opportunities exist **Shareholder Benefits** • Lessens return on investment • Reduces inclination to hold or increase investment **Company Esteem** • Lowers ratings for stocks • Raises cost for borrowing • Diminishes reputation • Lowers appeal as a possible employer

---

3. Write the mission statement.

   Tip: Record the completed mission statement on a flipchart page and post it so the Kaizen team can easily view it.

   a. Build the "to" component of the mission statement.

      Tip: The *to* portion of a mission statement states the improvement of a business result sought.

1) Review the business result you identified in Doing Substep 2.

    Tip: Typically, there is more than one. Narrow the list to the most relevant business result; this will be the one that the work process problem most affects and the business itself is most concerned about. For example, high unit cost shrinks profit margins but may also cause reduced market share by forcing noncompetitive pricing. If the business's driving concern is inadequate profit margins, use narrowed profit margins as the business result you will improve. If the current business driver is lost sales, use noncompetitive pricing. (See the scope document, Item A9, for the company's current business driver.) A mission statement may target more than one business result for improvement as long as each result relates to a business driver and is produced by the work process problem you identified.

2) Flip the selected business result to form a positive statement.

    Tip: For example, "shrinks profit margins" becomes "increases profit margins," and "restricts growth by limiting the output of existing plant and equipment" becomes "expands growth by increasing the output of existing plant and equipment."

3) Record the improvement in a *to* statement.

    Tip: For example, "expands growth by increasing the output of existing plant and equipment" becomes "to expand growth by increasing the output of existing plant and equipment." Make sure the statement is grammatically correct and reads easily. Adjust the wording if needed.

b. Build the "by" component of the mission statement.

   Tip: The *by* portion of a mission statement states the elimination or reduction of the work process problem you identified (e.g., increased accidents, elevated unit cost, poor timeliness of delivery).

1) Review the work process problem you identified in Doing Substep 1.

    Tip: Typically, there is more than one. Narrow the list to the most relevant problem, which is the one that most affects the business result you intend to improve. For example, assume you conclude that waste is causing the following work process problems: high unit cost, long cycle time, limited throughput, and high defect rates. If you chose narrowed profit margins as the business result to improve, select unit cost as your work process problem since it most affects profit margins. If you chose customer dissatisfaction with a product, then choose high defect rates as your work process problem. It *is* acceptable to attack more than one work process problem in an event. Be sure, however, that there is a connection between the work process problems you select and the business results you intend to improve.

2) Flip the selected work process problem.

Tip: Take the negatively stated work process problem and flip it to form a positive statement. For example, "high unit cost" becomes "low unit cost," "long cycle time" becomes "short cycle time," and "poor first-time quality" becomes "good first-time quality."

3) Record the improvement in a *by* statement.

Tip: For example, "low unit cost" becomes "by lowering the unit cost." Make sure the statement is grammatically correct and reads easily. Adjust the wording if needed.

4) Add the name of the work process.

Tip: To finish the *by* statement, add the name of the work process the team will improve (e.g., "by lowering the cost of the *trailer preventive maintenance process*," or "by reducing cycle time of the *TEOS purity testing process*").

c. Specify the "for" component of the mission statement.

Tip: The *for* component of the mission statement identifies for whom the team is trying to make this improvement. The beneficiaries will always be one or more of the following: the company, its customers, its employees, its shareholders, its suppliers, or the community. As a default, consider using "[name of host company] and all its stakeholders."

d. Construct the complete mission statement.

Tip: Put the *to*, *by*, and *for* components together to form a complete mission statement. For example:

▪ To increase profits and elevate customer satisfaction with on-time delivery by lowering the cost and reducing the cycle time of the nonflammable blending process for ABC Gases and all its stakeholders.

▪ To elevate customer satisfaction with the quality of our products by increasing the accuracy of the TEOS purity testing process for Tempe Chemicals, Inc., and all its stakeholders.

▪ To elevate customer satisfaction with our responses to their questions by reducing the frequency with which we fail to answer customer queries for Customer Services, Inc., and all our stakeholders.

Following Up Substeps

1. Verify that the mission statement is complete and consistent.

a. Ensure that the mission statement is complete.
Tip: The mission statement is complete if it has *to*, *by*, and *for* components.

b. Ensure that the mission statement is internally consistent.

1) Test the *by* component of the mission statement against the *to* component.

   Tip: Answer the question: "If I made the work process improvement stated in the *by* component of the mission statement, is it reasonable to believe that it would produce the improvement in business results specified in the *to* component?" Apply the following rule.

   Rule:

IF	the work process improvement stated in the *by* component of the mission statement would produce the improvement in business results specified in the *to* component
THEN	the mission statement is internally consistent
ELSE	the mission statement is not internally consistent
and	you must adjust the components of the mission statement to make it internally consistent.

2) Adjust the components of the mission statement to make it internally consistent.

   Tip: Rework the components of the mission statement by repeating the Doing Substeps. First, confirm that the work process problem is correctly identified. If it is not correctly identified, redefine the work process problem. Next, confirm that the business result harmed by the work process problem is correctly identified. If it is not correctly identified, reconsider the affect the target work process problem has on business results. Once you have reworked the draft mission, redo Following Up Substep 1.

c. Verify that the team's mission statement is externally consistent.

   Tip: The mission statement must be consistent with the expectations of the key stakeholders as expressed in the strawperson direction. Otherwise, the key stakeholders must approve a revision of their expectations.

   1) Test the external consistency of the mission statement.

      Tip: Compare the strawperson mission statement and the mission statement developed by the team. Apply the following rule.

      Rule:

IF	the strawperson mission statement and the team-drafted mission statement are the same
THEN	the team's mission statement is externally consistent
ELSE	the team's mission statement is not externally consistent
and	you must resolve the discrepancy between the strawperson mission statement and the team's mission statement.

2) Resolve the discrepancy between the strawperson mission statement and the mission statement drafted by the team.

Tip: Apply the following rules to either resolve the discrepancy or determine that the Kaizen event must be canceled. Be sure you explore all options for adjusting the mission statement before canceling the event. Also be sure to consult all parties before canceling the event. However, be clear in your own mind and make it clear to others that it is far more costly in material resources and participant goodwill to complete a Kaizen event that will fail due to a faulty mission than it is to terminate an event that has just begun.

Rule 1:

IF   the strawperson mission statement contains additional details about the work process or business results the event must achieve

and   the added details in the strawperson mission statement are *not* inconsistent with the results of the walk through

THEN   integrate the added details as stated in the strawperson mission statement into the team's mission statement

and   proceed with the Kaizen event.

Rule 2:

IF   the direction specified in the strawperson mission statement is inconsistent with the results of the walk through

THEN   obtain authorization from the event coordinator and the manager of the target work process to change the mission statement for the event to match that developed by the team based on the walk through.

Rule 3:

IF   the direction specified in the strawperson mission statement is inconsistent with the results of the walk through

and   authorization to change the event's mission statement to match that developed by the team based on the walk through is not obtained

THEN   do not proceed with the event

and   explain to all stakeholders why the event must be canceled

and   cancel the Kaizen event.

2. Update the Kaizen event documentation.

   Tip: Record the team-defined mission statement on a new flipchart page; post it where the performers of the target work process and the Kaizen team can easily view it as the event progresses. Also record the mission in the electronic form provided in the Kaizen Tool Kit (Direction for the Kaizen Event).

Check Steps

Use the following checklist to verify that the step was done correctly.

Benchmark	√
Getting Ready Substeps	
1. Reviewed the structure of a mission statement.	☐
2. Reviewed how to build a mission statement.	☐
Doing Substeps	
1. Identified the work process problem.	☐
2. Identified the affected business result.	☐
3. Wrote the mission statement.	☐
Following Up Substeps	
1. Verified that the mission statement is complete and consistent.	☐
2. Updated the Kaizen event documentation.	☐

Tips

- The mission statement should be valid, easily understood, connect with current business priorities, and identify a work process and business result that knowledgeable people, such as the key stakeholders and the employees of the work process, can readily recognize.

Step D1-S4. Set Goals for the Kaizen Event

Preview

This step uses the results of the walk through to set measurable targets for eliminating waste in the target work process. These targets, when realized, produce the work process improvement identified in the event's mission statement. Goals provide:

- an immediate focus for the team's work, and
- a pathway to realizing the team's mission.

Getting Ready Substeps

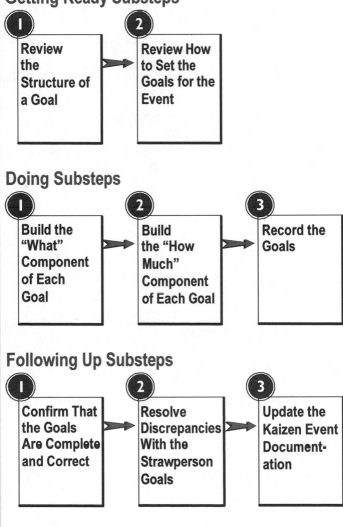

1 Review the Structure of a Goal

2 Review How to Set the Goals for the Event

Doing Substeps

1 Build the "What" Component of Each Goal

2 Build the "How Much" Component of Each Goal

3 Record the Goals

Following Up Substeps

1 Confirm That the Goals Are Complete and Correct

2 Resolve Discrepancies With the Strawperson Goals

3 Update the Kaizen Event Documentation

Purpose

To set measurable targets for eliminating waste in the target work process using the results of the walk through. These targets, when realized, produce the work process improvement identified in the event's mission.

Benefit

- Provides an immediate focus for the team's work by selecting which types of waste the team will remove during the event.

- Identifies a pathway to realizing the team's mission by specifying the targets which, when achieved, produce the work process improvement specified in the team's mission.

Application

Use this knowledge immediately after you build the mission statement.

Performer

Kaizen leader, co-leader, and team. The performers must be proficient in clarifying, confirming, constructively criticizing, and hitchhiking.

Resources

People

- Designated event coordinator
- Kaizen team
- Manager of the target work process

Information, Knowledge, and Training

- Complete, consistent, and verified scope document
- Mission statement
- Strawperson direction for the event
- Waste observed during the walk through categorized by type
- *Working With Others* (J.S. Byron and P.A. Bierley, Hope, ME: Lowrey Press, 2003) - teaches how to get (clarify and confirm) and give (constructive criticism and hitchhiking) ideas and information in ways that build collaboration and elevate results

Materials, Tools, and Other Resources

- Space, equipment, and supplies to support the team's work

  Room/Tables/Chairs
  - Chairs
  - Meeting area for the full team
  - Tables
  - Wall space for hanging storyboards and materials
  - Wheelchair-accessible areas
  - Wheelchair-accessible tables

  Equipment - General
  - Computer printer or access to one
  - Copier or access to one

  - Flipchart easels or hangers
  - Laptop computer with Microsoft Office 2000® and Adobe Acrobat Reader® 4.0 or higher
  - LCD computer projector
  - Overhead projector
  - Projection screen

  Equipment - Safety
  - Clothing
  - Earplugs
  - Gloves
  - Hard-hats

  - Safety glasses
  - Safety shoes

  Supplies
  - Flipchart markers
  - Flipchart pads
  - Masking tape
  - Multicolored Post-its® - 3"x5"
  - Name tags
  - Notebooks
  - Pens and pencils
  - Printer paper (white and colored)
  - Scissors
  - Transparency film (for a copier)

- Kaizen Tool Kit
  - Direction for the Kaizen Event (includes mission statement, goals for the event, and do's and don'ts)

Output

- Goals for the event
- Updated Kaizen event documentation

Method

Getting Ready Substeps

1. Review the structure of a goal.

   Tip: A goal has two components: a "what" component that states the waste you will reduce and a "how much" component that tells to what extent the team will reduce it (see Exhibit 1, next page).

Exhibit 1. Components of a Goal	
What	**How Much**
Eliminate or reduce a type of waste	The amount or degree to which the team will reduce the type of waste

For example:

- Reduce setup time [what] by 65% [how much].
- Reduce unnecessary processing [what] by 25% [how much].

2. Review how to set goals for the event.

    Tip: Write a goal for each of the five major sources of waste observed in the walk through. Use the Waste Observed During the Walk Through Categorized by Type document, developed during *Step D1-S2. Walk Through the Target Work Process*, to identify the top five sources of waste. Add to this list of goals any additional goal stated in the strawperson direction that is *not contradicted* by the results of the walk through. This means you accept any goal from the strawperson direction as long as the team did not observe facts in the workplace that suggest that the problem the goal targets does not exist. Construct each goal by creating and joining two components: a *what* component that states the waste to be removed or reduced and a *how much* component that specifies the extent to which you will reduce it.

Doing Substeps

1. Build the "what" component of each goal.

    a. Identify the five most observed forms of waste in the work process.

      Tip: Use the categorized list of waste examples the team recorded after its walk through of the target work process to identify the five forms of waste that have the most observations associated with them. For now, use the Example: Waste Observed During the Walk Through Categorized by Type - ABC Gases (pages 237–38) to learn how to define goals. The most observed forms of waste in that example are: travel/transport, setup, wait, hazard, and interruption.

    b. Write the *what* component for each goal.

      Tip: The what component restates the category of waste that you will reduce or eliminate and is preceded by the word "reduce" or "eliminate." Use the word "reduce" if you are not totally removing the waste from the work process.

      Example:

      - Reduce travel and transport...

- Reduce setup...
- Reduce wait time...
- Eliminate hazard items.
- Reduce interruptions...

2. Build the "how much" component of each goal.

   Tip: Whenever possible, express *how much* or *how well* as a measure (e.g., a percentage, an absolute number). If the goal states that the waste will be *eliminated*, it is assumed that the how much is 100%; therefore, the phrase "by 100%" need not be stated in the goal. In instances where information is limited, make your best guess as to the possible amount of improvement you can make, and adjust the target when you have completed *Task D2. Evaluate the Target Work Process*.

   Example:

   - Reduce travel and transport by 25%.
   - Reduce setup by 50%.
   - Reduce wait time by 50%.
   - Eliminate all hazard items.
   - Reduce interruptions by 50%.

3. Record the goals.

   a. List the goals set from the walk through on a flipchart page.

   b. Add any additional goals from the strawperson direction not already listed, if appropriate.

   Tip: Ask yourself: "Is there any goal in the strawperson direction that the organization wished us to work on that will be missed if we just pursue the goals the team has defined?" If the answer is yes, add any goal that appears in the strawperson list that is not contradicted by the observations made during the walk through. Frequently, a business will ask that productivity be improved or unit cost be reduced, and this will be reflected in the strawperson goals. Poor productivity or high unit cost are not forms of waste; they are the result of waste. However, as long as you judge that the waste removal specified in the team-defined goals will produce these results, add them as goals to the team's list, since it will make the final list of goals "face valid" to the key stakeholders. As the key stakeholders develop greater understanding of Kaizen event goals, this type of adjustment should be eliminated. Remember, however, *do not* add any goal from the strawperson direction that information gathered during the walk through indicated is invalid.

c. Add any goals suggested by the work process being performed intermittently.

Tip: Intermittent work processes start and then stop *between* operations,[1] usually until a worker is free to complete the next operation. If there is intermittence, you will have documented the delays that occur between work operations on your work process map (*Step D1-S1. Build a Description of the Target Work Process*, page 209). Determine whether these delays are relevant to the work process problem you are correcting or to the waste you observed. If the delays are relevant, add a goal targeting the removal of or reduction in delays *between* work process operations to your list.

Following Up Substeps

1. Confirm that the goals are complete and correct.

a. Make sure each goal statement is complete.

Tip: Each goal must state *what* waste will be reduced and by *how much*. Remember, if the goal states that the waste will be eliminated, it is assumed that the how much is 100% and therefore it need not be stated. Also, you may leave off an estimate of the amount of change if you have *absolutely no information* with which to work. This happens most often with goals specified by the key stakeholders and adopted from the strawperson direction.

b. Make sure the goals accomplish the mission.

Tip: Waste causes a work process problem that, in turn, produces a shortcoming in business results. Your mission statement promises better business results by improving the work process problem that is hurting them. Your list of goals must eliminate those types of waste that are at the root of the work process problem. Ask yourself: "If the team accomplishes these goals, is it reasonable to believe that it will produce the work process improvement promised in the mission?" Use only the goals that target a specific type of waste or the reduction of intermittence in completing this test. If you conclude that the team-defined goals will produce the work process improvement, then the goals are correct. If you conclude that these goals will not produce the work process improvement, then have the team identify what additional forms of waste need to be reduced or eliminated to accomplish the work process improvement. Repeat Doing Substeps 1 through 3 to set goals for each of these forms of waste and redo Following Up Substep 1.

2. Resolve discrepancies with the strawperson goals.

Tip: If one or more of the strawperson goals were rejected by the team, then you have a discrepancy between the goals set by the team and the direction set by the key stakeholders. Apply the following rules to either resolve the discrepancies or determine that the Kaizen event must be canceled. Be sure you

---

[1] Delays that occur *during* operations are identified as instances of waste and categorized under the form of waste named Interruption.

explore all options for adjusting the goals before canceling the event. Also be sure to consult with all parties prior to canceling the event. However, be clear in your own mind and make it clear to others that it is far more costly in material resources and participant goodwill to pursue a goal that is known to be invalid than to terminate an event that has just begun.

Rule 1:

IF	the strawperson direction includes one or more goals not included in the goals set by the team
THEN	notify the event coordinator and the manager of the target work process that a problem designated for improvement in the scope document is not present in the workplace
and	request authorization to work on the goals set by the team.

Rule 2:

IF	the strawperson direction includes one or more goals not included in the goals set by the team
and	authorization to work on the goals set by the team is not provided
THEN	do not proceed with the event since, based on the information you have, you are being asked to do something that cannot be done
and	explain to all stakeholders why the event must be canceled
and	cancel the Kaizen event.

3. Update the Kaizen event documentation.

   Tip: Record the team-defined goals on a new flipchart page; post this below the mission statement so that the performers of the target work process and the Kaizen team can easily view the direction for the event as it proceeds. Also record the goals in the electronic form provided in the Kaizen Tool Kit (Direction for the Kaizen Event).

Check Steps

Use the following checklist to verify that the step was done correctly.

Benchmark	√
Getting Ready Substeps	
1. Reviewed the structure of a goal.	☐
2. Reviewed how to set the goals for the event.	☐

Continued...

Benchmark (continued)	√
Doing Substeps	
1. Built the "what" component of each goal.	☐
2. Built the "how much" component of each goal.	☐
3. Recorded the goals.	☐
Following Up Substeps	
1. Confirmed that the goals are complete and correct.	☐
2. Resolved discrepancies with the strawperson goals.	☐
3. Updated the Kaizen event documentation.	☐

Tips

- Be sure that the goals you set are achievable since specifying unachievable goals means you will always fail, and that is destructive to morale. If you want to adopt the concept of stretch goals, then think of "stretch" as meaning what gets achieved rarely—*not never*.

Step D1-S5. Define the Do's and Don'ts

Preview

This step clarifies what the Kaizen team may and may not do as it improves the target work process. Clarifying the do's and don'ts helps ensure that the Kaizen team abides by the constraints set by the key stakeholders.

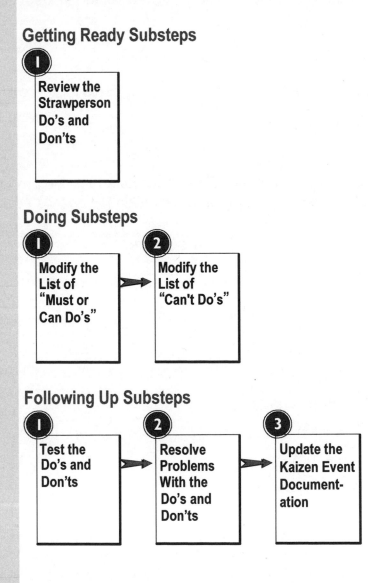

Getting Ready Substeps

1 Review the Strawperson Do's and Don'ts

Doing Substeps

1 Modify the List of "Must or Can Do's" → **2** Modify the List of "Can't Do's"

Following Up Substeps

1 Test the Do's and Don'ts → **2** Resolve Problems With the Do's and Don'ts → **3** Update the Kaizen Event Documentation

Purpose

To understand what the Kaizen team may and may not do as it improves the target work process.

Benefit

Helps ensure that the Kaizen team abides by the constraints set by the key stakeholders.

Application

Use this knowledge immediately after you set the goals for the event and before you evaluate the target work process.

Performer

Kaizen leader, co-leader, and team. The performers must be proficient in clarifying, confirming, constructively criticizing, and hitchhiking.

Resources

People

- Designated event coordinator
- Kaizen team
- Manager of the target work process

Information, Knowledge, and Training

- Complete, consistent, and verified scope document
- Goals for the event
- Mission statement
- Strawperson direction for the event
- *Working With Others* (J.S. Byron and P.A. Bierley, Hope, ME: Lowrey Press, 2003) - teaches how to get (clarify and confirm) and give (constructive criticism and hitchhiking) ideas and information in ways that build collaboration and elevate results

Materials, Tools, and Other Resources

- Space, equipment, and supplies to support the team's work

  Room/Tables/Chairs
  - Chairs
  - Meeting area for the full team
  - Tables
  - Wall space for hanging storyboards and materials
  - Wheelchair-accessible areas
  - Wheelchair-accessible tables

  Equipment - General
  - Computer printer or access to one
  - Copier or access to one

  - Flipchart easels or hangers
  - Laptop computer with Microsoft Office 2000® and Adobe Acrobat Reader® 4.0 or higher
  - LCD computer projector
  - Overhead projector
  - Projection screen

  Equipment - Safety
  - Clothing
  - Earplugs
  - Gloves
  - Hard-hats
  - Safety glasses

  - Safety shoes

  Supplies
  - Flipchart markers
  - Flipchart pads
  - Masking tape
  - Multicolored Post-its® - 3"x5"
  - Name tags
  - Notebooks
  - Pens and pencils
  - Printer paper (white and colored)
  - Scissors
  - Transparency film (for a copier)

- Kaizen Tool Kit
  - Direction for the Kaizen Event (includes mission statement, goals for the event, and do's and don'ts)

Output

- Do's and don'ts
- Updated Kaizen event documentation

Method

Getting Ready Substeps

1. Review the strawperson do's and don'ts.

   Tip: The strawperson do's and don'ts lists steps, resources, or coordination that the team either must or may use in doing its work (must or can do's) and actions the team cannot do (can't do's). (See example in Exhibit 1, next page.) The list was produced from the scope document in *Milestone B. Analyze Whether to*

Conduct the Kaizen Event (page 116). Record the strawperson do's and don'ts on a flipchart page and review the list with the team.

Exhibit 1. Example of Strawperson Do's and Don'ts	
Must or Can Do's	**Can't Do's**
■ Wear prescribed safety gear at all times and follow safety procedures. ■ Check with maintenance before moving any machinery or storage areas. ■ Make sure the process you observe follows prescribed ISO-9000 procedures. ■ Filling customer-owned containers must remain a priority.	■ The event may not continue past Friday noon. ■ Don't sacrifice quality.

Doing Substeps

1. Modify the list of "must or can do's."

   Tip: Ask the team whether it discovered any additional steps, resources, or co-ordination that it must or may use. For example, the team might uncover that it must check with accounting before eliminating information from any forms used in the target work process. Add any new "do's" the team discovered to the list. Consider with the team whether, based on new information, any item on the list can be removed. Discuss the information and, if the team believes the item may be removed, circle it. Verify the deletion with the event coordinator before executing it.

2. Modify the list of "can't do's."

   Tip: Ask the team whether it has discovered any information that suggests it should change the list of "can't do's." For example, the team might uncover that some of the forms used in the target work process are government-mandated; therefore, the team must add to its list of can't do's "cannot eliminate any government-mandated forms in reducing paperwork." Add newly identified re-strictions to the list. Circle any items the team believes it can delete. Verify the suggested deletions with the event coordinator before executing them.

Following Up Substeps

1. Test the do's and don'ts.

   Tip: The do's and don'ts make sense if they give the team the latitude it needs to accomplish the event's goals. Ask yourself: "If the team abides by the do's and don'ts as specified, is it reasonable to believe that it would have the latitude it needs to reach its goals?" Then apply this rule.

> ***Rule:***
>
> | IF | you cannot reasonably expect the team to accomplish its goals if it abides by the event's do's and don'ts |
> |---|---|
> | THEN | the do's and don'ts are in conflict with achieving the event's goals |
> | and | you must resolve the conflict between the latitude the team needs to accomplish its goals and the do's and don'ts as specified |
> | ELSE | proceed to updating the Kaizen event documentation. |

2. Resolve problems with the do's and don'ts.

   Tip: Check with the event coordinator and the manager of the target work process to resolve any problems. Apply this rule to determine what action to take following your discussions.

> ***Rule:***
>
> | IF | the do's and don'ts are in conflict with achieving the event's goals |
> |---|---|
> | and | a correction of the do's and don'ts for the event is not authorized |
> | THEN | do not proceed with the event since, based on the information you have, you are being asked to do something that cannot be done |
> | and | explain to all stakeholders why the event must be canceled |
> | and | cancel the Kaizen event. |

3. Update the Kaizen event documentation.

   Tip: Record the team-defined do's and don'ts on a new flipchart page; post this below the mission statement and goals for the event as a reminder to the team of the constraints under which it must operate. Also record the do's and don'ts in the electronic form provided in the Kaizen Tool Kit (Direction for the Kaizen Event).

Check Steps

Use the following checklist to verify that the step was done correctly.

Benchmark	√
Getting Ready Substep	
1. Reviewed the strawperson do's and don'ts.	☐
Doing Substeps	
1. Modified the list of "must or can do's."	☐
2. Modified the list of "can't do's."	☐
Following Up Substeps	
1. Tested the do's and don'ts.	☐
2. Resolved problems with the do's and don'ts.	☐
3. Updated the Kaizen event documentation.	☐

Tips

- Use a fail-safe approach in defining do's and don'ts. For example, if, after full discussion with the event coordinator, there remains any doubt that a constraint exists, assume that it does exist and include it in your list of do's and don'ts.

Task D2. Evaluate the Target Work Process

Preview

This task produces an exact measure of the types and amount of waste occurring in the target work process. This information:

- identifies specific behaviors that, if changed, will eliminate waste, and

- establishes a baseline against which to measure the Kaizen event's achievements.

Getting Ready Steps

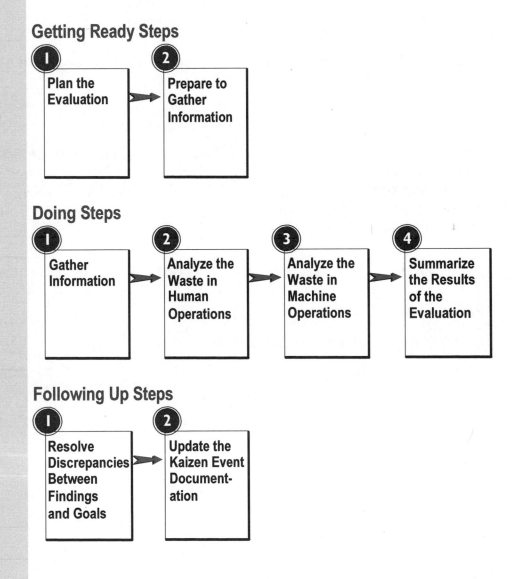

1 Plan the Evaluation

2 Prepare to Gather Information

Doing Steps

1 Gather Information

2 Analyze the Waste in Human Operations

3 Analyze the Waste in Machine Operations

4 Summarize the Results of the Evaluation

Following Up Steps

1 Resolve Discrepancies Between Findings and Goals

2 Update the Kaizen Event Documentation

267

Purpose

To produce an exact measure of the types and amount of waste occurring in the target work process.

Benefit

- Identifies specific behaviors that, if changed, will eliminate waste.
- Establishes a baseline against which to measure the Kaizen event's achievements.

Application

Use this knowledge after you have focused the Kaizen event and before you generate ideas about how to improve the work process.

Performer

Kaizen leader, co-leader, and team. The performers must be proficient in clarifying, confirming, constructively criticizing, and hitchhiking; detecting and recalling features of people and settings (observation skills); and performing simple inferencing—that is, use the guidance of a rule to determine what action or decision is appropriate in a given circumstance.

Resources

People

- Designated event coordinator
- Kaizen team
- Manager of the target work process
- Performers of the target work process

Information, Knowledge, and Training

- Description of the target work process
- Do's and don'ts
- Goals for the event
- Mission statement
- Safety rules
- Work standards for the target work process

- *Working With Others* (J.S. Byron and P.A. Bierley, Hope, ME: Lowrey Press, 2003) - teaches how to get (clarify and confirm) and give (constructive criticism and hitchhiking) ideas and information in ways that build collaboration and elevate results

Materials, Tools, and Other Resources

- Space, equipment, and supplies to support the team's work

Room/Tables/Chairs

- Chairs
- Meeting area for the final report to all stakeholders
- Meeting area for the full team available every day
- Multiple small group meeting areas
- Tables
- Wall space for hanging storyboards and materials
- Wheelchair-accessible areas
- Wheelchair-accessible tables

Equipment - General

- Calculators
- Computer printer or access to one
- Copier or access to one
- Digital camera

- Flipchart easels or hangers
- Laptop computer with Microsoft Office 2000® and Adobe Acrobat Reader® 4.0 or higher
- LCD computer projector
- Overhead projector
- Projection screen
- Stopwatches
- Tape measures
- Wheels for measuring travel distances

Equipment - Safety

- Clothing
- Earplugs
- Gloves
- Hard-hats
- Safety glasses
- Safety shoes

Supplies

- Clear tape

- Clipboards
- Erasers
- Flashlights
- Flipchart pads
- Flipchart markers
- Flow pens
- Graph paper
- Masking tape
- Multicolored Post-its® - 3"x5"
- Name tags
- Notebooks
- Pens and pencils
- Printer paper (white and colored)
- Ruler
- Scissors
- Small tool kit (screwdriver, pliers, wrench)
- Transparency film (for a copier)
- Utility knife

- Kaizen Tool Kit

  - Guide: Distance Measurement Role
  - Guide: Documentation Role
  - Guide: Machine Observer Role

  - Guide: Photographer Role
  - Guide: Process Observer Role
  - Guide: Spaghetti Charting Role

- Guide: Timekeeper Role
- Guide: Understanding the Forms of Waste
- Guide: Utility Role
- Guide: Workplace Layout Role
- Machine Analysis Sheet
- Machine Observations Data Sheet
- Parking Lot Issues
- Process Analysis Sheet
- Process Observations Data Sheet
- Sharpening Observation Skills Exercise
- Summary of Findings

Output

- Machine Analysis Sheet and related charts
- Parking Lot Issues updated with waste removal opportunities that cannot be pursued in the current event
- Process Analysis Sheet and related charts
- Summary of findings
- Updated Kaizen event documentation
- Updated mission and goals

Method

Getting Ready Steps

1. Plan the evaluation.

   Tip: Your plan must answer five questions: (1) how many observations will the team make of the target work process?, (2) what operations will it observe?, (3) which operators? (4) in what order?, and (5) who will perform each role in making the observations?

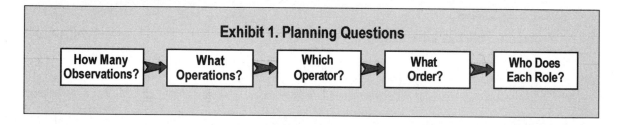

Exhibit 1. Planning Questions

How Many Observations? → What Operations? → Which Operator? → What Order? → Who Does Each Role?

   a. Decide the number of observations to complete.

   Tip: Multiple observations build confidence in the findings of the evaluation as you can average times across instances. As a result, your findings are less vulnerable to error due to observing an unusual execution of the work process. If the work process is short (i.e., less than 1.5 hours in cycle time), you have the option of doing multiple observations. However, do not exceed four hours in completing your observations.

b. Identify the operations to observe.

    Tip: The team will make observations of each work activity depicted in the work process map. Occasionally, you may sample the work performed in a work process that produces products in a batch and, from these partial results, estimate measurements for the total cycle of performance. For example, you may measure the performance of half a batch through an entire work process and then double your findings to estimate the measurements for the entire work cycle. Be certain that the portion of the batch you observe requires the same time to process as the portion you do not observe. If the units in a batch require different periods of time to process, include in the portion you observe representatives of the units that require less time and those that require more time so that you can correctly estimate the cycle time for processing the entire batch.

c. Identify the specific performer the team will observe.

    Tip: There may be more than one performer completing each work activity depicted in the work process map. These operators may be working in parallel or completing their tasks on different shifts. You must decide which of the different operators doing the same activity you will observe. In making your selection, you need to ensure that you observe the work activity performed *according to the current work standard* and that its cycle time is typical for the workplace. Ask knowledgeable people on the team to identify a performer to observe who is competent, motivated, and gets the job done at a typical speed.

d. Decide the sequence in which the team will observe workstations.

    Tip: Usually, the sequence of observations matches the flow of the work process. There are two circumstances when the sequence does not match the normal flow of work. The first is when the team's size permits parallel observations; the second is when a particular operation is performed on a special schedule.

    Typically, the team's size is not sufficient to conduct simultaneous observations of different operations. However, if the team is large enough, you can save time by doing some of the observations in parallel. Be sure that the observers are able to understand the work even though they will see it performed out of sequence. Use the work process description to provide them context for what they will observe.

    In the second circumstance, one operation may be performed on a less frequent schedule than the remaining operations in a work process. Consequently, you may need to observe a work operation out of sequence. For example, if an operation uses equipment that requires scheduled access, you may need to observe that operation when it is scheduled—which may or may not conform to where it logically occurs in the work process.

e. Assign team members to the information-gathering roles.

1) Decide which roles are needed.

   Tip: There are nine possible roles (see Exhibit 2). Not all roles are performed in every evaluation. For example, the machine observer role is rarely used. Check the event's mission and goals and the results of the walk through. Apply the team's resources where the best chance exists for accomplishing the improvements it seeks. Review each of the nine roles and determine which ones the team needs to perform.

Exhibit 2. Information-Gathering Roles		
Role	**Description**	**Guide**
Distance Measurement	Measures the distance a performer moves while executing his or her job using a distance wheel	Page 285
Documentation	Enters the process and machine observation information into the electronic forms contained in the Kaizen Tool Kit	Pages 286–90
Machine Observer	Describes each work activity executed by the machine using the Machine Observations Data Sheet so the team has a detailed understanding of machine operations	Pages 291–93
Photographer	Creates a photographic record of the event by taking digital pictures before, during, and after the team has made its improvements	Page 294
Process Observer	Describes each work activity executed by the performer using the Process Observations Data Sheet so the team has a detailed understanding of the work performed by employees	Pages 295–97
Spaghetti Charting	Charts the movements of the operators as they transport, travel, and search in the performance of their jobs	Pages 298–99
Timekeeper	Measures the time it takes to complete a work activity using a stopwatch so that the cycle time of each work activity is known	Page 300
Utility Role	Gathers documents supplied to and produced at the workstation as well as other critical information (e.g., list of tools used, list of quality inspection points)	Pages 301–02
Workplace Layout Role	Prepares a diagram showing the position of the workstations, equipment, and inventory used to complete the work process	Pages 303–04

2) Decide the number of people you must assign to each role.

   Tip: If the team is observing the work process together, one workstation at a time, assign one team member to each role required for completing the evaluation. On the other hand, if the team is splitting into subteams to observe different operations in parallel, assign as many team members to each role as there are subteams.

3) Make assignments.

Tip: Consider your team members and identify who you think would best perform each role. For the process and machine observer roles, select people familiar with the work process. If this is not possible, be sure to have the performer or machine operator call out the name of each task as it begins so the observers can record the activity on their observation sheets. Typically, the Kaizen co-leader is charged with performing the documentation role.

f. Record the evaluation plan.

Tip: Record the plan on a flipchart page using the format in Exhibit 3.

Exhibit 3. Suggested Outline for the Evaluation Plan				
			Role Assignments	
Order	**Operation**	**Performer**	**Role**	**Who**
1			Distance measurement	
2			Documentation	
3			Photographer	
Etc.			Etc.	

2. Prepare to gather information.

a. Prepare observers.

Tip: Before you begin, post the evaluation plan in full view of the team. Print sufficient copies of the guide for each role you will use so that you can supply one to each team member performing a role.

1) Review the evaluation plan with the team.

Tip: Tell the team the number of observations it will make of the work process and why. Review the proposed evaluation plan with the team. Get the team's feedback and adjust the plan as required.

2) Educate team members about their roles.

Tip: Distribute the role guides to team members. Have the person read his or her guide. Ask for and answer any questions team members have. Consider doing an exercise to sharpen observation skills with the team (see Guide: Sharpening Observation Skills Exercise, pages 305–08).

3) Equip the observers with the resources needed to do their jobs (Exhibit 4, next page).

Exhibit 4. Resources Needed by Each Information-Gathering Role

Role	Resource
Distance measurement	Measurement wheel
Machine observer	20 blank copies of the Machine Observations Data Sheet
Photographer	Digital camera
Process observer	20 blank copies of the Process Observations Data Sheet
Spaghetti charting	20 copies of the workplace layout sheets
Timekeeper	Stopwatch
Workplace layout role	Graph paper, blank paper, pencil, eraser, ruler

4) Explain the order in which assignments are executed.

Exhibit 5. Order in Which Information-Gathering Roles Are Executed

Before Observing the Work Process	While Observing the Work Process	After Observing the Work Process
■ Workplace layout role ■ Photographer	**Human Operations** ■ Distance measurement ■ Process observer ■ Photographer ■ Spaghetti charting ■ Timekeeper ■ Utility role	■ Documentation[1] ■ Photographer
	Machine Operations ■ Machine observer ■ Photographer ■ Timekeeper ■ Utility role	

[1]The documentation role may begin while observing the work process, especially if the work process includes a large number of tasks. The person performing the utility role provides the documenter the Process and Machine Observations Data Sheets as each is completed.

b. Complete before-observation assignments.

Tip: Have the team members performing the workplace layout and photographer roles complete their assignments. Remind the person doing the workplace layout role to produce 20 copies of the layout and provide the copies to the team member who will do the spaghetti charting. Also, you need to prepare the performer or machine operator for the observations by the team. If required, arrange with the person to say aloud the name of each task performed when it begins. Have the name of each task said aloud if the process or machine observer is unfamiliar with the work, or the work is largely mental in nature (e.g., computing numbers, evaluating a purchase request).[1]

Doing Steps

1. Gather information.

   a. Gather information about the human operations of the work process.

   Tip: Record the steps done by each performer, the time to complete each step, and any distance traveled by the performer on the Process Observations Data Sheet. Follow the guidance provided in the role descriptions for the roles involved in observing human operations. These roles are listed in Exhibit 5, page 274, under the heading "Human Operations."

   b. Gather information about the machine operations of the work process.

   Tip: If you are doing formal machine observations (i.e., recording each operation and measuring time and distance), you will record the steps performed by the machine, the time to perform each step, and any distance traveled by the machine on the Machine Observations Data Sheet. Follow the guidance provided in the role descriptions for the roles used in completing machine observations. These roles are listed in Exhibit 5, page 274, under the heading "Machine Operations."

   As stated earlier, formal machine observations are rarely performed. However, *you should always* make observations about machine-related issues such as breakdowns, slow processing speed, and problematic machine design that causes unnecessary setup or creates ergonomic concerns. Have team members note these observations, as you and the team will use them to uncover opportunities for eliminating waste in the work process.

   c. Document the observations.

   1) Enter the process observations into the Process Analysis Sheet.

   Tip: Follow the guidance provided on pages 295–97. It instructs you to record each work activity observed, its ending time, and distance traveled. You will then assign the activity and the time expended in performing it to either the value-added category or to a type of waste. See an example of a Process Analysis Sheet on page 309.

   2) Enter the machine observations into the Machine Analysis Sheet.

   Tip: Follow the guidance provided on pages 286–90. It instructs you to record each machine activity observed, its ending time, and the distance

---

[1]For other suggestions about evaluating office work processes, see Customizing the Kaizen Process, pages 393–96 and 408–13.

traveled by the machine or one of its major components. You will then assign the activity and the time expended in performing it to either the value-added category or to a type of waste.

2. Analyze the waste in human operations.

   a. Verify that the team observed a typical execution of the work process.

   Tip: You must confirm that the work you observed was executed according to the work standard and at a typical speed. Check the work as described on the Process Observations Data Sheet against the work as described in the work standard or the work process description and observed on the walk through. Verify that the cycle time the team observed was typical by checking it against the times recorded on the work process map. Apply the following rule to what you uncover.

   Rule:

   IF   the work the team observed was executed according to the official work standard or was consistent with the work as described in the work process description and observed on the walk through

   and   the observed cycle time of human operations is not much different from the cycle time of human operations reported on the work process map (less than 15% different)

   THEN   the team observed a typical execution of the work process

   ELSE   the team observed an unusual performance of the work process.

If the team observed an unusual execution, you need to explore with the team how and why it differed. If the work was not performed as required by management, make a second observation of the work with a performer who executes the operations according to the work standard. If the cycle time was different, look for reasons to explain why it differed. Frequently, the team will clarify that the time observed is actually more accurate than the time it previously reported. Sometimes the team will clarify that the discrepancy is due to an unusual event—for example, a rare power failure or faulty part. You may be able to adjust the observations you made by eliminating the unusual event from your measurements—e.g., by extracting the time spent waiting for re-establishing power after a power failure or the time needed to replace a defective part. But you must be *absolutely sure* that the event is unusual and that its presence does distort the measurement of the work process. Make a record of any adjustments of this type so that you can report them to the stakeholders when you communicate the results of the Kaizen event.

b. Prepare a visual display of performer movements.

Tip: The person performing the spaghetti charting role completes this step. He or she selects up to five sheets of the spaghetti chart and copies each onto an overhead transparency. The person overlays the transparencies on a copy machine and makes a single transparency from them.

c. Compute the value-added ratio.

Tip: The value-added ratio of human operations is computed automatically in the Process Analysis Sheet provided with the Kaizen Tool Kit. It is displayed at the bottom of the Process Analysis Sheet. See an explanation of the value-added ratio in the *Glossary* if you need to compute it manually.

d. Compute the distribution of work time by value added or waste category.

Tip: The percentage of work time by category (i.e., value added and type of waste) is automatically computed in the Process Analysis Sheet. The distribution of work time by value added or waste category is graphically displayed both in the bar chart and pie chart sections of the Process Analysis Sheet. If you need to compute it manually, sum the total time recorded under each category to which a work activity was assigned. Divide each sum by the total cycle time for the work you observed and multiply that result by 100%. This will give you the percentage of total cycle time of human operations that was value added and the percentage of time for each category of waste the team observed. With this information, you can construct a bar or pie chart manually.

e. Compute the total distance traveled by workers while executing the work process.

Tip: The total distance traveled is computed automatically in the Process Analysis Sheet and reported at the bottom of the Distance column. If you need to compute it manually, sum the distances reported alongside each work activity and report this sum as the total distance traveled.

f. Communicate observations to the team.

Tip: Print a copy of the Process Analysis Sheet and charts for each team member and distribute them to the team members. Make an overhead transparency of the last page of the Process Analysis Sheet and the pie chart.

3. Analyze the waste in machine operations.

Tip: If you did not perform machine observations in the formal sense of recording each operation and measuring time and distance, you still need to analyze the team's notes about machine-related issues such as breakdowns, slow processing speed, and problematic machine design that causes unnecessary setup or creates ergonomic concerns. Integrate these notes into a summary list of observations and go to Doing Step 4, page 279. If you did formal machine observations, follow the guidance below to analyze your findings.

a. Verify that the team observed a typical execution of machine operations.

   Tip: You must confirm that the machine-implemented work was executed according to the functional specifications for the machine and at a typical speed. Check the operations manual for the machine and compare the Machine Observations Data Sheet against the work as described in it. If there are no documented functional specifications, use the experience of team members familiar with the work process and your observations from the walk through. Verify that the cycle time the team observed was typical by checking it against the times recorded on the work process map. Apply the following rule to what you uncover.

   Rule:

IF	the machine-implemented work was executed according to the functional specifications for the machine or was consistent with the experience of team members familiar with the work process and your observations from the walk through
and	the observed machine cycle time is not much different from the machine cycle time reported on the work process map (less than 15% different)
THEN	the team observed a typical execution of the work process
ELSE	the team observed an unusual performance of machine operations.

   If the team observed an unusual execution of machine operations, you need to explore with the team how and why it differed. If the exploration confirms the accuracy of what the team observed or suggests an adjustment that would correct for an unusual event, you do not need to repeat the observation. If you make an adjustment in the measurements, be sure to record what you did so that you can report the corrections to the stakeholders when you communicate the results of the Kaizen event.

b. Compute the value-added ratio.

   Tip: The value-added ratio for machine operations is computed automatically in the Machine Analysis Sheet provided with the Kaizen Tool Kit. It is displayed at the bottom of the Machine Analysis Sheet. See an explanation of the value-added ratio in the *Glossary* if you need to compute it manually.

c. Compute the distribution of machine operations by value added or waste category.

   Tip: The percentage of machine time by category (i.e., value added and type of waste) is automatically computed in the Machine Analysis Sheet. The distribution of time by value added or waste category is graphically displayed both in the bar chart and pie chart sections of the Machine Analysis Sheet. If you need to compute it manually, sum the total time recorded under each category to which a machine operation was assigned. Divide each sum by the total cycle time for machine operations and multiply that result by 100%. This will give you the percentage of machine-executed cycle time that was value added and the percentage of time for each category of waste the team observed. With this information, you can construct a bar or pie chart manually.

d. Compute the total distance traveled by the machine while executing its tasks.

Tip: The total distance traveled is computed automatically in the Machine Analysis Sheet and reported at the bottom of the Distance column. If you need to compute it manually, sum the distances reported alongside each machine activity and report this sum as the total distance traveled.

e. Communicate observations to the team.

Tip: Print a copy of the Machine Analysis Sheet and charts for each team member and distribute them to the team members. Make an overhead transparency of the last page of the Machine Analysis Sheet and the pie chart.

4. Summarize the results of the evaluation.

a. Set up a flipchart page with the heading "Findings."

Tip: Use this sheet to record the judgments made by the team as it reviews the data it collected. See Exhibit 6 for an example.

b. Summarize the evaluation of performer movement.

Exhibit 6. An Example of a Summary of Findings

Findings

Movement

- 1,255 feet of distance per batch
- Great amount of distance in travel/transport
- More orderly than chaotic
- A great deal of motion
- Repetitive motion on hooking pigtails to cylinders and removing cylinder caps; each hook-up activity required a lot of hand movement

Status of Human Operations

- 02:19:30 cycle time
- 0% value-added ratio
- Wait (65% of cycle time)
- Setup (20% of cycle time)
- Unnecessary processing (8% of cycle time)
- Travel/transport (6% of cycle time)

Status of Inventory

- Not a significant issue at this time

Status of Machine Operations

- Measurement of machine operations not completed
- Vacuum machine was old and underpowered for its job, increasing the time required to reach target vacuum levels

Status of Workplace/Work Process Hazards

- Repetitive motion on hooking pigtails to cylinders and removing cylinder caps
- Operator not wearing earplugs

1) Create a section titled "Movement" on the flipchart page.

2) Characterize the distance covered by the performer.

   a) Tell the team the total distance covered during the execution of the work process. Locate this total at the bottom of the Process Analysis Sheet. Record it on the flipchart under the title "Movement."

   b) Record the team's judgment of distance.

   Tip: Have the team characterize the total distance the worker covers using a phrase like "a great amount," "a moderate amount," or "a small amount" to represent its judgment.

3) Characterize the orderliness of the observed movement.

   a) Display the transparency depicting the overlay of five pages of spaghetti charting.

   b) Ask the team to characterize the orderliness of movement as depicted in the overlaid spaghetti charts.

   Tip: Offer the team the following rule to guide its judgment.

   Rule:

IF	the paths of movement depicted on the transparency appear tangled and criss-cross like spaghetti in a bowl
THEN	the performer's movement is more chaotic than orderly
ELSE	the performer's movement is more orderly than chaotic.

   c) Record the team's judgment of the orderliness of movement.

4) Characterize the amount and significance of motion.

   Tip: Motion refers to bending, turning, sitting, standing, lifting, and similar behaviors.

   a) Poll the team for any observations of motion by the workers.

   Tip: Frequently, performer motion is too brief in duration to be captured on the Process Observations Data Sheet. Therefore, you need to direct the team to reflect back on the motion it observed during its observations so this form of waste is fully considered.

   b) Record the team's characterization of motion.

   Tip: Have the team characterize the motion it observed using one of the following phrases: "a great deal," "a moderate amount," or "little motion." Note the team's judgment on the flipchart page along with examples of the motion the team observed.

c. Summarize the status of human operations in the work process.

1) Create a section titled "Status of Human Operations" on the Findings flipchart page.

2) Record the cycle time for human operations.

3) Record the value-added ratio.

4) Record the top five sources of waste in human operations.

   a) Display the overhead transparency of the pie chart depicting the distribution of value-added activity and each type of waste.

   b) Rank the types of waste based on each type's percentage of cycle time.

   c) List on the flipchart page the five types of waste with the most presence in the work process in descending order. Include next to the name of the type of waste its percentage of cycle time.

d. Summarize information about inventory.

   1) Create a section titled "Status of Inventory" on the Findings flipchart page.

   2) Have the team member who performed the workplace layout role present information about inventory.

   Tip: The person should tell the number of locations at which inventory is maintained, where each is located, what is maintained at each location, and how much inventory is stored (e.g., enough for one day, one week, etc.).

   3) Have the team discuss the significance of inventory from a waste perspective.

   Tip: All inventory is waste in the sense that it absorbs resources (e.g., space and the money required to maintain it) and does not materially change the product. One way to evaluate the significance of inventory is to understand the level of inventory present versus the demand for it. For example, for a given item, is there inventory sufficient to meet one hour's demand, one day's demand, one week's demand, or one month's demand? The longer the period of time, the greater the degree of waste in inventory. If the inventory requires special storage arrangements or occupies space that would otherwise be used to satisfy unmet demand for products, then the inventory contributes relatively more waste since special arrangements mean added cost and inability to satisfy demand means lost opportunity for revenue.

   4) Note under the title "Status of Inventory" the team's judgment about the status and significance of inventory in the work process.

   Tip: Have the team characterize the status and significance of inventory as "great," "moderate," "little," or "not a significant issue at this time." Note the team's judgment on the flipchart page.

e. Summarize observations about machine operations.

1) Create a section titled "Status of Machine Operations" on the Findings flipchart page.

2) Decide how you will evaluate the status of machine operations.

Tip: You will *always* review the team's observations about machine-related issues such as breakdowns, slow processing speed, and problematic machine design that causes unnecessary setup or creates ergonomic concerns. Summarize the problems that the team's observations suggest and record this summary under the title "Status of Machine Operations." If the team also implemented formal machine observations, complete Steps 3) through 5); otherwise, go to Step f and summarize observations about workplace or work process hazards.

3) Record the cycle time for machine operations.

4) Record the value-added ratio.

Tip: Value-added ratio is computed by the Machine Analysis Sheet and reported at the bottom of the sheet.

5) Record the top five sources of waste in machine operations.

a) Display the overhead transparency of the pie chart depicting the distribution of value-added activity and each type of waste.

b) Rank the types of waste based on the percentage of cycle time accounted for by each.

c) List on the flipchart page the five types of waste with the most presence in the work process in descending order. Include next to the name of the type of waste its percentage of cycle time.

f. Summarize observations about workplace or work process hazards.

1) Create a section titled "Status of Workplace/Work Process Hazards" on the Findings flipchart page.

2) Record the hazards observed by the team.

Tip: Poll team members for their observations about hazards. Note the observations. Refer to the Process and Machine Analysis Sheets for any items classified as hazards as an aid in refreshing the team's memory.

Following Up Steps

1. Resolve discrepancies between findings and goals.

a. Confirm that the event's goals are consistent with the results of the evaluation.

1) Display the goals for the Kaizen event.

2) Decide if the Kaizen goals are consistent with the major sources of waste found during the evaluation.

   Tip: Review the sources of waste listed in the summary of findings. You need to look at the categories of waste listed under the sections recording the status of human operations and the status of machine operations. If any of the sources of waste listed in these sections is not addressed by a team-defined goal, you have a discrepancy.

3) Resolve discrepancies between the evaluation findings and the goals.

   Tip: Apply the following rules.

   Rule 1:

IF	the existing event goals are not consistent with the waste identified during the evaluation
and	the goals based on the evaluation would be consistent with the current mission of the event
THEN	add new goals for the event using the waste identified in the evaluation
and	eliminate any goals not supported by the findings of the evaluation.

   Rule 2:

IF	the existing event goals are not consistent with the waste identified during the evaluation
and	the goals based on the evaluation would not accomplish the current mission of the event
THEN	redefine the mission and goals for the event using the waste identified by the evaluation of the work process
and	verify with the event coordinator and the manager of the target work process that the new direction for the event is acceptable before proceeding.

   Rule 3:

IF	you redefined the mission and goals for the event based on the findings of the evaluation
and	the event coordinator or the manager of the target work process rejects the new mission and goals for the event
THEN	do not proceed with the event since, based on the information you have in hand, you are being asked to do something that cannot be done
and	explain to all stakeholders why the event must be canceled
and	cancel the Kaizen event.

b. Augment the event's goals with new opportunities.

Tip: List other opportunities for waste elimination suggested by the summary of findings. Be sure to include the opportunities for waste elimination the team uncovered from workers. Append to the event goals any new goals reflecting those opportunities that seem doable by the team in the current event. Record the waste removal opportunities that *cannot* be pursued in the current event in the electronic form titled "Parking Lot Issues" located in the Kaizen Tool Kit. These opportunities will be communicated to stakeholders at the end of the event.

2. Update the Kaizen event documentation.

Tip: Document the summary of findings using the electronic form in the Kaizen Tool Kit. Update the mission or goals of the event if either was modified.

Check Steps

Use the following checklist to verify that the task was done correctly.

Benchmark	√
Getting Ready Steps	
1. Planned the evaluation.	☐
2. Prepared to gather information.	☐
Doing Steps	
1. Gathered information.	☐
2. Analyzed the waste in human operations.	☐
3. Analyzed the waste in machine operations.	☐
4. Summarized the results of the evaluation.	☐
Following Up Steps	
1. Resolved discrepancies between findings and goals.	☐
2. Updated the Kaizen event documentation.	☐

Tips

- Be systematic and thorough in completing the evaluation as it ensures the validity of your findings, and these findings are the basis for all the team's work from this point forward.

Guide:
Distance Measurement Role

Task

To report the distance a performer covers while executing his or her job.

Steps

1. Learn how to operate the distance wheel.

   Tip: You will use a distance wheel to measure distance. Become familiar with how to operate it, read its display, and return its counter to zero.

2. Attend to the performer continuously.

   Tip: Position yourself so that you can see what the performer is doing at all times.

3. Detect when distance must be measured.

   Tip: Distance must be measured whenever the performer moves from his or her workstation to some other location, between locations away from the workstation, or back to the workstation.

4. Measure the distance moved.

   Tip: Start the wheel at the point at which the performer begins walking. Walk the process following the performer. Complete the measurement to the point of destination, thereby producing a measurement for one segment of travel.

5. Shout out the distance displayed on the measurement wheel when asked.

   Tip: The process observer will announce "Distance" when he or she is ready to record the distance. Report the distance in feet when in the United States and in meters when elsewhere. Reset the wheel to zero after each report.

6. Repeat Steps 3 through 5 until the performer states that his or her job is done.

Tips

- Measure and report the distance for one segment only.

Guide:
Documentation Role

Task

To enter the process and machine observations into the electronic forms provided in the Kaizen Tool Kit.

Steps

1. Prepare to document observations.

    Tip: Verify that the computer you are using has Microsoft Office 2000® and Adobe Acrobat Reader® 4.0 or higher installed and that you have a copy of the Kaizen Tool Kit.

2. Receive the Process Observation or Machine Observation Data Sheets before you begin.

    Tip: The person performing the utility role should supply you with the observation sheets as these are completed.

3. Enter process or machine observations.

    Tip: Follow the directions in Guide: Complete a Process Analysis or Machine Analysis Sheet, beginning on page 287.

4. Print the analysis sheet.

    Tip: Follow the directions in Guide: Print the Analysis Sheet (beginning on page 289) to print the Process or Machine Analysis Sheet. Before you begin, be sure you entered all the observations and assigned each observation to a category of value added or waste.

5. Print the pie chart of process or machine observations.

    Tip: To locate the pie chart, look for the tab labeled "pie chart" located at the bottom of the screen displaying the Process Analysis Sheet or the Machine Analysis Sheet. Click on the tab, and the pie chart will be displayed.

Guide:
Complete a Process Analysis or Machine Analysis Sheet

Your Action...	Computer's Response...
1. Open the Kaizen Tool Kit.	Displays the title screen for the Kaizen Tool Kit.
2. Click on the title screen.	Displays the table of contents.
3. Click on electronic forms.	Displays the list of electronic forms.
4. Locate the analysis sheet (process or machine) you want to complete and click on the tool icon.	Displays the analysis sheet.
5. Save the analysis sheet under a new name to the folder on your hard disk where you are storing the event's documentation. Consider using the location and date of the event plus "PAS" for a Process Analysis Sheet or "MAS" for a Machine Analysis Sheet. For example, Memphis 12-03-99 PAS.xls.	Places the analysis sheet on your hard disk, allowing you to save the information you enter.
6. The analysis sheet contains four documents: the observation data sheet, the analysis sheet, a bar chart, and a pie chart. Click on the tab at the bottom of the screen that is labeled either PROCESS ANALYSIS SHEET or MACHINE ANALYSIS SHEET.	Displays the analysis sheet you selected.
7. Note the identifying information at the top of the form. It includes: "Process Observed," "Facility," "Completed By," and "Date." Click on each of these cells and enter the required information.	Displays the text you entered.
8. Point your mouse to the cell under the title "Activity" alongside the step you are documenting and click the left mouse button. *Be certain* that you begin with Step 1. Sometimes the spreadsheet opens with the cursor on another row.	Places the cursor in the cell.
9. Enter the text of the activity.	Displays the text you entered.
10. Press the TAB key.	Moves cursor to cell under "End Time."
11. Enter the end time of the activity in hours, minutes, and seconds, placing a colon between each segment. For example, if the activity ended at the 20-second mark, enter 00:00:20.	Displays the text you entered.

Continued...

Complete a Process Analysis or Machine Analysis Sheet (continued)

Your Action...	Computer's Response...
12. Press the TAB key.	Moves cursor to cell under the next column to the right.
13. Enter the distance that was traveled for this activity. Enter a number only.	Displays the number you entered.
14. Move your cursor to the cell under the Duration column that is on the same row (or Step number) as the activity you are recording. Click the left mouse button. You might have to shift the screen over. To do this, look down to the right of the screen. You will see a slide bar with an arrow to the right. By clicking the arrow, you can shift the screen over so you can view the Duration column.	Makes the cell active and alerts the software that you will now assign the activity to either value added or a category of waste.
15. Note that each column to the *left* of the Duration column is labeled with a type of waste or value added. Locate the column to which you will assign the activity and press the text label at the top of the column. For example, press WAIT. If you make a mistake in assigning the time to a column, just click the cell with the time in it and press the delete key. Then, go back to the duration column, click the cell once, and reassign the time to the correct column.	Assigns the duration time to the category of value added or waste depending on which column you selected.
16. Repeat Steps 8 through 15 until all the activities have been entered. *Regularly save* the binder to ensure that you do not lose information if there is a power failure or your computer otherwise fails.	Displays the information you entered.
17. Save the binder when you are finished.	Saves the binder with the information you entered.

Guide:
Print the Analysis Sheet

Your Action...	Computer's Response...
1. Locate the analysis spreadsheet you want to print on your computer's hard disk.	Displays the name of the file.
2. Open the analysis spreadsheet.	Displays the contents of the spreadsheet.
3. The analysis sheet contains four documents: the observation data sheet, the analysis sheet, a bar chart, and a pie chart. Click on the tab at the bottom of the screen that is labeled either PROCESS ANALYSIS SHEET or MACHINE ANALYSIS SHEET.	Displays the analysis sheet you selected.
4. Point your mouse to the menu option titled "File" and then to the option "Print Preview."	Displays page 1 of the spreadsheet as it will appear when printed.
5. Press the PgDn key until you get to the last page on which you entered an activity. Write down the page number that appears on the bottom left of the screen.	Displays page with page number at the bottom left of the screen.
6. Press the PgDn key until you get to the last page of the spreadsheet. On this page the total for each column is displayed. Write down the page number that appears on the bottom left of the screen.	Displays page with page number at the bottom left of the screen.
7. Point your mouse to the top menu option titled "Close" and click the left mouse button.	Displays the analysis sheet.
8. Point your mouse to the menu option titled "File" and then to the option "Print."	Displays a form titled "Print."
9. Look at the center left area of the form titled "Print Range." Click on the word "Page(s)."	The radial button to the left of "Page(s)" is highlighted, and your cursor is placed into the "From:" field.
10. Type the number one (1) in the space to the right of "From:."	The number "1" appears in the space.
11. Press the TAB key.	Cursor moves to the space to the right of the label "To:."
12. Type the number of the last page on which you entered an activity in the space to the right of "To:."	The number you type appears in the space to the right of the word "To:."
13. Click "OK."	Prints the pages you specified.

Continued...

Guide:

Print the Analysis Sheet (continued)

Your Action...	Computer's Response...
14. Repeat steps 8 and 9.	Displays a form titled "Print." The radial button to the left of "Page(s)" is highlighted and your cursor is placed into the "From:" field.
15. Type the number of the last page of the spreadsheet, which you identified in Step 6, in the space to the right of the label "From:."	The number appears in the space.
16. Press the TAB key.	Cursor moves to the space to the right of the label "To:."
17. Type the number of the last page in the space to the right of "To:."	The number appears in the space.
18. Click "OK."	Prints the final page of the analysis sheet.

Guide:
Machine Observer Role

Task

To describe each work activity executed by the machine.

Steps

1. Gather paper copies of the Machine Observations Data Sheet.

   Tip: Be sure to have at least 20 blank data sheets. A blank Machine Observations Data Sheet is provided in the Kaizen Tool Kit. Become familiar with the different sections of the data sheet (see example on page 293). Note that the main section of the sheet has four columns headed Step, Machine Operation, End Time, and Distance.

2. Attend to the machine continuously.

   Tip: Position yourself so that you can see what the machine is doing at all times and can hear what the operator says.

3. Detect when a new machine operation begins.

   Tip: Be sure to look for any shift in the action of the machine. For example, if the machine is drilling holes and then begins to remove spurs from the edges of the holes, that signals that a new machine operation has begun. If the operator is announcing the machine operations, simply listen for the next announcement.

4. Record the name and number of the machine operation.

   Tip: Record the name of the activity in the Machine Operation column. Use one of the following verbs or verb phrases to start the name of the activity, if possible: "moves to... [where]," "waits for [what]," "searches for [what]," "inspects [what]," "reworks [what]," or "sets up [what]." Otherwise, use the name for the activity the operator offers or what common sense suggests. Be clear. Waiting is considered an activity and should be recorded whenever observed.

   After you record the name of the activity, record the number of the activity in the Step column. Be sure to number the steps consecutively.

Continued...

Guide:
Machine Observer Role (continued)

5. Ask for and record the time in the End Time column when ready.

   Tip: An operation ends if the machine stops or begins a new operation. Ask the timekeeper for the time by saying loudly: "Time." Record the time in hours, minutes, and seconds in the format 00:00:00.

6. Record the distance the entire machine or a major component of it travels.

   Tip: Estimate distances using feet in the United States and in meters elsewhere. Be consistent in your estimates.

7. Give the person doing the utility role each observation sheet as completed.

8. Repeat Steps 3 through 7 until all machine operations are complete.

Tips

- Write clearly or print if your handwriting is not easy to read.

Machine Observations Data Sheet

Process Observed:		Completed By:	
Facility:		**Date:**	

Step	Machine Operation	End Time 00:00:00	Distance

Page ____ of ____

Guide:
Photographer Role

Task

To develop a visual record of the event by taking pictures with a digital camera of workers, the team, and the workplace.

Steps

1. Take before photos of the workplace.

   Tip: Use a digital camera so that the images can be stored electronically and transmitted by e-mail. Take 12 to 15 pictures. The use of video in addition to photos is helpful. Follow the same guidance to take videos. Once you have completed the before pictures, give the camera to the Kaizen co-leader to download the pictures to the laptop computer on which he or she is documenting the event.

   a. Mark an "X" on the floor at the position you stand when you take each picture so that after photos can be taken from the same perspective. Use masking tape.

   b. Take pictures; check their quality by previewing them using this feature of the digital camera.

   c. Retake pictures that are not clear.

2. Take during photos.

   Tip: Take pictures of performers as they do their jobs and the team as it performs the event. Check the quality of the pictures by previewing them. Retake pictures that are not clear.

3. Take after photos of the workplace.

   a. Position yourself at each mark you put down in Step 1a.

   b. Check whether the picture is framed the same way as in the before picture.

   Tip: A picture is framed the same way if it includes the same area of the workplace as previously photographed and it is taken from the same position, with the camera held at the same orientation (i.e., vertically or horizontally).

   c. Take pictures; check their quality.

   d. Retake pictures whenever necessary.

4. Take a photo of the Kaizen team for use in the storyboard.

Guide:
Process Observer Role

Task

To describe each work activity executed by the performer.

Steps

1. Gather paper copies of the Process Observations Data Sheet.

   Tip: Be sure to have at least 20 blank data sheets. A blank Process Observations Data Sheet is provided in the Kaizen Tool Kit. Become familiar with the different sections of the data sheet (see example on page 297). Note that the main section of the sheet has four columns headed Step, Activity, End Time, and Distance.

2. Attend to the performer continuously.

   Tip: Position yourself so that you can see what the performer is doing at all times and hear what the performer says.

3. Detect when a new activity begins.

   Tip: Be sure to look for any shift in the focus or action of the worker. If, for example, he or she is operating on one component of a product and then begins to work on another, that is a signal that a new work activity has begun. If the action of the worker changes—for example, from sorting applications to reading applications—that too is a signal that a new work activity has begun. If the performer is announcing each task as it is performed, simply listen for the next announcement.

4. Record the name and number of the activity.

   Tip: Record the name of the activity in the Activity column. Use one of the following verbs or verb phrases to start the name of the activity, if possible: "moves to... [where]," "waits for [what]," "searches for [what]," "inspects [what]," "reworks [what]," or "sets up [what]." Otherwise, use the name for the activity the performer offers or what common sense suggests. Be clear. Waiting is considered an activity and should be recorded whenever observed.

   After you record the name of the activity, record the number of the activity in the Step column. Be sure to number the steps consecutively.

Continued...

Guide:
Process Observer Role (continued)

5. Ask for and record the time in the End Time column when ready.

   Tip: Ask the timekeeper for the time by saying loudly: "Time." Record the time in hours, minutes, and seconds in the format 00:00:00.

6. Ask for and record the distance in the Distance column when ready.

   Tip: Ask the distance measurer for the distance by saying loudly: "Distance." Record distance in feet in the United States and in meters elsewhere.

7. Give the person doing the utility role each observation sheet as completed.

8. Repeat Steps 3 through 7 until all human operations are complete.

Tips

- Write clearly or print if your handwriting is not easily readable.

	Process Observations Data Sheet		
Process Observed:		**Completed By:**	
Facility:		**Date:**	
Step	**Activity**	**End Time 00:00:00**	**Distance**
	Page ____ of ____		

Guide:
Spaghetti Charting Role

Task

To illustrate the movement of the performer as he or she executes assigned tasks.

Steps

1. Get 20 copies of the workplace layout form.

    Tip: You will use one page to trace the movement for up to 25 activities. After every 25 activities, trace the performer's movements on a different copy of the workplace layout.

2. Stand next to the person doing the process observations.

    Tip: You need to see the number of the activity the process observer is recording and when the process observer begins a new data sheet, since he or she will change data sheets approximately every 25 activities.

3. Label a blank workplace layout sheet.

    Tip: The team may need to see the correspondence between the tracings on the spaghetti chart and the steps the performer was executing. You must indicate the range of work activities for which each sheet records movement. Write at the top of the sheet "Activities 1 to 25," for example.

4. Detect when to chart movement.

    Tip: Chart movement whenever the performer moves from his or her workstation to some other location, or between locations away from the workstation, or back to the workstation.

5. Chart movement.

    Tip: Walk the process following the performer, drawing a line on the workplace layout sheet to depict the direction the worker travels.

6. Repeat Steps 2 through 5 until the work process is done.

Continued...

Guide:
Spaghetti Charting Role (continued)

7. Prepare a visual display of performer movements.

   Tip: When the process observations are complete, select up to five sheets of the spaghetti chart and copy each onto an overhead transparency. Overlay the transparencies on a copy machine and make a single transparency of them. The person who leads the summary of findings activity will display this transparency to the team so it can judge the orderliness of performer movement.

8. Provide the visual display of operator movements to the Kaizen leader.

Tips

- Spaghetti chart whenever the distance measurer measures distance. Both roles are activated whenever the worker moves from his or her workstation to some other location, or between locations away from the workstation, or back to the workstation.

Guide:
Timekeeper Role

Task

To report the ending time for each work activity using a stopwatch.

Steps

1. Position yourself next to the process or machine observer.

   Tip: You must position yourself next to the process or machine observer so that you can detect when he or she writes down a new activity.

2. Start the stopwatch exactly when the process or machine observer announces "Start."

   Tip: Listen for the announcement. Start the watch immediately and keep the stopwatch running *continuously* once started.

3. Note the time on the stopwatch when the observer begins to record a new activity.

   Tip: Detect when the observer records a new activity by watching the person's clipboard. When he or she begins to record a new activity, note the time displayed on your stopwatch.

4. Shout out the time when requested by the observer.

   Tip: Report to the observer the time you noted when he or she began writing the new activity (Step 3). Initially, you will probably report the time in seconds, as beginning tasks may not require more than a few seconds to complete. Once the work goes past one minute, begin reporting the time in minutes and seconds. Once the first hour of time has expired, report each new time in hours, minutes, and seconds.

5. Repeat Steps 3 and 4 until the work process is done.

Tips

- Speak the time clearly.
- Be attentive to the recording activities of the process or machine observer.

Guide:
Utility Role

Task

To support information gathering by collecting information not assigned to other roles and helping document process and machine observations.

Steps

1. Understand your role.

   Tip: You will gather documents supplied to produced at the workstation as well as other critical information (e.g., list of tools used, list of quality inspection points). Read the tasks below to understand your role. Use the form on the next page (Utility Information Recording Sheet) to document the information you uncover.

2. Collect input documents—that is, documents received by a performer prior to starting his or her work.

   Tip: Ask the performer *before he or she begins to do the work* if there are any documents that he or she must receive before beginning the work. Record the names of each document and get a copy of each if possible.

3. Collect output documents—that is, documents produced by the performer during the completion of his or her work.

   Tip: Note any documents that the performer produces during the observed work. Wait until the performer completes the work cycle, then obtain and record the names of each document and get a copy of each if possible.

4. Collect written guidance.

   Tip: After the work cycle is complete, check with the performer for any written guidance he or she may have at the workstation. Obtain a copy if possible.

5. List the tools performers use to complete their jobs.

6. Document inspection points for the work process.

7. Take completed Process and Machine Observations Data Sheets from the process and machine observers to the documenter for computer entry.

Tips

- *Do not interrupt* the flow of work.

Utility Information Recording Sheet

Instruction: List names of documents you collect and attach. List the names of tools used by performers and the locations of inspection points where products or services are checked.

Input Documents	Output Documents

Guidance Documents

Tools

Inspection Points

Guide:
Workplace Layout Role

Task

To prepare a diagram showing the position of the workstations, equipment, and inventory used to complete a work process.

Steps

1. Prepare a workplace layout sheet.

    a. Draw the perimeter of the main work area and label its dimensions on graph paper.

    b. Divide the page into four quadrants.

    Tip: Draw a straight line from top to bottom at the center of the perimeter and then from left to right, again at the center (Figure 1). Number each of the quadrants beginning with the quadrant in the upper right, moving to the quadrant in the upper left, then the lower left, and ending with the lower right quadrant (see Figure 1).

    If the work process is performed in more than one noncontinuous space, create a layout to represent the main area in which the work is executed. Draw an arrow off this main area to a connector (see below) for each other area a performer must travel to in doing the work; label each connector appropriately (e.g., "To Administration Office"). If the worker performs one or more tasks in an area outside the main area (as opposed to just traveling to it and back), create a layout for that area as well.

Figure 1. Prepare a Workplace Layout Sheet

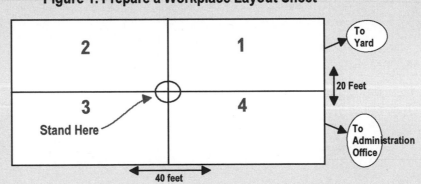

Continued...

Guide:
Workplace Layout Role (continued)

2. Diagram the workplace.

   a. Stand in the center of the workplace with graph paper and pencil.

   b. Draw items in the workplace.

      Tip: Look to Quadrant 1 of the work area and draw squares or rectangles to represent any machines, work tables, desks, computer stations, or tool centers. Label each. Place them on the graph paper in their correct position relative to the center of the work area and to each other. For inventory areas, use a triangle (Δ) to depict the area, and report a count or estimate of the number of pieces stored if possible. Also record how long it would take for the level of stored inventory to be depleted given the typical operation of the work process.

      If there is no room to record the inventory numbers on the layout, label each storage area with a letter (A, B, C, etc.); use a separate page to list the storage areas containing inventory and record the amount of inventory on this separate page.

   c. Repeat Step 2b for the remaining quadrants (2, 3, and 4) of the work area.

3. Provide team members with the workplace layout.

   Tip: Make a copy of the layout for each team member and 20 additional copies for the person performing the spaghetti charting role. Distribute the copies to the team.

Sharpening Observation Skills Exercise

Instructions

1. Ready the team for the exercise.

   a. Tell the team that the purpose of this exercise is to sharpen its observation skills. Explain that what is important in making observations is detecting and recording the details of what you observe. This exercise practices seeing and recording worker activities.

   b. Tell the team that it will be observing the Kaizen co-leader who will roleplay a worker doing a job. The co-leader will announce the beginning of work by saying "Start" and the end of work by saying "Finished."

   c. Each person should detect and record every activity he or she observes. Each activity should be stated in a "verb plus object" format—e.g., "Plugs in the projector" or "Opens the door."

   d. When the exercise is over, we will compare what the team has detected and recorded with a complete list of activities performed by the worker.

   e. Ask for and answer any questions the team has about the exercise.

   f. Provide the team with pads and pencils.

   g. Have the team assume positions that will allow each member to observe all the worker behaviors.

2. Signal the Kaizen co-leader to execute his or her role.

   Tip: The Kaizen co-leader should follow the guidance in Worker Role in the Sharpening Observation Skills Exercise, page 307, in performing his or her role.

3. After the demonstration is complete, instruct team members to review what they recorded, edit it as they see fit, and number the activities. Give them five minutes to complete this task.

Continued...

Sharpening Observation Skills Exercise (continued)

4. Debrief the exercise.

   a. Ask team members to tell the number of activities they recorded. Note the lowest and highest numbers and compute the average.

      Tip: Draw a horizontal line on a flipchart page. Record the low number at the left end of the line, the high number at the right end, and the average number at an appropriate point along the line.

   b. Ask team members to share some of the activities they recorded. Note whether the team members used the "verb plus object" format.

   c. Display the visual that depicts the complete list of activities the worker demonstrated.

      Tip: This visual is contained in the Kaizen Tool Kit with the materials for this exercise. A copy of it is provided on page 308.

   d. Ask team members to compare their lists of activities to the visual to see whether their lists are similar to that displayed. After a few minutes, get their judgments. Explore with them any barriers they experienced in producing a complete list of activities and offer coaching, as appropriate, to enable the team members to improve their skills in detecting and recording work.

Guide:
Worker Role in the Sharpening Observation Skills Exercise

Task

To set up the simulated workplace and execute the work activities listed below.

Steps

1. Set up the workplace.

   Tip: You need two tables, three chairs, two pads of paper, and two pencils. Position the equipment as shown in Figure 1.

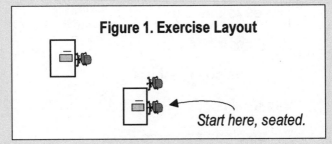

Figure 1. Exercise Layout

Start here, seated.

2. Execute the following steps exactly as listed when the Kaizen leader signals you to begin.

   a. Say "Start" loudly.

   b. Push chair back from table.

   c. Stand

   d. Turn right.

   e. Move to chair blocking progress.

   f. Move chair out of the way.

   g. Move to second table.

   h. Pull chair back.

   i. Position yourself to sit.

   j. Sit down.

   k. Pull self and chair to table.

   l. Pick up pencil.

   m. Check off items on pad.

   n. Put down pencil.

   o. Push back chair.

   p. Stand up.

   q. Say "Finished" loudly.

Tips

- Practice performing the list of activities.
- *Do not* interrupt the flow of work once begun. Follow the guidance above *exactly*.

Visual for Sharpening Observation Skills Exercise

List of Worker Activities

1. Pushes chair back from table.

2. Stands.

3. Turns right.

4. Moves to chair blocking progress.

5. Moves chair out of the way.

6. Moves to second table.

7. Pulls chair back.

8. Positions self to sit.

9. Sits down.

10. Pulls self and chair to table.

11. Picks up pencil.

12. Checks off items on pad.

13. Puts down pencil.

14. Pushes back chair.

15. Stands up.

Example:

Process Analysis Sheet

Process Observed: Cylinder Preparation
Facility: Oakland, CA

Completed By: JPV
Date: 08/09/01

Step	Activity	End Time 00:00:00	Distance	Value Added	Motion	Travel/ Transp.	Unnec. Process.	Hazard	Wait	Delay Inter.	Search	Inspect	Rework	Setup	Duration
1	Goes to front office	0:00:12	34.00			0:00:12									0:00:12
2	Gets orders	0:00:25	36.00			0:00:13									0:00:13
3	Separates orders	0:01:20					0:00:55								0:00:55
4	Keys in blend sheet information	0:02:15					0:00:55								0:00:55
5	Re-works blend sheet information	0:02:40											0:00:25		0:00:25
6	Keys in blend sheet information	0:03:15					0:00:35								0:00:35
7	Keys in blend sheet information	0:03:50					0:00:35								0:00:35
8	Keys in blend sheet information	0:04:24				0:00:34									0:00:34
9	Keys in blend sheet information	0:04:49					0:00:25								0:00:25
10	Keys in blend sheet information	0:05:34					0:00:45								0:00:45
11	Prints blend sheet	0:05:52					0:00:18								0:00:18
12	Gets blend sheet off printer	0:06:40	11.00			0:00:48									0:00:48
13	Goes back to office	0:06:59	11.00			0:00:19									0:00:19
14	Separates blend sheets from paper	0:07:40					0:00:41								0:00:41
Totals		1:30:14	875	0:00:00	0:00:00	0:08:06	0:08:34	0:00:00	0:00:00	0:00:00	0:00:00	0:00:00	0:00:25	1:13:09	1:30:14

IF THESE TWO NUMBERS DO NOT AGREE, RECHECK DURATION DISTRIBUTIONS

Value-Added Ratio = 0:00

Process Cycle Time 1:30:14

Task D3. Solve the Performance Issue

Preview

This task conceives and selects the best ways to achieve the Kaizen event's goals. It:

- enables the team to make improvements to the work process during the event,
- identifies improvements that team members can make after the event to further benefit the business, and
- strengthens the team's sense of ownership for making the business better.

Getting Ready Steps

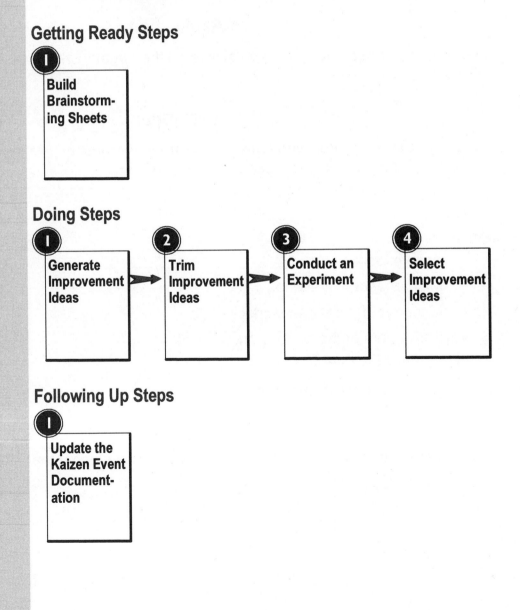

1 Build Brainstorming Sheets

Doing Steps

1 Generate Improvement Ideas

2 Trim Improvement Ideas

3 Conduct an Experiment

4 Select Improvement Ideas

Following Up Steps

1 Update the Kaizen Event Documentation

Purpose

To conceive and select the best ways to achieve the Kaizen event's goals.

Benefit

- Enables the team to make improvements to the work process during the event.
- Identifies improvements that team members can make after the event to further benefit the business.
- Strengthens the team's sense of ownership for making the business better by engaging team members in thinking about the sources of waste in the work process and uncovering ways to eliminate them.

Application

Use this knowledge after you have evaluated the target work process and before you take action to improve it.

Performer

Kaizen leader, co-leader, and team. The performers must be proficient in clarifying, confirming, constructively criticizing, and hitchhiking.

Resources

People

- Kaizen team
- Maintenance supervisor
- Manager of the target work process
- Performers of the target work process
- Safety supervisor
- Work standards supervisor

Information, Knowledge, and Training

- Contractual agreements (e.g., with customers, unions) that affect the target work process
- Description of the target work process
- Do's and don'ts
- Goals for the event
- Government regulations applicable to the target work process

- Integrated list of improvement ideas obtained from workers in the target work process
- Machine Analysis Sheet and related charts
- Mission statement
- Procedure for modifying work process or workplace layout standards
- Process Analysis Sheet and related charts
- Safety rules
- Summary of findings
- Work standards for the target work process
- *Working With Others* (J.S. Byron and P.A. Bierley, Hope, ME: Lowrey Press, 2003) - teaches how to get (clarify and confirm) and give (constructive criticism and hitchhiking) ideas and information in ways that build collaboration and elevate results

Materials, Tools, and Other Resources

- Space, equipment, and supplies to support the team's work

Room/Tables/Chairs

- Chairs
- Meeting area for the final report to all stakeholders
- Meeting area for the full team available every day
- Multiple small group meeting areas
- Tables
- Wall space for hanging storyboards and materials
- Wheelchair-accessible areas
- Wheelchair-accessible tables

Equipment - General

- Calculators
- Computer printer or access to one
- Copier or access to one
- Digital camera
- Flipchart easels or hangers
- Laptop computer with Microsoft Office 2000® and Adobe Acrobat Reader® 4.0 or higher
- LCD computer projector
- Overhead projector
- Projection screen
- Stopwatches
- Tape measures

- Wheels for measuring travel distances

Equipment - Safety

- Clothing
- Earplugs
- Gloves
- Hard-hats
- Safety glasses
- Safety shoes

Supplies

- Clear tape
- Clipboards
- Erasers
- Flashlights
- Flipchart pads

- Flipchart markers
- Flow pens
- Graph paper
- Masking tape
- Multicolored Post-its® - 3"x5"

- Name tags
- Notebooks
- Pens and pencils
- Printer paper (white and colored)
- Ruler

- Scissors
- Small tool kit (screwdriver, pliers, wrench)
- Transparency film (for a copier)
- Utility knife

- Kaizen Tool Kit
  - Design of the Experiment
  - Guide: Designing the Experiment
  - Parking Lot Issues
  - Prioritized List of Process and Workplace Improvement Ideas
  - Results of the Experiment

Output

- Prioritized list of process and workplace improvement ideas
- List of improvement ideas selected for execution in the event
- Design of the experiment
- Results of the experiment
- Updated Kaizen event documentation

Method

Getting Ready Steps

1. Build brainstorming sheets.

   Tip: Brainstorming sheets focus the work of the team as it generates improvement ideas. Two sheets are created for each goal. The first sheet names the goal and lists below it examples of the waste the goal targets for reduction. The second sheet, titled "Ideas," is used to record the improvement ideas the team generates or collects from other sources (Exhibit 1).

   Build brainstorming sheets for each of the event's goals using the example in Exhibit 1 as your guide. Have the team identify examples of the waste specified in the goal statement from the analysis sheets. Direct team members to look for the most resource-consuming instances of waste.

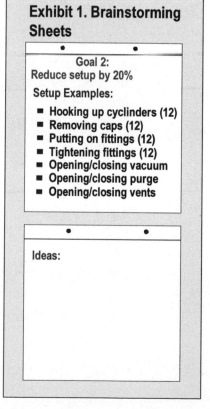

Exhibit 1. Brainstorming Sheets

Goal 2:
Reduce setup by 20%

Setup Examples:
- Hooking up cyclinders (12)
- Removing caps (12)
- Putting on fittings (12)
- Tightening fittings (12)
- Opening/closing vacuum
- Opening/closing purge
- Opening/closing vents

Ideas:

Doing Steps

1. Generate improvement ideas.

   a. Select one goal on which to focus.

   b. Brainstorm improvement ideas.

   Tip: Brainstorming is a method for producing ideas by just saying whatever comes into your mind. It is fast, easy to do, and produces good ideas.

   1) Explain the task to the team.

   Tip: The team's task is to generate as many solutions as possible within a set time period by accepting and recording on their notepads whatever ideas come to mind.

   2) Review the rules of brainstorming.

   Tip: Share the following rules with the team and make sure that team members understand each rule.

   - Say whatever comes into your head.
   - Do not judge an idea during brainstorming.
   - Keep generating ideas until time is up.

   3) Set a time limit.

   Tip: Set five minutes to produce ideas. Let the team know that it will return later to discuss each idea.

   4) Complete the brainstorming activity.

   Tip: Direct the team to look at the brainstorming sheet for the selected goal and focus on the examples. Tell team members to generate ideas when you indicate "Start" and record their ideas on their notepads. After five minutes, you will ask each team member for his or her ideas. Ask for and answer any questions. Remind the team members to write down whatever comes to their minds, stressing that "every idea is worth considering." Say "Start." After five minutes, gather the team's ideas. Record each idea as stated by a team member on the "Ideas" flipchart page. Precede it with a letter (A, B, C, etc.). Be sure that, as ideas are shared, the team restrains itself from making judgments.

   c. Add improvement ideas from other sources.

   1) Add ideas obtained from workers in the target work process.

   Tip: Have team members review the integrated list of improvement ideas previously developed. This list includes ideas that workers submitted both prior to the event and during the personal interviews conducted as part of the walk through. Ask the team to identify any ideas that relate to the selected goal that have not been included on the list. Add these ideas to the list of possible solutions.

2) Add ideas uncovered from best practice databases or other knowledge resources.

Tip: Review the contents of the best practice databases or other resources where improvement ideas are stored. Identify any ideas that relate to the selected goal that have not been included on the list of ideas. This effort will be limited by time and the ease with which these knowledge resources can be accessed. Assign this step to the Kaizen co-leader. Add the ideas he or she uncovers to the list of possible solutions.

d. Repeat Steps a through c until all goals have been addressed.

Tip: If an idea contributes to more than one goal, list it under each goal it benefits. This information will be important later when the team prioritizes solutions.

e. Expand thinking about solutions.

Tip: See if there are other approaches to reducing waste in the work process that the team may not have considered and add them to the list of improvement ideas. For example, have the team think about how the process is currently divided among workers. Could dividing the process differently reduce one or more of the types of waste targeted for reduction? Consider how workstations are designed. Could combining workstations or configuring them as an inverted "U" help realize the team's waste reduction goals?

Also encourage the team to challenge assumptions, especially regarding whether particular operations are needed at all. For example, we have repeatedly encountered work processes where maintaining either paper-based or electronic tracking systems has been performed because workers and managers assumed that the information being recorded was vital to someone. In many of these cases, when we explored the need for the information with the people thought to use it, we discovered that the contents were never accessed. Through open discussions, we have been able to bring all the involved parties to the point of seeing that the system itself was all waste.

2. Trim improvement ideas.

Tip: Trimming eliminates ideas that the team judges not worth further consideration.

a. Select a goal on which to focus.

b. Verify that the team has a common understanding of each improvement idea.

Tip: Use your clarifying and confirming skills to explore each idea and verify that team members have a common understanding of what it means. Hold off any constructive criticism and hitchhiking by the team until it is clear that the idea is understood.

c. Delete those ideas that the team determines are not effective, are too costly, would harm safety, negatively affect a customer value, or violate a contractual agreement or government regulation.

Tip: The team eliminates ideas that, upon reflection, do not make good business sense or are disallowed by law or contract. Ask the team to identify any ideas it judges are not effective, are too costly, would harm safety, negatively affect a customer value, or would violate a contractual agreement or government regulation. Ask team members to use constructive criticism to raise their concerns and hitchhiking skills to improve suspect ideas. If there is uncertainty about the effectiveness of an idea, consult the Process or Machine Analysis Sheet to estimate an idea's effect on reducing waste or consider doing an experiment (see Step 3, below) to test whether the improvement produces benefits. If there is uncertainty about an idea's effect on safety, consult with the safety supervisor for his or her advice. If there is uncertainty about what customers' value, refer the team to the list of customer values posted in the meeting room. If there is uncertainty about an idea's compliance with existing contracts or government regulations, consult with the manager of the target work process or the person responsible for ensuring compliance with government regulations. Cross out any ideas the team considers not worth further consideration even after improvement.

d. Delete those ideas that would violate one of the do's and don'ts governing the event.

Tip: Be sure to test whether you can get permission to do the idea before discarding it. Frequently, constraints can be renegotiated if there is good reason to justify a change. Check with the appropriate party (e.g., the maintenance supervisor, manager of the target work process, work standards supervisor) to discuss what is possible.

e. Repeat Steps 2a through 2d until you have considered all goals.

3. Conduct an experiment.

Tip: An experiment may be required to confirm the effectiveness of an improvement idea either because the team is uncertain or because the management of change process for the business requires it. For guidance, see *D3-S3. Conduct an Experiment* beginning on page 323.

4. Select improvement ideas.

a. Decide whether the team can perform all the remaining improvement ideas.

Tip: Before you proceed to select improvements that the team will execute in the event, verify that you *cannot* perform all the remaining ideas. Sometimes it is possible to do all the ideas generated for *all* goals. For example, you may have a large team which can be divided into subteams to work on multiple ideas at one time, or none of the ideas may take much time to execute. For whatever reason, if it is true that you can execute all the remaining ideas, you *do not need* to select ideas. Instead, go directly to the Following Up Steps.

b. Prepare the team for rating improvement ideas.

1) Review the criteria for rating improvement ideas.

   Tip: Begin with the rating criteria listed in Exhibit 2. Modify, delete, or add criteria as appropriate given the unique requirements of the event. List each criterion and its meaning on a flipchart page so that the team may view it as it makes its selections.

Criterion	Meaning
Doable	An idea for which the team has (or can get) the authority and resources needed to execute it and that can be executed during the time remaining in the event
Effective	An idea that will significantly remove or reduce the targeted waste
Cost Reasonable	An idea that produces a dollar benefit greater than the cost of implementing it
Safety Sensitive	An idea that either increases safety in the workplace or does no harm to the current level of safety
Value Enhancing	An idea that Improves the satisfaction of customer values other than the values immediately benefited by the removal the targeted waste

Exhibit 2. Rating Criteria

2) Explain the rating method the team will use.

   Tip: Use either a verbal or visual rating approach. For the verbal approach, explain that team members assign each improvement idea a score from 1 (lowest rated) to 3 (highest rated). In deciding on the rating for each idea, team members should judge how well each satisfies the rating criteria the team adopted. When voting, each team member will be asked to voice his or her rating for each improvement idea. The Kaizen leader records the ratings assigned by team members.

   In the visual approach, the team uses Post-its® to assign ratings to each idea. In this method, each team member has three Post-its® to assign; when voting, the team member goes to the list of improvement ideas and places one or more Post-its® by the idea(s) for which he or she wishes to vote. A team member may give one idea all three votes or split his or her votes among multiple ideas.

c. Prioritize the improvement ideas.

1) Select a goal on which to focus.

2) Direct the team to evaluate how well each idea satisfies the rating criteria.

   Tip: Tell the team members to consider one improvement idea at a time and go down the rating criteria, asking themselves how well the improvement idea satisfies each criterion. When done, each team member should decide what rating (from 1 to 3) or how many votes (from 0 to 3) he or she wishes to give the idea.

3) Gather and total the team's ratings.

   Tip: If you are using voice voting, ask each team member to say what rating he or she assigned each idea and record it. If you are using Post-its®, have each team member come up to the list of improvement ideas for the goal under consideration and assign his or her Post-its®. Once the voting on a particular goal is finished, sum the votes assigned to each idea.

4) Rank the ideas using the total score each idea received.

   Tip: Rank the ideas in ascending order. The idea having the highest score is given the rank "1," the idea with the next highest score is ranked "2," and so on. The rank of "1" means that the idea has the highest priority for implementation. If more than one idea has the same total score, ask the team to make a choice between the two, placing one ahead of the other. If the team cannot do so, assign the ideas the same rank.

5) Repeat Steps 1) through 4) until the improvement ideas for all goals are ranked.

   Tip: See Example: List of Prioritized Process and Workplace Improvement Ideas, page 322.

d. Select the improvement ideas to implement in the event.

1) Identify the "home run" ideas.

   Tip: Home run ideas are ones that have been rated highly and have impact across a number of goals. By doing one of these ideas, you are able to advance the achievement of many goals. If you have any home run ideas, select them for execution by tagging them with an asterisk (*). Review what resources (e.g., people, time, materials) will be required to execute these selected ideas and judge whether the team has any remaining resources with which to execute more than these ideas. If the team has remaining resources, continue the selection process. Otherwise, go to Step 4e (page 320).

2) Select the highest ranked remaining idea for each goal by tagging it with an asterisk (*).

Tip: These ideas, in addition to the home run ideas, become the first set of ideas to be executed by the team. Judge whether the team has resources remaining with which to execute more than the asterisked ideas. If the team has resources to implement more ideas, continue the selection process; otherwise, go to Doing Step 4e (below).

3) Select additional improvement ideas to accomplish goals that are not realized by the first wave of improvements.

a) Determine if any goal will remain unrealized after executing the improvement ideas selected thus far.

b) Select the highest remaining priority improvement idea for that goal.

c) Judge whether the team can execute more than this additional idea.

Tip: If the team cannot do more improvements, then go to Step 4e, below.

d) Repeat actions a) through c) until enough improvements have been selected to accomplish every goal, or the team has selected all the ideas it is capable of accomplishing within the event.

e. List the selected improvement ideas on a separate flipchart page.

Tip: Create a flipchart page that lists all the improvement ideas that the team will execute during the event. List them in the order that the team will execute the ideas. Use the format depicted in Exhibit 3. This list will make it easier for the team to see what it must get done during the event and track its progress. Consider preparing this flipchart during a team break. Post it in full view of the team and the employees performing the target work process.

Exhibit 3. Format for the List of Selected Improvement Ideas	
Improvement Idea	**Goal Affected**
Hand tools and toolbox for fill area	1, 4
Storage bins for red cap and plugs at manifolds	1, 4
Tool belt	2, 4
Etc.	

Following Up Steps

1. Update the Kaizen event documentation.

Tip: Use the electronic form provided with the Kaizen Tool Kit to record the improvement ideas generated by the team. Include the ranking each idea received and place an asterisk by the ideas selected for execution during the event (see example on page 322). Exclude from the list those ideas the team judged as not worth further consideration. Also document the results of experiments conducted by the team using the electronic form provided in the Kaizen Tool Kit. Finally, add to the Parking Lot Issues electronic form those ideas the team felt were effective but could not be implemented during the event.

Check Steps

Use the following checklist to verify that the task was done correctly.

Benchmark	√
Getting Ready Steps	
1. Built brainstorming sheets.	☐
Doing Steps	
1. Generated improvement ideas.	☐
2. Trimmed improvement ideas.	☐
3. Conducted an experiment (if required).	☐
4. Selected improvement ideas.	☐
Following Up Steps	
1. Updated the Kaizen event documentation.	☐

Tips

- Challenge responsibly the traditional way work has been done in the workplace. This means using your clarifying and confirming skills to understand the reasons why work has been done a certain way and your constructive criticism and hitch-hiking skills to generate better ideas collaboratively.

- Be open to all sources of ideas.

- Recognize that good solutions must not only promise benefit but be recognized and accepted by all the people the ideas will affect. The higher the level of involvement incorporated in identifying and testing solutions to eliminate waste, the greater the likelihood the ideas will be accepted and used.

Example:
List of Prioritized Process and Workplace Improvement Ideas

Improvement Idea	Priority
Goal 1: Reduce travel time by 60%	
A. Eliminate compressor in fill room and move to Raleigh	4
B. Sample at point of fill/eliminate transport of cylinders to lab	3
*C. Move storage to fill room	2
*D. Hand tools and toolbox for fill area	1
E. Storage bins for red cap and plugs at manifolds	6
F. 90° valve opener/closer	5
G. Eliminate manifold #7 to increase storage space in flammable fill by 300 square feet	7
H. Eliminate manifold #9 to increase storage space in flammable fill by 300 square feet (install cut-off valves and proper piping)	8
Goal 2: Reduce setup time by 30%	
*A. Hand wheels with soft seat washers (look at quick connect valves)	1
B. Reduce leak checks on line	10
C. Correct cylinders through access	11
D. Eliminate delays from gas supplier	8
E. Eliminate stenciling of cylinders	6
F. Eliminate full/empty tags	9
G. Improve lighting	5
H. Eliminate tool cabinets	4
I. Increase vacuum capacity (decrease the number of vacuums required per line)	7
*J. Investigate data from monitoring unit (validate to eliminate vacuum and purge)	2
*K. Tool belt	3
Goal 3: Eliminate all identified hazards	
*A. Eliminate manifold #7 to increase storage space and improve safety by eliminating the hazard created by storage at front of dock and remaining clutter	1
Goal 4: Improve productivity by 30%	
A. All brainstormed ideas contribute to this goal	
Goal 5: Eliminate excess assets/inventory by $50,000	
*A. Remove excess cylinders, possibly 300	1

*Selected.

Step D3-S3. Conduct an Experiment

Preview

This step tests the effectiveness of an improvement idea in eliminating waste. An experiment:

- provides the information needed to evaluate an improvement idea,

- minimizes the risk of negative consequences and wasted resources should the improvement idea not be effective, and

- often generates additional information that allows the team to develop better solutions.

Getting Ready Substeps

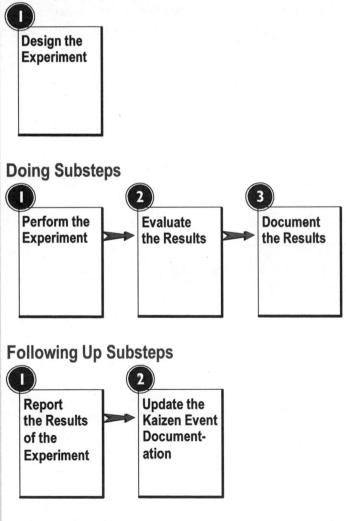

1 Design the Experiment

Doing Substeps

1 Perform the Experiment

2 Evaluate the Results

3 Document the Results

Following Up Substeps

1 Report the Results of the Experiment

2 Update the Kaizen Event Documentation

Purpose

To test the effectiveness of an improvement idea in eliminating waste.

Benefit

- Provides the information needed to evaluate an improvement idea.
- Minimizes the risk of negative consequences and wasted resources should the improvement idea not be effective.
- Often generates additional information that allows the team to develop a better solution.

Application

Use this knowledge whenever you are uncertain about the effectiveness of an improvement idea or the risks associated with trying it. Use it when a company's management of change procedure requires that an experiment be conducted prior to the approval of a change.

Performer

Kaizen leader, co-leader, and team.

Resources

People

- Kaizen team
- Maintenance supervisor
- Manager of the target work process
- Performers of the target work process
- Safety supervisor
- Work standards supervisor

Information, Knowledge, and Training

- Contractual agreements (e.g., with customers, unions) that affect the target work process
- Description of the target work process
- Goals for the event
- Government regulations applicable to the target work process

- Integrated list of improvement ideas obtained from workers in the target work process
- Machine Analysis Sheet and related charts
- Mission statement
- Procedure for modifying work process or workplace layout standards
- Process Analysis Sheet and related charts
- Safety rules
- Summary of findings
- Work standards for the target work process

Materials, Tools, and Other Resources

- Space, equipment, and supplies to support the team's work

Room/Tables/Chairs

- Chairs
- Meeting area for the final report to all stakeholders
- Meeting area for the full team available every day
- Multiple small group meeting areas
- Tables
- Wall space for hanging storyboards and materials
- Wheelchair-accessible areas
- Wheelchair-accessible tables

Equipment - General

- Calculators
- Computer printer or access to one
- Copier or access to one
- Digital camera

Flipchart easels or hangers

- Laptop computer with Microsoft Office 2000® and Adobe Acrobat Reader® 4.0 or higher
- LCD computer projector
- Overhead projector
- Projection screen
- Stopwatches
- Tape measures
- Wheels for measuring travel distances

Equipment - Safety

- Clothing
- Earplugs
- Gloves
- Hard-hats
- Safety glasses
- Safety shoes

Supplies

- Clear tape
- Clipboards
- Erasers
- Flashlights
- Flipchart pads
- Flipchart markers
- Flow pens
- Graph paper
- Masking tape
- Multicolored Post-its® - 3"x5"
- Name tags
- Notebooks
- Pens and pencils
- Printer paper (white and colored)
- Ruler
- Scissors
- Small tool kit (screwdriver, pliers, wrench)
- Transparency film (for a copier)
- Utility knife

- Kaizen Tool Kit
  - Design of the Experiment
  - Guide: Designing the Experiment
  - Results of the Experiment

Output

- Design of the experiment
- Results of the experiment

Method

Getting Ready Substeps

1. Design the experiment.

   Tip: Develop the design with the Kaizen team so that the design benefits from the thinking of all team members. Build the design on a flipchart page first. Use the Guide: Designing the Experiment, page 330, to generate your design on the flipchart. Once the design is complete, enter it into the electronic form titled "Design of the Experiment" provided in the Kaizen Tool Kit. Print the design and share it with the people who need to review and approve it.

   a. Title the experiment.

   Tip: The title states the purpose of the experiment. Review the idea to be studied. Ask yourself what the purpose of the experiment is. Identify what it will decide. For example, "Determine the accuracy of ABC purity testing equipment" or "Measure the travel reduction of relocating XYZ tools." Record the title on a flipchart page.

   b. Record the team members who will do the experiment and how long the experiment will take.

   c. Define the hypothesis of the experiment.

   Tip: The hypothesis tells the results you expect to find. It has two components. The first component states *what* you will do; the second component states what *result* you believe it will produce. Use this format: "If we [do what?], then we will observe [what results?]." Example: "If we compare the new ABC purity testing equipment against the old purity testing equipment, then we will find that the new equipment is no less accurate than the old"; or "If we move the XYZ tools to a location five feet to the right of the existing workstation, then we will reduce travel by 20% and cycle time for the work activity by 10%." Formulate the hypothesis, then record it on the flipchart page.

   d. Specify the resources to be used.

   Tip: List any equipment, materials, or supplies you require to perform the experiment.

e. Define the measures and decision rule.

Tip: List each measurement you will take. State the decision rule that will determine whether the results of the measurements prove your hypothesis. The decision rule is written in the form of an "IF...THEN" statement: "If we observe that [improvement idea] causes [desired results], then we will conclude that [improvement idea] is effective." For example, "If we observe that moving the XYZ tools to a location five feet to the right of the existing workstation reduces travel by 20% and cycle time for the work activity by 10%, then we will conclude that moving the XYZ tools is an effective improvement idea."

f. Specify the method to be used.

1) Identify what will be done.

2) Identify where it will be done.

3) Identify who will be doing the improvement that will be measured.

4) Identify when the test will be executed and for how long or how many cycles.

5) Identify when and how you will take measurements.

6) Identify what, if any, extraneous factors will be measured so that their influence on the success of the idea can be determined (e.g., willingness of people to try the idea, quality of input resources).

g. Finalize the design.

Tip: Review the design and decide if it tests the hypothesis you have defined and whether the method you describe is doable. Also confirm that the experiment satisfies any management of change requirements. Once the design is final, document it using the electronic form in the Kaizen Tool Kit.

h. Get approval to complete the experiment.

Tip: Print the description of the experiment and share it with the manager of the target work process. Get his or her approval to perform the experiment. Ask who else should review the experiment before it is executed and check with these parties as well.

Doing Substeps

1. Perform the experiment.

Tip: Assemble the resources needed for the experiment. Conduct it as described in the method section of your design. Collect measurements. If you need to adjust the method, be sure to record the adjustments and correct the design description. Also, before making any adjustments, make sure the revised method still allows you to test the hypothesis as it is defined and that the decision rule stated in the design can still be applied.

2. Evaluate the results.

Tip: Document the results on the flipchart page you used to record the design of the experiment. Compare the observed results to the expected results stated in the hypothesis. Decide whether the results support the hypothesis by applying the decision rule specified in your design. Extract any learning that the experiment sparked about the problem the experiment is addressing or the solution it tested.

3. Document the results.

Tip: Document the results of the experiment by completing the remaining sections of the electronic form in which you recorded the experiment's design. See example on page 331.

Following Up Substeps

1. Report the results of the experiment.

Tip: Print and distribute copies of the results of the experiment to the team. Have the team review and discuss the findings. Adjust the write-up as required based on the team's feedback. Share the results with the manager of the target work process and any other party who reviewed the experiment's design. Finally, post a copy of the results in a place where the performers of the target work process can view it.

2. Update the Kaizen event documentation.

Tip: Revise the documentation of the results of the experiment if needed.

Check Steps

Use the following checklist to verify that the step was done correctly.

Benchmark	√
Getting Ready Substeps	
1. Designed the experiment.	☐
Doing Substeps	
1. Performed the experiment.	☐
2. Evaluated the results.	☐
3. Documented the results.	☐
Following Up Substeps	
1. Reported the results of the experiment.	☐
2. Updated the Kaizen event documentation.	☐

Tips

■   Make sure you only need to do the experiment once. Be thorough in answering the design questions. Involve people with expertise about the hypothesis you are testing regardless of whether they are on the Kaizen team. Verify that your experiment satisfies any management of change requirements.

Guide:
Designing the Experiment

Title	Enter the experiment title.
Conducted By	List the team members who will conduct the experiment.
Total Time	Enter the total time the experiment is expected to take.
Hypothesis	Enter the results you expect to find.
Resources	List the equipment, materials, and other resources needed to do the experiment.
Measure	List each measurement you will take.
Decision Rule	Identify how you will decide if the results from the experiment are sufficient to conclude that your hypothesis has been proven true.
Method	Describe the experiment.
	Identify what will be done.
	Identify where it will be done.
	Identify who will be doing the improvement that will be measured.
	Identify when the test will be executed and for how long or how many cycles.
	Identify when and how you will take measurements.
	Identify what, if any, extraneous factors will be measured so that their influence on the success of the idea can be determined (e.g., willingness of people to try the idea, quality of input resources).

Example:

Results of the Experiment

Title	Determine whether using the new Carl Fischer test machine would reduce setup and cycle time and improve safety without compromising the accuracy of TEOS purity testing equipment.
Conducted By	J.P. Vitalo; F. Butz
Total Time	1.5 hours
Hypothesis	If we compare the new Carl Fischer test machine to the SM2K test machine, then we will observe 10% less setup time, 2% reduced cycle time, and at least equivalent accuracy with the new Carl Fischer test machine.
Resources	New Carl Fischer test machine and the SM2K test machine, TEOS sample
Measure	▪ Measure the difference between the Carl Fischer purity results and the SM2K purity results. ▪ Measure the setup time required for using the Carl Fischer machine.
Decision Rule	If we find that the purity measurements produced by the Carl Fischer are consistent with the SM2K and we find that the setup time is 10% less for the Carl Fischer machine and that this reduced setup time shortens cycle time by 2%, then replacing the SM2K machine with the Carl Fischer machine is an effective improvement idea. Also, since the Carl Fischer has fewer valves, it requires less maintenance and offers fewer openings through which leaks of hazardous material may occur. Therefore, we will also know that it provides a safer testing option.
Method	We received eight TEOS samples from the lab in test beakers. We took the test solutions over to the SM2K and ran the purity test on each sample. Next, we took the samples of TEOS to the Carl Fischer machine, extracted a measure of the TEOS from each sample, and injected the solution into the machine. This was done for all eight samples. Both machines report the parts per million of water in each sample. We compared the results from the Carl Fischer machine to the results from the SM2K. We also observed the time required to inject the machines. We had, from our process observations, the time required to draw samples. We checked the consistency between the Carl Fischer and the SM2K readings. The tests were done by the lab manager in the testing lab. The tests were completed on Wednesday morning. We controlled for differences in samples by using the same sample in each machine. We also controlled for operator factors by having the same person execute the testing on each machine.
Results	We found that the new Carl Fischer machine gave us readings equivalent to the SM2K. Setup time and cycle time were reduced as expected.
Conclusion	The new Carl Fischer machine does reduce setup and cycle time and improves safety without compromising the accuracy of TEOS purity testing.
Learning	No additional learning. Improvement idea executed as expected.

Task D4. Act to Improve the Target Work Process

Preview

This task implements the selected improvement ideas. It eliminates waste, achieves the event's goals, and realizes its mission. The task also provides satisfaction and fulfillment to the team as it sees its efforts translated into results.

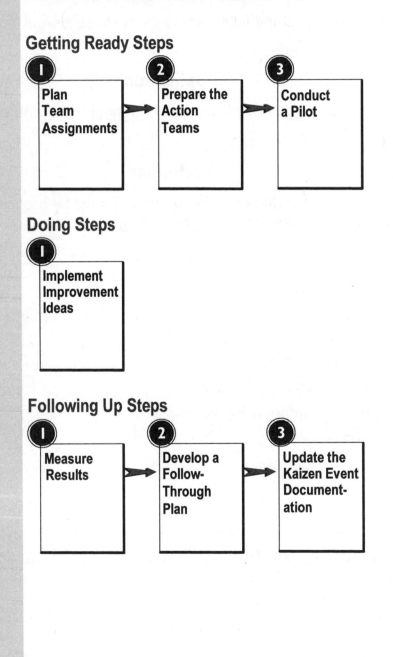

Getting Ready Steps

1 Plan Team Assignments → **2** Prepare the Action Teams → **3** Conduct a Pilot

Doing Steps

1 Implement Improvement Ideas

Following Up Steps

1 Measure Results → **2** Develop a Follow-Through Plan → **3** Update the Kaizen Event Documentation

Purpose

To execute the selected improvement ideas successfully.

Benefit

- Makes the changes in the work process and workplace that eliminate waste, achieve the event's goals, and realize its mission.

- Provides satisfaction and fulfillment to the team as it sees its efforts translated into results.

Application

Use this knowledge after you have selected the work process and workplace improvements you will make.

Performer

Kaizen leader, co-leader, and team. The performers must be proficient in clarifying, confirming, constructively criticizing, and hitchhiking.

Resources

People

- Kaizen team
- Maintenance supervisor
- Manager of the target work process
- Performers of the target work process
- Safety supervisor
- Work standards supervisor

Information, Knowledge, and Training

- Complete, consistent, and verified scope document
- Contractual agreements (e.g., with customers, unions) that affect the target work process
- Description of the target work process
- Do's and don'ts
- Goals for the event
- Government regulations applicable to the target work process

- List of improvement ideas selected for execution in the event
- Machine Analysis Sheet and related charts
- Mission statement
- Parking Lot Issues
- Procedure for modifying work process or workplace layout standards
- Process Analysis Sheet and related charts
- Results of experiments (if completed)
- Safety rules
- Work standards for the target work process
- *Working With Others* (J.S. Byron and P.A. Bierley, Hope, ME: Lowrey Press, 2003) - teaches how to get (clarify and confirm) and give (constructive criticism and hitchhiking) ideas and information in ways that build collaboration and elevate results

Materials, Tools, and Other Resources

- Space, equipment, and supplies to support the team's work

Room/Tables/Chairs
- Chairs
- Meeting area for the final report to all stakeholders
- Meeting area for the full team available every day
- Multiple small group meeting areas
- Tables
- Wall space for hanging storyboards and materials
- Wheelchair-accessible areas
- Wheelchair-accessible tables

Equipment - General
- Calculators

- Computer printer or access to one
- Copier or access to one
- Digital camera
- Flipchart easels or hangers
- Foam board 3'x5' (1/4")
- Label maker
- Laminator
- Laptop computer with Microsoft Office 2000® and Adobe Acrobat Reader® 4.0 or higher
- LCD computer projector
- Overhead projector
- Projection screen
- Stopwatches

- Tape measures
- Telephone for conferencing
- Wheels for measuring travel distances

Supplies
- Clear tape
- Clipboards
- Colored tape
- Double-sided tape
- Erasers
- Flashlights
- Flipchart markers
- Flipchart pads
- Flow pens
- Graph paper
- Laminating sheets
- Magnifying glasses

- Masking tape
- Multicolored Post-its® - 3"x5"
- Name tags
- Notebooks
- Pens and pencils
- Printer paper (white and colored)
- Roll of white paper (34"x44")
- Ruler

- Scissors
- Small tool kit (screw-driver, pliers, wrench)
- Transparency film (for a copier)
- Utility knife

Food

- Lunch
- Morning and after-noon snacks

- Special dietary needs (e.g., kosher food, low salt)

Recognition/Awards

- Certificates of recognition
- Dinner as a team one evening during the event
- Gifts to recognize team contributions

- Kaizen Tool Kit

  - Action Plan Template
  - Design of the Pilot
  - Example: Action Plan
  - Guide: Building an Action Plan
  - Guide: Planning the Pilot

  - Results of the Pilot
  - Summary of Monetary Benefits
  - Summary of Operating Improvements
  - Template for Leave-Behind Measure

Output

- Changes in the work process and workplace
- Design of the pilot (if a pilot is completed)
- Follow-through plan
- Leave-behind measure

- Results of the pilot (if a pilot is completed)
- Summary of monetary benefits
- Summary of operating improvements
- Updated Kaizen event documentation

Method

Getting Ready Steps

1. Plan team assignments.

   a. Create action teams.

      Tip: Action teams take responsibility for executing improvement ideas. You will establish an action team to implement each improvement idea. Complete this responsibility the night before the team meets to make changes.

1) Select an improvement idea.

2) Form the goal for the improvement action.

   Tip: A goal focuses planning. Write each goal statement on a flipchart page so that you can display it to the team. Use the guidance in Exhibit 1 to write a complete goal statement. Write the "So That," "Conditions," and "Standards" sections for each goal exactly as stated in Exhibit 1.

Exhibit 1. Guide for Stating the Goal of an Improvement Action	
Component	**Contents**
To	The goal that the change advances
For	Who is to benefit; same as in the mission statement for the event
By	The improvement to be implemented
So That	"The mission of the event is achieved"
Conditions	"All do's and don'ts are satisfied"
Standards	• "Change idea executed as planned [yes] • Waste reduction specified in goal accomplished [yes]"

Goal
  To: Reduce wait time by 35%
  For: ABC Gases and all its stakeholders
  By: Hooking the unused vacuum pump in tandem to the current vacuum pump to speed the vacuum and purge operations
  So That: The mission of this event is realized
  Conditions: All do's and don'ts are satisfied
  Standards: 1. Change idea executed as planned
  2. Waste reduction accomplished

3) Determine the number of people needed to execute the idea.

   Tip: Consider the workplace feature or work process activity to be altered. Review the information about that feature or activity that was collected during the evaluation. This information is recorded on the Process or Machine Analysis Sheets. Use this information to determine the number of people needed to implement a change idea.

4) Determine the mix of expertise needed to execute the idea.

   Tip: Check with team members knowledgeable of the work process if you are uncertain about what expertise is required to execute a change.

5) Form an action team.

   Tip: Form an action team to execute the idea by identifying team members with the mix of expertise needed to make the change. Assign these team members to the action team.

6) Repeat Steps 1) through 5) to create an action team for each improvement idea.

b. Create a "What, Who, When" chart.

1) On a flipchart page, create three columns and head the first "What," the second "Who," and the last "When."

2) Record each change idea (what), the people implementing it (who), and the time by which the idea should be executed (when) in the appropriate columns.

Tip: The order of execution should correspond to the priority ranking given each selected change idea unless there is a necessary sequence to the actions as, for example, if one action prepares the way to execute another action.

c. Obtain the team's feedback on the plan.

Tip: Share the assignments with the team at the next team meeting. Display the What, Who, When chart and explain its contents and reasoning to the team. Obtain the team's feedback on the time needed to execute the idea and the appropriateness of the people assigned to each task.

d. Adjust assignments as needed by updating the What, Who, When chart.

2. Prepare the action teams.

Tip: Prepare action teams by handing off to each team its goal and supporting the teams in building action plans if they are needed. An action plan *is needed* when the team is implementing a large change or a change that will affect important elements of the work process. Any improvement that will be piloted before it is fully implemented in the workplace also requires a detailed, documented action plan. *For ideas that are simple and limited in effect, no action plan is needed.* The action teams implementing these improvements should talk through the action after they receive their goals so that all team members understand what the team will do.

a. Gather the action teams.

Tip: Gather only the action teams that have nonduplicating members since a team member can only do one assignment at a time. Once these teams have completed their work, repeat Step 2 until all actions are carried out.

b. Hand off a goal to each action team.

Tip: Do this hand-off in a large group so that every team member knows what other members will be doing. Display the goal for each action team's assigned improvement. Explain the goal. Ask for and answer any questions team members have about each goal.

c. Create action plans.

Tip: Action plans guide the execution of process improvements. Decide which action teams need to prepare action plans and have only these action teams prepare plans. The remaining action teams should talk through what they will do and begin their change-making assignments.

Before introducing action plans, prepare a transparency of the template of an action plan (Exhibit 2) to display to the team. Use the electronic copy of the template provided in the Kaizen Tool Kit. Also print a copy of the Guide: Building an Action Plan (page 345) and the example of an action plan (page 346) for each team member. An electronic copy of these materials is also provided in the Kaizen Tool Kit.

Exhibit 2. Action Plan Template

Goal
To:
For:
By:
So That:
Conditions:
Standards:

Plan

Getting Ready Steps

1. [Action]
2. [Action]
3. Etc.

Doing Steps

1. [Action]
2. [Action]
3. Etc.

Following Up Steps

1. [Action]
2. [Action]
3. Etc.

Resources

People
Information
Equipment, Materials, Etc.

Problems/Solutions

Possible Problem   *Fix*

1. [Problem]   1. [Action]

Fallback

What the team will do if it is prevented from executing the change

1) Introduce the concept of action plans.

Tip: Display the template of an action plan and distribute the copies of the Example: Action Plan. Tell the team that action plans guide the execution of improvement ideas. They allow action team members to (1) coordinate their efforts so that together they achieve their goal and (2) anticipate and prevent problems that might cause failure.

Point out that not every improvement idea requires a formal action plan. Large changes or changes that will affect important elements of the work process should get detailed planning. Any improvement that will be piloted before it is fully implemented in the workplace also requires a detailed, documented action plan.

For ideas that are simple and limited in effect, however, simply talk through the action within the team so that all members understand what the team will do.

Direct the team to review the action plan example. Use the example to walk the team through the different parts of the plan. Ask for and answer any questions team members may have.

2) Have each action team create its action plan.

   Tip: Distribute a copy of the Guide: Building an Action Plan to each person. Review the guide's contents with the action team members and ask for and answer any questions they may have. Direct each action team that needs to prepare a plan to identify a person to record the plan on a flipchart page and post it where the entire Kaizen team can view it when finished. This will share thinking with all team members and enable them to comment on each plan. Provide each action team with the materials it needs to build its plan (e.g., flipchart pages, markers). Tell the teams they have 15 minutes to build their plans. Circulate among the action teams, observing their progress and providing coaching as needed. Use the Guide: Checking an Action Plan (page 347) to help you evaluate how well a plan is formed. Be sure that every plan includes whatever actions, data collection, or approvals are required by the work site to establish a new work standard. Refer to the management of change procedure you gathered when preparing for the event (*Milestone C. Prepare for the Kaizen Event*) to refresh yourself on these requirements.

3) Have each action team present its action plan.

   Tip: If time permits, have each action team present its plan to the Kaizen team as a whole for feedback. Be sure that team members use their clarifying, confirming, constructive criticism, and hitchhiking skills during the exchange.

3. Conduct a pilot.

   Tip: Do a pilot whenever (1) you have an improvement idea for which some element of information or knowledge is missing that is needed for the full-scale use of an idea, (2) the management of change procedure for the workplace requires it, or (3) a one-step rollout of the idea across the entire workplace does not seem to be the best way to implement the change. For detailed guidance on conducting a pilot, see *Step D4-S3. Conduct a Pilot* (beginning on page 373).

Doing Steps

1. Implement improvement ideas.

   Tip: Direct each action team to implement its assignment. Circulate among the action teams, observing their progress and providing coaching as needed. Have the action teams regroup as the full Kaizen team at half-day intervals to share progress and provide each other with feedback. Help the teams detect when assistance is needed to overcome barriers to making an assigned change and obtain it. Record the completion of improvements by printing "Done" next to the corresponding action on the What, Who, When chart. Be sure that the action teams document any information about the execution of the change that is required for achieving acceptance of the change as a new work process or workplace standard. As assignments are completed and people become free, form new action teams as necessary. Have these teams do action plans, if needed, and release them to execute their improvements.

Following Up Steps

1. Measure results.

   Tip: For detailed guidance, see *Step D4-S1 Measure Results* (pages 351–71).

2. Develop a follow-through plan.

   Tip: The plan should include a leave-behind measure with which performers may track the continued use of improvements, an assignment for getting the Kaizen improvements incorporated into the work standards, the identification of replication opportunities, and an action list specifying what needs to be done to transform soft into hard monetary benefits. It should also identify improvement ideas for execution after the event. You will share this follow-through plan with the stakeholders when you communicate the results of the Kaizen event.

   a. Prepare a leave-behind measure.

      Tip: Create a visual display to help track and report the continued use of work process and workplace improvements (see Exhibit 3, next page). Establish a follow-through schedule for work process performers to meet and monitor the use of improvements. See an example of a completed leave-behind measure on page 349. Prepare your measure using the template provided in the Kaizen Tool Kit, print it, and distribute it to the team. If possible, have a copy enlarged into a wall display and laminated. Hang the display in the workplace using a 3'x5' piece of foam board as a backing.

   b. Assign responsibility for obtaining changes to the work standards.

      Tip: Review the process for modifying work standards which you acquired prior to the event (see *Milestone C: Prepare for the Kaizen Event*).

1) Identify a Kaizen team member to lead in changing the work standards.
2) Ask the person to assume responsibility for spearheading the effort.
3) Determine a schedule for obtaining approval for the changes.

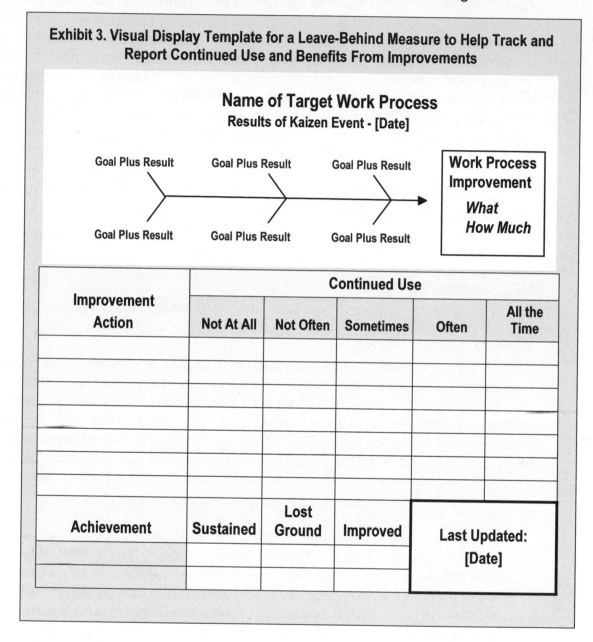

Exhibit 3. Visual Display Template for a Leave-Behind Measure to Help Track and Report Continued Use and Benefits From Improvements

Name of Target Work Process
Results of Kaizen Event - [Date]

Goal Plus Result   Goal Plus Result   Goal Plus Result

Work Process Improvement
What
How Much

Goal Plus Result   Goal Plus Result   Goal Plus Result

Improvement Action	Continued Use				
	Not At All	Not Often	Sometimes	Often	All the Time
Achievement	Sustained	Lost Ground	Improved	Last Updated: [Date]	

c. Identify replication opportunities.

Tip: Replication refers to propagating the use of the Kaizen improvements across all applicable work sites. Use the work process description to identify all other work sites where the work process you improved is also executed. List these sites and ask team members to review and verify or correct this list if needed.

d. List the actions needed to change soft to hard benefits.

Tip: If you reported soft monetary benefits from the Kaizen event, you need to understand the action required to transfer those soft benefits into hard benefits. It may be simply getting approval for a new work process standard. If so, Step 2b, above, will handle it. However, other actions may be required. For example, the business may need to dispose of excess inventory, sell accumulated scrap, redeploy staff to new and productive activities, or pursue sales now possible given increased throughput. For each soft benefit, identify the action needed to convert it into a hard benefit and who needs to take it.

Exhibit 4. Example of a List of Actions Needed to Transform Soft to Hard Benefits

Soft Benefit	Value	Action Needed	Responsibility
■ Equipment or Tools - reduced number of presses needed	$50,000	Sell the unneeded presses	Mike C., Materials Disposition Group
■ Facility - reduced square feet needed	$45,000	Move out of space	Sandra C., Manager of Work Process Betty V., Financial Office Sam W., Buildings and Maintenance
■ Added revenue - increased throughput permits satisfaction of unmet customer demand	$450,000	Sell added volume of output	Tyrone C., Manager of Marketing Betty V., Sales
Etc.			

e. Identify improvement ideas for execution after the event.

Tip: The plan should include any improvement ideas not executed in the event. Include no more than two items to be acted upon by individuals after the event. Consult your Parking Lot Issues list for possible post-event improvements. Remaining improvement ideas not included in the plan or executed in the event should be reported to the event coordinator and the manager of the target work process for later action. Each change listed in the follow-through plan should have an owner with a date for completion. *Be reasonable in setting dates*; review the workload team members have and set dates they feel are doable. Make sure each change has a goal. Use the guidance for defining a goal provided in this unit (page 337). Each person assigned a follow-through change should prepare an action plan as a first step.

3. Update the Kaizen event documentation.

Tip: Complete the Kaizen Summary (see example of a Kaizen Summary on page 184). An electronic Kaizen Summary form is provided in the Kaizen Tool Kit. Record on this form the follow-through action items, who is responsible for each, the date each item is to be completed, and its initial status as open. Update the leave-behind measure, as required, based on feedback from the team. Verify that the summaries of operating improvements and monetary results are complete and that the results of pilots are reported, if any were performed. Retain your follow-through plan as you will use it in *Milestone E. Institutionalize the Process Improvements*.

Reminder

The event is *not* complete. You must execute the Following Up Tasks of *Milestone D. Perform the Kaizen Event* (pages 171–77) to properly finish the event.

Check Steps

Use the following checklist to verify that the task was done correctly.

Benchmark	√
Getting Ready Steps	
1. Planned team assignments.	☐
2. Prepared the action teams.	☐
3. Conducted a pilot (if required).	☐
Doing Step	
1. Implemented improvement ideas.	☐
Following Up Steps	
1. Measured results.	☐
2. Developed a follow-through plan.	☐
3. Updated the Kaizen event documentation.	☐

Tips

- Be thorough and involving throughout the action phase. Success depends on systematic planning, openness to feedback and ideas, and disciplined follow through.

Guide:
Building an Action Plan

Step	Done?
1. Get into your action teams.	☐
2. Assign one person the role of recorder.	☐
3. Review your assigned goal for executing an improvement action.	☐
4. Generate the steps that will make the assigned change. a. Name the 5 to 10 major tasks that are required to complete this change. *Tip:* Do not worry about the order of the tasks at this point. Be sure, however, to generate *all* the tasks that seem to be needed. b. List the team's ideas on a flipchart page or white board. c. Order the tasks from first to last executed. *Tip:* Also, sort the tasks into getting ready, doing, and following up tasks. d. Refine the task list. *Tip:* Make sure each task is stated completely. A complete task statement has at least a verb and an object. For example, "Recruit forklift operators," *not* "Complete recruitment"; or "Plan project budget," *not* "Budget."	☐
5. Get feedback on your plan from the Kaizen leader or co-leader.	☐
6. Correct any deficits uncovered in the plan. *Tip:* For example, if the first step is not immediately doable, then identify what you must do prior to executing the first step and add that to the plan. Or if the last step does not produce the goal, identify what you must do after the last step to achieve the goal and add that to the plan.	☐
7. Identify and record any special resources needed to implement the idea.	☐
8. Identify and record any problems that may occur as you implement the idea.	☐
9. Identify and record next to each problem a brief statement of how the team will remedy the problem should it occur.	☐
10. Identify and record a fallback position for any problem that would make implementing the improvement impossible.	☐
11. Check that you have a complete plan. *Tip:* Compare your action plan to the example provided.	☐

Example:

Action Plan

Action Plan for Deploying the Unused Vacuum Pump

Goal

To:	Reduce wait time by 35%
For:	ABC Gases and all its stakeholders
By:	Hooking the unused vacuum pump in tandem to the current vacuum pump to speed the vacuum and purge operations
So That:	The mission of this event is realized
Conditions:	All do's and don'ts are satisfied
Standards:	1. Change idea executed as planned
	2. Waste reduction accomplished

Plan

Getting Ready Steps

1. Obtain work permit.
2. Obtain vacuum line blueprints.
3. Obtain work safety procedures.
4. Gather safety equipment.
5. Acquire a ladder.
6. Acquire wrenches.
7. Gather pipe fittings.
8. Gather pipe threader, solder, and torch.

Doing Steps

1. Test spare vacuum pump to make sure it operates.
2. Service the pump (perform basic maintenance).
3. Trace the pipeline to find best tie-in location.
4. Connect the two vacuum lines together.

Following Up Steps

1. Verify that the system works.

Resources

People

Nathan H., Maintenance
James L., Fill Operator
Thomas C., Fill Operator

Resources (cont'd)

Information

- Vacuum line blueprints
- Work safety procedures

Equipment, Materials, Etc.

▪ Ladders	▪ Pipe fittings	▪ Solder
▪ Wrenches	▪ Torch	▪ Pipe threader

Problems/Solutions

Possible Problem / Fix

Vacuum pump does not operate — Troubleshoot and repair

Fallback

If we can't get the idle pump to work, the team's fallback plan is to purchase a replacement pump for the unit currently in use. The pump is 25 years old and is grossly underpowered for its current workload. The team has found that we could obtain a new vacuum pump that could pump three times the cubic feet per minute of the current unit for a cost of $2,800. The team has checked this with the plant manager, and he is willing to purchase the new pump if the team can't get the idle pump to work.

Guide:
Checking an Action Plan

Instructions: Respond to each question. Treat "unknown" as a "no" in this decision aid. If you respond "yes" to all questions, then conclude that the action plan is sound; otherwise, the action plan needs correction.

Statement	Yes	No
1. Is the first task in the plan immediately doable?	☐	☐
2. Does the last task in the plan produce the goal?	☐	☐
3. Are the tasks of similar size or difficulty?	☐	☐
4. Are there getting ready tasks that prepare for execution?	☐	☐
5. Are there doing tasks that guide execution?	☐	☐
6. Are there following up tasks that finish off the job?	☐	☐
7. Are the steps of the action plan correctly sequenced? *Tip:* Use the Guide: Testing the Sequence of Steps in an Action Plan to judge if the steps of the plan are correctly sequenced.	☐	☐
8. Does the plan identify the resources needed to complete the improvement, including people, information, equipment, and materials?	☐	☐
9. Does the plan identify potential problems to execution and possible solutions?	☐	☐
10. Does the plan identify a fallback position should one or more of the problems not be solvable?	☐	☐

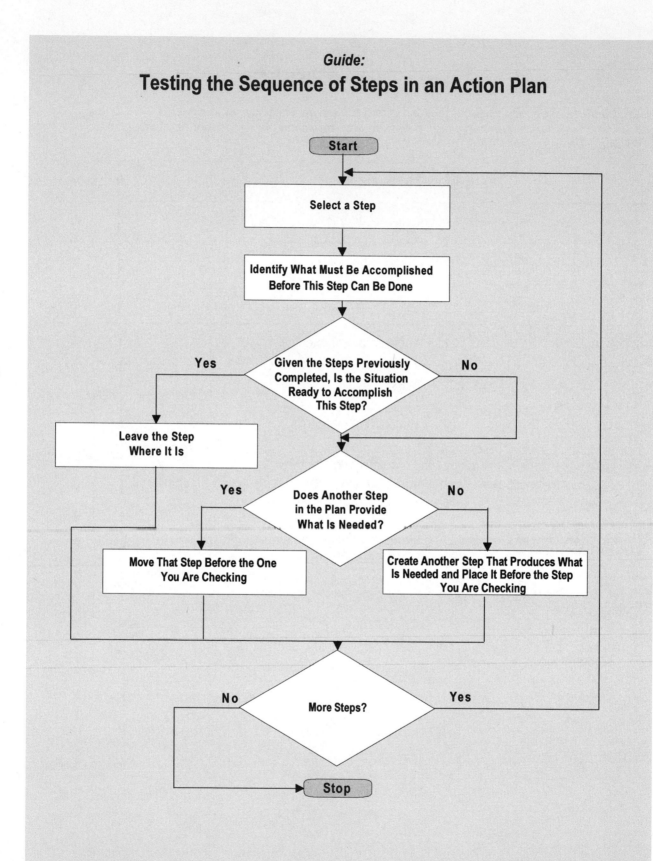

Guide:
Testing the Sequence of Steps in an Action Plan

Example:
Leave-Behind Measure

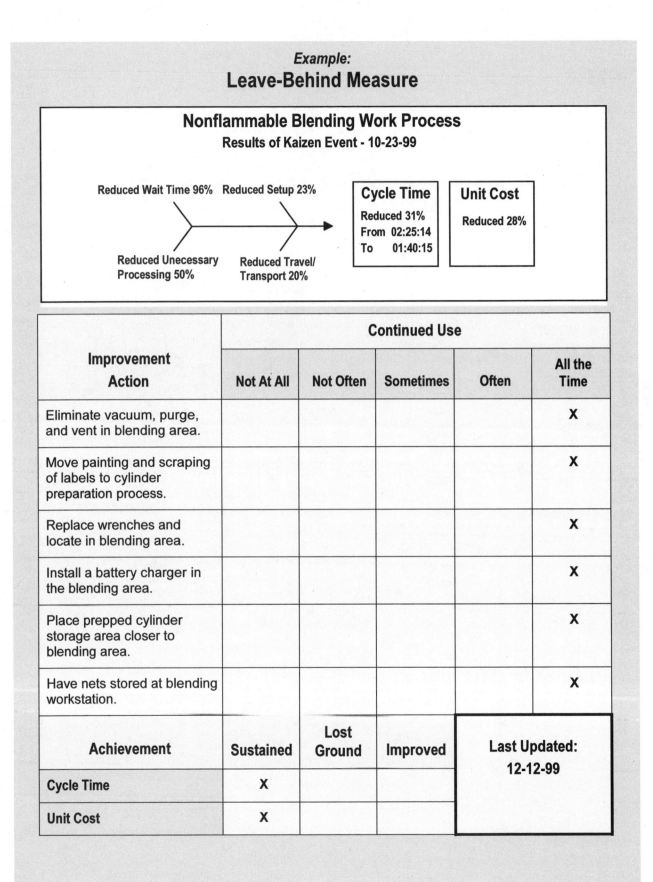

Nonflammable Blending Work Process
Results of Kaizen Event - 10-23-99

Reduced Wait Time 96%   Reduced Setup 23%

Reduced Unecessary Processing 50%   Reduced Travel/ Transport 20%

Cycle Time
Reduced 31%
From 02:25:14
To   01:40:15

Unit Cost
Reduced 28%

Improvement Action	Continued Use				
	Not At All	**Not Often**	**Sometimes**	**Often**	**All the Time**
Eliminate vacuum, purge, and vent in blending area.					X
Move painting and scraping of labels to cylinder preparation process.					X
Replace wrenches and locate in blending area.					X
Install a battery charger in the blending area.					X
Place prepped cylinder storage area closer to blending area.					X
Have nets stored at blending workstation.					X
Achievement	**Sustained**	**Lost Ground**	**Improved**	**Last Updated:** 12-12-99	
Cycle Time	X				
Unit Cost	X				

Step D4-S1. Measure Results

Preview

This step detects and quantifies the work process and business benefits produced by the Kaizen event. It provides the information needed to judge whether the event achieved its mission and goals.

Getting Ready Substeps

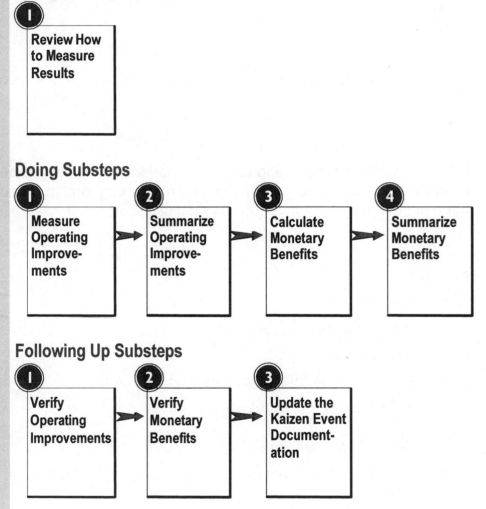

① Review How to Measure Results

Doing Substeps

① Measure Operating Improvements

② Summarize Operating Improvements

③ Calculate Monetary Benefits

④ Summarize Monetary Benefits

Following Up Substeps

① Verify Operating Improvements

② Verify Monetary Benefits

③ Update the Kaizen Event Documentation

Purpose

To detect and quantify the work process and business benefits produced by the Kaizen event.

Benefit

Provides the information needed to judge whether the event achieved its mission and goals.

Application

Use this knowledge after you have completed making the improvements you selected for execution during the event.

Performer

Kaizen leader, co-leader, and team. The performers must be proficient in clarifying, confirming, constructively criticizing, and hitchhiking, and in detecting and recalling features of people and settings (observation skills).

Resources

People

- Comptroller
- Designated event coordinator
- Kaizen team
- Manager of the target work process
- Performers of the target work process

Information, Knowledge, and Training

- Contractual agreements (e.g., with customers, unions) that affect the target work process
- Description of the target work process
- Do's and don'ts
- Goals for the event
- Machine Analysis Sheet and related charts
- Mission statement
- Procedure for modifying work process or workplace layout standards
- Process Analysis Sheet and related charts
- Safety rules

- Summary of Findings
- Work standards for the target work process
- *Working With Others* (J.S. Byron and P.A. Bierley, Hope, ME: Lowrey Press, 2003) - teaches how to get (clarify and confirm) and give (constructive criticism and hitchhiking) ideas and information in ways that build collaboration and elevate results

Materials, Tools, and Other Resources

- Space, equipment, and supplies to support the team's work

Room/Tables/Chairs

- Chairs
- Meeting area for the final report to all stakeholders
- Meeting area for the full team available every day
- Multiple small group meeting areas
- Tables
- Wall space for hanging storyboards and materials
- Wheelchair-accessible areas
- Wheelchair-accessible tables

Equipment - General

- Calculators
- Computer printer or access to one
- Copier or access to one
- Digital camera

- Flipchart easels or hangers
- Laptop computer with Microsoft Office 2000® and Adobe Acrobat Reader® 4.0 or higher
- LCD computer projector
- Overhead projector
- Projection screen
- Stopwatches
- Tape measures
- Wheels for measuring travel distances

Equipment - Safety

- Clothing
- Earplugs
- Gloves
- Hard-hats
- Safety glasses
- Safety shoes

Supplies

- Clear tape

- Clipboards
- Erasers
- Flashlights
- Flipchart pads
- Flipchart markers
- Flow pens
- Graph paper
- Masking tape
- Multicolored Post-its® - 3"x5"
- Name tags
- Notebooks
- Pens and pencils
- Printer paper (white and colored)
- Ruler
- Scissors
- Small tool kit (screwdriver, pliers, wrench)
- Transparency film (for a copier)
- Utility knife

- Kaizen Tool Kit
  - Summary of Monetary Benefits
  - Summary of Operating Improvements

Output

- Summary of monetary benefits
- Summary of operating improvements

Method

Getting Ready Substeps

1. Review how to measure results.

   Tip: The approach involves four steps: (1) measure operating improvements, (2) summarize operating improvements, (3) calculate monetary benefits, and (4) summarize monetary benefits (Exhibit 1). Measure operating improvements by repeating the evaluation of the target work process and calculating the differences between what you observed during the first evaluation and what you now observe. Add to this information changes in other operating factors (e.g., inventory levels, space usage) and summarize all the operating improvements produced by the Kaizen event. Next, calculate the monetary benefits resulting from these changes. There are four components to monetary benefits: (1) savings from human operations; (2) savings from machine operations; (3) savings from other operating improvements (e.g., materials, facility space); and (4) dollar gains resulting from added sales or profit. Estimate the value of each component and decide how much of the savings and dollar gains are hard (i.e., flow immediately to the business at the end of the event) and soft (i.e., not realized at the end of the event but could be realized with additional action). Finally, summarize all the monetary benefits produced by the Kaizen event.

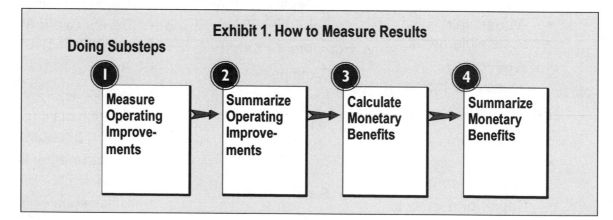

Exhibit 1. How to Measure Results

Doing Substeps

1. Measure operating improvements.

   a. Focus the evaluation of the target work process.

   Tip: Determine what components of the target work process to reevaluate. If your improvement actions affected the entire work process, then you need to reevaluate the entire work process; otherwise, focus your reevaluation on those components of the work process that have been changed.

b. Execute the evaluation.

   Tip: Use the guidance provided in *Task D2. Evaluate the Target Work Process* to produce the appropriate analysis sheet and related charts and a summary of findings.

c. Measure other improvements made in the target work process.

   1) Estimate inventory reductions.

      Tip: Determine whether any changes made to the work process reduced the need for inventory. If the changes affected inventory, determine how many items of each type of inventory were eliminated.

   2) Estimate reductions in the usage of materials or supplies.

      Tip: Determine whether your changes reduced the amount of materials or supplies consumed by the work process. If the changes made a reduction, identify the types of items reduced and by what amount over the course of the year. Your changes may not have reduced the quantity of materials or supplies used but may have allowed the use of less expensive products. In this case, find out the unit cost of the original type of product used and the unit cost of the new type. Then find out how many units of the product are used over the course of a year. This information will be important later when you summarize monetary benefits.

   3) Estimate reductions in energy and other utilities.

      Tip: Determine whether your changes reduced energy consumption. For this metric to be worth pursuing, you need to be able to estimate both the degree to which energy use was reduced and translate that reduction into a per unit of output measurement. If, for example, you could determine that it took nine kilowatts of power to produce one unit of output before a change was made, and, after the change, it required only eight kilowatts of power per unit of output, then information about energy reduction is worth pursuing. Consumption information is most likely available in work processes that make heavy use of energy. Even in these instances, however, the business may not be able to isolate the energy use of the work process you improved.

      Estimate reductions in other utility usage (e.g., water, sewage, telephone) if the event's improvements affected them and the effect was important to the business.

   4) Estimate reductions in facility space.

      Tip: Determine whether your changes reduced the amount of facility space required to operate the work process at a given level of output.

Compute any reduction in square feet. Obtain the original number of square feet of facility space needed to operate the work process and the number needed after the changes. Remember that any reduction in inventory also implies a reduction in space.

5) Estimate reductions in equipment and tools.

Tip: Determine whether your changes reduced the number of pieces of equipment or tools used to operate a work process at a given level of output. Identify the types of equipment or tools reduced and the quantity of reduction of each type.

6) Estimate reductions in scrap or waste generated by the work process.

Tip: Determine whether your changes reduced the amount of scrap or waste material generated by the work process. Identify the types of scrap or waste reduced and the quantity of reduction of each type.

7) Estimate reductions in contracted services.

Tip: Determine whether your changes reduced the amount of contracted services (e.g., waste hauling, facility maintenance, product transport) required by the work process. Identify the contracted services reduced and the quantity of reduction of each type.

d. Measure the improvement made to productivity.

Tip: As used in this document, productivity is the units of output produced for each unit of input. The unit of output and input may be a count (e.g., number of products per hour) or a dollar value (e.g., dollars produced per dollar spent). You could, for example, represent labor productivity as 12 units per person hour or as $318.18 in output value produced for $1 of labor cost—assuming that 12 units of output have a value of $7,000 and the cost of one person hour of work is $22 ($7,000 ÷ $22).

There are two types of productivity affected by events: labor and machine. Most commonly, you will report only labor productivity improvements.

1) Determine what units of output and input you will use to measure productivity (i.e., number produced per hour or dollar value of products produced per dollar of cost).

2) Locate the original rate of output per unit of input (i.e., rate *prior* to change).

3) Determine the new rate of output per unit input (i.e., rate *after* change).

e. Measure the improvement made to throughput.

Tip: As used in this document, throughput is the number of units of output produced per unit of time of work process operation. The number of units of output used is the output from *one production line on one shift*. If 1,200 cylinders are filled by one production line per shift and it takes one calendar week of operation to produce that output, then the throughput is 1,200 units per week. If that production line operated five days a week, you could also express the throughput as 240 units per day of work process operation (1,200 units per week ÷ 5 operating days per week).

1) Determine what time unit of work process operation to use in measuring throughput (e.g., one hour, one day, one week, one month, one year).

2) Locate the original rate of output from one production line on one shift per time unit of work process operation (i.e., throughput rate *prior* to change).

   Tip: If there are multiple production lines and shifts and these have different rates of throughput, then find the original rate of output of each production line on each shift for the unit of time you select. Average these rates of output to establish your rate of throughput prior to change.

3) Determine the new rate of output per time unit of work process operation (i.e., throughput rate *after* change).

2. Summarize operating improvements.

   a. Set up a flipchart display to record operating improvements.

      Tip: Exhibit 2 (next page) presents an example of a summary of operating improvements. Use the format of this example to organize your flipchart display. Be sure to enter the initial and final findings for each item relevant to your event. A blank electronic copy of the summary of operating improvements is in the Kaizen Tool Kit. If you have access to an LCD projector, you could fill out this form on a computer linked to the projector and display it on the screen for the team. Or you can print the electronic form, distribute it to the team, and have the team fill it out with you.

   b. Calculate the improvement percentages.

      Tip: For each item measured, enter the finding from the first evaluation into the Original Finding column and the result from the second evaluation into the Post-Change Finding column. If you use the electronic form in the Kaizen Tool Kit, the improvement percentages will be computed automatically. Otherwise, compute the differences between the original and post-change findings for each item (e.g., distances traversed, cycle time, value-added ratio, amount of each type of waste). Then divide each difference by the original value and multiply the answer by 100% to produce the improvement percentage. For example, if the first observation of the work process showed that travel/transport consumed 10 minutes of the cycle time for human operations and the post-improvement observation showed it consuming 3 minutes, then you would have produced a difference of 7 minutes (10 - 3) and made a 70% reduction in travel/transport ([7 ÷ 10] x 100%). Enter improvement percentages into the Improvement column.

Exhibit 2. Example of a Summary of Operating Improvements			
Work Process Element	**Original Finding**	**Post-Change Finding**	**Improvement**
Human Operations			
■ Distance (in feet)	6,000	120	98%
■ Cycle time	03:21:00	02:15:00	33%
■ Value-added ratio	0.02	0.44	2,100%
■ Travel/transport	00:44:13	00:16:12	63%
■ Motion	00:36:11	00:12:09	66%
■ Wait	00:02:01	00:02:01	0%
■ Interruption	0	0	0%
■ Search	0	0	0%
■ Inspect	00:26:08	00:17:33	33%
■ Rework	0	0	0%
■ Setup	01:18:23	00:27:00	66%
■ Unnecessary processing	00:10:03	0	100%
■ Hazard	3 found	3 removed	
Machine Operations			
■ No formal measurements of machine operations were completed. No changes observed.			
Other Operating Improvements			
■ Inventory (cylinders - empty units)	1,000	250	75%
■ Materials or supplies - plastic holders used per year	12,000	0	100%
■ Energy or other utilities	No effect	No effect	No effect
■ Equipment or tools (# of presses needed)	16	14	13%
■ Facility (square feet needed)	5,000	4,000	20%
■ Scrap or waste	No effect	No effect	No effect
■ Contracted services	No effect	No effect	No effect
■ Labor productivity (output units per person/hour)	12	16	33%
■ Throughput (units per line/shift/week)	1,200	1,600	33%

In the case of value-added ratio, labor productivity, and throughout, the calculation produces a negative improvement percentage because the post-change number is higher than the pre-change number. In these three instances, just omit the minus sign when manually computing these percentages. The electronic form provided in the Kaizen Tool Kit automatically makes this adjustment to its calculations.

1) Compute the difference produced for each item measured.

   Tip: Original finding - post-change finding = difference produced.

2) Compute improvement percentages.

   Tip: (Difference produced ÷ original finding) x 100% = improvement percentage.

3) Record the improvement percentages.

   Tip: Record the percentages in the Improvement column. Omit the minus sign when reporting the percentage for value-added ratio, labor productivity, and throughout if you have manually computed these values.

3. Calculate monetary benefits.

   Tip: This process (Exhibit 3) begins by determining the value of labor savings and machine savings, if machine observations were formally completed. Next the process calculates the savings from other operating improvements made and computes the dollar gains generated by event improvements. After each computation, it determines how much of the benefits should be categorized as hard and soft. Finally, the process documents whether the changes made by the event produced any new costs.

Exhibit 3. Calculate Monetary Benefits

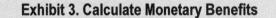

| Determine the Value of Labor Savings | | Determine the Value of Machine Savings | | Determine the Value of Other Operating Improvements | | Determine the Value of Revenue and Profit Gains | | Calculate New Costs Required by Improvements |

---

a. Determine the value of labor savings.

1) Calculate the amount of labor time saved.

   Tip: Labor time savings is the annual number of employee and contractor hours that was reduced by shortening the cycle time for human operations. *Do not report labor savings* if the time saved in human operations will be used inside the same work process to generate a greater level of output. In this case, capture the benefits of your labor savings as dollar gains through the sale of the additional outputs that will result from increased throughput (see Doing Substep 3d, page 363).

a) Obtain operating information from the team or work process manager.

Tip: You need to know how many days per year the work process operates. You already know how many lines and shifts exist (Item B8 of the scope document). Check with the team members for the number of days per year the work process is up. If it varies, get an average. If the team members are not sure, check with the work process manager.

b) Compute the time saved in human operations.

Tip: Look at the total reduction in the cycle time of human operations reported in your summary of operating improvements.

c) Compute the annual amount of labor time saved.

Tip: This calculation is done in two steps. First, determine how many work process cycles occur per year. Find out how many cycles of the work process are executed each day across all lines and shifts, then multiply this number by the number of days the work process is up during a year. Second, compute the total labor time reduced for one year by multiplying the number of work process cycles executed per year by the labor time the event reduced in one cycle. Report this result in hours so that you can easily compute its dollar value.

See an example of how to determine the amount of labor time saved in Exhibit 4.

Exhibit 4. Example of Calculating Labor Time Savings

Tim and his Kaizen team trimmed 2.5 hours from the work process cycle time. It was all in human operations. That work process ran on three lines and three shifts per day. On each line, the work process was executed two times per shift. Tim and his team sat down to figure out how much time they saved per year. First, the team figured out how many cycles of the work process occurred in one day. That was simple. It ran two times per day, line, and shift and there are three lines per shift. So, it ran six times per shift (2 runs per line x 3 lines) and 18 times per day (6 times per shift x 3 shifts). The company operated the process 365 days per year, so the team quickly determined that the work process executed a total of 6,570 cycles per year (18 cycles per day x 365 days). The team finished its calculations by determining that the event saved the company 16,425 labor hours per year (2.5 labor hours per day x 6,570 cycles).

---

2) Calculate the labor dollars saved annually.

Tip: Compute the dollar value of the labor time savings by multiplying the cost of labor per unit of time and the annual amount of time saved.

a) Obtain financial information from the work process manager or the comptroller.

Tip: Get the "loaded" hourly cost for each type of employee performing the work process (e.g., hourly staff and salaried staff). The loaded hourly cost includes not only the salary paid the performer but the value of fringe benefits and other costs the company may assign. Be sure to get the overtime rates if the work process uses overtime labor. Obtain the hourly rate for contract workers and their overtime rates.

b) Divide the labor time among the types of workers.

Tip: For example, if both employees and contract workers performed the work process, separate the total time saved into employee time and contractor time. Also, if the employee time you saved included both hourly and salaried employees, make this division as well. You need to break up labor time so that you can multiply the hours saved by the right pay rate.

c) Multiply the total hours of labor time saved per year by the pay rate appropriate to the performer group.

Tip: For example, use the loaded hourly cost for hourly employees, the loaded hourly cost for salaried employees, and the hourly rate for contract workers. Add these dollar computations together (if there is more than one performer group). The result of these calculations is the dollar value of the labor time the event's improvements reduced for one year of operation of the target work process.

Exhibit 5 provides an example of how to calculate labor dollars saved annually.

Exhibit 5. Example of Calculating the Labor Dollars Saved Annually

Tim and his Kaizen team now understood that they had saved the company 16,425 labor hours per year. The next question the team tackled was: "How much money was that?" They looked over the sources of labor for the work process. The performers were hourly workers and contractors. The team checked with the work process manager who told them that only a quarter of all the workers on the line were contracted. "The rest are ours." With this information, the team divided the total labor saved (16,425) into two bundles: hourly employees 12,318.75 hours (75% employees x 16,425 total hour saving per year) and contractors 4,106.25 hours (25% contractor workers x 16,425 total hour saving per year). Figuring the dollar savings was now easy to do. The loaded labor rate for hourly workers was $22.80 per hour so the team saved the company $280,867.50 per year in employee labor costs. The cost of contract workers was slightly less at $20 per hour so the savings were $82,125. Together, the total annual labor dollar savings from the event was an impressive $362,992.50.

---

3) Determine hard and soft labor dollar savings.

a) Identify the hard labor dollar savings.

Tip: Hard labor savings are cost reductions that begin when the event ends. This means money that would be spent in making the work process run is *not* spent. Be careful in assigning employee labor savings as hard when employees are redeployed to "other productive work." Make sure that this other work produces benefit for the company and that the company would have had to incur additional costs to execute that work had labor not been freed by the event.

b) Identify the soft labor dollar savings.

Tip: Soft labor savings are labor cost reductions that are not realized immediately when the event ends. This means that the level of spending on labor continues at the same rate as before the event. Essentially, any dollar labor savings that are not identified as hard savings become soft savings.

4) Document the labor dollars saved annually.

Tip: Record the labor dollars saved annually on a flipchart page identifying the total amount saved by performer group and how much of the total was assigned as hard or soft savings (see example in Exhibit 6).

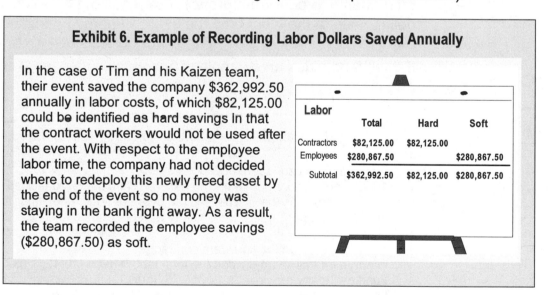

Exhibit 6. Example of Recording Labor Dollars Saved Annually

In the case of Tim and his Kaizen team, their event saved the company $362,992.50 annually in labor costs, of which $82,125.00 could be identified as hard savings In that the contract workers would not be used after the event. With respect to the employee labor time, the company had not decided where to redeploy this newly freed asset by the end of the event so no money was staying in the bank right away. As a result, the team recorded the employee savings ($280,867.50) as soft.

Labor	Total	Hard	Soft
Contractors	$82,125.00	$82,125.00	
Employees	$280,867.50		$280,867.50
Subtotal	$362,992.50	$82,125.00	$280,867.50

b. Determine the value of machine savings.

Tip: If your event focused on improving machine operations and you completed formal measurements of machine performance, you will need to determine and report the value of machine savings. For guidance, see Guide: Determining the Value of Machine Savings, beginning on page 369. If your event did not focus on improving machine operations or complete formal measurements of machine performance, proceed to the next substep.

c. Determine the value of other operating improvements.

1) Review the list of other operating improvements.

   Tip: These improvements are listed in your summary of operating improvements (example presented in Exhibit 2, page 358).

2) Compute the annual dollar savings from other operating improvements.

   a) Determine the cost of each operating item prior to the event.

      Tip: Find out from the work process manager or comptroller the cost assigned to the work process the year prior to the event for each item. You may need to do some computations if the cost information available is per unit and not an aggregate. For example, the person may know the cost per square foot of facility space or the cost per unit of a material used in the work process. If you receive a unit cost, multiply it by the number of units listed for the feature in the Original Finding column of your summary of operating improvements.

   b) Determine the annual savings.

      Tip: Compute the value of savings from each other operating improvement by multiplying the annual cost of the item by the improvement percentage listed for the item.

3) Assign savings to either hard or soft categories.

   Tip: Allocate the portion of savings realized immediately when the event ends to the hard savings category. Any dollar savings that are not identified as hard savings are assigned to soft savings.

4) Document the dollar value of savings from other operating improvements.

   Tip: Record the annual savings from each item on a flipchart page. Identify the item, the total amount saved, and how much of the total is hard or soft savings (see Exhibit 7, next page).

d. Determine the value of revenue and profit gains.

1) Review the possible sources of dollar gains an event may produce.

   Tip: Dollar gains are additional revenues and profits that come to the company as a result of actions taken in the event. Exhibit 8 (next page) lists some of the possible sources of dollar gains a Kaizen event may produce.

2) List the sources of dollar gains produced by your event.

3) Gather the information you need to compute dollar gains.

   Tip: You need information about each product whose sales, unit cost, or pricing your event affected. If the event produced a new use for an existing product as well as added throughput of the product for the current use, then you need sales, unit cost, and profit information about both the new and original uses of the product.

Exhibit 7. Example of Recording Savings From Other Operating Improvements

Tim and his Kaizen team were anxious to see the savings they produced from other operating improvements. Exhibit 2 (page 358) lists the other operating improvements their event generated. The team divided up the computing task. Mack and Jane dealt with inventory reductions. The work process originally required 1,000 empty cylinders

Non-Labor	Total	Hard	Soft
Cyl.	$71,250	$71,250	$0
Space	$45,000	$0	$45,000
Etc.			

maintained in inventory at a cost of $95/unit. The annual inventory cost prior to the event was $95,000 (1,000 units x $95/unit). The event reduced inventory by 75% or $71,250 ($95,000 original cost x 75% improvement).

Benito and Nikki computed the facility space savings. They found that the work process is charged $45/square foot for facility space. The yearly cost for facility space was $225,000 before the event. The event produced a savings of $45,000 ($225,000 original cost x 20% improvement).

Item by item, the team computed the annual savings from each improvement and then allocated the savings to the categories of hard or soft.

You require both prior year information and projections for the subsequent year. The projections should reflect the effects of the Kaizen event only and not other market or business factors. For example, if the event produces greater throughput enabling a business to satisfy unmet demand for a product, then the portion of increased sales enabled by the Kaizen improvements should be reported. Do not report projected sales increases due to other reasons (e.g., a new plant coming online).

Exhibit 8. Possible Sources of Dollar Gains

Sustained Increases in Ongoing Revenue or Profit Due to...

■ Meeting unmet demand by improving throughput over the same production line

■ Enhancing value to the customer of an existing product or service, thereby supporting higher pricing

■ Elevating market share by enhancing product or service value to the customer

■ Selling a new product conceived during the event

■ Selling an existing product to new markets by uncovering a new use for the product during the event

One-Time Dollar Gains Due to...

■ Sale of assets no longer needed

If the Kaizen event enabled premium pricing by adding a customer-valued feature and held the unit cost of the product stable, then the event produced both an increase in revenues and profitability. Be sure to report both gains. Exhibit 9 list the types of information you need to collect.

Exhibit 9. Information Typically Needed to Compute Dollar Gains for Each Product Affected by the Kaizen Event

Item	Last Year[1]	Projection for Next Year
Sales Volume		
Price per Unit		
Profit per Unit		
Revenue From Sale of Freed Assets		

[1]New products or existing products sold for new uses will not have prior year information.

4) Compute the total annual dollar gains.

   Tip: See Guide: Computing Dollar Gains (page 371) for guidance on how to compute dollar gains.

5) Decide the hard and soft dollar gains.

   Tip: Allocate the portion of gains realized immediately when the event ends to the hard category. Any dollar gains that are not identified as hard are assigned to the soft category. For a gain to be categorized as hard, the increase in revenues and profits must begin immediately after the conclusion of the event. This means that there need to be orders in hand prior to the event that the Kaizen improvements now permit the company to fulfill and that, without the event, the company would not have been able to fill within the same reporting period. Other than the circumstance of existing orders that cannot be filled or the sale of freed assets before the end of an event, it is unlikely that any gains from an event can be counted as hard since increased sales revenues and profits require future action by the company (e.g., its salespeople) and customers.

6) Document the dollar gains from the event.

   Tip: Record the identified monetary gains from the event on a flipchart page. Identify the item, the annual amount gained, and how much of the total is hard or soft. See example in Exhibit 10, next page.

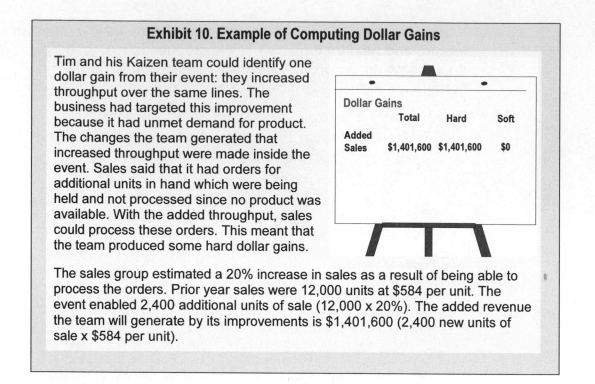

Exhibit 10. Example of Computing Dollar Gains

Tim and his Kaizen team could identify one dollar gain from their event: they increased throughput over the same lines. The business had targeted this improvement because it had unmet demand for product. The changes the team generated that increased throughput were made inside the event. Sales said that it had orders for additional units in hand which were being held and not processed since no product was available. With the added throughput, sales could process these orders. This meant that the team produced some hard dollar gains.

Dollar Gains	Total	Hard	Soft
Added Sales	$1,401,600	$1,401,600	$0

The sales group estimated a 20% increase in sales as a result of being able to process the orders. Prior year sales were 12,000 units at $584 per unit. The event enabled 2,400 additional units of sale (12,000 x 20%). The added revenue the team will generate by its improvements is $1,401,600 (2,400 new units of sale x $584 per unit).

e. Calculate new costs required by improvements.

Tip: List and total the items of new cost. Allocate the portion of the total to hard costs if the expenditures are made during the event; allocate them to soft costs if they will be made after the event. These new expenses will be subtracted from the total of savings and gains to determine the net monetary benefits from the event.

4. Summarize monetary benefits.

Tip: Complete the summary of monetary benefits. See Exhibit 11 (next page) for an example. A blank electronic copy of Exhibit 11 is in the Kaizen Tool Kit. The table automatically calculates totals. Include in your summary all savings and dollar gains generated by the Kaizen event.

Following Up Substeps

1. Verify operating improvements.

Tip: Review the summary of operating improvements with the team. Decide whether all improvements have been listed and properly documented. Add or correct any items as needed.

2. Verify monetary benefits.

Tip: Review the summary of monetary benefits with the team. Decide whether it includes all savings and gains generated by the Kaizen event. Decide whether all benefits have been properly computed. Add or correct any items as needed.

Exhibit 11. Example of a Summary of Monetary Benefits			
Monetary Benefit	**Total Value**	**Hard**	**Soft**
Labor Dollar Savings			
■ All workers	$362,993.00	$82,125.00	$280,868.00
Subtotals	$362,993.00	$82,125.00	$280,868.00
Savings From Other Operating Improvements			
■ Inventory - cylinders - empty units	$71,250.00	$71,250.00	$0.00
■ Materials or supplies - plastic holders used per year	$120.00	$120.00	$0.00
■ Energy or other utilities	$0.00	$0.00	$0.00
■ Equipment or tools - number of presses needed	$50,000.00	0.00	$50,000.00
■ Facility - square feet needed	$45,000.00	0.00	$45,000.00
■ Scrap or waste	$0.00	$0.00	$0.00
■ Contracted services	$0.00	$0.00	$0.00
Dollar Gains			
■ New sales to satisfy unmet demand	$1,401,600.00	$1,401,600.00	$0.00
Subtotals	1,930,963.00	1,555,095.00	375,868.00
Less New Expenses			
■ New tools	$260.00	$60.00	$200.00
Total Expenses	$260.00	$60.00	$200.00
Summary			
Net Benefits	$362,733.00	$82,065.00	$280,668.00

3. Update the Kaizen event documentation.

   Tip: Modify the summary of operating improvements and the summary of monetary benefits as needed based on team feedback.

Check Steps

Use the following checklist to verify that the step was done correctly.

Benchmark	√
Getting Ready Substeps	
1. Reviewed how to measure results.	☐
Doing Substeps	
1. Measured operating improvements.	☐
2. Summarized operating improvements.	☐
3. Calculated monetary benefits.	☐
4. Summarized monetary benefits.	☐
Following Up Substeps	
1. Verified operating improvements.	☐
2. Verified monetary benefits.	☐
3. Updated the Kaizen event documentation.	☐

Tips

- Be conservative in your estimate of all savings and gains. Credibility is as important to achieve as capturing every last dollar of value produced.

- Although we compute and report savings and gains for one year, these monetary benefits typically continue to be produced for multiple years. Understand this so that you can help others appreciate that the report you and the team will make is a "low end" estimate of the monetary benefits resulting from the Kaizen event.

Guide:
Determining the Value of Machine Savings

Steps

1. Calculate the amount of machine time saved.

   Tip: Machine time saved is the annual number of hours of machine operation that was reduced by shortening the cycle time. *Do not report machine savings* if the time saved in machine operations will be used inside the same work process to generate a greater level of output. In this case, capture the benefits of your machine savings as dollar gains through sale of the additional outputs that will result from increased throughput (see Doing Substep 3d, page 363).

   a. Obtain operating information from the team or work process manager.

      Tip: You need to know how many days per year the work process operates. You already know how many lines and shifts exist (Item B8 of the scope document). Check with the team members for the number of days per year the work process is up. If it varies, get an average. If the team members are not sure, check with the work process manager.

   b. Compute the time saved in machine operations.

      Tip: Look at the total reduction in the cycle time for machine operations reported in your summary of operating improvements.

   c. Compute the annual amount of machine time saved.

      Tip: This calculation is done in two steps. First, determine how many work process cycles occur per year. Find out how many cycles of the work process are executed each day across all lines and shifts, then multiply this number by the number of days the work process is up during a year. Second, compute the total machine time reduced for one year by multiplying the number of work process cycles executed per year by the machine time the event reduced in one cycle. Report this result in hours so that you can easily compute its dollar value.

2. Calculate the machine dollars saved annually.

   Tip: Compute the dollar value of the machine time savings by multiplying the cost of machine use per unit of time and the annual amount of time saved.

   a. Get the hourly operating cost for each type of machine performing the work process.

Guide:
Determining the Value of Machine Savings (continued)

b. Divide the machine time among the types of machines.

   Tip: Use your Machine Analysis Sheet to guide you in allocating cycle time reduction among the machines used in the work process.

c. Multiply the total hours of machine time saved per year by the rate appropriate to each machine.

3. Assign savings to hard and soft categories.

   Tip: Allocate the portion of savings realized immediately when the event ends to the hard savings category. Any dollar savings not identified as hard savings are assigned to soft savings.

4. Document the dollar value of savings from improvements in machine operations.

   Tip: Record the annual savings from machine operating improvements on a flipchart page. Identify the total amount saved and how much of the total is hard or soft savings.

Guide:
Computing Dollar Gains

Source of Gain	Method
Improved Throughput	Compute the expected increase in units sold as a result of the improved throughput. Multiply this increase by the price per unit. This will give you the revenue gain produced by the added throughput.
Higher Pricing	*Revenue Gain* Compute the difference in selling price enabled by the new product features. Multiply this price addition by the projected number of units to be sold annually. Deduct from this total gain in revenue any increased cost required to produce the enhanced product. *Profit Gain* Identify the difference in unit profit enabled by the new product features. Multiply this amount by the projected number of units to be sold annually.
Elevated Market Share	Identify the percentage of added market share due to actions taken in the Kaizen event. Compute the expected annual increase in units sold as a result of the improved market share. Multiply this unit increase by the price per unit. This will give you the revenue gain produced by the event-enabled increase in market share.
New Product Sales	Identify the expected number of units of the new product that the company will sell annually. Multiply this quantity by the price per unit. This will give you the revenue gain produced by the new product.
Sales of an Existing Product to New Markets	Identify the expected number of units of the product that the company will sell annually in its new market. Multiply this quantity by the price per unit. This will give you the revenue gain produced by the sale of the existing product to new markets.
Sale of Asset No Longer Needed	Obtain the sales price and cost of making the sale. Compute the gain by subtracting from the selling price any cost associated with selling the asset.

Note: This table presents simplified methods of computation. They do not address every nuance in computing gains but provide a good estimate. For example, when making a new product offering, it is possible that the new product will depress sales of an existing product. This loss in revenue should be subtracted from the gain in revenue produced by the new product that evolved from the Kaizen event.

Step D4-S3. Conduct a Pilot

Preview

This step implements an improvement for a portion of a work process or workplace. A pilot:

- allows you to introduce a work process or workplace improvement in a phased manner rather than all at once,
- provides insights and information that enable full-scale rollout of a change, and
- satisfies management requirements when a pilot is needed before implementing a systemwide change.

Getting Ready Substeps

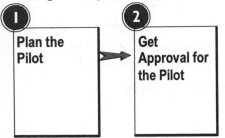

Doing Substeps

Following Up Substeps

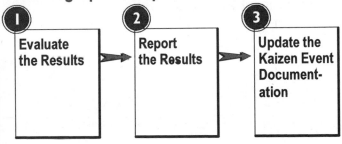

Purpose

To implement an improvement for a portion of a work process or workplace.

Benefit

- Allows you to introduce a work process or workplace improvement in a phased manner rather than all at once.
- Provides insights and information that enable full-scale rollout of a change.
- Satisfies management requirements when a pilot is needed before implementing a systemwide change.

Application

Use this knowledge whenever (1) you have an improvement idea for which some element of information or knowledge is missing that is needed for the full-scale use of an idea, (2) the management of change procedure for the workplace requires it, or (3) a one-step rollout of the idea across the entire workplace is not the best way to implement the change.

Performer

Kaizen leader, co-leader, and team.

Resources

People

- Kaizen team
- Maintenance supervisor
- Manager of the target work process
- Performers of the target work process
- Safety supervisor
- Work standards supervisor

Information, Knowledge, and Training

- Action plan for implementing the improvement
- Contractual agreements (e.g., with customers, unions) that affect the target work process
- Description of the target work process
- Goals for the event

- Government regulations applicable to the target work process
- Integrated list of improvement ideas obtained from the workers in the target work process
- Machine Analysis Sheet and related charts
- Mission statement
- Procedure for modifying work process or workplace layout standards
- Process Analysis Sheet and related charts
- Report of the results from an experiment on the improvement idea
- Safety rules
- Summary of findings
- Work standards for the target work process

Materials, Tools, and other Resources

- Space, equipment, and supplies to support the team's work

Room/Tables/Chairs
- Chairs
- Meeting area for the final report to all stakeholders
- Meeting area for the full team available every day
- Multiple small group meeting areas
- Tables
- Wall space for hanging storyboards and materials
- Wheelchair-accessible areas
- Wheelchair-accessible tables

Equipment - General
- Calculators
- Computer printer or access to one
- Copier or access to one
- Digital camera
- Flipchart easels or hangers
- Foam board 3'x5' (1/4")
- Label maker
- Laminator
- Laptop computer with Microsoft Office 2000® and Adobe Acrobat Reader® 4.0 or higher
- LCD computer projector
- Overhead projector
- Projection screen
- Stopwatches
- Tape measures
- Telephone for conferencing
- Wheels for measuring travel distances

Supplies
- Clear tape
- Clipboards
- Colored tape
- Double-sided tape
- Erasers
- Flashlights
- Flipchart markers
- Flipchart pads
- Flow pens
- Graph paper
- Laminating sheets
- Magnifying glasses
- Masking tape
- Multicolored Post-its® - 3"x5"
- Name tags

- Notebooks
- Pens and pencils
- Printer paper (white and colored)

- Roll of white paper (34"x44")
- Ruler
- Scissors

- Small tool kit (screwdriver, pliers, wrench)
- Transparency film (for a copier)
- Utility knife

- Kaizen Tool Kit
  - Design of the Pilot
  - Guide: Planning the Pilot
  - Results of the Pilot

Output

- Design of the pilot
- Results of the pilot

Method

Getting Ready Substeps

1. Plan the pilot.

   Tip: Use the guidance provided in Guide: Planning the Pilot (pages 381–82) to lead the team in thinking through its approach to the pilot. Record the team's thinking on a flipchart page. Be sure to incorporate any requirements specified in the work standards change procedure. Once the plan is complete, enter it into the electronic form provided in the Kaizen Tool Kit.

   a. Formulate the questions to be asked and answered by the pilot.

   Tip: Be sure to include questions to which key stakeholders will want answers as well as any questions dictated by the procedure for modifying work process or workplace layout standards.

   b. Identify the information the pilot needs to collect.

   Tip: This information includes the facts needed to answer the questions posed for the pilot as well as provide information required by the work standards change procedure.

   c. Decide the scope of the pilot.

   Tip: Where will the pilot take place? When will it begin? For how long will it be implemented? The typical length of a pilot is from one to three months. Set the period of the pilot so that there is sufficient time to uncover the information you need or to satisfy the time period prescribed in the work standards change procedure.

d. Identify who will implement the pilot.

Tip: Since pilots usually extend past the week of the Kaizen event, a special team may need to be identified to lead its implementation. Select team members based on expertise and availability.

e. Identify a source for each element of information needed.

Tip: List the source for each element of information and the method by which it will be collected, recorded, and retained. Answer the question: "Who or what can tell us the information we need to answer the questions we have posed?" The source may be a person, a machine measurement, or records maintained in the workplace.

f. Identify the method for acquiring the needed information.

Tip: The method should identify who will be responsible for collecting each item of information, when it will be collected, how it will be recorded, and where it will be stored. It should also identify the steps for summarizing and reporting the information, including who will perform these steps and when.

g. Define criteria for judging what the information says about each question to which key stakeholders want an answer.

Tip: For each question you must answer, state the decision rule that will determine the answer. The decision rule is written in the form of an "IF...THEN" statement: "If we observe [information found], then we will conclude [question plus answer]." For example, "If we observe no complaints from workers about problems in moving around the workplace as a result of moving the XYZ tools to a location five feet to the right of the existing workstation, then we will conclude that moving the XYZ tools does not disrupt traffic patterns in the workplace."

h. Adjust the action plan developed to guide the execution of the improvement.

Tip: The action plan was developed in *Task D4. Act to Improve the Target Work Process*, pages 339–40. Adjust the action plan so that it is consistent with the plan for the pilot. Make sure it contains steps for collecting the operating and impact information the pilot must produce.

i. Finalize the design.

Tip: Review the plan and decide if the pilot's scope is appropriate and whether it will produce answers to all the questions that need to be resolved. Also confirm that the pilot satisfies any management of change requirements. Once the design is final, document it using the electronic form provided in the Kaizen Tool Kit.

2. Get approval for the pilot.

Tip: Print the description of the pilot and attach a copy of the action plan for implementing the improvement. Provide these documents to the manager of the work process and obtain his or her approval. Ask who else should review the plan before it is executed and check with these parties as well.

Doing Substeps

1. Conduct the pilot.

Tip: Follow the action plan in implementing the improvement. Follow the plan for the pilot in collecting, recording, and storing information generated by the pilot.

Following Up Substeps

1. Evaluate the results.

   a. Analyze the information.

   Tip: Organize the information from the pilot. Relate the information you collected to questions the pilot must answer. Analyze the results, doing statistical tests as required. Summarize the findings with respect to each question the pilot must answer.

   b. Decide the answer to each question posed.

   Tip: Apply the decision rules established in the plan for the pilot.

   c. Extract and apply any learning from the pilot.

   Tip: A pilot may generate learning about how the improvement idea may be enhanced (e.g., resequence steps or reposition equipment) as well as how best to implement it (e.g., what training to provide performers). Apply the learning to improve the idea or the method for implementing the improvement throughout the workplace.

   d. Document the results of the pilot.

   Tip: Complete the remaining sections of the form included in the Kaizen Tool Kit. Record the results, conclusions about further rollout of the improvement, and any learning developed from the pilot.

2. Report the results.

Tip: Distribute print copies of the description of the pilot to the Kaizen team. Obtain feedback about what was found and concluded. Adjust the write-up of the pilot as needed. Provide a copy of the completed pilot information to each person who reviewed the plan for the pilot and post a copy in the workplace so that employees can view the results.

3. Update the Kaizen event documentation.

Tip: Modify the electronic form in the Kaizen Tool Kit based on feedback from the team or other stakeholders.

Check Steps

Use the following checklist to verify that the step was done correctly.

Benchmark	√
Getting Ready Substeps	
1. Planned the pilot.	☐
2. Got approval for the pilot.	☐
Doing Substeps	
1. Conducted the pilot.	☐
Following Up Substeps	
1. Evaluated the results.	☐
2. Reported the results.	☐
3. Updated the Kaizen event documentation.	☐

Tips

- Be thorough in answering the design questions. Involve people with expertise in planning the pilot. Make sure your design satisfies management of change requirements, if these exist.

Guide:
Planning the Pilot

Improvement	Enter the name of the improvement to be piloted.
Scope	■ Identify where within the workplace or with whom the improvement will be implemented. ■ Enter when the pilot will begin and for how long it will continue.
Conducted By	List the team members who will conduct the pilot.
Questions to Be Answered	Enter the questions to be asked and answered by the pilot (e.g., sustainability of the improvement; effects of the improvement on other operations, contractual agreements, or compliance with government regulations; what to keep in mind as the improvement is rolled out to the entire work process).
Information Needed	List the information needed to answer each question.
Sources and Methods	■ List the source for each element of information. The source may be a person, a machine measurement, or records maintained in the workplace. ■ Describe the method by which this information will be collected, recorded, and retained. Identify the steps for summarizing and reporting the information including who will perform these steps and when. Use the Method Questions for Planning a Pilot to help you describe the pilot's method (page 381).
Decision Rule	Identify how you will decide if the results from the pilot are sufficient to support further rollout of the improvement.
Action Plan	Attach a copy of the action plan for implementing the improvement idea.
Results	■ List the answers to each question documented above. ■ Add the results to this document when the pilot is completed.
Conclusion About Further Rollout of Improvement	■ State whether the results of the pilot support using the improvement throughout the workplace. ■ Add the conclusion to this document when the pilot is completed.
Learning	List guidelines derived from the pilot that would be helpful to follow in future implementations of the improvement.

Continued...

Guide:
Planning the Pilot (continued)

Method Questions for Planning a Pilot

Use the following planning questions to guide you in creating a detailed description of your method for ensuring that the information needed to answer the questions posed for the pilot is acquired, analyzed, and reported.

Collecting, Recording, Storing

- Who collects the information?
- When does he/she collect the information?
- How does he/she collect the information?
- How does he/she record the information?
- Where does he/she store the information once it is collected?

Summarizing

- Who summarizes the information?
- When does he/she summarize the information?
- How does he/she summarize the information? (List the steps the person should perform to summarize the information.)
- Where does he/she store the summarized information?

Reporting

- Who prepares the report?
- When does he/she prepare the report?
- How does he/she report the information (e.g., memo, annual report, posts on bulletin board)?
- To whom is the report communicated? By what date?

Milestone E. Institutionalize the Process Improvements

Preview

This milestone ensures that the improvements made by the Kaizen event generate maximum benefits for the business and its stakeholders. Institutionalization:

- sustains the use of the business improvements made during the Kaizen event,

- ensures the transfer of soft into hard benefits,

- replicates improvements across all workplaces where they are applicable, and

- supports the post-event execution of improvement ideas identified in the follow-through plan.

Getting Ready Tasks

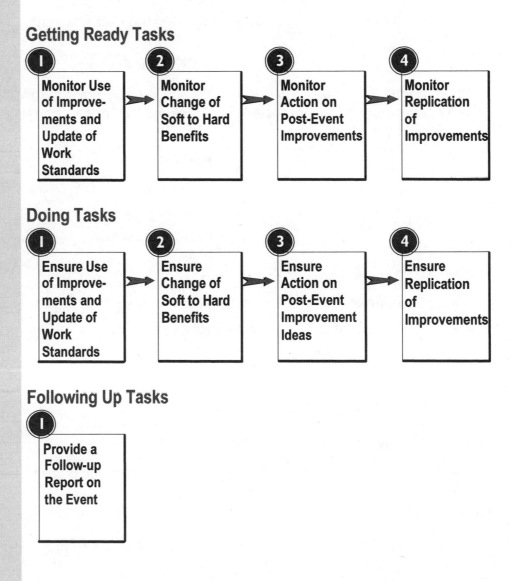

1 Monitor Use of Improvements and Update of Work Standards

2 Monitor Change of Soft to Hard Benefits

3 Monitor Action on Post-Event Improvements

4 Monitor Replication of Improvements

Doing Tasks

1 Ensure Use of Improvements and Update of Work Standards

2 Ensure Change of Soft to Hard Benefits

3 Ensure Action on Post-Event Improvement Ideas

4 Ensure Replication of Improvements

Following Up Tasks

1 Provide a Follow-up Report on the Event

Purpose

To ensure that the improvements made by the Kaizen event generate maximum benefits for the business and its stakeholders.

Benefit

- Sustains the use of the business improvements made during the Kaizen event.
- Ensures the transfer of soft to hard benefits.
- Replicates improvements across all workplaces where they are applicable.
- Supports the post-event execution of improvement ideas identified in the follow-through plan.

Application

Implement this task after you have completed the Kaizen event.

Performer

Kaizen leader and team. The highly interactive nature of this milestone requires that the leader be especially proficient in clarifying, confirming, constructively criticizing, and hitchhiking.

Resources

People

- Designated event coordinator
- Kaizen team
- Maintenance supervisor
- Manager of the target work process
- Performers of the target work process
- Safety supervisor
- Sponsor of the event
- Work standards supervisor

Information, Knowledge, and Training

- Contractual agreements (e.g., with customers, unions) that affect the target work process
- Follow-through plan
- Government regulations applicable to the target work process

- Parking Lot Issues
- Kaizen summary
- Summary of operating improvements
- Summary of monetary benefits
- Leave-behind measure
- Procedure for modifying work process or workplace layout standards
- Safety rules
- Work process improvements developed during the Kaizen event
- Work standards for the target work process
- *Working With Others* (J.S. Byron and P.A. Bierley, Hope, ME: Lowrey Press, 2003) - teaches how to get (clarify and confirm) and give (constructive criticism and hitchhiking) ideas and information in ways that build collaboration and elevate results

Materials, Tools, and Other Resources

- None.

Output

- A business encouraged to and supported in obtaining the best return from the benefits produced by the creative efforts of its employees during the Kaizen event

Method

Getting Ready Tasks

1. Monitor use of improvements and update of work standards.

   Tip: The Kaizen team should be sustaining its work process improvements by completing its post-event improvement meetings as scheduled and maintaining the information displayed in the leave-behind measure. Contact team members periodically to determine whether the meetings are being conducted as planned and the information required by the leave-behind measure is up to date. Also determine the status of continued use of the improvements in the workplace and their affect on work process performance. Finally, contact the person assigned responsibility for getting the Kaizen improvements incorporated into the work standards of the target work process and determine whether the process is occurring as planned.

2. Monitor change of soft to hard benefits.

   Tip: Contact team members and the work process manager periodically to get their perspectives on how improvements are progressing. In your conversations, find out the status of actions to transform soft into hard savings.

3. Monitor action on post-event improvements.

   Tip: The follow-through plan included two improvement ideas to be implemented after the event. Each improvement had an owner with a date for completion and a goal. Each person assigned a follow-through change prepares an action plan as a first step. Inquire about the status of the action plans and their implementation.

4. Monitor replication of improvements.

   Tip: Contact the sponsor of the Kaizen event periodically. Provide an update to him or her about the continued use of the Kaizen improvements, progress in realizing soft gains and executing post-event improvements, and any new ideas developed by performers of the target work process. Inquire about the status of replication of the Kaizen improvements to other work sites.

Doing Tasks

1. Ensure use of improvements and update of work standards.

   Tip: Help the team identify and remove obstacles to sustained use of the Kaizen improvements. Intervene as necessary to assist performers in getting support from their managers for decisions, actions, or resources needed to enable the business to continue to benefit from the Kaizen improvements. Credit the team's ongoing commitment and achievements and encourage the work process manager to do the same.

   Know where in the approval process the request for the work standards changes is and what is needed to move it forward so that you can advocate for action on the change request. Advance the approval process by encouraging, supporting, and otherwise influencing decision-makers to incorporate process improvements into the official work standards. The first level of advocacy is simply showing interest in the progress of the request and communicating to all parties the business benefits that are being delayed or lost as a result of inaction.

2. Ensure change of soft to hard benefits.

   Tip: Help the work process manager identify and remove obstacles to transforming soft to hard monetary benefits. Intervene as necessary with the manager's superiors to assist in getting decisions, actions, or resources needed to enable the business to reap *as real dollars* the soft benefits the Kaizen event produced.

3. Ensure action on post-event improvement ideas.

   Tip: Help the employees assigned responsibility for executing the improvement ideas complete their action plans. Assist them in identifying and removing obstacles to applying the improvements should any be encountered. Intervene as necessary to assist performers in getting support from their manager for decisions, actions, or resources needed to execute the improvements. Credit the workers' ongoing commitment and achievements and encourage the work process manager to do likewise.

4. Ensure replication of improvements.

   Tip: Help the sponsor of the Kaizen event identify and remove obstacles to replicating the Kaizen improvements to other work sites.

Following Up Tasks

1. Provide a follow-up report on the event.

   Tip: This written report should summarize the findings with respect to continued use of improvements made during the Kaizen event, adoption of new work standards, realization of soft monetary benefits, implementation of post-event improvements, and replication of improvements to other work sites. Do this report at the six-month anniversary of the Kaizen event. Include recognition for the additional monetary benefits produced by replication and by transforming soft to hard benefits. Direct the report to the sponsor of the Kaizen event, but share it with the Kaizen team and the manager of the target work process. Be sure to credit the contributions of all who helped sustain and increase the benefits from the Kaizen event.

Check Steps

Use the following checklist to verify that the milestone was accomplished.

Benchmark	√
Getting Ready Tasks	
1. Monitored use of improvements and update of work standards.	☐
2. Monitored change of soft to hard benefits.	☐
3. Monitored action on post-event improvements.	☐
4. Monitored replication of improvements.	☐
Doing Tasks	
1. Ensured use of improvements and update of work standards.	☐
2. Ensured change of soft to hard benefits.	☐
3. Ensured action on post-event improvement ideas.	☐
4. Ensured replication of improvements.	☐
Following Up Tasks	
1. Provided a follow-up report on the event.	☐

Tips

- Always remember that you are basically a coach and an advisor in this effort to institutionalize the improvements from the Kaizen event. You need to work *through other people* by helping them understand the business benefits of acting and enabling them to see how they can act to realize those benefits.

Customizing the Kaizen Process

Preview

This section presents advice on how to tailor the Kaizen process to meet different needs and how to position Kaizen within larger improvement initiatives.

Topics

First Things First

You seek to become a Kaizen leader and be able to produce the business benefits that Kaizen promises. Your challenge is to develop your skill in executing Kaizen. To guide your own development, you need to be able to detect how well you are achieving and, if your success is less than optimum, how you need to modify what you are doing. In trying to answer these questions, you face three unknowns:

1. What results should I expect to produce?

2. What process will generate these results?

3. Am I sufficiently proficient in using this process to produce its results?

If you can't answer these questions, your task in building your proficiency is much harder. For example, how will you detect if your results are less than optimum if you do not know what results to expect? How can you decide whether you took the right steps to produce the results if you do not know whether the process you used works? And, if you cannot answer the first two questions, the answer to the third question is neither possible nor important.

Following the *Kaizen Desk Reference Standard* eliminates the first two unknowns and puts you in a better position to manage your own development successfully. The process documented in this book has a known profile of results. Further, it has reliably produced these benefits both when executed by the people who developed it and by people who have been trained and certified in it. When you start your development efforts, you therefore understand what results you should realize and know what process will produce those results.

These "knowns" allow you to diagnose your own performance. First, you can compare what you produced to the results you should have produced. If there is no match, you can check what you did against what the process specifies. If there still is no match, you understand that you need to complete the process entirely. If there *is* a match, then you can focus on detecting in which tasks you require greater proficiency and drive your development efforts to build that proficiency.

If, however, you deviate from the *Kaizen Desk Reference Standard before* you achieve mastery, the task of managing and directing your own development is much harder. For example, if the results you produce are not satisfactory, was it because your changes to the process undermined its effectiveness, you failed to execute your new process well enough, or perhaps you failed to execute well enough the retained elements of the standard process? How will you know?

It is in the spirit of supporting your learning efforts that we encourage you to stick with the process until you can produce its results reliably. In this spirit we say, "first things first." Master the method presented in this book, then consider tailoring the process based on the new learning you will develop and the guidance provided in this unit.

Tailoring the Process

The most common reasons for modifying the Kaizen process are (1) the desire to accelerate Kaizen, (2) the need to address an "office" application, (3) the use of Kaizen within a just-in-time production system, and (4) the presence of a union within the work setting.

Accelerating Kaizen

There are two focuses for accelerating the Kaizen process—one seeks to shorten the period from request to completion; the other looks to shorten the week of the actual event.

Shortening the Cycle Time of the Kaizen Process

A first-time Kaizen event in a workplace can be conceived, planned, and executed within a five-week period *if* the requesting business, its people, and its business information are accessible when needed. The Kaizen event itself requires no more than five consecutive days. Subsequent events within the same workplace require less than five weeks, since some scope information will already exist and the amount of preparation needed to ready the work process performers and the Kaizen team will be reduced.[1]

Typically, however, the time period from conception to execution takes longer than five weeks because key people are inaccessible, the information needed to plan the event is not available, or the work schedules of proposed team members force a delay in scheduling the event. What can you do about these delays?

One solution to minimizing delays is to be proactive. Take the initiative in educating the business at the time it requests a Kaizen event that the simplest way to accelerate the cycle of performance is to ensure that the key requirements for a timely event are satisfied. The first of these requirements is the ready availability of the people most critical to defining and preparing the event—the designated event coordinator, the key stakeholders, and the proposed members of the Kaizen team. The second requirement is the need for quick access to business information—especially the work standards for the target work process. The third requirement for speed is prompt logistical support from the site where the event will be held. If these requirements are satisfied, the event can occur within five weeks at a maximum. You especially need to stress that control of this cycle time is in the hands of the business, not you as the Kaizen leader. Assuming that the business acts expeditiously, your preparation work will require no more than five person days of effort; the remaining time is a function of the business.

One solution you should *not* take is to succumb to pressure and jettison your process and your professionalism. Not infrequently, a business will attempt to resolve the problem of its people not being available by arguing that you really do not need

---

[1]See *Guidelines for the Sustained Use of Kaizen*, pages 400–04, for additional ways to shorten the cycle time for Kaizen events.

the information you seek because the problem is straightforward, the work process is simple, and everyone is ready to be cooperative. Here again leverage the *Kaizen Desk Reference Standard* to ensure your success. It is *your* work standard. Remind the business that conducting an event that will reliably produce its intended results requires the same discipline and adherence to a standard as producing any product right the first time. Stick to your process. The knowledge embedded within it and your commitment to put it in the service of people define you as a professional.

Shortening the Week of the Event

Sometimes the issue is not the cycle time from request to completion but the requirement that the event take five days. The performance of the event itself can be accelerated. The basic solution is to externalize setup for the event—that is, complete certain activities prior to the event so that they require less time within the week of the actual event. Using this approach, we have completed Kaizen events within three and a half days for a first-time event within a workplace and three days for follow-on events. The key elements to externalize are (1) building the work process description, (2) educating people about Kaizen, (3) teaching the concept of waste and the skill of detecting it, and (4) ensuring that the team has Working With Others skills.[2]

Building the Work Process Description

Do the work process description prior to the event, getting the information from the work standards and from interviews with at least two people knowledgeable of the target work process. One person should be the manager of the target work process; the second should be a performer of the work process. Collect information through telephone conversations, e-mail, or face-to-face conversations as practicable. Draft the description using the guidance in *Step D1-S1. Build a Description of the Target Work Process* and send it to the interviewees for confirmation or adjustment. Finalize the work process description prior to the event or prior to conducting a pre-event orientation should you plan to do one.

Preparing the People

Conduct a one-day pre-event orientation session with the key stakeholders, the performers of the target work process, and the proposed team. Break the session into two parts. Include all participants in the first part and use it to introduce the purpose of the proposed event, educate about Kaizen and how it is executed, and solicit feedback and ideas on how to make the event a success. Include only the Kaizen team in the second part of the session. Focus this meeting on teaching an abridged version of Working With Others skills, educating the Kaizen team about the concept of waste and how to detect it, and solidifying the team's learning by completing some components of the walk through of the target work process (all Getting Ready Substeps and Doing Substeps 1 and 2; see *Step D1-S2. Walk Through the Target Work Process*, pages 218–24). Before doing the walk through, review and confirm with the team the description of the target work process.

---

[2] These skills are delineated in J.S. Byron and P.A. Bierley, *Working With Others* (Hope, ME: Lowrey Press, 2003).

Together, these modifications allow you to complete *Task D1. Focus the Kaizen Event* and *Task D2. Evaluate the Target Work Process* in the first day of the actual event. Solving performance issues can begin the morning of the second day, with action to improve the work process starting in the afternoon and completing on the third day of the event. Depending on the scope of the actions you choose to implement, the close-out meeting with the team and the communication to stakeholders can occur either on the afternoon of Day 3 or the morning of Day 4.

If the requesting business decides to host a pre-event meeting, schedule it for the week before the Kaizen event so that the preparation work is fresh in the team members' minds.

Office Applications

Some people distinguish between "shop Kaizen" and "office Kaizen." They describe shop Kaizen as applying to manufacturing work processes and office Kaizen as applying to all else. We see only one Kaizen. The process described in this book applies to improving *all* work processes. We think the distinction of shop versus office misses the mark. The issue is not location or even industry, it is the nature of the work and the characteristics of the context in which the work is done.

Types of Tasks and Their Work Contexts

Psychologists distinguish between instrumental and cognitive tasks. Instrumental tasks are largely physical in nature and involve the manipulation of things (e.g., lifting, polishing, drilling, driving, sculpting). Cognitive tasks are largely mental in nature and involve the manipulation of information or knowledge (e.g., planning, evaluating, designing, deciding). The qualifier "largely" is used for two reasons. First, no task is purely one or the other by its content. Second, the performer may infuse a instrumental task with considerable cognitive components (see Exhibit 1 for an example). Shop or manufacturing work processes are dominated by instrumental tasks while office work processes are dominated by cognitive tasks.

Exhibit 1. The Difference a Performer Can Make

Hitting a baseball may seem a purely instrumental task, and, based on interviews, that is how Mickey Mantle approached it. On the other hand, Ted Williams approached the task very differently. Both players were exemplary hitters. Mantle was an intuitive performer who blended talent, practice, and strength to create skill and achievement. He could not, by his own admission, explain how he hit the ball; he just did. When he slumped, he would use trial and error to try different ways to break out of it. Mostly, he just kept trying and let things work themselves out. Williams was a knowledge-driven performer. He could explain in minute detail how he executed a particular swing and what swing he would use in a particular circumstance. If he slipped, he used his knowledge to detect the source of his batting problem and to devise a fix. Here are two performers executing the same instrumental task, yet one is infusing it with a great deal of cognitive components.

Notwithstanding the exceptions a performer's approach may create, instrumental and cognitive tasks have important differences (Exhibit 2, next page) and these differences are expressed in the work processes they execute. For example, cognitive tasks are not directly observable. By definition, cognitive work occurs in the mind of the performer. The product of these tasks is typically information in the form of a decision or document, or a service result (e.g., a customer satisfied with the response to his or her inquiry). In either case, the activity and result are not directly observable. You must do something additional to make them observable. For example, you must document the decision or elicit from the customer whether he or

Exhibit 2. Key Similarities and Differences Between Instrumental and Cognitive Tasks

Feature	Instrumental Tasks	Cognitive Tasks
Input	■ Predominantly physical materials ■ More likely to be precisely specified as to content and characteristics	■ Predominantly information which may be contained in a document or acquired by conversation ■ Less likely to be precisely specified as to content and characteristics
Output	■ Predominantly physical products ■ More likely to be specified precisely with respect to form, fit, finish, and function ■ Problems with outputs more easily observable	■ Predominantly information which may be in the form of a decision or a fact represented in a document or a report ■ Less likely to be precisely specified ■ Problems with outputs less easily detected as they tend to be judgments not standardized by explicit rules
Process	■ Readily observable ■ Predominately a sequence of actions guided by decisions	■ Not directly observable ■ Predominately a sequence of decisions which trigger actions
Feedback	■ Performance tracking and reporting are embedded in the work process and part of normal management activity ■ Performance feedback is frequently immediate and visible as the component either passes or fails inspection and the product is produced at its required volume and speed	■ Performance tracking frequently tied to personnel appraisal systems which may not be formalized and, even when formalized, may not be implemented as designed ■ Feedback is usually global—not instance-specific—and occurs at a few set dates during the year, although it may be provided more frequently
Work Context	■ Work standards more likely to exist ■ Production system is more visible as it is marked by workstations that have different tools or equipment arranged in a sequence that matches the flow of materials through the work process ■ Focus of performers is on output	■ Work standards less likely to exist ■ Production system is less visible, as work is frequently performed at a set of similar desks or work spaces with few cues as to the nature of the work or the flow between each space ■ Focus of performers is more likely on process

she is satisfied and then document that response. Further, work processes that are predominately cognitive are less likely to have precise specifications for inputs or outputs, work standards to govern execution, or process and output monitoring that feeds back information on the quantity and quality of performance.[3] Not infrequently, the workplaces within which these work processes occur permit more performer discretion in how work is accomplished. Performers become used to having such discretion and may even experience it as their right. When the work processes are in back office or support operations, the customer for the work may not be understood, and sometimes these processes are seen as functionally autonomous and not terribly responsive to others.

Implications for Kaizen

The Kaizen process documented in this book requires minor modification to accommodate the differences between cognitive and instrumental tasks (see Guide: Adjusting the Kaizen Process to Accommodate "Office" Work Processes, beginning on page 408). The characteristics of the typical work context hosting cognitively dominated work processes underscore caution and care during your performance of *Milestone B. Analyze Whether to Conduct the Kaizen Event* but no adjustments in its process. The typical office or service work process is less likely to be ready for a Kaizen event because its work process may not be standardized, there may be no measurements of its performance, and its people may not be aligned with respect to supporting such an event.

The nature of cognitive work results in some differences in the work process map produced in *Step D1-S1. Build a Description of the Target Work Process*. The map will depict more decisions and require additional documentation of the knowledge guiding those decisions. Decisions in a cognitively dominated work process are the equivalent of the critical material processing operations in a shop or manufacturing work process. Decisions constitute the activities of analysis and interpretation and direct the transfer or transformation of information or the execution of actions. Decision-making is the equivalent of the skillful actions of machine operators and craftspeople who shape with tools a raw or semi-finished material into a final product. The "tool" used by the cognitive task performer is knowledge, usually in the form of rules. For example, one task a personnel officer performs is to process retirements. As part of that activity, he or she needs to determine whether that worker qualifies for a pension. The officer begins with information about the worker including his or her age and length of service. The "tool" the officer uses to transform this information into a pension determination is a rule—let's say the rule of 80. This rule specifies:

IF   the worker is at least 50 years of age

and   the worker's length of service equals or is greater than 30 years

THEN   the worker qualifies for a pension.

---

[3]These observations are less applicable the more the work process is related to matters of legal or fiduciary responsibility—e.g., accounting, purchasing, medical testing, charting of the nation's waterways.

By applying this rule to the information the officer has, he or she fashions a judgment which is the output of the officer's task.

Apart from the heavy presence of decisions in the work process map, be prepared to document more information elements as information constitutes the major inputs and outputs of tasks in a cognitive work process. Our process already includes capturing this content as part of the descriptive information about each task. Just recognize that there will be more to capture.

The nature of cognitive tasks also requires two adjustments in *Step D1-S2. Walk Through the Target Work Process*. The first adjustment is mental in nature. You will need to remind yourself that the forms of waste you will observe in an office work process will usually involve working with information and especially the paper forms or software screens that carry information. Frequently, these forms or screens are poorly designed so that the sequencing and display of information neither coincides with the flow of work or enables speedy recognition of their contents, thereby causing search. Sometimes forms contain contents that are unnecessary and obscure the needed information, also causing search. Sharpen your understanding of transport as well to include moving information from one paper form to another or from a paper form to a computer screen. Consider completing incomplete information or correcting incorrect information as rework. Recognize that filling out forms or entering information into a computer screen is setup, but that entering the same information into multiple software applications because these applications do not "talk to" each other is unnecessary processing. Again, fix in your mind that, for office processes, information is the equivalent of the physical materials used in manufacturing processes.

The nature of cognitive tasks also requires adjusting how the walk through occurs. With cognitive work processes, you will have the performer do a "talk through" of his or her work, probably using the work process map as a guide. This is necessary since the worker's operations are largely mental and therefore not observable.

The mental nature of cognitive work also affects how you execute *Task D2. Evaluate the Target Work Process*. Again, since many of the operations the worker is performing are not directly observable, you need to ask the performer to do *introspective reporting*. In this method, the performer not only announces each task as it is started but says what he or she is thinking and deciding as the task is performed. Introspective reporting makes explicit to observers what they cannot see—namely, the mental work of the performer.

Altogether, the adjustments to the Kaizen process are minor as you will see by reviewing the Guide: Adjusting the Kaizen Process to Accommodate "Office" Work Processes, beginning on page 408.

Just-in-Time Production Systems

A just-in-time production system controls production to match the rate of customer demand known as *takt time*. Parts are pulled into and through the process at a pace consistent with takt time so that the output of the process emerges *just when the customer wants it*. Such systems are designed so that the component operations are balanced, meaning that the cycle time of performance for each operation matches the pace required of the overall system. In such systems, the concept of waste is not as critical as the concept of pace. As a consequence, Kaizen events in just-in-time production systems focus on:

- getting to takt time;
- speeding up to reach a new, faster takt time; or
- reducing the resources needed to sustain takt time.

If the work process is truly just-in-time and is not operating to takt, the primary concern of the Kaizen event must be to get the cycle time of the work process to match its required takt time. Correcting this problem becomes the work process improvement incorporated into the event's mission. The conduct of the event remains the same.

The other possible use of Kaizen in a just-in-time production system is to reduce the resources needed to sustain operations at takt. Resource consumption may be expressed in unit cost or overall cost of the operation of the work process. Again, no adjustment is needed, since you simply represent this work process improvement in the event's mission and accomplish it by applying the standard Kaizen process.

If the work process is just-in-time, it will *never be acceptable* to make changes that compromise the ability of the work process to operate at takt. Consequently, as you consider solutions to eliminating waste, you need to be sensitive to their effects on maintaining takt time.

Union Presence

The presence of a union does not require tailoring the Kaizen process since it already incorporates actions to connect with, engage, and involve all key stakeholders, including a union. But it is valuable to reinforce that, in our experience, the keys to winning union support for an event are to recognize and respect its rights and purposes within the workplace, to involve the union from the very beginning of the process, and to sustain that involvement throughout the event. As with every stakeholder, it is critical both to share the purpose and activities of the proposed event and personalize the value of the event. Personalizing requires you to understand what is important to the stakeholder and to be able to connect and communicate how the conduct and results of the event advance the stakeholder's purposes. It is also critical to respond to the stakeholder's feedback and find ways to address and resolve any concerns he or she has with regard to the event.

If you follow the process and emphasize in your conduct the points just made, you should find the union—and every other stakeholder—an ally in conducting a successful event.

Absence of a Standard Approach to Executing a Work Process

Many businesses, especially service and information businesses, cannot take advantage of Kaizen because they lack standardized procedures for accomplishing work. Sometimes the absence of a standard is simply the result of inattention. Sometimes it reflects a culture that is driven by a concern for individual preference rather than the achievement of a common goal. And sometimes standards do not exist because they establish accountability, and accountability is not desired.

If a company lacks a standard method for accomplishing a work process but will commit itself to establishing and enforcing the use of standards, you can help the company by applying selected elements of the Kaizen process. You can use the methods described in *Step D1-S1. Build a Description of the Target Work Process* to assist the company in creating its baseline standard. Once that baseline is established, you can apply Kaizen to improve it continuously. The approach requires the commitment of leadership, the participation of the performers of the work process, and the execution of the following tasks.

1. Identify the work process the company seeks to improve.

2. Build the overview of the target work process.

   Tip: Build the first part of the description of the target work process using input from all managers and performers of the work process. Resolve differences in the overview information, especially with respect to the purpose of the work process. Be sure to involve representatives from all interfacing work processes, and make sure that their expectations of the work process are incorporated in its purpose statement. Establish the resulting overview as the standard for the work process. Be sure that it is approved by the work process manager, his or her manager, and the manager who oversees all the organizations that interface with the work process.

3. Document the various ways the work process is performed.

   Tip: Map the different ways performers accomplish the work process to produce the *same* output. Have the sources of the information verify that the maps you produce for their approaches correctly represent what they do.

4. Evaluate the work process variations.

   Tip: Work with the performers of the work process to do the evaluation. Establish two criteria for decision-making: (1) the selected work standard must define a procedure that accomplishes the purpose of the work process as described in the overview, and (2) the selected work standard must minimize waste. Teach the performers about waste. With them, detect the waste in the various work process maps. Help them adopt, adapt, or otherwise devise a process that satisfies the decision-making criteria.

5. Establish the selected work process variation as the initial work standard.

    Tip: Using the results of the evaluation, have the performers decide on a work process map to serve as the source for the initial work standard. Ensure that a work standard consistent with the selected map is written. Work with the manager to determine when the work standard will be implemented, how performers will be prepared to use the standard successfully, and how compliance with the standard will be supported.

Once the work standard is established, we recommend not doing a Kaizen event immediately. Rather, allow the company six months or more to establish consistent execution of the work process and to develop an understanding of what kind of results the process is able to produce. After that point, you can be assured of the company's commitment to using standards and that performers of the work process have sufficient expertise in executing the process to support improving it.

Planning for a Stream of Events

There are two common circumstances under which a business considers a stream of Kaizen events. The first is where it experiences the benefits of a single Kaizen event and desires to reproduce those benefits with more events. The second is where the business is committed to a strategy of continuous improvement under whatever label (e.g., quality, lean manufacturing).

Success Breeds Reuse

Once a business sees the power of Kaizen to produce both monetary benefits and the elevated participation and excitement of employees, it seeks more events. It may, however, still be thinking tactically and not strategically. This means it sees events as a near-term vehicle for building its people and improving its operations rather than as a long-term strategy for transforming its culture and achieving its business intent (i.e., purpose, values, and vision).

Using Kaizen as a Continuous Improvement Strategy

This book presents Kaizen as a response to a need to correct problems with the performance of a work process. We chose this approach because it is the most frequent way in which Kaizen is first introduced into a workplace. However, Kaizen is actually a continuous improvement methodology. It is really intended for periodic reuse independent of anyone detecting a specific need to elevate the success of a work process. Its power is precisely in its ability to detect opportunity *on its own*. This power derives from the concept of waste and how Kaizen operationalizes that concept into a detection system that continuously uncovers where resources are not being applied in a value-adding manner. In other words, Kaizen is an *engine of insight* that can reveal opportunity not otherwise detectable. In this sense, Kaizen may be applied as a continuous improvement methodology throughout a workplace, incrementally moving it toward perfection.

Guidelines for the Sustained Use of Kaizen

Whether the business is thinking tactically or strategically, the sustained application of Kaizen provides opportunities for maximizing its benefits and economizing its resource use. To reap the added benefits of sustained use, you need to elevate your thinking about the application of Kaizen from solving work process problems to accomplishing a larger business purpose. If the company is thinking tactically, consider the current year's business driver as the appropriate reference point. If it is thinking strategically, connect the stream of Kaizen applications to accomplishing the company's purpose, values, and vision. From this vantage point, bound the application of Kaizen by clarifying the breadth of the company within which Kaizen will be applied and the goal that its application will achieve. With the purpose and scope of the initiative defined, focus the effort further by targeting the execution of Kaizen events. To accomplish this task, you need to engage, involve, and win the support of the leadership. Once aligned, leadership's tasks are to analyze which business components offer the greatest opportunities for elevating success and, using this information, sequence the stream of Kaizen events. The continuing task of leaders is to promote the effort throughout the company.

Once the direction of the effort is defined and promoted by leadership, the remaining employees of the enterprise are readied to participate. They too must be engaged and involved in the project. Their perspectives on how the effort is bound and the proposed sequencing of events needs to be heard and integrated into a final direction. Once rollout is begun, events are conducted and their results shared and leveraged. The entire undertaking is recycled periodically so that the energy of participation is sustained, the focus is fresh and relevant to the business's purposes, and the learning from the prior period of performance is translated into a still more effective next period of performance. The major tasks that establish a sustained use of Kaizen are: (1) bound the application of Kaizen, (2) align leadership, (3) target the application of Kaizen, (4) ready membership, (5) conduct the Kaizen events, (6) leverage the results, and (7) recycle the initiative.

Task 1. Bound the Application of Kaizen

Bounding the application means specifying the purpose the sustained use of Kaizen will serve and deciding where within the company you will execute Kaizen events.

Formulate the purpose the sustained application of Kaizen will realize by defining a goal for the initiative. Use the format of a goal for an improvement action (*Task D4. Act to Improve the Target Work Process*, page 337) to assist you. Make the *to* component the business benefit you seek to produce for the company and its stakeholders—whether tactical or strategic. Make the *by* component "the sustained application of Kaizen" within whatever section of the company it will be applied. Be sure to include at least one benefit for each stakeholder in the *so that* component.

Specify in the *conditions* component whatever the do's and don'ts for this initiative are, and establish in the *standards* component the key success criteria that will be used to judge the effectiveness of the initiative.

Once the purpose of the initiative is defined, decide whether the effort will be companywide or be executed within one or more of its components. If the initiative will not be companywide, we recommend that the scope of application should be no narrower than a single business and certainly can be a division of businesses within a company. We define a "business" as a set of components that are dedicated to conceiving, developing, and executing commercial transactions that transform input resources into a product or service output and exchange that output with a customer for some desired resource, usually money. Businesses service a market—meaning they support a customer within a geographical region in accomplishing his or her purpose by providing a needed resource (i.e., a product or service).

A business is our recommended scope for several reasons.

- Only at the level of a business are all the components needed for successful commerce present. Improvement efforts that do not span the business have highly restricted potential for benefiting the company's overall success or its bottomline.

- Companies are most likely to assign businesses the status of "profit centers," meaning that only at the level of a business are you likely to obtain the financial information you need to compute monetary benefits.

- The leadership position in charge of a business is usually high enough on the executive ladder to command the attention, control the resources, and win the alignment needed to sustain the effort and leverage its benefits.

Look for businesses where there is growth potential or competition is keen and maximizing efficiency is critical to success so that the benefits of Kaizen will have their greatest impact.

Task 2. Align Leadership

Despite 75 years of efforts to transform companies from a top-down to a flat management configuration with high levels of employee involvement, most businesses remain essentially top down. Hence, before proceeding further in your effort, you must first obtain the commitment of leadership to the goal of the initiative, to the sustained use of Kaizen as the means to realizing that goal, and to the actions leadership needs to take to support the effort. At a minimum, these actions require that leadership (1) be knowledgeable of the Kaizen method and its results, (2) participate in sequencing the execution of Kaizen events, (3) support the effort by delegating authority and assigning resources, (4) promote the effort through sustained communication of its purpose and results, (5) recognize the contributions and achievements by employees, and (6) take those actions necessary to transform soft to hard monetary benefits.

Begin by aligning leaders with using Kaizen to accomplish the company's purpose. This will require educating leaders about the goal the company seeks to realize and about Kaizen, its method and impact, and how it can enable the company to achieve its goal. Continue the education by focusing on the roles leaders must perform to ensure the effort's success. Aligning leaders will also require working through any concerns leaders have and enabling them to personalize the importance of supporting this effort for the company and all its stakeholders. Once aligned, involve leadership in the task of sequencing the application of Kaizen.

Task 3. Target the Application of Kaizen

Start with profiling each business within which Kaizen will be applied. Use Section A of the Kaizen scope document as a guide (see *Milestone A. Document a Scope for the Kaizen Event* and *Task A1. Understand the Scope Document*). Add to this information an end-to-end map of the business's value stream. Use the guidance in *Step D1-S1. Build a Description of the Target Work Process* to describe the value stream. Build the overview for the business's value stream just as you would build the overview of a target work process. Map the sequence of actions required to execute a business; more specifically, to conceive, develop, and execute commercial transactions that transform input resources into a product or service output and exchange this output with a customer for consideration. By necessity, this will be a multi-departmental map and include the organizations responsible for business planning, marketing, sales, production, distribution, and customer support. Focus this map on a single product, but not necessarily a single model. Resourcing functions (e.g., human resources, information technology, finance) and back office operations (e.g., billing, collections) may also be represented on the map.

Using the map as your reference, involve stakeholders in assessing where in the work flow the greatest initial benefits are likely to be reaped from applying Kaizen. Leveraging their input and existing performance information, scan for areas where problems or inefficiencies occur or where there may be lost opportunity due to bottlenecks or variability in performance. Begin with the components that make the greatest contribution to cost or consequence in terms of quality, timeliness, and competitiveness of products. Build a prioritized list of target work processes using the results of this assessment. Create a schedule for introducing Kaizen into these work processes and begin to prepare a scope document Section B for each one.

If the business is large or complex, you will need to do several levels of mapping before you get to work process components appropriate for Kaizen (remember it needs to be four hours or less in cycle time).

As you proceed down to the work process level, be sure to involve the managers of these work processes in the selection activity and to document the reasons for selecting each work process as a host for a Kaizen event. Also identify with the manager a designated event coordinator who will be the point of contact for the Kaizen leader.

Task 4. Ready Membership

With leadership's commitment and action, the next step is to align membership. This is simply a larger version of the preparation efforts you need to do for any Kaizen event (see guidance in *Milestone C. Prepare for the Kaizen Event*). You need to understand stakeholders so that you can communicate effectively with them and constructively involve them in the initiative. All stakeholders need to understand the purpose and scope of the initiative, their roles within it, and why performing these roles is critical to the company's success. They also need to understand how the initiative serves their purposes and addresses their concerns. As well, you need to gather and integrate into the plan their perspectives on focus and direction so that the effort leverages their knowledge as well as the knowledge of leadership, and their participation allows them to own the effort going forward along with leadership.

Stakeholders who will become participants of Kaizen events require additional education about Kaizen. Look to the one-day pre-event orientation session described on pages 392–93 for ideas about this preparation. Assume that you will identify prospective Kaizen leaders from participants to events. Prepare them for the leader role by using the *Kaizen Desk Reference Standard*; consider augmenting this with formal training in the Kaizen process. Check our website for details about Kaizen training (http://www.vitalentusa.com).

Task 4. Conduct the Kaizen Events

Use the guidance in this book to conduct your events. The cycle time for performance will be accelerated by the work already accomplished in focusing the effort and readying the people.

Task 5. Leverage the Results

Establish a vehicle for broadly communicating the results of each Kaizen event. Consider a initiative-wide newsletter. Also consider creating a intranet site to share results, recognize the contributions of employees, announce new events, and help in leveraging learning from events. You may want to establish a best practice site for registering improvements developed in Kaizen events and make it accessible across the company.

Be certain to track and report the initiative-wide cumulative results from the events, including such facts as:

- number of events,
- number of people participating in events,
- cumulative monetary benefits (soft and hard),
- percentage of soft benefits transformed into hard benefits, and
- the cumulative cost of the initiative.

Include a sample of comments from participants as well as the average rating of events on Items 2, 6, and 7 of the Kaizen Participant Feedback Form (see *Milestone*

D. Perform the Kaizen Event, pages 175–76 and 186–88). Also include recognition for the contributions of performers to the success of the initiative.

Task 6. Recycle the Initiative

Set a yearly date for a renewal exercise in which each business reviews its goals for the prior year, what it achieved, why, what it learned, and how to leverage its learning into next year's efforts. Out of the exercise should come the objectives for the following year, the priority list of work processes on which to focus Kaizen, and actions that leverage the prior year's learning to ensure better achievement. SRLD[SM] (Status, Reason, Learning, Direction) is an excellent tool for guiding the renewal activity.[4]

Building the High-Performing Organization

There is a third and somewhat paradoxical way to employ Kaizen broadly in a business. It is to use Kaizen to produce transformational change.

Kaizen by definition pursues small changes that progressively move toward perfection. But the incremental nature of its improvements relates to work process change. When a Kaizen event is conducted according to the standard in this book, it has another level of impact which is not necessarily incremental. Kaizen attracts and develops people who are capable of creating and sustaining high performance. By its nature, it draws to it people who are achievers at heart—people who are internally driven to make a difference, to perfect something. These people are focused on their work, frustrated by waste, and delighted by the opportunity to improve what they are about so that it excels. Their pursuit of excellence is only excited more with each step toward its achievement. Equally important, Kaizen attracts people who also are inclusive in their thinking and doing. Kaizen, as defined in this book, demands a broad view of the connection of an activity to all activities that surround it and so it builds into its fact-finding steps to describe the context within which the target work process operates. It also constructs its teams to include people who speak from the different perspectives that populate the workplace, and it pursues its solutions with an openness to every voice. People who find Kaizen a gratifying experience are not only pioneering in their attitudes but inclusive in their disposition.

The kind of people that Kaizen attracts and develops are the heart and soul of high-performing organizations (HPOs). The broad and sustained application of Kaizen can lead to a rapid emergence of the central element needed for a company to become high performing.

High-Performing Organizations

In 1997, Vital Enterprises embarked on an extensive research effort to summarize the literature on what was thought to differentiate the very best commercial enterprises from all others. Our first task was to formulate a definition of such high-performing

---

[4] R.L. Vitalo and P.A. Bierley, *Mining Learning From Performance*, Hope, ME: Lowrey Press, 2003.

organizations. Our second task was to develop an understanding of the formative factors that create and sustain such an enterprise.

HPO Defined

We distilled this literature and augmented it with both outcome research from allied areas such as psychology and our own experience. From this effort, we anchored our definition of an HPO in its ability to produce extraordinary results for all stakeholders (i.e., customers, shareholders, employees, communities, and suppliers).[5] We developed the definition further by elaborating what "extraordinary results" meant. HPOs are the vital few companies that account for most of the change that occurs in each industry, market, and region. Their extraordinary results extend beyond customer service and shareholder gain. HPOs are said to fulfill societal and industry ideals by becoming agents and models of constructive innovation and by being places where people can learn, achieve, and grow. Although these companies produce extraordinary results, they do not necessarily have unbroken records of success. Indeed, HPOs may experience setbacks at different points in their history. What HPOs do consistently display is the ability to sustain performance *over time* and *over changing market circumstances*. Their record of achievement has a positive slope over decades. And, even more significantly, they produce benefits for all stakeholders *inclusively*—not for the benefit of management at the expense of employees and shareholders, or for employees and shareholders at the expense of suppliers and the community.

Formative Factors

Our research identified one source for the success of HPOs and three principles that govern their operation.

One Source

People make the difference in any enterprise, and they alone determine whether an HPO exists or fails to exist. The right people, therefore, are the single source for achieving all the esteemed benefits produced by an HPO. They are the heart, head, and sinew of such companies. It is from their substance that all other elements of an HPO emerge.

The right people have these qualities: (1) they align to a purpose larger than self-interest, (2) they are teamed in their performance, (3) they are energized from within, (4) they have or acquire whatever expertise their tasks demand, and (5) they are always pioneering. People who create and sustain HPOs align to a business intent that commits to commerce through excellence and to producing benefits for all stakeholders *inclusively*. They team with the other members of the business they implement as well as across the company. Their inner desire to produce excellence energizes their performance. Their first step in every endeavor is to acquire the knowledge and proficiency needed to execute their tasks. Throughout, they are

---

[5]Vitalo, R.L., *The High-Performing Learning Organization* (Hope, ME: Vital Enterprises, 1997).

pioneering, driving to achieve the previously unachievable, to probe new opportunities, and to create new benchmarks of accomplishment.

The enlightening yet disturbing implication of this single source of effect is that *you cannot change your company without changing its people*.

Three Principles

The three principles that explain the performance of an HPO describe its relationship with the people who power it, clarify what these people focus on, and explain how they view the rest of what surrounds them.

Principle 1 asserts that the right people are the origin and end of the HPO. This means that aligned, teamed, energized, capable, and pioneering people create HPOs, and that, reciprocally, HPOs attract, nurture, and develop these people. The relationship is circular and self-sustaining. An HPO *never* acts in a way that compromises this relationship.

Principle 2 states that enterprise and learning are the only activities on which people in an HPO focus. Their single imperative is *to maximize enterprise through learning*.

Principle 3 declares that all elements other than people are optional. If these elements exist, it is on a "just-in-time" and "only-for-so-long-as-useful" basis. This paraphernalia includes structure, strategy, systems, procedures, equipment, tools, and facilities.

The Role of Kaizen

The methodology of Kaizen documented in this book encourages the development of the right people, the right focus, and the right attitude toward all else.

The Right People

Kaizen is a teamed activity that aligns performers to a larger purpose of advancing business success and benefiting all stakeholders. It attracts people energized by the opportunity to make a difference and equips them with knowledge and skills that empower them to realize that opportunity. Further, it encourages performers to challenge the usual way of performing work and to devise better methods that enhance the value of work from the perspective of the customer. Every one of its features draws to it the kind of people who are the single source of effect in creating and sustaining the HPO's extraordinary results. Kaizen provides these people an opportunity to exercise their qualities and grow in their capability, involvement, and contribution. If allowed its full impact, the broad application of Kaizen acts to nourish the seeds of an HPO's creation and propagate them throughout the workplace.

The Right Focus

Each Kaizen event roots its direction in producing business benefits and uses learning as its means of achieving those benefits. Its very substance emphasizes a focus on enterprise and learning. Moreover, its leave-behind measure and the follow-up team meetings it fosters sustain and enhance the presence of the right focus in each workplace it enters.

The Right Perspective

Kaizen continuously challenges people to question the value of each element in a work process. It raises the question of necessity for every action and every resource. In this way it eliminates "sacred cows" and reinforces the third principle of an HPO, that all elements other than high-performing people are optional. From a Kaizen perspective, each element in the workplace either adds value as defined by the customer or it is waste, and all waste is to be eliminated. There are no products or product features that *must* exist, or production or delivery methods that *must* be used, or paraphernalia of any sort that *must* be present. Similarly, there are no roles, structures, or divisions of responsibility that are givens.

Kaizen, then, can be a means to the strategic business goal of becoming an HPO. Each event, when completed as described in this book, is itself a mini-HPO in that it is *"governed by purpose and powered by teamed, capable people who use learning to achieve extraordinary results for all stakeholders."* A stream of events with a company-wide scope can be used to model and teach the principles of an HPO and attract, develop, and elevate the contribution of the kind of people needed to power one.

What Kaizen Cannot Do

Kaizen is a tool, a technology. When performed according to the guidance in this book, every element of it is consistent with the model of an HPO and, as just stated, each event is itself a mini-HPO. But Kaizen as a technology is fundamentally paraphernalia. As such, its utility depends on the people who champion and apply it. This is the implication of the HPO model that most authors miss. Most consultants seem to believe it is possible to build an HPO by establishing its paraphernalia. They seem to think that if we build the artifacts, then the artifact builders will appear. In essence, these authors propose to use external conditions to shape the right people into being. This is self-contradictory. The right people are intrinsically motivated—not externally driven. Further, there is no evidence that values can be embedded in people—certainly not in adults. People must embrace them. We can assist each other in the process of developing the right stuff, but we cannot command it. We may model values and encourage their incorporation, but, ultimately, the act of incorporating values is a matter of personal choice. Some people will experience the personal qualities encouraged by Kaizen as meaningful to them and worth their investment and sacrifice; others will not. And that is their right.

The bottomline is that Kaizen can help you uncover the right people in your organization and can help encourage and develop those people, but it will not transform the wrong people into the right people. Further, if the "wrong" people are at the top of your organization, Kaizen will never be allowed to have its full impact, and your business will not become an HPO.

Guide:
Adjusting the Kaizen Process to Accommodate "Office" Work Processes

Kaizen Process	Guidance
Milestone A. Document a Scope for the Kaizen Event	▪ No adjustments needed. ▪ Pay special attention to Items B14 and B14a of the scope document. These items document the interfaces between the target work process and other work processes and identify organizations that must be consulted before the target work process may be modified. Work processes that generate information or service outputs are frequently back office or support functions, and their content and procedures are sometimes controlled by the other organizations in whose service they operate.
Task A1. Understand the Scope Document	▪ No adjustments needed.
Milestone B. Analyze Whether to Conduct the Kaizen Event	▪ No adjustments needed. ▪ Because work processes that generate information or service outputs are frequently undocumented and lack measurements, you need to be especially careful in evaluating the presence of a work standard and the inclination of management and performers to apply a standard and measure performance. ▪ You also need to evaluate the presence and impact of software systems—specifically, whether these systems so constrain the target work process that meaningful change is not possible. It is not uncommon that waste within the target work process is a product of the design of software support systems, yet control of the design of the software resides outside the work process. ▪ Some work processes that generate information or service outputs occur over long cycle times because they are intermittent. An intermittent work process starts then stops between operations. The actual time spent in executing the process is much less than its cycle time. For example, a personnel appraisal work process typically has a cycle time of one year, but the actual time spent in executing the process may be no more than three to four hours total. There may be a meeting to establish appraisal goals, a second meeting to provide feedback at the half-year mark, and a third meeting to provide final feedback and the appraisal rating. Pay attention to intermittence when evaluating whether the team can observe the operation of the target work process within the time available during a Kaizen event. ▪ In evaluating the business case, consider not only the direct cost of operating the work process but also the cost of poor performance. We had an office work process that was small in total operating cost, but, because of its tardiness, it required the company to use expedited delivery procedures to meet strict timeliness requirements. Its products were being shipped internationally, and expedited delivery resulted in a highly significant cost which the Kaizen event could eliminate.

Continued...

Guide:
Adjusting the Kaizen Process to Accommodate "Office" Work Processes (continued)

Kaizen Process	Guidance
Milestone C. Prepare for the Kaizen Event	■ No adjustments needed.
Milestone D. Perform the Kaizen Event	■ No adjustments needed.
Task D1. Focus the Kaizen Event	■ No adjustments needed.
Step D1-S1. Build a Description of the Target Work Process	■ No adjustments are needed to building the overview of the target work process. ■ Be prepared to document more decisions in your work process map. Work processes that emphasize cognitive tasks are predominately a sequence of decisions which culminate in some action. These decisions are more complex and have a greater effect on results than the actions the decisions trigger. Document both what the decision is and the knowledge that should guide decision-making. Use the Guide: Documenting Decision Logic (pages 412–13) to assist you in documenting each decision. Be sure to note when there is no formal knowledge defined to guide decision-making; the absence of such knowledge can have a significant impact on waste. ■ In completing the descriptive information about each task, be prepared to document more information elements, as information constitutes the major inputs and outputs of tasks in a cognitive work process. ■ The flow of processes that generate an information or service output frequently mirrors the flow of documents from input to output. For example, a purchase request comes in, a purchase order or notice of rejection goes out, and the steps in between evaluate the information contained in the request document to arrive at its final disposition. You may find that tracing the path of input documents and the transformation of the information they contain into outputs is an aid to understanding the flow of work.
Step D1-S2. Walk Through the Target Work Process	■ Your walk-through plan will likely use "talk through" as a method for cognitive tasks in that you cannot observe these activities being performed. Much of the talk through may occur as you map the work process especially if you do a thorough job in documenting the knowledge that guides decision-making.

Continued...

Guide:

Adjusting the Kaizen Process to Accommodate "Office" Work Processes (continued)

Kaizen Process	Guidance
Step D1-S2. Walk Through the Target Work Process (continued)	■ You will still want to observe the work area in which each task or decision is executed and have a performer lead you through how he or she moves between tasks. You will want to observe any storage areas that are accessed, software screens that the performer must work with in doing his or her job, and forms or other media that convey information inputs or outputs. ■ Remind yourself that the forms of waste you will observe in an office work process will usually involve working with information and especially the paper forms or software screens that carry information. Frequently these forms or screens are poorly designed so that the sequencing and display of information neither coincides with the flow of work or enables speedy recognition of their contents thereby causing search. Sometimes forms contain contents that are unnecessary and obscure the needed information, also causing search. Sharpen your understanding of transport as well to include moving information from one paper form to another or from a paper form to a computer screen. Consider completing incomplete information or correcting incorrect information as rework. Recognize that filling out forms or entering information into a computer screen is setup but that entering the same information into multiple software applications because these applications do not "talk to" each other is unnecessary processing. Again, fix in your mind that, for office processes, information is the equivalent of the physical materials used in manufacturing processes.
Step D1-S3. Build the Mission Statement	■ No adjustments needed.
Step D1-S4. Set Goals for the Kaizen Event	■ No adjustments needed.
Step D1-S5. Define the Do's and Don'ts	■ No adjustments needed.

Continued...

Guide:
Adjusting the Kaizen Process to Accommodate "Office" Work Processes (continued)

Kaizen Process	Guidance
Task D2. Evaluate the Target Work Process	▪ Since the most significant work is mental, observing the performance of a task has limited utility. Modify the observation part of the evaluation accordingly. Consider using introspective reporting. In this method, the performer not only announces each task as it is started but says what he or she is thinking and deciding as the task is performed. Such reporting makes explicit to observers what they cannot see directly—namely, the mental work of the performer.
Task D3. Solve the Performance Issue	▪ No adjustments needed.
Step D3-S3. Conduct an Experiment	▪ No adjustments needed.
Task D4. Act to Improve the Target Work Process	▪ No adjustments needed.
Step D4-S1. Measure Results	▪ No adjustments needed.
Step D4-S3. Conduct a Pilot	▪ No adjustments needed.
Milestone E. Institutionalize the Process Improvements	▪ No adjustments needed.

Guide:
Documenting Decision Logic

Task

To record the ideas that guide making a decision.

Steps

1. Name the decision and state its importance.

2. List the outcomes that the decision may conclude.

3. List the factors the person must consider in making the decision.

   Tip: Name each factor *and* identify what about each factor the decision-maker should evaluate. For example, in deciding the approval of a purchase order, one factor to consider might be total cost, and the person making the decision might need to pay attention to whether the cost is above or below $25,000.

4. Describe the flow of decision-making.

   Tip: Each decision has a beginning and follows a sequence in which factors are considered. This flow is important to capture because it may evidence waste. If the flow is simple, as in the example on page 413, you may describe it in a statement. If it were complex, you should document it using a graphical method such as a series of decision trees (see below).

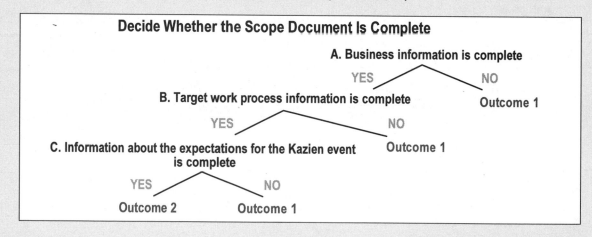

Decide Whether the Scope Document Is Complete

A. Business information is complete — YES / NO → Outcome 1

B. Target work process information is complete — YES / NO → Outcome 1

C. Information about the expectations for the Kazien event is complete — YES → Outcome 2 / NO → Outcome 1

Tips

- Since work standards frequently lack documentation for decisions, your documentation provides work aids that can ensure consistent excellence in decision-making by performers. In this sense, your knowledge documentation has a "poka yoke" or mistake-proofing use.

Continued...

Guide:
Documenting Decision Logic (continued)
Example

Decision

Decide whether the written scope document is complete.

Importance

Ensures that you have the information you need to evaluate the scope.

Possible Outcomes

1. Conclude that the scope document is not complete and obtain the missing information.

2. Conclude that the scope document is complete and proceed to evaluate its consistency.

Decision Factors

A. Basic business information is complete (yes, no).

   Tip: Use the Scope Statement Checklist, Basic Business Information section (page 83), to decide whether the business information is complete. If each item in the section listed is checked, then the business information is complete; otherwise, it is not.

B. Target work process information is complete (yes, no).

   Tip: Use the Scope Statement Checklist, Target Work Process Information section (pages 83–84), to decide whether the target work process information is complete. If each item in the section listed is checked, then the target work process information is complete; otherwise, it is not.

C. Information about the expectations of the key stakeholders for the Kaizen event is complete (yes, no).

   Tip: Use the Scope Statement Checklist, Expectations for the Kaizen Event section (page 84), to decide whether the information describing the expectations for the event is complete. If each item in the section listed is checked, then the information about stakeholders' expectations is complete; otherwise, it is not.

Decision Flow

Consider each decision factor in the order it is listed (i.e., from A through C).

Ending Note: Of Sanctity and Sacrilege

In the Preface to this book, we began by telling you what Frank Butz constantly reminds us: that Kaizen is about people. We said that although Kaizen's immediate focus is on improving work processes and business results, its energy, heart, and lasting benefits are in enabling people to emerge as productive achievers—at least when Kaizen is performed according to the standard established in this book. Herein lives the potential for sacrilege.

Of Sanctity

The people whom Kaizen attracts are the very best among us. They are achievers excited by the opportunity to create excellence. In our experience, they are frequently ignored in their workplaces except when a crisis occurs. Then they are the people to whom others turn to fish them out of difficult waters. The "system" quickly learns that these people march to a different drummer. Their beat emphasizes results, not politics. The system also learns that it does not need to reward these people because they are internally driven. They do not seek status and privilege, so rewarding them by elevating them is unnecessary—indeed, it would be dangerous, at least in companies where "getting along" is more important than getting better. Now do not misunderstand: these people get along fine socially; they just have a difficult time in saying the emperor has clothes when he does not.

For every one of these truly exceptional people, there are many others who also desire to achieve but who—for whatever reason—have had their drive dulled by Dilbert-like work settings. These individuals come alive when they see the potential of Kaizen to create opportunities to make a difference. Their spirits soar and their initiative is reborn. Witnessing their renewal and hearing their expressions of appreciation for once again finding satisfaction in their work is humbling because what unfolds in front of you is life in all its preciousness. Its significance is far greater than you and certainly far greater than Kaizen. It is the light, the fire, the thrill that can elevate all of us together as people. This is what is sacred: seeing life reignited.

And Sacrilege

What is not sacred is seeing the opportunities and improvements of these people co-opted by others whose intents are not inclusive but exclusive and whose abilities, despite their positions of higher status and authority, are inferior. These are the people who kick off the initiative, take credit for its achievements, and carefully avoid allowing it to grow to the point where it might threaten the status quo. They promise up front their endorsement, resources, and support. They champion its initial results. But they never stay the course to the point where they and their peer group must change. Before that point is reached, the brakes are applied, and the light, the fire, and the thrill are dimmed. This is the sacrilege: seeing life snuffed.

Your Choice

The human spirit is sacred. You may create circumstances where that spirit can be beckoned, excited, and inspired. Kaizen, when practiced as described in this book, has that effect. It attracts and develops people who can create and sustain extraordinary results, not just for themselves but for others as well.

If you are an individual contributor seeking to develop your ability to make change that benefits others as well as yourself, we applaud you, we pledge our support to you, and we hope that you will use our method and share with us what you learn.

If you are a leader of an enterprise that seeks to be high performing by providing value to its customers, competing on the basis of excellence, and benefiting all stakeholders inclusively, we applaud you as well and pledge our support to you and our hope that you will use our method and share with us what you learn.

But if you are a person whose pursuit is exclusive, and whom, for whatever reason, does not want the byproduct of an involved, excited, and pioneering workforce, then we say—"Use some other method to make change. Use the traditional Japanese approach of a knowing sensei, directing and correcting the performance of unknowing performers. *Do not use our method!*" We have no desire to participate in sacrilege.

Glossary

Action plan
A plan used to guide the execution of process improvements. It contains the goal for the improvement, a list of steps to follow in implementing the improvement, a statement of the resources needed to make the improvement, the identification of potential problems the team may encounter and possible solutions, and a fallback solution should the problems prevent the team from making the improvement.

Action team
A subset of Kaizen team members who are assigned responsibility to implement a specific improvement.

Attending
To fully focus both physically and mentally on another person or a group of people. Attending signals your readiness to relate to and work with the individual or team, places you in a position to observe and listen to the individual or team, and triggers reciprocal attending from the individual or team.

Backbone work process
The set of operations in a mixed model work process through which every variation of a product must pass, in exactly the same way, in order to be produced.

Batch output
A unit of output composed of more than one instance of a product or service. For example, a batch output might be a pallet of cylinders, a carton of eggs, or a suite of related customer services.

Best practices database
A repository, usually electronic, where guidelines for the best way to perform work are stored. These guidelines are derived from practices developed and tested in the workplace or from outside sources. Each best practice is a recommended best way to execute a particular task.

Brainstorming
A method for generating ideas that asks people to say or record whatever comes into their minds. It requires people to suspend judgment and accept uncritically the ideas that emerge.

Business
A set of components that are dedicated to conceiving, developing, and executing commercial transactions that transform input resources into a product or service output and exchange this output with a customer for some desired resource, usually money.

Business driver
The priority near-term focus for a business with respect to improving its operations and the results it produces. Common examples are growing revenues, improving profit margins, winning additional market share, satisfying customers, and elevating employee involvement.

Business intent
The purpose, vision, and core values that explain why a company exists and the ultimate direction it seeks to realize.

Business, name of

The organization responsible for planning, resourcing, selling, producing, and distributing the final product or service output to which the target work process contributes and supporting the customers who purchase it. This is the entity credited with the revenues from the sale of the final product or service and controls the expenditures associated with producing and delivering it.

Business result

A measure of the effect business performance has on some dimension important to one or more of its stakeholders, its customers, its owners, its employees, its suppliers, the finance industry, and the communities within which it operates. Some key measures of business results are customer reaction, financial results, employee reaction, shareholder benefits, and company esteem. Each of these areas has a variety of possible specific indicators. For example, customer reaction may be indicated by satisfaction with a product or service as measured by ratings or repeat purchase rates for a product or service. Any time a company fails to achieve its targeted level of achievement in one or more key success areas, it has a business problem.

Capital-intensive industry

An industry in which the largest source of operating cost is material assets or their operation (e.g., plant, equipment, utilities). Power generation and automobile manufacturing are two examples of capital-intensive industries.

Cell

A series of workstations arranged in a tight sequence, typically in a "U" shape, where one or more performers execute a set of related work activities.

Cognitive tasks

Tasks that involve the mental manipulation of information or knowledge. Include tasks such as diagnosing, assessing, goal setting, forecasting, planning, evaluating, and designing, among others.

Company

A commercial enterprise that applies resources to accomplish targeted results for its owners and stakeholders. A company is composed of one or more businesses.

Cost of a Kaizen event

In general, the cost of an event is computed by calculating participant salaries for the week of their participation, consultant costs, travel and accommodation expenses, and any special expenses (e.g., equipment rentals, meals).

Cost reasonable

A rating criterion for an improvement idea. Refers to an improvement idea that produces a dollar benefit greater than the cost of implementing it.

Cycle time

The rate at which a unit of product exits a work process. A unit is one completed output but not always one item. For example, a unit of output might be a pallet of cylinders or a carton of eggs. Note that cycle time *is not* the time it takes one piece to move all the way through the work process. This is termed *lead time*, and it is usually longer than cycle time because in most work processes pieces of finished products wait in inventory along the production line.

Decision rule

Identifies the results that the measurements taken in an experiment must produce for the experimenter to conclude that the hypothesis is true. The decision rule is written in the form of an "IF...THEN" statement: "If we observe that [improvement idea] causes [desired results], then we will conclude that [improvement idea] is effective." For example, "If we observe that moving the XYZ tools to a location five feet to the right of the existing workstation reduces travel by 20% and cycle time for the work activity by 10%, then we will conclude that moving the XYZ tools is an effective improvement idea."

Doable	A rating criterion for an improvement idea. Refers to an improvement idea for which the team has (or can get) the authority and resources needed to execute it during the event and that can be executed during the time remaining in the event.
Effective	A rating criterion for an improvement idea. Refers to an improvement idea that will significantly remove or reduce the targeted waste.
End-to-end work flow map	A graphic that depicts a work flow beginning with raw materials entering the business and ending with the delivery of a product or service to a customer. The map shows, *at a minimum*, the name of the work process, each operation in it, and the sequence in which the operations are performed.
Experiment	A test under controlled conditions that is made to demonstrate a known truth, examine the validity of a hypothesis, or determine the efficacy of something previously untried.
Extraneous factors	Causes that are not part of your hypothesis but that may affect the measurement of its validity. For example, you may think that computers are a more effective teaching tool than other forms of instruction. You would hypothesize that students taught by computer will achieve scores 10% higher, on average, than students taught without computers. Your measure is test scores on an achievement test. Your decision rule is that if students taught by computers achieve an average test score 10% higher than students taught without computers, then computers are more effective than other forms of instruction. One extraneous factor you need to control is the learning ability of the students receiving each teaching approach. Some students learn faster than others. Unless you make sure that the learning abilities of the students receiving each teaching approach are similar, you will not be sure that the results you find for the superior teaching approach are simply due to having better learners.
Factor cost	The expense associated with each element that contributes to production (e.g., labor, equipment, raw materials).
Full-time equivalent	A way of counting employees based on each employee's level of employment. For example, a full-time employee counts as 1, a half-time employee counts as 0.5, and a person who works two days a week is counted as 0.4.
"Go-to" people	Individuals in a company whom others identify as having exceptional expertise in some area.
Gross margin (as a percentage)	Total revenue minus cost of goods sold divided by total revenue. This result is multiplied by 100%. Total revenue and cost of goods sold are reported in a company's quarterly and yearly financial statements.
Hard savings or dollar gains	The yearly cost reductions or revenue increases that flow immediately after the Kaizen event concludes and require no additional actions beyond the event to be realized. These are also referred to as *hard benefits*.
Hazard	Any observed workplace conditions or worker behaviors that could result in harm.

High-performing organization (HPO) A company that is governed by purpose and powered by teamed, capable people who use learning to achieve extraordinary results for all stakeholders (i.e., customers, shareholders, employees, communities, and suppliers).

"Home run" ideas Improvement ideas that have been rated highly and have impact across a number of goals. By implementing one of these ideas, you are able to advance the achievement of many goals.

Hypothesis Something taken to be true for the purpose of investigation; an assumption to be tested by study or experimentation.

Icebreaker exercise An activity used to create comfort in a work group and advance the work that the group has assembled to complete.

Industry group A sector of the economy made up of businesses that make similar products or offer similar services. A company may have multiple businesses within it and therefore belong to more than one industry group. For example, General Electric is in the home appliance industry, the health care equipment industry, and the financial services industry, among others.

Inferencing The process that applies knowledge to the facts of a situation and makes a decision or chooses an action. The simplest inferencing begins by verifying that a set of conditions are true and, if they are, adopting the decision or choice to which they point. This inferencing method is called *modus ponens*.

Inputs The information or materials that trigger the work process (e.g., customer order); control its execution (e.g., work instructions, product design); or are used to form the final output of the process (e.g., empty cylinders, customer specifications).

Inspect Checking for error in a component, product, or activity. It is waste because production cost is added.

Instrumental tasks Tasks that involve the physical manipulation of materials. These include such tasks as lifting, polishing, drilling, driving, and sculpting.

Interfaces The work processes and departments with which the target work process interacts. These are organizational components, separate from the target work process, from which it gets, gives, or uses something in common as it performs its work.

Intermittent work process A process that starts then stops somewhere between operations, as opposed to *within* an operation. This start-stop quality is usually due to workers being assigned to multiple work processes so that they are only available part of the time for each. Intermittence is most common in office work processes where, for example, information to be processed remains in someone's in-basket until he or she is free to attend to it.

Interruption Stoppage in work activity due to some external factor (e.g., machine breakdown, request for information). It is waste because production time is lost during the period of interruption.

Introspective reporting A method for understanding cognitive tasks wherein the performer not only announces each task as it is started but says what he or she is thinking and deciding during the performance. Introspective reporting makes explicit to observers what they cannot see for themselves—the mental work of the performer.

Inventory	The quantity of goods and materials on hand; stock. Inventory includes work in progress that is temporarily stored at or between workstations, finished products stored at the end of the work process, and supplies or materials used to make the outputs of the work process.
Just-in-time production system	A method by which production is controlled by the rate of customer demand known as *takt time*. Parts are pulled into and through the process at a pace consistent with takt time so that the output of the process exits just when the customer wants it.
Kaizen	Pronounced *Ki-zen*, the word is constructed from two Japanese ideographs, the first of which represents change and the second goodness or virtue. Kaizen is commonly used to indicate the long-term betterment of something or someone as in the phrase *Seikatsu o kaizen suru* which means to "better one's life." As we use the term, it refers to a method that strives toward perfection by eliminating waste. It eliminates waste by empowering people with tools and a methodology for uncovering improvement opportunities and making change.
Kaizen news	The name we give to the daily agenda and progress report the Kaizen leader or co-leader produces for the team and performers of the target work process.
Key stakeholder	A subset of all stakeholders who either have authority over whether the event happens or whether the changes proposed for the target work process get implemented. The key stakeholders to an event usually include, at a minimum, the sponsor of the event, the manager of the target work process and his or her manager, and the head or his or her designee of each organization outside the target work process that must be consulted before the target work process may be modified. *See also Stakeholder.*
Labor dollar savings	The annual dollar value saved by reducing the time required by human operations in the target work process.
Labor productivity	As used here, the units of output produced for each unit of labor expended. The unit of output and input may be a count (e.g., number of products per hour) or a dollar value (e.g., dollars produced per dollar spent). You could, for example, represent labor productivity as 12 units per person hour or as $318.18 in output value produced for $1 of labor cost—assuming that 12 units of output have a value of $7,000 and the cost of one person hour of work is $22 ($7,000 ÷ $22).
Lead time	The time it takes one piece of output to move all the way through the work process. Lead time is usually longer than cycle time because, in most work processes, pieces of products or the execution of a complete service waits along the production line—that is, the incomplete output sits without work being performed on it for periods of time.
Lean manufacturing	An outgrowth of the quality movement. A production philosophy that focuses on achieving efficiencies through maximizing value-adding activities and minimizing—and ultimately eliminating—waste. *See also Quality.*
Leave-behind measure	A visual display used to support the sustained use of process improvements initiated during the Kaizen event. It depicts the event goals and the work process results they produce using a fishbone graphic. Below the graphic, it lists the individual improvements made by the team and provides a place for recording the degree to which each improvement continues to be used in the workplace and the results the sustained improvements are producing.

Loaded labor cost	The hourly cost of labor including salary, the value of fringe benefits, and other costs the company may assign.
Location(s) of execution	Location(s) where the target work process is performed.
Machine	A mechanically or electrically driven device that accomplishes a task by virtue of its construction or software programming.
Management of change	The name frequently given to the procedure by which a work standard or instruction is officially modified.
Mixed model work process	A mixed model work process either (1) produces multiple outputs each of which is a variation on one basic product (e.g., cylinders filled with different gases, passenger vehicles including two-door and four-door models) or (2) produces a single output from different inputs (e.g., customer requests for replacement of a Model 213 coffee carafe originating from telephone calls, website orders, and letters). In each case, the existence of variation in outputs or inputs requires the work process to vary.
Motion	Changes in position by the worker (e.g., turning, bending, lifting) while he or she is at the workstation. It is waste because production time is lost during movement.
Multiple role or department	A work process in which the work is performed by a set of people who have different jobs and may work in different departments. In the map depicting such a work process, the flow of work moves up and down between departments or roles as well as horizontally.
Net margin (as a percentage)	Net income divided by total revenue. This result is multiplied by 100%. Net income and total revenue are reported in a company's quarterly and yearly financial statements.
Opportunity for improvement (in a work process)	The amount of improvement available in a work process expressed as a percentage; the higher the percentage, the greater the opportunity. To compute the opportunity for improvement, subtract the value-added ratio from 1 and multiply it by 100%. For example, if the value-added ratio is 0.097, then the opportunity for improvement is 90.3% ([1 - 0.097] x 100% = 90.3%).
Outputs	The information, materials, or service outcomes that are the expected final results of executing the work process (e.g., a cylinder filled with gas, a trailer loaded with products, an updated database, an approved credit application, a customer satisfied with the resolution of his or her complaint).
Overview (of a work process)	The first component of a work process description. The overview information includes the name of the target work process and its purpose; its inputs, outputs, locations of performance, cycle time, and takt time; and the names of the other work processes or departments with which the target work process interrelates.
Parent work process	The larger work process within which the target work process operates.
Payback period	The period of time at the end of which a party expects to reap full benefit from some action.

Personal protective equipment	Clothes and other paraphernalia (e.g., earplugs, safety glasses, safety shoes) designed to protect one from hazards in the workplace.
Poka yoke	Means mistake proofing in Japanese. Refers to a device or procedure that assists in preventing innocent mistakes.
Productivity	The units of output produced for each unit of input. The unit of output and input may be a count (e.g., number of products per hour) or a dollar value (e.g., dollars produced per dollar spent).
Profit	As used here, the amount of money left after subtracting the cost of goods sold from sales revenue.
Purpose (of a work process)	A set of facts that provide a quick understanding of the work process. The purpose statement has five components labeled "to," "for," "by," "so that," "conditions," and "measures." The *to* tells you what is produced; *for* tells you for whom it is produced; *by* is the method of production and, as such, restates the name of the work process itself; *so that* identifies the benefits the output should provide; *conditions* tells the requirements the work process must satisfy; and *measures* lists the indicators management uses to determine how well the work process is performing.
Quality	A group of methods (e.g., total quality management, robust quality, statistical quality control, lean manufacturing) that share a core premise and approach. The premise is that companies that best satisfy the real needs of their customers achieve the greatest success. The core approach focuses on customer requirements and drives to continuously improve their satisfaction by involving all employees in problem-solving activities.
Quality management system (QMS)	The process used to develop, maintain, and modify official work standards or instructions. A management of change procedure is the part of a QMS that handles the modification of a standard. A QMS may also include procedures for disseminating standards, teaching workers how to perform consistent with standards, and ensuring compliance with them.
Replication	The transfer of process improvements developed for a target work process in one location to other sites within a business where the same work process is performed.
Return on investment	The ratio of the dollar value of benefits for a defined period of time to the dollar value of costs for the same period of time.
Revenue	As used here, any money coming to the company through the sales of products or other assets or through investment strategies that manage financial assets.
Revenue center	The organization within a company to which revenues for a product or service are credited. In small companies, the company as a whole may be a single revenue center. In large, horizontally structured companies, revenue centers are considered separate businesses.
Rework	Behavior required to reprocess a product or product component to salvage a defective unit or part. It is waste because production cost is added.

Safety sensitive A rating criterion for an improvement idea. Refers to an improvement idea that either increases safety in the workplace or does no harm to the current level of safety.

Search Behavior required to locate some needed resource (e.g., a person, tool, part, or piece of information). It is waste because production time is lost during the search.

Service-intensive industry An industry in which the largest source of operating cost is labor. Engineering and management services and health care are two examples of service-intensive industries.

Setup Labor required to ready a performer or machine to execute a task. Setup is waste because production time is lost during the preparation period.

Single-role work process A work process in which all work is accomplished by one person or by a set of people who have the same job.

Soft savings or dollar gains The yearly cost reductions or revenue increases that require some additional action beyond the Kaizen event to realize (e.g., redeployment of workers to other productive tasks, review and approval of a new work standard, additional sales to benefit from greater throughput). These are also referred to as *soft benefits*.

Sponsor of the event The person who is requesting that a Kaizen event be performed and has the standing in the organization to authorize and provide resources for it.

Stakeholder An individual or group that may either affect the success of an event or be affected by its occurrence.

Storyboard A visual display that presents information about the direction, participants, and results of a Kaizen event. The display is intended to stand on a table or be mounted on a wall. The storyboard presents the mission, goals, and do's and don'ts of the event; before, during, and after photos of the target work process; a team photo with names; and the Kaizen Summary.

Strawperson direction A tentative statement of the mission, goals, and do's and don'ts for the event derived from the scope document.

Stretch goals State targets for results that represent the upper limit of what is achievable. These are results that get achieved rarely, but not never.

Takt time The rate at which a unit of product must exit a work process to satisfy customer demand. Takt time is computed by dividing the number of product or service output units customers demand over a given period of time (e.g., a day or week) by the total available production time for the period. For example, if customers demand 240 widgets per day and the factory operates eight hours per day (480 minutes), takt time is 30 widgets per hour or 1 widget every two minutes. If customers want two new products designed per month and the company operates 160 hours per month, the takt time is a new design every 80 hours.

Throughput The units of output produced per unit of time of work process operation.

Travel/transport	Movement by a worker from his or her workstation to another place. If the worker is moving parts, materials, and information around the workplace, it is called transport; otherwise, it is travel. Both are waste because production time is lost during travel or transport around the plant.
Unit cost	The average cost to produce a unit of output from a work process.
Unnecessary processing	Work done that is not needed to produce the product or service as required by the customer. Such processing may be done at the discretion of the worker or required by the work instruction. It may even modify the output, but it will do so in a way that a well-informed and reasonable customer does not value. It is waste because production cost is added unnecessarily.
Value-added ratio	The relative presence of value-adding work to total work. To compute the value-added ratio, divide the total value-added time by the total cycle time. For example, if the amount of work judged value added accounts for 398 seconds and the total cycle time for a process is 4,096 seconds, then the value-added ratio would be 0.097 (398 ÷ 4,096 = 0.097). You can compute the percentage of cycle time during which work is adding value to the output by multiplying the value-added ratio by 100%. In the above example, only 9.7% of total work process activity, as measured in time, is adding value (0.097 x 100% = 9.7%). One use of the value-added ratio is to compute the opportunity for improvement.
Value adding or value-adding work	Any activity done right the first time that materially changes a product or service in a way for which a well-informed and reasonable customer is willing to pay.
Value chain	A sequence of activities in which each activity adds value to an input resource as it passes through a business to become its product or service output. (Defined in M. Porter, *Competitive Advantage: Creating and Sustaining Superior Performance* [New York: The Free Press, 1985].)
Value stream	The sequence of actions required to execute a business—i.e., to conceive, develop, and execute commercial transactions that transform input resources into a product or service output and exchange this output with a customer for a desired resource, usually money.
Wait	Delay in a work activity until some needed resource becomes available or authority to proceed is received. It is waste because production time is lost during the waiting period. In contrast to intermittence, wait occurs after an operation is begun (*see also Intermittent work process*).
Waste	Any activity that is *not* value-adding. Waste does not materially change a product or service output in a way for which a well-informed and reasonable customer is willing to pay or makes such a change as a result of rework.
Work center	A place where a single operator executes a work activity. Also termed a workstation.
Work process	A sequence of activities that accomplish a task and produce an output.
Work process description	A graphical representation of a work process made up of two components: an overview and a work process map.

Work process map The second component of a work process description. The work process map includes the name of the target work process, its total cycle time and takt time, the name of each operation that executes the work process and its cycle time and position within the sequence of work, the roles or departments responsible for doing each operation, and other descriptive information about each operation. The operations that execute the work process are arranged in a sequence of rectangular boxes connected by arrows. Each box is labeled with the name of a work activity. The sequence shows the flow of work from beginning to end.

Work process problem An unwanted feature of the current work process operation (e.g., cycle time too long, defects too many, throughput too low, excess inventory, unit cost too high, product not delivered when needed).

Work standard The procedure a company has formally established as the correct way to execute a task.

Workplace A physical setting in which there is one or more workstations or cells.

Workstation A place where a single operator executes a work activity. Also termed a work center.

Index

A

D

Defining do's and don'ts, *see Do's and don'ts*

Description of the target work process
 and scope document, 96, 100
 as an output, 192, 199
 as part of focusing the Kaizen event, 193
 as part of preparing for the event, 167, 199–202
 as required documentation, 176–77, 211
 building a, *see Building a work process description*
 components of, 199
 example of building a, 31–33
 sources of information for, 201
 use in evaluating the target work process, 271, 276
 use in setting goals, 258
 use in walk through, 218–19, 221

Design of the Pilot, *see Pilot*

Designated event coordinator, *see Event coordinator*

Direction for the Kaizen event
 as an output, 192,
 as required documentation, 176–77, 251, 259, 265
 confirm internal consistency, 193–94
 defining the direction for the event, 189–95
 do's and don'ts, *see Do's and don'ts*
 example of a direction following a walk through, 37
 example of a final direction, 43
 example of a strawperson direction, 26
 goals, *see Goal*
 how to prepare and print, *see Building the mission statement, Setting goals, and Do's and don'ts*
 mission, *see Mission statement*
 strawperson direction, 113–16, 117

Distance measurement role
 guidance for, 285
 resources needed by, 274

Documentation
 ensure completeness, 176–77
 Kaizen Tool Kit, 7
 output of Kaizen event, 13, 19, 176–77
 source for mining learning, 62–63, 175
 update, 194, 211, 225, 251, 259, 265, 284, 320, 328, 344
 use in communication, 59–61, 172 (storyboard)
 use in providing feedback, 14

Documentation role
 guidance for, 286–90
 resources needed by, 274
 when role is performed, 274
 and utility role, 301

Documenting scope for the Kaizen event
 application of, 68
 benefit from, 68
 check steps for, 78
 confirm the accuracy of the draft scope document with each stakeholder, 76–77
 confirm who the key stakeholders are, 76
 confirm with the source that the documented scope is accurate, 74–75
 coordinate the verification process with the event coordinator, 75–76
 distribute the verified scope, 77
 Example: ABC Gases Kaizen Event Scope Document, 86–90
 gather the scope information, 72–75
 Guide: Deciding Whether the Scope Document Is Verified, 85
 Guide: Explaining What Kaizen Is, 79–80
 Guide: The Event Coordinator Role, 81
 Guide: The Role of Providing Scope Information, 82
 judge whether you have verified the scope document, 77
 Kaizen Tool Kit support for, 68–69
 learn about the business requesting the Kaizen event, 69
 learn the expectations of the Kaizen event, 73–74
 method for, 69–77
 obtain the basic business information, 72–73
 obtain the target work process information, 73
 outputs of, 69
 prepare the source of the scope information, 71–72
 prepare yourself to gather the scope information, 69
 purpose of, 68
 resources needed for, 68
 Scope Statement Checklist, 83–84
 tips for, 78
 understand the scope document, 69, *see also Understanding the scope document*
 verify the scope information, 75–77
 work with the event coordinator, 69–71, 75–76

Do's and don'ts
 application of, 262
 benefit from, 262
 check steps for, 265–66
 description of, 263
 documentation of, 265
 example of, 37, 43, 264
 Kaizen Tool Kit support for, 263
 method for, 263–65
 modify the list of "can't do's," 264
 modify the list of "must or can do's," 264
 output of, 263
 performer of, 262
 purpose of, 262
 resolving problems with do's and don'ts, 265
 resources needed for, 262–63
 review the strawperson do's and don'ts, 263–64

Acknowledgments

This book exists for one reason only—the excitement and growth we have seen in the people whom we have trained. Their response to the Kaizen method we shared with them and their use of it as a vehicle for personal growth and professional contribution excited us to produce and publish this book. To these people who have inspired us with their commitment to achievement through substance, we express our deep appreciation.

We would especially like to recognize those persons who have pioneered the introduction of Kaizen in their workplaces—Mark Guy, Real LeJeune, Brian Crowe, Mike Frotten, and Don Roll—and into new business units and market regions—Joe Cirafesi, Mark Anderson, and Mark Reed.

Finally, we want to recognize Jim Byron and Chris Bujak, two leaders whose guts, determination, and talent have brought measurable and profound benefit to their fellow employees and the customers and shareholders of the companies they serve. Their initiative, perseverance, and genuine competence has empowered the learning and change efforts of thousands of fellow workers who, in turn, have provided tens of millions of dollars in benefits to their companies.

In terms of producing this book, we owe gratitude and appreciation to our editor, Nita Congress, who has painstakingly applied her expertise to enhance its readability and logic. We also benefited from the editorial contributions of Patricia Bierley and Elizabeth Vitalo.

Authors

Raphael L. Vitalo, Ph.D.

Raphael L. Vitalo received his doctorate in psychology from the University of Massachusetts at Amherst. He has authored over 50 professional articles, technical reports, and chapters in the areas of psychology, organizational consulting, work process improvement, information systems, and artificial intelligence. Over his 20 years of consulting experience, he has designed, managed, and implemented over 350 projects serving public and private companies in the areas of organizational effectiveness, performance management, workforce productivity, business process reengineering, knowledge engineering, information systems design, and expert systems development. Dr. Vitalo has trained Kaizen leaders in the United States and Europe. He is currently the president of Vital Enterprises.

Frank Butz

Frank Butz is Senior Tool Expert for Air Products and Chemicals, Inc., a global supplier of industrial gases and chemicals. He has been implementing Kaizen since 1997 and has conducted over 100 Kaizen events. In addition, he has developed and implemented a comprehensive training and certification program which, to date, has

prepared more than 60 Kaizen leaders for his company. Mr. Butz is also a tool expert in workplace organization and visual controls and total productivity management and has consulted with the Northeastern Pennsylvania Industrial Resource Center on the application of Kaizen and other lean manufacturing methodologies.

Joseph P. Vitalo

Joseph P. Vitalo is a certified Kaizen leader and trainer who is also trained in demand flow technology and workplace organization and visual controls. He has planned and led Kaizen Events in the United States, Canada, Europe, and the United Kingdom. His last 22 events produced total annualized savings of $1.8 million. He has co-led Kaizen leader training events which have prepared more than 30 new Kaizen leaders. Mr. Vitalo is currently a consultant and trainer with Vital Enterprises.

User Evaluation and Feedback Form

We seek your feedback in our effort to continuously improve the effectiveness of this book in supporting you and others in learning and applying Kaizen.

Please complete the electronic questionnaire and provide your ideas on how this book may be improved to serve you better. Print and mail the questionnaire or fax your feedback to: Raphael L. Vitalo, Ph.D., Vital Enterprises, 777 Hatchet Mountain Road, Hope, Maine 04847 (Fax: 207-763-3710). As an alternative, visit our website and complete the feedback form online. By providing feedback on the *Kaizen Desk Reference Standard* online, you will have the opportunity to become a member of our website and obtain access to our Kaizen Forum and other services dedicated to supporting new learning by users of the *Kaizen Desk Reference Standard*. For more details about these services, see our website.

INSTRUCTIONS Answer each question by checking the appropriate box.	Yes 1	2	3	4	No 5

A. Judge the Acceptability of the Book

	Yes 1	2	3	4	No 5
1. Is its appearance attractive?	☐	☐	☐	☐	☐
2. Is it logically organized?	☐	☐	☐	☐	☐
3. Does it offer the right knowledge?	☐	☐	☐	☐	☐
4. Is it easy to use?	☐	☐	☐	☐	☐

STOP   **Have you used the Kaizen Desk Reference Standard?**

	Yes	No
	☐	☐

If *Yes*, please answer the following questions. If *No*, stop here.

B. Judge the Usefulness of the Book

	Yes 1	2	3	4	No 5
1. Does it help you educate yourself about Kaizen?	☐	☐	☐	☐	☐
2. Does it help you complete a Kaizen scope statement?	☐	☐	☐	☐	☐
3. Does it help you verify a Kaizen scope statement?	☐	☐	☐	☐	☐
4. Does it help you analyze whether to conduct a Kaizen event?	☐	☐	☐	☐	☐
5. Does it help you build a description of the target work process?	☐	☐	☐	☐	☐
6. Does it help you complete a walk through of the target work process?	☐	☐	☐	☐	☐
7. Does it help you focus a Kaizen event with respect to building a mission, setting goals, and defining do's and don'ts?	☐	☐	☐	☐	☐
8. Does it help you evaluate the presence of waste in the target work process?	☐	☐	☐	☐	☐
9. Does it help you generate ways to eliminate waste in the target work process?	☐	☐	☐	☐	☐
10. Does it help you implement process improvements to the target work process?	☐	☐	☐	☐	☐
11. Does it help you measure and report the results of the Kaizen event?	☐	☐	☐	☐	☐
12. Does it help you ensure the use of process improvements past the Kaizen event?	☐	☐	☐	☐	☐

What, if any, features of this book are value-adding to your efforts?

What, if any, features of this book do not add value or take away value?

Please provide any suggestions for improving the book's value to you.

Thank you for your feedback!

Please return to: Raphael L. Vitalo, Ph.D., Vital Enterprises, 777 Hatchet Mountain Road, Hope, Maine 04847
Fax 207-763-3710

Benefit From Other Vital Enterprises Offerings

Check out our website at www.vitalentusa.com for Kaizen:

- Member Services
- Business Services
- Related Performance-Improving Products

Our intent is to connect with people committed to getting a task done right the first time and, in that process, to grow in capability and provide benefits both for them and others. Offering the *Kaizen Desk Reference Standard* is one means to accomplish our purpose. Consider our other offerings as you seek to make a difference using Kaizen.

Member Services

Product Forums

Our website hosts interactive forums, each focused on supporting the successful application of a specific Vital Enterprises product. These forums permit members to ask application questions about each product, share their learning, and receive support for their achievement efforts. The authors of each product participate in the forum focusing on the use of their work. By purchasing the *Kaizen Desk Reference Standard,* you qualify as a member of our website and have access to the Kaizen forums.

Additional Learning Resources

You will find other knowledge (e.g., lessons, guides) and information products (e.g., case studies) available on our website that can assist you in your efforts. All these resources are available free of charge. Some are available for download, others for use online.

Business Services

Use our services to support your internal development and business improvement efforts.

Plan

Allow us to assist you in planning your sustained use of Kaizen to elevate your company to high performance.

Demonstrate

Have us lead initial events to demonstrate live the power of Kaizen and introduce your work teams to its basic concepts and tools.

Train

Use us to train and coach your people to lead events that will provide them with growth and satisfaction as they generate real and significant business benefits for your company.

We stand ready to place our expertise and products in the service of your efforts to benefit your enterprise and all its stakeholders. We can accelerate your success, as we have for others.

Benefit From Other Vital Enterprises Offerings

Related Performance-Improving Products

Kaizen Team Manual

by Raphael L. Vitalo, Ph.D., Joseph P. Vitalo, and Frank Butz

The *Kaizen Team Manual* prepares team members to participate in Kaizen events implemented according to the *Kaizen Desk Reference Standard*. It orients team members to what Kaizen is and how it is performed. It teaches them about waste and how to detect it. It informs them about their possible roles in the Kaizen event and equips them to execute those roles. The manual accelerates the Kaizen process by allowing team members to prepare for the event prior to its execution. It supports learning and retention of Kaizen knowledge and skills by functioning as a resource to which team members may refer after the event is complete.

Sold in sets of two manuals.

Working With Others Training Program

by James S. Byron and Patricia V. Bierley

This one-day training course prepares participants to work with others in ways that elevate the success of all. It teaches skills that enable participants to understanding the ideas and information others are sharing and to express their own ideas in ways that keep group members connected and moving toward their common goal. The Working With Others (WWO) skills are clarifying and confirming, which together build an accurate picture of what another person is sharing; and constructive criticism and hitchhiking, which allow a person to add his or her ideas in a way that generates better solutions while maintaining positive relationships. The training is conducted in an action learning format where participants take up and solve a problem together while learning and applying the WWO skills. The materials include a problem to be solved, but are structured to allow you to substitute another problem specific to the context in which the training is conducted. Simultaneously, you can both build the skills of your workforce and solve a real business problem.

Includes an Instructor Guide, a Participant Coursebook, a set of WWO Cards, and the WWO Instructional Tools, a CD-ROM that includes visuals, handouts, and other instructional aids.

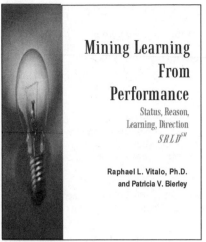

Mining Learning From Performance

by Raphael L. Vitalo, Ph.D., and Patricia V. Bierley

This half-day training course prepares participants to develop ideas from their last effort to do a task and use them to produce a better next effort. The four-step method taught is Status, Reason, Learning, Direction (SRLD^{SM}). It may be applied on an individual or team basis. The learning produced becomes better practices that may be shared with others to leverage benefits across a company. SRLD^{SM} provides each learner an engine to power the continuous improvement of his or her own performance and to generate knowledge worthy of sharing with others.

Includes an Instructor Guide, a Participant Coursebook, and SRLD^{SM} Instructional Tools, a CD-ROM that provides visuals, a learning development template, and other instructional aids.

Gathering Practical Knowledge

by Raphael L. Vitalo, Ph.D., and Patricia V. Bierley

This half-day training course prepares participants to rapidly acquire practical knowledge from an expert. Practical knowledge is ideas that guide the performance of some task. The training builds on the participants' knowledge of Working With Others (WWO) skills by providing them with an understanding of what elements of knowledge one needs to do a task and how they can use their WWO skills to gather and verify that knowledge efficiently. Teaching Gathering Practical Knowledge (GPK) skills offers a powerful method for accelerating the transfer of learning and expertise throughout a workforce. It also builds the foundation for representing knowledge and populating best practice databases with content people can really use.

Includes an Instructor Guide, a Participant Coursebook, a set of GPK Skill Cards, and the GPK Instructional Tools, a CD-ROM that includes visuals, handouts, and other instructional aids.

To get the latest information about our member services, business services, and performance-improving products, visit us online at www.vitalentusa.com.

All performance-improving are products published by Lowrey Press, a division of Vital Enterprises. Lowrey Press is committed to providing people with knowledge to power their achievement and success.

Warning! Before Breaking the Seal on the Kaizen Tool Kit, Read the Following .

Before breaking the seal on the Kaizen Tool Kit CD-ROM packet included with this book, read the licensing agreement printed below. This is a license agreement between you and Vital Enterprises - Hope, Maine 04847. By opening the accompanying software packet, you acknowledge that you have read and accept the following terms and conditions. If you do not agree and do not want to be bound by such terms and conditions, promptly return the book and the unopened software packet to the place you obtained them for a full refund.

License Agreement

Vital Enterprises - Hope, Maine 04847 END-USER LICENSE AGREEMENT

1. License Grant. Vital Enterprises (VE) grants to you (either an individual or entity) a nonexclusive license to use one copy of the enclosed software program(s) (collectively, the "Software") solely for your own personal or business purposes on a single computer (whether a standard computer or a single workstation component of a multiuser network). The Software is in use on a computer when it is loaded into temporary memory (i.e., RAM) or installed into permanent memory (e.g., hard disk, CD-ROM, or other storage device). VE reserves all rights not expressly granted herein.

2. Ownership. VE is the owner of all rights, title, and interest, including copyright, in and to the compilation of the Software recorded on the CD-ROM. Copyright to the individual programs, forms, or other contents on the CD-ROM is owned by the author or other authorized copyright owner of each program. Ownership of the Software and all proprietary rights relating thereto remain with VE and its licensors.

3. Restrictions on Use and Transfer.

(a) You may only (i) make one copy of the Software for backup or archival purposes, or (ii) transfer the Software to a single hard disk, provided that you keep the original for backup or archival purposes. You may not (i) rent or lease the Software, (ii) install the software on a server, (iii) copy or reproduce the Software through a LAN or other network system or through any computer subscriber system or bulletin-board system, or (iv) modify, adapt, or create derivative works based on the Software.

(b) You may not reverse engineer, decompile, or disassemble the Software. You may transfer the Software and user documentation on a permanent basis, provided that the transferee agrees to accept the terms and conditions of this Agreement and you retain no copies. If the Software is an update or has been updated, any transfer must include the most recent update and all prior versions.

4. Restrictions on Use of Individual Programs. You must follow the individual requirements and restrictions detailed for each individual program in the "Kaizen Tool Kit" section of this Book. These limitations are contained in the individual license agreements recorded on the CD-ROM. By opening the software packet(s), you will be agreeing to abide by the licenses and restrictions for these individual programs. None of the material on this disk(s) or listed in this Book may ever be distributed, in original or modified form, for commercial purposes.

5. Limited Warranty.

(a) VE warrants that the Software and CD-ROM are free from defects in materials and workmanship under normal use for a period of sixty (60) days from the date of purchase of this Book. If VE receives notification within the warranty period of defects in materials or workmanship, VE will replace the defective CD-ROM.

(b) VE AND THE AUTHOR OF THE BOOK DISCLAIM ALL OTHER WARRANTIES, EXPRESS OR IMPLIED, INCLUDING WITHOUT LIMITATION IMPLIED WARRANTIES OF MERCHANTABILITY AND FITNESS FOR A PARTICULAR PURPOSE, WITH RESPECT TO THE SOFTWARE, THE PROGRAMS, THE SOURCE CODE CONTAINED THEREIN, AND/OR THE TECHNIQUES DESCRIBED IN THIS BOOK. VE DOES NOT WARRANT THAT THE FUNCTIONS CONTAINED IN THE SOFTWARE WILL MEET YOUR REQUIREMENTS OR THAT THE OPERATION OF THE SOFTWARE WILL BE ERROR FREE.

(c) This limited warranty gives you specific legal rights, and you may have other rights which vary from jurisdiction to jurisdiction.

6. Remedies.

(a) VE's entire liability and your exclusive remedy for defects in materials and workmanship shall be limited to replacement of the Software, which may be returned to VE with a copy of your receipt at the following address: Disk Fulfillment Department, Attn: Vital Enterprises, 777 Hatchet Mountain Road, Hope, Maine, 04847 or call 1-207-763-3758. Please allow 3-4 weeks for delivery.

This Limited Warranty is void if failure of the Software has resulted from accident, abuse, or misapplication. Any replacement Software will be warranted for the remainder of the original warranty period or thirty (30) days, whichever is longer.

(b) In no event shall VE or the author be liable for any damages whatsoever (including without limitation damages for loss of business profits, business interruption, loss of business information, or any other pecuniary loss) arising from the use of or inability to use the Book or the Software, even if VE has been advised of the possibility of such damages.

(c) Because some jurisdictions do not allow the exclusion or limitation of liability for consequential or incidental damages, the above limitation or exclusion may not apply to you.

7. U.S. Government Restricted Rights. Use, duplication, or disclosure of the Software by the U.S. Government is subject to restrictions stated in paragraph (c) (1) (ii) of the Rights in Technical Data and Computer Software clause of DFARS 252.227-7013, and in subparagraphs (a) through (d) of the Commercial Computer—Restricted Rights clause at FAR 52.227-19, and in similar clauses in the NASA FAR supplement, when applicable.

8. General. This Agreement constitutes the entire understanding of the parties and revokes and supersedes all prior agreements, oral or written, between them and may not be modified or amended except in a writing signed by both parties hereto which specifically refers to this Agreement. This Agreement shall take precedence over any other documents that may be in conflict herewith. If any one or more provisions contained in this Agreement are held by any court or tribunal to be invalid, illegal, or otherwise unenforceable, each and every other provision shall remain in full force and effect.

Installation

Insert the CD-ROM into your computer drive, and the Kaizen Tool Kit installation program will open automatically. If it does not, locate the autorun.exe file on the CD, then double click on the file. This action will initiate the installation of the Kaizen Tool Kit. Answer the prompts as they appear. Once the installation is completed, a shortcut icon will appear on your desktop. Clicking on this icon will open the Kaizen Tool Kit and provide you access to its contents.

For best experience in using the tool kit, deselect the Adobe Reader General Preference viewing option labeled "Open Cross-Document Links in Same Window." For Acrobat Reader 5.0, do this by choosing Edit from Acrobat's top Menu, then Preferences, then General. Select Option from the left panel listing, then make sure ***no*** checkmark appears next to "Open Cross-Document Links in Same Window." If a checkmark is present, click on the option to remove it, then choose "OK" to save your settings.